PERSONAL ADJUSTMENT, MARRIAGE, AND FAMILY LIVING

SIXTH EDITION

Prentice-Hall, Inc., Englewood Cliffs, New Jersey

PERSONAL ADJUSTMENT, MARRIAGE, AND FAMILY LIVING

SIXTH EDITION

Judson T. Landis
Professor Emeritus of Family Sociology
Research Associate, Institute of Human Development
University of California at Berkeley

Mary G. Landis

PERSONAL ADJUSTMENT, MARRIAGE, AND FAMILY LIVING SIXTH EDITION

by Judson T. Landis and Mary G. Landis

Supplementary: TEACHERS GUIDE

Design by Craven & Evans, Creative Graphics
Cover photos by Catherine Ursillo

© 1975, 1970, 1966, 1960, 1955, 1950 by Prentice-Hall, Inc., Englewood Cliffs, New Jersey 07632.
All rights reserved. No part of this book may be reproduced in any form or by any means without permission in writing from the publisher.
Printed in the United States of America
10 9 8 7 6 5 4
ISBN 0-13-657338-X

PRENTICE-HALL INTERNATIONAL, INC., *London*
PRENTICE-HALL OF AUSTRALIA, PTY. LTD., *Sydney*
PRENTICE-HALL OF CANADA, LTD., *Toronto*
PRENTICE-HALL OF INDIA PRIVATE LTD., *New Delhi*
PRENTICE-HALL OF JAPAN, INC., *Tokyo*

RELATED PRENTICE-HALL BOOKS

BUILDING A SUCCESSFUL MARRIAGE,
    by Judson T. Landis and Mary G. Landis

CAREERS: EXPLORATION AND DECISION,
    by Jack L. Rettig

EXPLORING HOME AND FAMILY LIVING,
    by Henrietta Fleck and Louise Fernandez

FOOD AND YOUR FUTURE,
    by Ruth Bennett White

LIVING WITH YOUR FAMILY,
    by Henrietta Fleck, Louise Fernandez, and Elizabeth Munves

MAKING HEALTH DECISIONS,
    by Ben C. Gmur, John T. Fodor, L. H. Glass, and Joseph J. Langan

TEEN-AGERS' GUIDE FOR LIVING,
    by Judson T. Landis and Mary G. Landis

UNDERSTANDING AND GUIDING YOUNG CHILDREN,
    by Katherine Read Baker and Xenia F. Fane

YOU AND YOUR FOOD,
    by Ruth Bennett White

PICTURE CREDITS

Sculpture by Gustav Vigeland, Photography by David Finn in *Embrace of Life,* published by Harry N. Abrams—pages xxii, 138, 232.

Intimacy by Ossip Zadkine, Musée des Beaux-Arts, La Chaud-de-Fonds, Switzerland—page 60.

Family Group (Detail) by Henry Moore, with permission of the sculptor and The Tate Gallery, London—Title page and page 338.

A.A.M.P.E.R., 28   Richard Adler, 4   Allegheny College (Meadville, Pa.), photo by Ben Spiegle, 143   American Basketball Association, 21   American Cancer Society, 114, 116   Christa Armstrong, 127 (bottom right), 284 (top)   American Telephone and Telegraph Company, Long Lines Dept., 54, 364   H. Darr Beiser, 404   Bergen Evening Record Corporation, 372   Bergen Pines County (N. J.) Hospital, photo by Richard A. Mendez, 53   Bigelow-Sanford, Inc., 65   *Chicago Sun-Times* Syndicate, George Lichty, 180   Bob Combs from Rapho Guillumette, 30   Douglas Cory from DPI, 258   Jim Cron from Monkmeyer Press Photo Service, 284 (bottom)   Jim Dallas Studios for *DuPont Magazine,* 407 (left)   Phoebe Dunn from DPI, 160   Robert De Gast from Rapho Guillumette, 209   DPI, 6   Du Pont Company, 12   The Equitable Life Assurance Society of the United States, 20, 93, Ford Motor Company 290, 300   Mimi Forsyth from Monkmeyer Press Photo Service, 31, 62, 96, 219, 247, 311, 340, 367, 391   Edward Gallob from DPI, 326   General Motors Acceptance Corporation, 24   Gerber Products Company, 76, 360 (left)   Don Getsug from Rapho Guillumette, 236   The B. F. Goodrich Company, 397   John C. Goodwin, 272   Joel Gordon, 169, 228, 406   Ted Grant from DPI, 195   Rapho Guillumette, 10, 22, 79   Hackensack (N. J.) Hospital, 350   Michal Heron from Monkmeyer Press Photo Service, 68, 74   Ideal Basic Industries, Inc., 356   Hank Ketcham, 77   Paulo Koch from Rapho Guillumette, 280   © Ray Lain, Agent Steve Satterwhite, 176   Judson T. Landis, 2, 347, 355, 373 (left)

Freda Leinwand from Monkmeyer Press Photo Service, 17, 108   Jan Lucas from Rapho Guillumette, 234, 344   University of Maine at Orono, 43   Manchester College (Ind.), 56, 70   Merck & Co., Inc., 288   Lew Merrim from Monkmeyer Press Photo Service, 267   Lida Moser from DPI, 150, 187   Dan Nelkin, 399   North Bergen (N. J.) High School, George Mattei, PRELUDE, 211   One-A-Day Vitamins Plus Iron, 165   Christy Park from Monkmeyer Press Photo Service, 379   Rondal Partridge, 81, 103 (left), 111, 154, 242, 265, 275, 323, 328, 331, 360 (right), 369 (right), 373 (right), 381, 382, 384, 392, 411   Peace College (Raleigh, N. C.), Pam Walters, 182   Pepsi-Cola Company, 151, 179   Rice Council of America, 361   Bruce Roberts from Rapho Guillumette, 185   Pemberton Robinson from DPI, 140   Hugh Rogers from Monkmeyer Press Photo Service, 173   Steve Satterwhite, 298   Saturday Evening Post, 164, 216, and Jerry Marcus, 241, 249   Sybil Schackman from Monkmeyer Press Photo Service, 127 (top right)   Warren Schloat Associates, Inc., 38, 82, 95, 103 (right), 129, 131, 133, 145, 168, 200, 215, 252, 269, 333, 352, 395, 408   Flip Schullse from Black Star, 118   Charles Schulz, 19, 34, 40, 48, 50, 66, 120   Sealy Incorporated, 342   Sybil Shelton from Monkmeyer Press Photo Service, 46, 89, 124, 295   Jon Sinish from DPI, 92   Bob S. Smith from Rapho Guillumette, 127 (left)   Southwest Junior High School, Reading, Pa., 369 (left)   Eileen Spingler, 69   Jerrold Stefl, 191, 197, 256   David Strickler, 67   Sherry Suris from Rapho Guillumette, 25, 229   Texas Eastern Transmission Corporation, photography: Don Klumpp, 189   United Nations, 407 (right)   Waldorf College (Forest City, Iowa), photo by Robert Evenson, 49, 105   Xerox Corporation, 161

PREFACE

This book offers factual material, some interpretations of research findings, and possibly some insights useful to people meeting the challenges of young adulthood. It is organized primarily for study and classroom discussion but is addressed also to out-of-school youth who are, or soon will be, forming their own family units. This sixth edition has been rewritten in view of social changes occurring in this decade. We have tried to eliminate stereotyped references to male and female roles.

We work with the concept of growth tasks, recognizing that at each age in life we all must make special kinds of growth appropriate to that age. Healthy personality development can proceed more readily when young people perceive that their parents and others of all ages must cope with new experiences that test and baffle them, just as one must do during the teens. People who understand the breadth of these lifelong growth requirements can approach their own problems with relative objectivity and confidence. Part I explores the concept of personality growth in some depth.

Part II considers the dating stage of life. Emphasis is upon dating as a learning experience in preparation for wise mate selection. Part III deals with the approach to marriage in general. This discussion considers the question of age for marriage, with emphasis on maturity and readiness for adult responsibility as a prerequisite for marriage. Discussions of "danger signals" are designed to help people become alert to elements in a relationship that may serve as warnings against unwise mate choice and future marriage failure. Further, our view is that young people with a realistic concept of marriage as a lifetime cooperative partnership will tend to approach marriage with some caution and to build more successful marriages.

Part IV gives a realistic picture of what it means to be married with emphasis upon the areas that require special understanding and growth if the marriage is to be a happy one. We have added two new chapters, "Sexual Adjustment in Marriage" and "Adjusting to Divorce." These two new chapters should give young people added insight into marriage adjustment as well as into the problems adults and their children go through in adjusting to a failed marriage.

Part V deals with approaching parenthood and the personality growth of young children. The purpose here is twofold: students with insight into the needs of little children will better understand their own personality growth and needs; moreover, many of them will soon be parents, and their study now of what parenthood requires can help them prepare to function adequately as parents. In addition, students who understand the implications of becoming parents may approach marriage more cautiously. Indeed, increased perception of and knowledge about *all* aspects of marriage, parenthood, and family living should function as a deterrent to too youthful marriage. Such knowledge should help to decrease the rate of marriage failure in our society.

The first five editions of this book were written by Judson T. and Mary G. Landis, a husband and wife team for 43 years. Following Mary's untimely death from cancer, the sixth edition was prepared by Judson T. Landis, Janet Landis Summers, and Grace Watterson Landis.

We are indebted to the many young people who have talked with us or written letters to us explaining their viewpoints about the subjects included in this book. They challenge our thinking and offer us new insights. We continually learn from them.

Many teachers have offered helpful criticisms after using the several editions. Every teacher who has been willing to give us candid comments on the flaws and the strengths of the first five editions has helped immensely in this revision. We want to express our special appreciation for their contribution.

Judson T. Landis

CONTENTS

part one **Understanding Yourself and Others** 1

1 Family Interaction 2

Unique Task of Your Age, 3　Growth at Each Age Basic to Later Stages of Life, 3　Freedom of Choice During the Teen Years, 5　You Live in a Family, 7　Growth Tasks of Parents, 8　Looking Ahead — Marriage, 8　Looking Ahead — Marriage Versus Singleness, 9　The Implications of Marriage, 9　Family Functions, 11　Families Give Physical and Social Heritage, 11

2 What You Are 17

Our Basic Needs, 18　Ups and Downs, 20　What Do You Do? 23　Yet Each Individual Remains Unique, 24　Growth Tasks Ahead, 25　Range of Development in Individuals, 26　Social Differences Characteristic of Each Sex, 27　Accepting Individual Differences, 27

3 How We Meet Our Problems 30

Direct Attack, 31　Detour, 32　To Give Up or to Take Action, 33　Retreat, 35　Rationalization, 36　Daydreaming, 37　Fear, 39　Meeting Problems, and Health, 41　Meeting Problems, and Personality Growth, 42　Focus on You, 43

4 Getting Along With Others 46

Important Personality Traits, 47   Some Habits That Hinder, 47
Some Habits Worth Cultivating, 52   Focus on You, 57

part two Social Life and Dating 61

5 Dating 62

Uncertainties in the Dating Period, 63   Some Rules That Help in Dating, 64   Who Asks? 67   Who Pays? 67   Blind Dates, 68
To Be More Successful in Dating, 69   Focus on You, 71

6 Functions of Dating 74

Discovering Oneself, 75   Becoming Realistic About the Other Sex, 77   Discovering Families, 78   Discovering and Understanding the Need for Love, 80   Recognizing Danger Signals in a Relationship, 82   Contribution of Dating Steadily, 87
Some Negative Aspects, 88   In Summary, 89   Focus on You, 90

7 Decisions About Premarital Standards 92

Responsibility Parallels Growth—Into Freedom, 93   Moral Definitions, 94   Responsibility to Self, 95   Responsibility for the Other Person, 97   Motivations for Premarital Sexual Intercourse, 98   Negative Aspects of Premarital Sex, 98   Responsibility to Self Versus Responsibility for Another Person, 100   Premarital Pregnancy, 101   Responsibility to a Child and to Society, 102   Living According to Personal Standards, 104

8 More Decisions: Alcohol, Smoking, Drugs 108

Alcohol, 109   Research Findings About Alcohol, 109   Implications of the Facts About Alcohol and Alcoholism, 112   Smoking, 114   Why People Start or Stop Smoking, 115   Living in a Drug-oriented Society, 117   Use and Abuse of Drugs, 118   Your Policy About the Use of Drugs, 119   Personal Problems and Drugs, 120   Confusion About Addicting and Non-addicting Drugs, 121   In Conclusion, 122

9 Family Understanding During the Dating Years 124

Basic Causes of Conflict, 125   What of the Young People? 126   Parents and Dating, 126   The Family Car, 128   Hours to Be In, 129   Disagreement Over Your Clothes and Hair, 130   Parents Cannot Always Discuss Their Worries, 131   Some Young People Demand Too Much, 132   Establishing and Maintaining Good Communication, 134   Focus on You, 134 part three   **Looking Toward Marriage**   139

10   **Dating Becomes Mate Selection**   140

Family Background Affects Marriage, 141   What Traits Do You Consider Most Desirable in a Mate? 145   Marriageability, 146   Do Your Personalities Fit? 148   What About Recreational Interests? 149   What About Friends and Social Interests? 151   Parental Approval, 152   Homogamy in Mate Choice, 154   Differences May or May Not Matter, 155   Mixed Marriages, 155   Dating, Mate Choice, and Marriage Success, 157

11   **Maturity for Marriage**   160

Maturity for Marriage, 161   Some Problems That Go With Age at Marriage, 163   Age of Marriage and Divorce, 166   School Policies Toward High School Marriages, 168   Your Long-range Goals, 169   Marrying to Avoid Separation, 170   Focus on You, 170

12   **Engagement**   173

Length of Courtship and Adjustment in Marriage, 174   Being Well Enough Acquainted, A Crucial Factor, 175   Agreement During Engagement and Agreement in Marriage, 176   Readiness for Engagement, 178   Purpose of the Engagement, 178   Danger Signals During Engagement, 179   Failure to Recognize Danger Signals, 181

13 **Engagement (continued)** 187

Breaking Engagements, 188   Broken Hearts Do Heal, 188   Issues to Be Discussed During Engagement, 191   Engagement as Preparation for Marriage, 192   In Summary, 194

14 **Religion and Marriage** 197

Religion and Relationships Within the Family, 198   Religion and Family Background, 200   Agreement on Religion, 201   Marriages of People of Different Religious Faiths, 203   Focus of Problems, 204   Kinds of Solutions, 205   Jewish-Gentile Marriages, 205   Conclusion, 206

15 **Is It Love?** 209

Components of Love, 210   Physical Attraction, 210   Satisfaction of Personality Needs, 211   Sharing, 212   We Look at Our Relationships With Others, 213   Value of Love Experiences, 214

16 **Marriage Customs and Laws** 219

Physical and Mental Qualifications for Marriage, 220   Age for Marriage, 223   Marriage of Relatives, 223   Interracial Marriages, 224   Void and Voidable Marriages, 225   Getting Married, 225   The Marriage Officiant, 227   Premarital Examination, 227   Planning the Wedding, 227   The Honeymoon, 229

part four **When You Marry** 233

17 What It Means to Be Married 234

Most Marriages Are Happy, 235   But All Marriages Require Adjustment, 235   Areas Requiring Adjustability, 237   Adjustment Takes Time, 237   We Need to Be Realistic, 239   Chief Types of Adjustment, 240   Tabling Differences, 243   Time to Adjust and Happiness in Marriage, 243   Importance of Adaptability, 244   Conclusions, 245

18 What About Quarreling? 247

Quarreling in Marriage, 248   What Is Quarreling? 248   Function of Quarreling in Early Marriage, 248   Discovering Areas of Difference, 250   Quarreling May Become Habitual Behavior, 251   As a Tension Reliever, 251   Cumulative Effect of Quarreling, 253   Physical Factors and Quarreling, 253   The Family Conference, 254

19 Sexual Adjustment in Marriage 258

Sex as a Part of the Total Marriage Relationship, 259   Biological Basis for Sexual Drive, 260   Social Conditioning About Sex, 260   Time to Adjust in Sex, 261   Some Specific Problems in Sexual Adjustment, 262   Summary, 265

20 You and Your In-laws 267

The Family Pattern, 268   Growth Tasks for All at This Stage of Life, 271   The In-laws as Scapegoats, 273   Unsuccessful Attitudes, 274   Success With the In-laws, 274   Living With Parents, 275   Some Suggested Rules for Guidance in In-law Relationships, 276   Happiness in Marriage and In-law Adjustment, 277

21 Making Decisions About Finances 280

Money Problems in Marriage, 281   Agreement During Engagement and Agreement in Marriage, 282   Threefold Nature of Financial Problems, 283   Growing Together on What Is Valued, 284   Who Should Control the Money, 286   Some Questions to Be Faced, 287   What About Budgeting? 288   The Need to Be Realistic About Expenses, 290   Your Budgeting, 291   Conclusions, 292

22 Family Economics 295

Every Home Needs a Consumer Expert, 296   The Wife as the Consumer Expert, 296   Getting Consumer Information, 296   Some Considerations for Buying, 297   Judging Values, 299   Buying Credit, 299   The Dollar Cost of Credit, 302   Buying Security, 303   Life Insurance, 304   G.I. Insurance, 305   Pointers in Buying Life Insurance, 306   Renting or Buying a Home, 307

23 Avoiding Divorce 311

Marriage Failure Comes Early, 312　Why Unhappy Marriages Continue, 313　The Decision to Divorce, 314　Divorce Laws, 315　No-fault Divorce, 317　Conciliation Courts, 318　What Is Divorce? 319　Causes of Divorce, 319　Specific Personality Traits and Divorce, 321　Lack of Preparation for Marriage as a Cause of Divorce, 323　Alternates to Divorce, 323

24 Adjusting to Divorce 326

Divorce May Offer New Hope, 327　Marrying After Divorce, 329　Children and Divorce, 331　Conclusion, 335

part five When You Become a Parent 339

25 Approaching Parenthood 340

Positive Rewards of Parenthood, 341　Being Realistic About Parenthood, 341　Parenthood as Crisis, 342　Parenthood as a Profession, 343　How Can One Prepare? 343　Approaching the First Child's Birth, 346　Preparing Prospective Parents for the Birth, 347　Presence of the Father at the Birth, 348　Stages of the Birth Process, 349　Understanding Each Other During Pregnancy, 351

26 New Parents and Emotional Growth of Children 355

The Child Needs Love, 356   Changes in Attitudes About Infant Care, 357   Each Child Grows in His or Her Own Way, 358   Basic Aims of Child Rearing, 359   Sense of Proportion, 359   Forming Good Habits, 360   Bedtime Habits, 362   Eating Habits, 362   Family Table Talk, 363   Overall Goals, 364

27 Discipline and Guidance in Child Development 367

Consistency in Child Rearing, 368   Lack of Guidance Means Trouble for a Child, 368   Self-confidence, 371   Value of Praise, 372   Constructive Versus Destructive Training, 373   Agreement Between Parents, 374   Perspective on Discipline and Guidance, 377

28 The Second Baby 379

Older Children React in Various Ways, 380   Understanding the Child's Feelings, 381   What Can Be Done About It?, 382   Sex and Reproduction, 383   Parents' Uncertainties as Children Grow Up, 388   Parent-child Understanding, 389

29 **Adoption** 391

Adopting Children, 392   Unsound or Sound Motives for Adopting, 393   Honesty About Adoption, 394   Feelings About Adoption, 394   Children Born to Unmarried Mothers, 395   More Reforms Needed, 396

30 **The Successful Family** 399

Happiness of Children, 400   Factors Making for Unhappiness During Childhood, 401   Helping Children When a Loved One Dies, 403   Facing Your Vocational Future, 405   Working Mothers, 406   Parents in the Happy Family—Middle and Later Years, 408   How Sons and Daughters Can Help Parents, 409   Remarriage of Parents and Grandparents, 409   Grandparents—Old Age, 410   The Happy Family, 412

Index   416

PERSONAL ADJUSTMENT, MARRIAGE, AND FAMILY LIVING

SIXTH EDITION

part one

UNDERSTANDING YOURSELF AND OTHERS

The first cry of a newborn baby
in Chicago or Zamboango,
in Amsterdam or Rangoon,
has the same pitch and key,
each saying, "I am!
I have come through!
I belong!
I am a member of the family!"

　　Carl Sandburg

1 Family Interaction

After studying this chapter, you will be able to

1. Identify stereotyped ideas about people in various age groups.
2. Express ways in which you are more free to concentrate on your own growth now than you will ever be again.
3. List advantages of marriage and singleness.
4. Discuss effects of heredity and environment on physical characteristics and on personality.

A tendency exists in our society to divide life into compartments and to view each stage of life, and the people who are in that stage, as separate and distinctly different from all other age groups. We speak of "teenagers," of "young adults," of "parents," of "the middle aged," of "grandparents," as if each group belonged to a different species, with entirely different feelings, problems, and needs.

This tendency to stereotype people according to their age group creates misunderstandings among people. It is easy to misjudge the motives and the actions of people whom we have put into a common bin with all others of the same age. This kind of age-stereotyping in our society probably has some of its basis in the defensive need of insecure individuals to wall themselves in with their own kind; necessarily they must then wall others out by casting them into separate and typical molds. They can thus escape the challenge of trying to understand and respond to the feelings of members of stereotyped groups. By this time in your life, you have probably felt discriminated against for being a "teenager." It is safe to say that your mother has felt that she was typed as a "housewife" or as a "working mother" or as a "middle-aged woman." Your father may feel typed as a "breadwinner." Your grandmother or grandfather may feel discrimination in much the same way that you do. They are stereotyped as "old" and therefore assumed to be out of touch or out of date, just as you may feel misjudged because of the connotations that the term "teenager" has for some segments of our society.

To become more effective in our relationships with others and in our personal development, we must appreciate the fact that categorizing individuals is not realistic. You are first of all yourself; you are a "teenager" only secondarily. You will not be a basically different person in ten, twenty, or thirty years. Each of us lives with certain needs and feelings throughout life. If we are aware of this, we can better understand some of our own motives and actions as well as those of the people around us.

The stereotyping of individuals tends to be reinforced because, while needs and feelings remain the same, circumstances of life change. Responsibilities become greater and directions in life more fixed. Freedom of choice and action decreases in some ways as people advance through the stages of life. The specific growth tasks required of each age are different.

UNIQUE TASK OF YOUR AGE

During the teen years, people rapidly change physically, emotionally, and socially, and such changes require many adjustments that put pressure upon the individual. The need for making adjustments and finding solutions to problems is not unique to your age; but what is unique is that now your most legitimate concerns are with yourself. Your special task is to think first of your own physical, mental, emotional, and social growth, and to find out who you really are and in what directions you want your life to move. Never again will you be so free to concentrate on your own development.

GROWTH AT EACH AGE BASIC TO LATER STAGES OF LIFE

You are now basically the same person you will be later when circumstances have changed and others see you as one caring for children and doing housework at home, or as one working to support a family and worrying and hoping your children won't make the same mistakes you made. The things you feel strongly about now, your necessity to love and to be loved, and your desire to be successful in what you attempt, are a part of you. Your response to the pressures of these requirements in your nature will be a factor in your life, whether you are in your teens, twenties, forties, or sixties.

While basically you will be the same person throughout life, specific responsibilities and living tasks will change as you progress from one age to another. The demands that life makes shift emphasis with

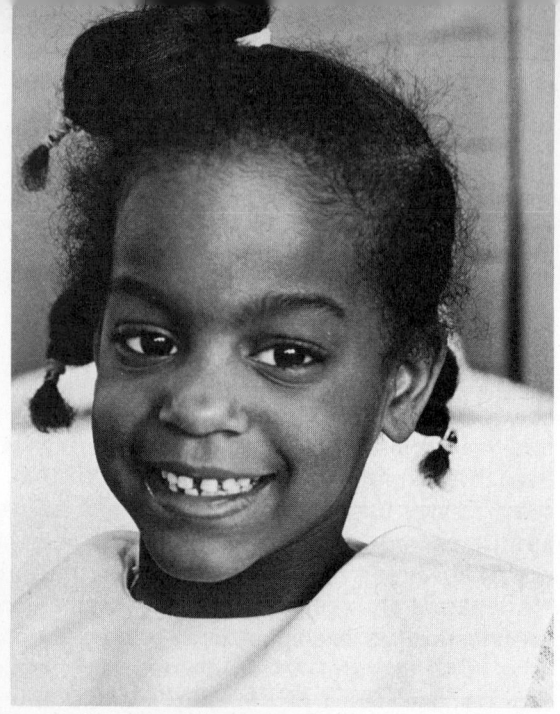

Each person is a unique individual. We are only secondarily members of groups.

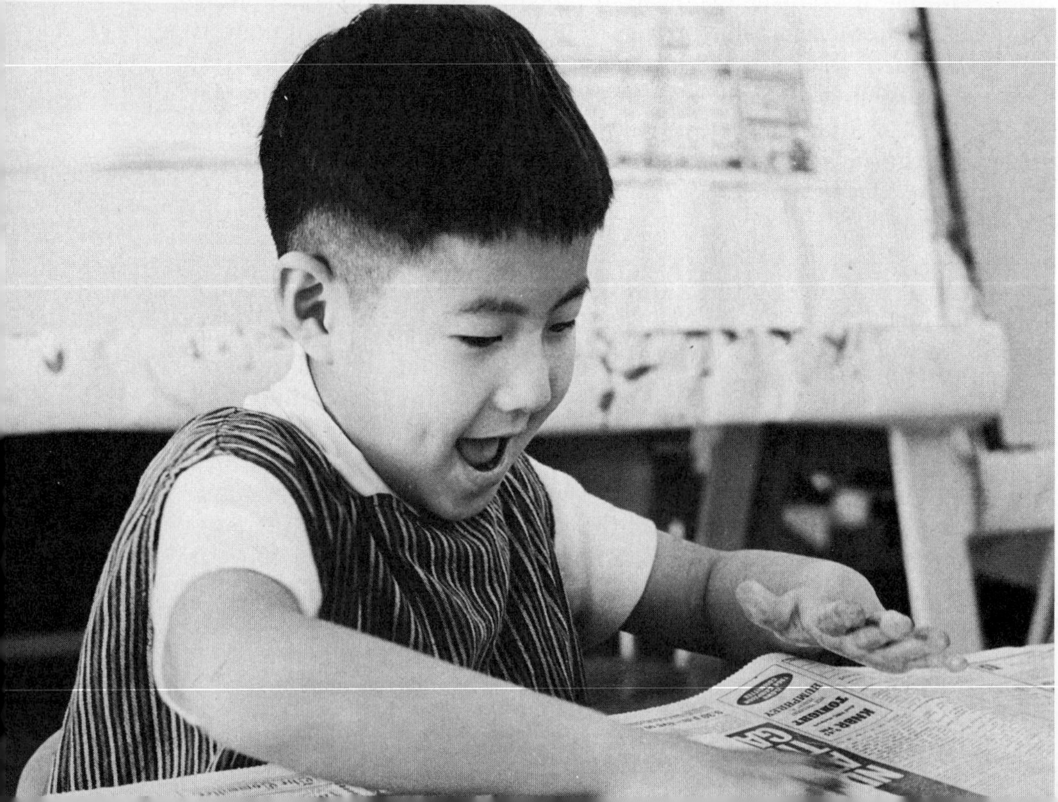

each age. The habits of thought, the responses to pressures, and the ways of meeting problems that you are developing will greatly affect the way you are able to function when you find yourself in each new stage of life. Each part of life will be more satisfying if you have accomplished the required growth in the preceding stage.

From infancy to grandparenthood, well-being depends largely upon successful relationships with other people. An infant responds to loving care with physical and emotional growth and becomes a healthy, happy baby and young child. In later childhood and in adolescence, satisfactory growth—physical, mental, and emotional—includes creating good relationships with other people. Later, the person ready for growing into new stages becomes a successful marriage partner, then a parent who can contribute to the emotional growth of the children, and finally a grandparent who can experience old age with a measure of equanimity, being a positive factor in the lives of others.

FREEDOM OF CHOICE DURING THE TEEN YEARS

The special advantage of the teen years is that one is, in general, free to make choices and later reject them if they prove to have been mistakes. Policies and habits can be changed more easily now than later; mistakes in judgment or in action can be corrected now as they could not be later. The challenge is to do as much testing and experimenting as necessary in order to be sure of your own identity and directions in life, without closing off important options in the process. The word "option" is used in the business world to refer to deals or agreements in which one has the privilege of taking or leaving a specified advantage or of buying or not buying certain property. As long as one holds an open option, there is freedom to make a different decision on the matter without any penalty. In business, options are usually obtained by legal agreement, but during the teen years, there are a number of valuable options that one holds automatically. In these matters, you have the great advantage that these options have no specified date of being closed to you. They remain open until you choose to close them by making decisions having a permanent effect. Let us examine some of these open choices.

1. *Freedom to choose among many kinds of people in making friends.* You need not yet be "typed" and confined to one group; there is still time to assess a variety of friendships.
2. *Freedom to test one's interaction with people of the other sex.* As long as one is not yet married, there is still time to find a partner with whom the most satisfactory marriage and family life is possible; one is not yet positively committed to trying to make the best of a bad choice.

3. *Freedom to develop one's intellectual ability, to get an adequate education and preparation for a lifework.* As long as one is in school, has not dropped out or failed all school subjects, one can still overcome obstacles and go ahead to get a good education. One's educational options remain open.
4. *Freedom to have satisfactory relationships with parents.* If misunderstandings and conflicts are building up with parents while you are trying to grow up, ways can be found to cope with the problem. There is still time, as long as you try to communicate with your parents and are not cut off totally from them.
5. *Freedom to choose a lifework, to follow a policy that gives you a chance to discover the kind of work you want to do for the rest of your life.* There is still time to make sure that you do not trap yourself in work that gives no real satisfaction or sense of achievement. The best possible way to keep this option open is to continue with your education and to take as wide a variety of courses as possible. Some people decide on a lifework too soon and narrow their studies accordingly, taking it for granted that they have known for years what they wanted to be when they grew up. Any choice made early in life probably needs rethinking during the teen years when there is still time to change your goals and your plans.

In the teen years many choices are open to us before boundaries to our world become limiting to our potential.

6. *Freedom in general from serious handicaps that limit your choices and satisfactions in living.* You have probably not yet formed habits that handicap you physically, that would be hard to break later. You see many people in later stages of life who struggle against physical handicaps brought on by unwise use of drugs, tobacco, and alcohol. They may feel their handicap deeply, but have long since given up trying to break habits that became established when they were in their teens. Believing their courses of action were only temporary and of no permanent significance, these people closed their options before they realized the implications. *You* can keep your options open. It is never too *late* to become a smoker, or to drink excessively, or to take risks with drugs, but it can be too soon. It is appropriate that you examine your beliefs and standards of behavior and try to learn what you support and what you oppose in the world. You can do this without acting out each phase of your testing to the extent that you break laws, making a record that you would have to live with.

As long as important choices have not been made and habits established, one remains free, with a minimum of handicaps. You still have time to keep problems within limits that you can live with. Later chapters will consider in greater detail the areas of free choice that are now open to you.

YOU LIVE IN A FAMILY

Our discussion thus far may seem to assume that you are now on your own in organizing and living your life and getting on with growing up and determining your future. But most of our readers are living in families, coping with the complications as well as enjoying the advantages that come with living with parents and brothers or sisters.

Conflicts and misunderstandings arise in families during these years. Some parents find it hard to realize that their children are growing up, and they try to exercise too much control for too long a time. Some children become aggressive in asserting their independence before they have reached a level of maturity consistent with the independence they want.

It would be easier for all if it were possible to mark a date on a calendar and say, "On that day, I will be grown up." Then on that day, parents could relax, and their children could take over all responsibility for their own lives without help or interference. On the surface, this might seem desirable; but there are many factors that would prevent such a thing from happening.

People mature at varying rates. Two children in the same family may differ greatly in the rate of their physical and emotional growth.

Also, an individual may be far more mature physically than emotionally or mentally. One who is making excellent progress toward maturity may still lack judgment, and need only time to learn from experience. If growth tasks have been accomplished since infancy, most people in the teens have developed some maturity. They will be learning to accept and adjust to their weaknesses or liabilities and to know what assets and abilities they can count on. They will be challenged by the present and will be able to look ahead and begin to make realistic plans for the future.

GROWTH TASKS OF PARENTS

One of the growth tasks of your parents at their stage of life is to find out when to relinquish authority and when to retain responsibility if they are to be adequate as parents. They have no very helpful guide any more than you do. Being parents of teenaged people is a new and often difficult experience for them. They may be as involved with trying to define their present roles as their children are in trying to define theirs. Each may be unaware that the other also is struggling to adjust to the requirements of a stage of life that makes new demands.

LOOKING AHEAD—MARRIAGE

Most people hope to marry and have a home of their own. The way we live in the present—whether we are happy or unhappy, friendly or unfriendly, cheerful or moody, gracious in speech or sarcastic, responsible or irresponsible—may seem unrelated to marriage, but will have much to do with the happiness or unhappiness of life in the future.

A student who was listening to a discussion on what kind of people make the best husbands or wives said, "But why talk about that now? I am not going to marry for eight or ten years yet, and I don't believe in crossing bridges until I get to them." However, this same student hoped someday, ten or twelve years in the future, to be a surgeon, and had thus far chosen the correct courses in preparation for college entrance. By so doing, one would be sure of being ready for the chosen profession.

Many people are as illogical as this. They know that months or years of training are necessary before one is ready for any good job or profession, but they do not realize that it is just as important to be ready for the lifetime job that marriage is. If one is ill-prepared and cannot cope, problems that arise in marriage are much more difficult than those one could encounter in an unsuitable occupation. It is much simpler to change jobs than to change life's circumstances after one is married.

LOOKING AHEAD—MARRIAGE VERSUS SINGLENESS

Society does not force people to enter a certain vocation such as medicine, law, or electronics. Society does put pressures on people to marry. Those who wish to remain permanently single often feel pressure to marry, although they may have doubts about whether or not they want to marry. Social attitudes may be changing enough so that now there may be less of this pressure on people. In the past, 95 percent of women in the United States married at least once by the age of forty, and 92 percent of men by age forty-five and older married or had been married. The percentage of men and women who have married has increased during the past twenty years. With the acceptance of the idea that society should not pressure all to marry, however, it is possible that the percentage who marry in the future will decrease.

As you read and study during this course, you may decide that marriage is not for you, at least not in the foreseeable future. Singleness has many advantages in that one can live a more self-centered life, be more independent in pursuing vocational and avocational interests, and avoid many adjustments required in marriage and parenthood. Married people must learn to live cooperatively if they are to be happy, and they must be willing to live unselfishly if they are to be successful as marriage partners and as parents. Marriage requires more of the individual than some people can give or are willing to give.

Statistics on mortality show that married people have a lower death rate at every stage of life than do single people or those whose marriages have been broken by death or divorce. These facts are explained in many different ways: married people have someone to care for them, to fulfill their emotional and physical needs, and to show concern with health or illness. Probably one of the largest factors in explaining the lower death rate of the married is that there is a selective process operating. More who remain single may be physically or emotionally handicapped.

THE IMPLICATIONS OF MARRIAGE

People who approach marriage carefully and with an understanding of its implications, and who have grown up to the point of being able to fulfill the many kinds of responsibilities that come with marriage, usually find that a good marriage enhances all of life. Such individuals are more likely to be successful in any job or profession than those committed to an unsatisfactory marriage. Failing marriages contribute disorder and trouble to society and to individuals. Good marriages lead to happy families, with children who can meet life with confidence, and adults who are happy and better able to meet their responsibilities within and outside the family at each stage of life.

Marriage and parenthood require the best that one can give. Children reared in happy homes are given the strength to face life with confidence.

Most people never think of the broad social purposes of marrying and creating a family. It is natural to think mostly in terms of one's own experiences, of one's expectations and hopes for personal happiness. But in reality, marriage does have implications, as we have said, far beyond the two people involved. The whole of society is interested in each marriage, because it is through the social unit of the family that the continuity of society is maintained. Families produce new generations of individuals, and through these, new members pass on not only physical life, but knowledge, customs, traditions, and intellectual, emotional, and spiritual endowments.

The values of our culture and of individual families are powerful factors in the growth and development of each new generation. In some periods of time there was little change from one parent generation to the next, values and beliefs being passed on relatively intact. Today, many of the values of the older generation are being seriously questioned by members of the younger generation; it remains to be seen which of the established values will disappear from our culture and which will be found to be valid and allowed to survive. Nevertheless, in the process of examining and assessing the values of your parents, you are probably discovering how powerful the beliefs and attitudes of the parental family are in the life of each person. It will be the same when you are a parent; your children will have to face and come to terms with the values by which you live. That is only one aspect of the wide, social implications of two people falling in love and deciding to marry.

FAMILY FUNCTIONS

When you have such thoughts as, "I'm certainly going to do things differently from the way my parents did, when I raise children," or "I think my parents used good sense. I hope I can do as well as they have done," you are recognizing the meaning of the family as an ongoing institution in our society.

The specific functions of the family may be listed in three chief divisions. They are (1) to provide physical care for children; (2) to nurture the growth of personality and to equip the children to live successfully in their social environment; and (3) to meet the emotional needs of adults as well as children.

Most families are well aware of the obligation to fulfill the physical function. The majority of parents do their best to clothe, feed, and shelter their children; but when it comes to contributing consciously to the personality development of their children and of each other, a wide variation appears in what people know or understand about family relationships.

FAMILIES GIVE PHYSICAL AND SOCIAL HERITAGE

The most obvious gift from your parents is *physical inheritance.* It matters to you how you look: the color of your eyes and hair and complexion, the shape and size of your nose, and whether you are tall or short. And you recognize that some special characteristics are yours because of the family into which you were born. John's father and grandfather are both over six feet tall, and John, at sixteen, is bothered because he is not yet as tall as his father; but he knows the chances are good that before he finishes growing he will at least equal his father's height.

If brown eyes are characteristic of most of the members of a family, it is easy to see that they are an inherited trait. However, many other characteristics are not inherited, even though it is true that one might not have had them had one been born and reared in a different family. Although the most obvious gifts from our families have to do with physical makeup, some *habits of behavior* are passed on also.

The social environment in the family establishes relationships that extend beyond the individual to the family that he or she in turn will have.

Whether you are the type whose brain works faster than your muscles or the type who acts instantly and thinks later; whether you habitually "fly off the handle" when things go wrong or whether you take things calmly and try to achieve your goals through tact and persuasion —you have these and many other characteristics at least in part, because of the family into which you were born. Each family has its own characteristic way of meeting life situations, its own pattern of behavior within the family. On your street, the houses or apartment buildings may look alike, the children go to the same school, people travel the same route to go to work, and people may have similar equipment with which to do housework. Yet out of these houses will come all types of people. You have only to look at your classmates to see the great variations that exist among individuals. Some seem to be better able to meet life situations; they are happier, or kinder, or better organized in their work habits than others.

Doubt exists about many characteristics: they may or may not be largely due to *biological inheritance*. About others we can be quite sure. For example, we know that the characteristics of the vocal cords and the cavities of the head that determine voice quality, and the curliness or straightness of hair are inherited. The limits of tallness or shortness are set this way, and so is bone structure—whether one is big-boned or small-boned and delicately built. Inheritance determines one's potential muscular coordination, that is, whether one is awkward or adept in activities that require balance and timing. The kind of intelligence we have is due to heredity; we vary in our ability to learn.

The processes of heredity are covered in biology courses. In our present discussion, we may review briefly the formula by which heredity operates. When two parent cells join to form a new individual, there are minute pairs of particles called *chromosomes* in the father cell (sperm) and in the mother cell (ovum) that unite. Each chromosome carries innumerable *genes,* which are responsible for inherited traits. For example, genes for eye color present in the chromosomes of both parents provide a wide range of possible eye colors for their child. The new individual's eyes may turn out to be much like those of one parent, or may be entirely different, because chance has a great deal to do with determining which genes will dominate or whether genes will pair in such a way as to produce a new color or blending of colors. Because genes are innumerable, all kinds of combinations are possible. That is why in some families we see contrasts in physical characteristics. A pair of parents may have one child with blue eyes, another with brown eyes, and others with gray or hazel eyes. In the same family are found redheads, blonds, and brunettes.

The genes that operate to determine physical features have done their work by the time two parent cells have united and a new individual begins growth. From that time forward, *environment* begins its work. Development can be affected by the physical environment before birth: extreme malnutrition, some diseases of the mother, or certain drugs can affect the growth of the unborn child. After birth, we continue to be susceptible to the effects of factors in the physical environment, such as the food we eat and our exposure to disease. We also begin to form habits, ways of responding to others, all of our personality traits. Our development in one direction or another is affected by the patterns of behavior in our family.

A child is quick-tempered just like one of the parents or has a sense of humor like a grandparent; one child may be nervous and get upset just like one parent does; three children show musical ability. Can we say for sure which of these are inherited traits, or to what extent they are due to the life experiences of the individuals?

Some inherited characteristics are certainly modified by the conditions under which the individual lives, or by the environment. Malnutrition may prevent one from growing to full potential height, and may hamper muscular coordination. One who has naturally good coordination may not develop it, while some other person who has less natural ability may, through practice, excel in activities that require muscular coordination. Because of differences in opportunity and motivation, wide differences exist in the degree to which individual intellectual abilities are developed. One with superior intellectual capacity may make little use of it because of lack of opportunity, while one with less natural ability may achieve superiority because of better opportunities in life or because of greater incentive to achieve.

We do know that whatever our inheritance, we can do much for ourselves and for others in our family to help influence development in a satisfactory direction. Personalities develop; behavior patterns become set; habits of emotional response become established—all as an outgrowth of family association. Thus, by the time you became a high school student, your family had given you not only the physical appearance you inherited, which had, no doubt, already been modified by the habits of eating and sleeping with which you grew up, but also the personality, which is much more important to your success in life than is the color of your hair or your stature.

You also have affected the personalities of the other members of your family. Your parents are not the same people they would have been had you not been born. Living with you has definitely influenced the directions of their growth. Each of us is a part of the environment of those with whom we live.

QUESTIONS FOR REVIEW

1. What do you understand to be the meaning of the statement that people tend to be stereotyped by age groups?
2. Can you give some examples of stereotyped ideas about people of different age groups, such as "all teenagers are. . ."? Do these ideas have any basis in fact?
3. How does this stereotyping affect relationships between people?
4. Do you see any connection between this age-grouping tendency and the "generation gap" often referred to in the press and in public discussions?
5. Can you give a possible explanation of the motivation behind such stereotyping?
6. Have you ever felt discriminated against because people see you first as a "teenager" and do not see you as an individual?
7. Can you think of examples of circumstances in which other people are discriminated against because of stereotyping?
8. Discuss some needs that are the same for all age groups in society.
9. In what ways are you now more free to concentrate on your own growth than you will ever be again?

10. Can you predict what you will be like when you are older by the personality characteristics you have at present? In what ways?
11. As they look to the future, what advantages do teenagers have over older people?
12. List several specific choices that may set the direction of one's life.
13. What habits formed early in life may be emotional or physical handicaps in later years?
14. Discuss some special growth tasks required of both children and parents when children reach adolescence. How are these growth tasks parallel?
15. Even though most of you do not plan to marry for some time, why should young people be concerned about what makes for successful marriage and parenthood?
16. What percentage of men and women eventually marry? Do you think a larger percentage of the population marries than is actually qualified? Explain.
17. What are some of the advantages of living a single life? Of being married?
18. Why do married people of all ages have lower death rates than do the single of the same ages?
19. Can you explain why people may not look upon preparing for the career of marriage in the same way that they view a career in teaching, medicine, manufacturing, accounting, or police work?
20. Why is the preparation for marriage important from society's viewpoint?
21. What are the chief functions of the family?
22. Name some of the physical characteristics children receive from their parents.
23. What characteristics in people are determined largely by their environment as children? Does environment have a greater effect than heredity?

ACTIVITIES AND PROJECTS

1. Imagine that you are twenty years older. Write a short discussion of a difficult day you have just had in your relationships with one or more of your children. What went wrong from your viewpoint? How does it look to your child?
2. Chapter 1 says that adequate growth achieved in each stage of life contributes to growth in successive stages. Can you think of a difficult situation you have encountered lately, your handling of which will contribute to the way you can meet a problem in the future? Analyze your constructive or destructive actions.
3. Make a list of the necessary preparation and qualifications for entering each of the following fields of endeavor: teaching, medicine, marriage, skilled labor.
4. Have you ever analyzed the ways in which your family differs from others'? To get a picture of your family's contribution to you, write a paragraph summarizing the main physical characteristics of your family and another paragraph describing some of the distinctive social traits of members of your family.

WORDS AND CONCEPTS

At the end of each chapter, you will find a list of some words and terms used in the text. Make use of a dictionary and the discussion in the chapter to gain an understanding of the broad concepts as well as the usage of the words and terms listed.

biological inheritance
category
chromosomes
connotations
continuity
culture
discrimination
environment
family values
genes
implications
institution
motivation
nurture
option
ovum
permanent significance
physical environment
potential
species
sperm
stereotype
tendency
traditions

What You Are

2

After studying this chapter, you will be able to

1. List some common needs basic to personality development.
2. Identify possible causes for ups and downs in feelings of physical and/or emotional well-being.
3. Describe constructive and destructive ways of reacting to a bad day.
4. Discuss the range of normal physical development during adolescence and the social differences characteristic of each sex.

Now is a good time to take a clear look at the person you are. You can add up the things that are on the credit side of your personality and balance them against traits or habits that are liabilities. This honest evaluation is basic for those who want to go ahead meeting life situations with confidence. You may feel handicapped by some of the traits that you now have as part of your personality.

Perhaps something often goes wrong in your relationships with others. When one can recognize one's strong and weak points, one is ready to do something about the traits that clearly need to be changed. All of us have some of the same feelings and needs. It is because we are seeking to satisfy these needs that we behave as we do.

If these needs have been met all the way along, a person is much more likely to have developed a well-balanced personality, and to be able to have mutually rewarding relationships with others. If personality needs have not been met, one may have developed habits of action or ways of feeling and thinking that are handicaps in daily living.

OUR BASIC NEEDS

First, *everyone needs to feel respected and valued by others.* For children, a consciousness of the love of parents is of fundamental importance to emotional growth. If your parents have loved you well enough to work with you as well as for you, to spend time with you because they liked your company—if they let you know that they have felt good about having you in the family—you probably have grown up with certain attitudes that are a help to you in getting along with other people. But you still want to feel that those less prejudiced than your parents like you, too.

At some time, you have been rebuffed by someone and made to feel rejected. That experience is always hard to take. Nevertheless, it happens at least a few times to everyone. No one goes through life without ever being unwanted or left out.

The important thing is whether you can use such experiences constructively so that they occur less frequently or whether you take them in such a way that they mar your personality, which consequently may cause them to occur even more often. The following chapter will discuss some of the constructive and destructive ways in which people sometimes react when faced with problems.

Second, *each person needs the satisfaction of achievement in at least one activity or part of life.* In some, this need is excessive. They are too competitive. Their satisfaction comes, not from the pleasure of achievement, but from feeling that they have outdone others. An element of competition exists in almost all of our efforts. We play to win. But more essential to happiness and effectiveness in life is the knowledge that we have certain skills and abilities and that we can call upon these when we need them. If a person is excessively competitive, it may mean that actually that person is not confident of this ability and must excel in order to prove that there is no inadequacy.

When we have learned by experience that we have certain abilities or that we can do some things well, it becomes easier to give to others the recognition they need for their abilities or capacities. No one is able to achieve in all things. Abilities vary, but every person has some aptitude for excellence in one or more areas. If you study yourself, you can make the most of the aptitudes that you have.

Third, *all of us have a gregarious side to our nature; we need the companionship of others.* You know how important your friends are to you—the group of people with whom you spend your free time. The person who has always lived in the same town and has always attended school with the same people may not be aware of the special effort it takes to become acquainted with others. But the young person who moves into a new community and school in the middle of the school year or changes schools within the community has to make use of certain effective techniques in association with others in order to establish an individual position. The one who is successful in becoming established in a new group has developed a skill that will be useful all through life, and such a person will be better able to make new friends in any situation, whether or not he or she is a newcomer.

Sometimes, people are not forced by circumstances, such as a change in school or in residence, to branch out in their associations. They become too dependent upon a certain few people and associate exclusively with a limited number. Consequently, they miss the development that comes with knowing and enjoying many different types of people.

Fourth, *we all need new experiences, or adventure.* People try in all kinds of ways to satisfy their need for adventure. One reason that newcomers to a school find so much satisfaction in making friends is that the experience is new and different. True, such an experience is not always easy. It calls upon abilities and powers that the person may not have known existed. However, to find and use new abilities brings a sense of achievement and satisfaction.

A great part of the fascination of travel is the expanded experience that it offers. One needs to cultivate the ability to take advantage of new experiences. Most of us have a tendency to be provincial, but we get a lot more out of life if we overcome that tendency. We need not be

Each of us needs friends. We want to feel that we are liked and valued. In what other ways do our friends meet our needs?

like one boy whose parents took him on a European trip. While the rest of the party enjoyed the special foods of each country, he was not willing to do any adventuring in his eating. He longed only for such foods as hamburgers. Most people may not travel far from home, but those who are awake to opportunities will find many new and constructive experiences in their own community.

Some people try to satisfy their need for new experiences by going recklessly against the standards of society, rather than adventuring in acceptable ways. An immature person may get a thrill out of throwing a rock through a window and then running away before being caught. Another person with the same urge toward adventure may explore unknown and interesting parts of the city.

One high school student may get pleasure from driving a car or a motorcycle at reckless speeds, ignoring traffic regulations and taking chances with accidents or death; while another who is more mature may become an expert driver who has complete control of the machine.

Thus, in seeking to find satisfactions for the needs that are common to us all, we may use means that are constructive. Such means contribute to growth and make us more effective in daily living. Or we may resort to courses of action that seem satisfactory at the moment, but that will eventually bring defeat because they create problems and consolidate destructive personality traits.

UPS AND DOWNS

Another way in which you may be like many others is in a tendency to have "good days" or "bad days" without knowing the reason for such feelings.

Perhaps something goes wrong at home before breakfast. You get a late start to school, and then you fail a test in the first-hour class, and a teacher makes a remark to you that seems unfair. It's a bad day! You overhear someone making an unkind comment about you as you enter the school building, and you begin to feel that you have not a friend in the world and that life is not worth living.

Some people go through cycles in their feelings. When they are feeling low, they look for the cause in the happenings of their day. When they feel better, they believe it is because the world is treating them right for a change. Others manage to keep their feelings on a fairly even keel and to meet the different occurrences in their daily lives without wide swings in their emotions.

Moods are sometimes due to physical causes. If one is not up to par, has lost sleep, or has been missing meals, making up for it with the kinds of snacks that add nothing to good nutrition, the resulting physical condition may be reflected in emotional life. Nutritionists have found that emotions are affected by deficiencies in some of the necessary food elements. Not having enough food containing protein such as meat and eggs, or not having enough of the vitamins and minerals found in

Many different types of activities offer opportunities for the satisfaction of our need to achieve.

green and yellow vegetables and in fruit, can cause deficiencies that affect one's emotions and disposition. There are good reasons to eat a good breakfast and to choose an apple rather than candy when one is hungry between meals.

Also, girls sometimes feel depressed when physical changes are taking place in connection with the menstrual cycle. At such a time, it may be hard to recognize feelings as temporary and due to physical causes.

Conversely, physical well-being is affected by emotional behavior. A person who allows himself or herself to become discouraged and upset over trifles, and makes it a practice to fly into a rage or give way to crying spells when things go wrong may begin to have physical symptoms such as loss of appetite, indigestion, or sleeplessness.

It is not always possible to put a finger upon the exact cause of a feeling of depression, but it is profitable to learn when to ignore such feelings and how to minimize them by filling the time with constructive activities. You can learn not to attach too much importance to your tem-

We have our ups and downs, but as we become mature we learn how to cope with our moods.

porary moods. You can develop the ability to look at situations that affect you and decide whether there is an actual cause for discouragement or unhappiness. When there is a real problem causing discouragement, help is sometimes available through counselors at school. One who can discuss problems with parents may find help from them.

WHAT DO YOU DO?*

Below is a list of things college students have told us that they do when they have had a bad day and need to get rid of their unpleasant feelings. Read the list and mentally, or on a separate sheet of paper, check whether these ways of expressing feelings are desirable or undesirable. Which of these do you find yourself using? Have you found some constructive ways, not listed here, for working off feelings?

If I'm feeling low or have had a bad day, I

1. become moody.
2. argue and quarrel.
3. show temper.
4. engage in sports and games.
5. take a walk.
6. throw or break things.
7. work or study.
8. talk things over with a good listener.
9. get sarcastic.
10. cry.
11. ride or drive.
12. slam doors or drawers.
13. play a musical instrument or sing.
14. watch television or go to a movie.
15. listen to records.
16. blame others.
17. do things for others.
18. take out anger on pets.
19. sulk and am rude to others.
20. smoke or drink.
21. overeat.
22. drive recklessly.
23. read a book or magazine.

* If you have not read or studied our book *Building Your Life* (Englewood Cliffs: Prentice-Hall, Inc., 1964), read the section "Physical and Mental Health," pages 221–281. That discussion may help you toward a better understanding of yourself and your ways. The list on this page is adapted from that book, page 241.

Although some interests remain constant, every stage of life has growth tasks and adjustments.

YET EACH INDIVIDUAL REMAINS UNIQUE

Thus far, this chapter has been considering ways in which we all tend to be alike in basic needs. Yet as you observe the great variations among people, the differences in their responses and in their physical growth and intellectual ability may seem greater than the similarities. You are probably especially aware of the specific ways in which you feel that you are different.

It is true that although basic needs are similar, and even ways of reacting to these needs tend to be similar, we are more concerned about characteristics that make each of us an individual with a unique identity. For each person, there is a normal rate of physical development, and this rate may differ greatly from that of another person of exactly the same age. The same is true of intellectual ability and development. Throughout life, we must achieve certain physical, emotional, intellectual, and social growth tasks appropriate to each specific age; and we achieve these successive levels of development according to our own individual abilities and experiences. There is no absolute standard at any given point by which to measure the progress one is making.

WHAT YOU ARE

GROWTH TASKS AHEAD

Perhaps if we look at the close relationship between physical factors and emotional functioning of another age group, an understanding of growth requirements or developmental tasks becomes more clear. For example, you probably know some people in the grandparent stage of life. To you, they may seem to be just there, fixed, unchanging, with all their responses to life's experiences long since permanently engraved. However, if you could see beyond surface appearances into their feelings, you would discover that they are in a stage very much like your own. They are experiencing physical changes that are new to them. They are finding it necessary to come to terms with these changes and to try to understand and cope with emotional reactions that accompany physical changes.

Often a connection exists between our emotions and our physical condition.

For example, older people who are accustomed to feeling strong and energetic find it no easier at their age, than you would find it now, to have their energy limited or to cope with recurring illnesses that block their ability to carry out plans and projects. They also must adjust to changes in their appearance. Just as it matters to you now to have an attractive appearance, so it will matter regardless of your age. At older ages, one must adjust to the fact that appearance has changed, that what was considered beauty or handsomeness has altered. The older person must now reassess goals and determine what values are basic to happiness. This person has the same challenge here that you have in your teens. The older person who is achieving the growth tasks required of that age is coming to terms with physical facts of life and the emotional complications accompanying physical changes.

The person who during the teens can develop an understanding and acceptance of his or her own physical makeup and the close tie between his physical and emotional nature, has a great advantage for all of life. Adjustments in the future stages will be less difficult.

RANGE OF DEVELOPMENT IN INDIVIDUALS

There is a very wide range of *normal physical development* during the teens. For example, some girls enter puberty at ten or eleven. Their figures show distinctly feminine characteristics, and they begin to menstruate. They may also start to become very much interested in boys and in social life. Others reach this stage of physical and emotional development as much as five or six years later.

There are advantages and disadvantages for a girl either way. One who develops at the youngest age may easily make mistakes in behavior and accumulate some regrets because her physical development has outpaced her experience in making choices. On the other hand, she has an advantage in that she does begin to gain social experience and may at fifteen or sixteen show more poise and social finesse than the late-developing girl. The late developer has some advantages, however. She has more time for growing up while she observes and learns from the experiences of others. She has more years in which to develop her scholastic abilities and meet other responsibilities before she becomes involved with physical changes and the emotional and social complications accompanying these changes.

An equally wide range exists in normal development of boys. The boy's masculine physical characteristics may develop at any time from twelve to sixteen years of age. He may begin to have nocturnal emissions as early as ten or as late as eighteen, according to the rate of physical maturing normal for him.

It is sometimes difficult for people to accept these differences and to recognize that for boys as well as for girls there are both advantages and disadvantages in being an early developer or a late developer physically. There is no "right" age for reaching each successive stage in physical maturing; it is important to accept one's own unique physical endowment. In some other aspects of development, our growth is more within our own control and direction than in the physical.

SOCIAL DIFFERENCES CHARACTERISTIC OF EACH SEX

A major difference appears during the teens between girls as a group and boys as a group in their social development, although the difference between the sexes may not actually be much, if any, greater than the normal variations within each sex. In general, regardless of the age at which physical development occurs, girls tend throughout the teens to be more "social" in their development than boys. Regardless of her physical characteristics, a girl may be more interested in the prestige of dating or having an active social life than in satisfying any physical urges toward a boy. The opposite emphasis may be more nearly true of the boy. Strong physical drives developing during these years may be a boy's compelling motivation toward dating.

This natural difference complicates association between boys and girls in high school. Each one naturally interprets the actions and words of the other in terms of his or her own feelings and experience. Neither is likely to be aware of the variance of communication between them. Such a simple word as "date" may not, therefore, have the same connotation for a boy that it has for a girl.

ACCEPTING INDIVIDUAL DIFFERENCES

Problems that arise in families and in communities are in some cases due to a lack of understanding of the normal aspects of development of young people. Unfortunately, a tendency exists to judge everyone by inflexible standards. The young person who develops early—or late—may meet criticism or misunderstanding. Even parents may expect the same kind of behavior and attitudes from two or more children, each of whose development is very different from that of the others.

An understanding of the normality of differences in physical, emotional, intellectual, and social growth will help you in your teens to accept your own present stage of growth. You can then work toward an ever-improving balance between what you are as a unique individual and the kind of life you want to live.

Not everyone has the same talents.

Whatever problems of adjustment one has at this stage of life, there is the helpful fact that all one's associates are confronted with the same kinds of tasks in living. Everyone is trying to gain social experience, to function well in a group. Everyone suffers embarrassment at times. No one is absolutely confident, no matter how confident some people may appear to be. Each one's challenge should be to understand and accept comfortably one's own special characteristics. To be depressed or discouraged over failures of any kind, whether in friendships, studies, or physical appearance, only wastes energy that might be used to make progress toward becoming more successful in one's situation.

QUESTIONS FOR REVIEW

1. Why is it valuable to look critically at your own personality?
2. What are four personality needs that we all have?
3. What may be indicated by excessive competitiveness with others?
4. In what ways do people show the gregarious side of their natures?
5. Give examples of constructive ways in which young people fulfill their desire for new experiences. Give examples of destructive ways.
6. Are you aware of the cause of your problems if you are having a "bad day," or do you feel that everyone else is out of step? Are you aware of the true reason for this type of behavior?
7. List several factors that may cause people to have ups and downs in their feelings of physical and/or emotional well-being.

WHAT YOU ARE

8. Do you recognize any types of behavior given on page 23 as characteristic when you are feeling low? What would you add to the list?
9. What are some of the special changes grandparents have to face and adjust to? How are their problems of adjustment parallel to yours?
10. What is the range of normal physical development during adolescence?
11. What might be some special problems of boys or girls who develop physically at twelve or younger? At sixteen or older?
12. How do boys and girls tend to differ in their emotional development?

ACTIVITIES AND PROJECTS

1. Examine the extent of your friendships. Are you depending upon an exclusive few for your social life, or do you make an effort to branch out and add new friends?
2. List some opportunities for new experiences that are available in your community. Try to look at your town or city as if you were a traveler seeing your community for the first time. Are you, as a native, missing some opportunities for constructive adventure?
3. Write a few paragraphs describing a person who has developed undesirable personality traits that are related to unfortunate family conditions.
4. In a good home economics book, look up the elements of a balanced diet. What are the four basic food groups and the recommended daily amounts? Does your diet include some of all the foods required?

WORDS AND CONCEPTS

basic needs
competitive
constructive
cope
cycles
destructive
gregarious

menstrual cycle
moods
nocturnal emissions
prestige of dating
provincial
puberty
social development

How We Meet Our Problems

After studying this chapter, you will be able to

1. List some common ways of coping with problems, and characterize their positive and negative aspects.
2. Explain why it is important for one to analyze how problems are met.
3. Analyze what connection exists between how you meet your problems and your success in friendships and in marriage.
4. List the steps involved in meeting problems constructively.

How well you fit into a group, how well you get along with your family and with other people, and how well you will do as a marriage partner or as a parent depend largely upon how you meet your problems. You have already developed some habitual ways of reacting; but through conscious effort, it is possible to modify behavior patterns that have been built up during childhood. Let us consider some kinds of situations and responses involved in associating with others.

Have you ever figured out how you act when things fail to go as you wish? Most of us have observed how others behave in such circumstances more than we have observed ourselves. You have experienced feelings of frustration, whether or not you called them that. How you adjust to the frustrating circumstances is an important key to understanding your personality.

Imagine that, as one is traveling toward a destination, a roadblock is encountered. What one does may be compared with the ways in which people react when faced with problems. Four common ways of coping with barriers are we may make a direct attack; we may detour; we may stand still; or we may retreat. How can we apply these various solutions to the ways we meet problems?

DIRECT ATTACK

In many instances, barriers are not really insurmountable; they only seem to be. Sometimes, we can overcome the obstacles and achieve the goal by making a direct attack. We may give up too easily and look for what seems to be an easy way out rather than face the problem and overcome the difficulty.

A high school boy wanted to be a debater. When he tried out for the team, the coach thought he was a hopeless prospect. He was shy, had a high-pitched voice, and his posture was poor. Although he was given little encouragement, he persisted. He studied the performance of successful speakers and accurately sized up his own weaknesses and strengths. Then he spent many hours mastering all the facts on the subjects for debate so when he spoke it could be with confidence. He worked at developing good posture and at speaking clearly and distinctly.

We meet problems in different ways. With maturity, the direct attack may or may not be the best way.

By his junior year, he made the varsity team, and in his senior year, he was on the winning team in his state league. As an adult, he became a very good lawyer. He achieved such success because he was able to figure out his weaknesses and his strengths, and was willing to work intelligently to develop the abilities that he had. He made a direct attack upon his problem.

Direct attack is often the best way to meet problems; nevertheless, one needs to be realistic in evaluating situations. It may be necessary to change either the tactics or the goal. A little boy who could not get the front door open banged his head against the glass panel in the door until he cracked the glass and cut his head. He too was using the method of direct attack, but a less painful and more effective way of meeting the problem would have been to detour—he could have gone around to another door that was not locked.

There are many cases of people who believe they must have a certain type of education and enter a certain work or profession who persist in the direct attack when a careful study of the facts would show that they should change their goal or their method of achieving the goal. Sometimes, a family puts pressure upon a child to be a doctor, secretary, homemaker, lawyer, or engineer, when the abilities are such that this person would be far more useful and successful in work of a different nature. So, although direct attack is often the best way to handle problems, it is equally important to study the situation that confronts you in order to make a wise decision.

DETOUR

If we encounter a roadblock when traveling, a well-marked detour is usually available. However, with many problems that we face, no such detour is provided. In many situations we may have to think for a long time before we know what to do. Sometimes, we do little rational thinking about a problem; we give in to frustration, or we attempt to relieve our feelings the way the small boy did when he cracked the door glass with his head.

One of the most common detours is called *compensation*. People compensate by adopting a substitute activity when they are blocked. Compensation restores one's confidence and helps overcome feelings of inferiority that may have resulted from having experienced failure or defeat.

A boy with an intense desire to excel in sports may not be heavy enough or fast enough to be a good football player. However, he may become proficient in such activities as handball, skiing, or swimming, and so satisfy his desire to engage in sports.

Most of us know people who have compensated for defects in ways that are constructive. We have observed the crippled person who has a gracious charm that attracts all acquaintances, the blind person whose sensitivity to touch and sound brings enjoyment of pleasures denied to many who see, or the person with an extremely homely face whose kindness and friendliness have brought popularity or endearment.

Some people, however, compensate in ways that are undesirable. A child who faces defeat, or who is misunderstood and feels unloved by family, may turn to delinquency.

The bully on a grammar school playground is almost always one who is unhappy and unable to face the failures in some part of everyday living. This person expresses unhappiness by trying to make others unhappy or to hurt them, and acts this way because of not knowing how to meet everyday problems constructively.

The little child who feels inadequate and tries to compensate by being tough may, later on, be a rigid parent who must dominate spouse and family. This person, unable to listen to anyone else or to consider their needs, is still struggling with feelings of weakness that do not allow facing the possibility of being revealed as wrong.

People who feel awkward in social situations sometimes become aggressive and loud in public, or they may be sarcastic and belittling in their conversation. They may be extremely critical of the efforts and achievements of others. Often they are not aware of the true reason for their behavior.

We see then that compensation, like direct attack, may be desirable or undesirable according to the circumstances and the methods used.

TO GIVE UP OR TO TAKE ACTION

Some people who find themselves unable to cope with life's situations, who are either fearful or blocked in their efforts to achieve desired goals, react by just giving up and withdrawing from situations that would force them to grow. Sometimes, so many new and puzzling situations face a young person that it is a temptation to have a general "sit-down strike" against maturing. In such persons, behavior becomes fixed at a childish level of development and remains there.

An example of this may be a girl who, because she feels inadequate, refuses to become involved in social life. She clings to the safety of her mother or father, rather than developing a social life among her schoolmates. Later years may find such a girl the spinster devoting herself to her aging parents, excluding any individual life of her own. She may never recognize what was wrong. She may believe that she remained single because her parents needed her or because the "right man" failed to come along. If she marries, she may become the kind of mother who, in her fifties, clings to her children excessively in an attempt to control them. She may try to keep their first loyalty to her rather than to their own mates and children.

Anne felt that she was not very successful at parties. If the parties included dancing or any games that involved choosing partners, she was usually among the last chosen. She was wise enough to know that her solution was not in staying at home and avoiding parties. She attended class parties and any others to which she was invited, hoping to become more successful. But instead of working at learning to be gracious and friendly toward others, she tried to hide her feelings of failure by being highly critical of others. She would comment upon Sally's poor taste in dress, and smile in a superior way at Jane's awkwardness on the dance floor. She would criticize the ideas the committee used in decorating for the party, and make fun of the silly games that some people chose to play. She succeeded only in adding to her handicaps by becoming known as sharp-tongued and critical.

Helen was no prettier than Anne, no better at games or dancing, and she felt that her overweight was a serious handicap. She, too, was often among the last ones chosen. But she met her problem more constructively than Anne did. She was helped by a counselor to appreciate the fact that to many people social success does not come easily, that for most of us it requires some effort. She made it a point to give compliments rather than criticisms; she tried hard to cultivate an interest in whether others were having a good time, instead of centering all her thoughts on how she was doing. She attended the after-school dancing class that was open to all, and worked at becoming a better-than-average dancer. Eventually, she found that boys like to dance with a good dancer who has a pleasant smile, even if she is not among the prettiest girls at the party. Of course, she did not suddenly become sensationally popular, but she gradually overcame her handicaps and was able to make a satisfactory social life for herself. She met her problem constructively instead of resorting to behavior that would only have increased her unhappiness.

It is not desirable to escape from meeting challenging or pressing situations in life by giving up and making excuses for failure. One thing of which we may be sure is that all people in their teens are going through the same process of meeting new situations, developing new skills, and testing their ability. The difficulties that crop up along the way are not the unique trials of any one person, but are common to all who make their way successfully into adulthood.

Table 1 FACTORS THAT MAY LEAD TO FEELINGS OF INFERIORITY

Circumstance	Boys (Percent)	Girls (Percent)
My physical appearance	28	27
My lack of social skills	14	13
My lack of popularity	12	14
My poor grades	13	10
Being left out of activities	8	14
My lack of athletic ability	7	5
The appearance of my home	5	4
The way my family acts	3	5
My clothes	3	4
My lack of mechanical ability	6	3

Sometimes it is helpful to know that other people worry about the same things that we worry about. Purdue University polled high school students in all parts of the country, asking them which of the above things were most likely to make them feel inferior. Notice that about the same things bother both the boys and girls. (Adapted from *Purdue Opinion Panel*.)

RETREAT

Another way in which some people react when they face a serious problem is to retreat, or turn back, from the problem. This is called *regression*—to "regress" is the opposite of to progress. It usually means turning back to a less mature stage of development.

The student who, after high school graduation, goes to college and finds that college work is difficult and that high school friends are missed sometimes tries to solve the problem by packing and returning to the familiarity and security of the hometown. A boy who does not regress openly may spend too much time fooling around until his grades get so low that he must drop out and go back to his earlier activities at home. The young wife who faces adjustments with her husband may meet the situation by packing up and going home to mother.

Such people are reacting just as the child does who runs home and refuses to play the game when it does not go according to personal wishes.

Retreat is seldom a good way to meet situations. Sometimes, you may find that you have made a mistake in trying to achieve a certain goal, and it may be necessary to back up before going ahead again. As with a traveler, it may be necessary to turn around and backtrack to find another road that will furnish a detour around the barricade. In these cases, retreat is only a temporary and constructive part of advance. In regression, the individual tends to return to and remain at a state of adjustment not consistent with age and experience.

Resorting to temper tantrums, throwing things, breaking dishes or furniture, calling names, driving at excessive speeds, or trying escape through alcohol or drugs, are all forms of regressive behavior.

RATIONALIZATION

We sometimes explain our weaknesses and failures by giving excuses that may be socially acceptable but that are in reality an attempt to hide even from ourselves the true reason for failure. This way of explaining things is *rationalization*.

If Jane fails to make the grade on a history test, she may say that history is not a practical subject and that she spends her study time on something more useful. Perhaps she will claim that the teacher is prejudiced against girls and wouldn't give her a good grade no matter what she did to deserve it.

If Jim gets a traffic ticket, he may say, "The cop was cruising today just looking for a victim, and I happened to come along."

One who is disappointed with low grades in school may say, "Who wants to be a grind? I can't spend all my time studying. I get more out of life than people who worry about grades do," and so on.

Someone asks, "But why not rationalize if it saves face and helps one through unpleasant situations?" From that viewpoint, it is true that to rationalize can be a temporary help, but rationalization is not an honest facing of reality; it is an attempt to fool oneself and others about the reasons for failure. Before we can solve a problem, we must face it squarely. As long as we rationalize, we limit progress toward solving problems.

If Jane says, "I fooled around and didn't study my history, and it showed up on the test. I think I can do better this term," and if Jim admits, "I was going fifty in a thirty-five-mile zone when the cop caught up with me; it cost me fifteen dollars that I can't afford," they will be making progress toward overcoming faults. Rationalization does not solve anything. At best, it only postpones facing issues.

People who will not take the responsibility for their own failures often look about for people, circumstances, or even things upon which to project the blame. The very small child will say, "The dog did it," or, "You bumped my arm and made me spill it." A girl who was known by others to be unfriendly and distant often complained that other people were unfriendly and treated her coldly. She assigned to other people the trait that she could not admit that she possessed. Naturally, this was easier than to assess her own shortcomings.

Evidence of a healthy maturity is the ability to make an honest appraisal of one's behavior and to accept responsibility for that behavior. When you can look objectively at your acts and say, "I made a mistake and brought this unpleasant situation on myself," you are in a good position to begin to overcome the cause of the trouble. To face the facts squarely and decide what you can do to remedy an unsatisfactory situation is to act constructively. Feelings of frustration and unhappiness begin to disappear when you are working at doing something about a problem; but to alibi and place the blame elsewhere may only increase a feeling of defeat and unhappiness. Often one does not even believe one's own excuses and suspects that others, too, may not be accepting the habitual weak alibis.

DAYDREAMING

When some people meet baffling or unsatisfactory circumstances, they attempt escape through daydreaming. In their imagination, they accomplish what they have failed to do in practice. The person who does not make friends with the opposite sex may escape into imagination and build daydreams about being the most popular person in school.

Most of us have done some daydreaming, and it is not harmful unless it is used as a habitual method of escape when problems arise.

A type of daydreaming can be used constructively if the dreaming becomes a means to an end rather than an end in itself. When your wishes are blocked, you can do some dreaming as you make plans to solve the problem. The person who does not have enough friends can

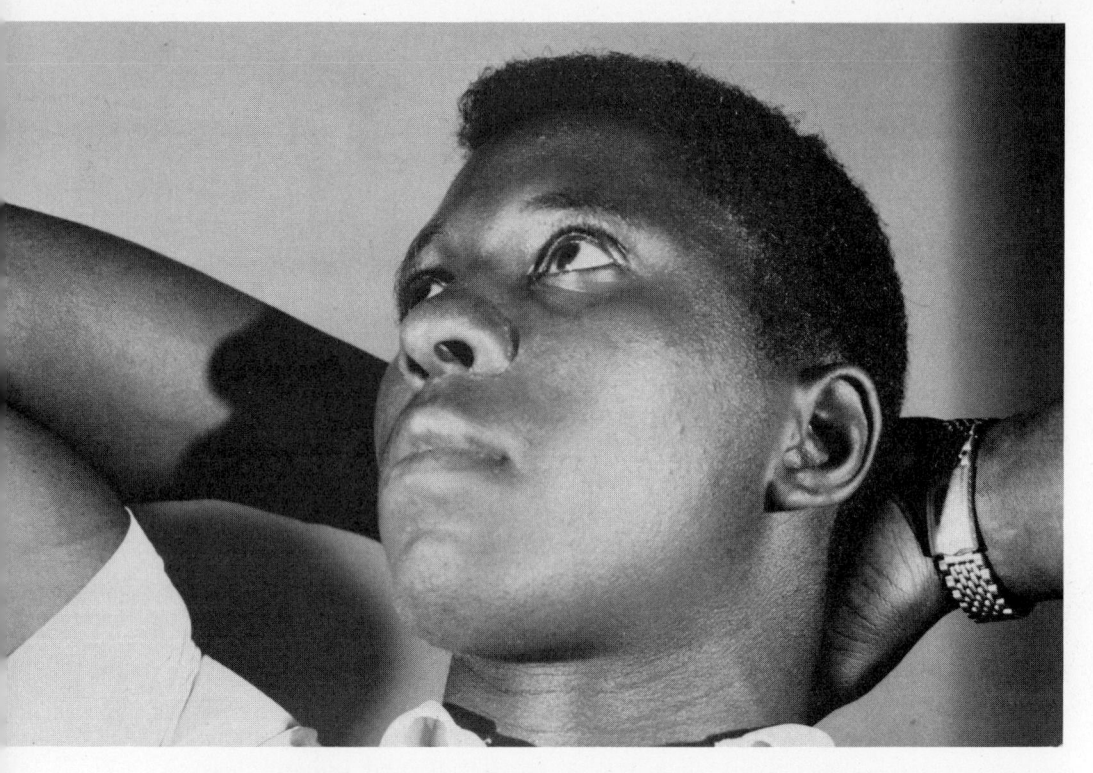

How might daydreaming be channeled toward constructive ends? Can it ever be a desirable method of meeting problems?

dream—if one goes on to plan a constructive policy that will be helpful in becoming more desirable as a friend or more adept in social situations. This would include a careful look at one's own behavior to determine why one is not liked and a course of action to overcome the faults. However, if overdone, daydreaming, or escaping into fantasy, may lead the individual into a world so far removed from reality that this person becomes unable to meet problems in any constructive way.

Can you identify the following examples of behavior in light of the discussion thus far?

1. John says, after failing a test, "I would have passed the test, but my brother kept the television on all evening, so I couldn't study."
2. Nancy explains her failure to get dates with, "My ideals and standards are high, so boys are uncomfortable around me; they like the girls who don't care what they do."
3. After failing to make the lead in the senior play, Jane explained, "I did not really want the lead. I have so much work to do that I would not have had time to practice."

4. When Allen failed to make the basketball team, he stayed home for three days, refusing to speak to anyone.
5. When Mr. Jones was accused of a questionable business deal, he defended his action by saying, "Business is business, you know."
6. When Henry failed his history and English tests, he took all of his books home and said he was quitting school.
7. Mary's mother and father were constantly quarreling and threatening to get a divorce. Mary went to a show almost every evening, and during the daytime, imagined that she was the heroine in the movies she had seen.
8. Mr. Johnson says, "Why should I work hard? A man has to have pull to get ahead in this world, and I don't know the right people."
9. Bill dials the number of a friend. Upon getting a busy signal for the third time, he jumps on his bike and rides over to the friend's house.
10. Sue, after sideswiping a tree with the car, says, "It wouldn't have happened if the brakes had worked better. Why do we have to have such an old car, anyway? All our friends have better cars."
11. When Helen was called on the foul that put her out of the game, she slammed the ball on the floor so hard that it bounced into the gallery.
12. Jim remarked at the dinner table, "I just know I am going to wake up with a headache tomorrow; I have to give a special report in my history class."

FEAR

Fear is a useful emotion; it serves us well many times in life. The physical reaction to fear is a quick increase in energy that can enable one to accomplish physical feats that normally would be impossible. We all know that in times of sudden danger we can run faster, jump farther, lift or move heavier objects than we normally could have done. Even when we are not faced with sudden danger, fear of consequences helps us to use wisdom in our actions.

But almost all people have some fears that do not serve a useful purpose. As people reach true maturity, they gradually eliminate the fears that are useless or destructive. They learn by experience that some fears are groundless and may be dismissed and that others must be met and overcome.

Many of us fail to recognize our fears for what they are. We may rationalize rather than admit that we are allowing our actions to be controlled by fear. People who have had a fear of dogs since childhood may explain their refusal to let their children have a dog by saying that dogs are dirty or that they are too expensive to feed.

Coping with fears

First of all, it is necessary to examine fears objectively. There is a difference between being courageous and being foolhardy. The person who is not an expert swimmer is not being fearful, but is using common sense, when limiting swimming to familiar waters or to pools where lifeguards are on duty. The most expert swimmers are careful to follow the rules of safety, such as swimming with a companion, and going into the water only when in good physical condition. We need, then, to distinguish between fears that serve a useful purpose and those that handicap us and ought to be eliminated.

It is wise initially to look for the cause of the fear. Such fears as of animals, or of the dark, or of lightning and thunder or wind, are often the result of some unpleasant experience in early childhood; or the fear may have been "caught" from a mother or father or from an older sibling who had such a fear and communicated it by fearful actions. One can examine such fears and decide rationally that they have no sensible basis, and then begin to overcome them.

The average person comes face to face with some measure of fearfulness. You may feel like resisting some kinds of new experience even though you want very much to do the thing that you hesitate to do. Perhaps it is hard to ask for or accept a first date, or you may fear competitive situations that might show you up before others. Such fears are sometimes not recognized. Rather, one may have vague feelings of anxiety or uneasiness in such situations.

It would be far easier to overcome such feelings if a person could realize that one's own inadequacies are seldom as apparent to others as they are to oneself. People go through life conscious of the things they cannot do as well as others, or imagining that others notice their faults and weaknesses, although those around them may not observe such faults or failures. Often, it is only in our own minds that we are inadequate. Those who can resist allowing actions to be controlled by a fear of failure often will find satisfaction and pleasure in achieving success.

It is important to overcome fears, for, if left unchecked, they may contribute to the development of undesirable personality traits of various kinds. The habitual sulker, the bully, the person who gives way to outbursts of temper, and the nervous or moody person often are the victims of fears that they are meeting negatively instead of meeting constructively.

MEETING PROBLEMS, AND HEALTH

It is not uncommon that small children who are starting school will develop a stomachache or headache as the time approaches to go to school. They may be dreading the new experience ahead of them and react with physical symptoms. This is not only true of small children; it has happened to every one of us.

Most of us could smile sympathetically when as children we read in *Winnie the Pooh* of Piglet, who, when faced with the problem of the Heffalump, thought perhaps it would be wise to "go straight home and to bed with a headache."

Players often find it impossible to eat before a game. You may have heard someone say, "I get a headache if I have to give a report before the class." What can they do about it?

The wise parent of the small child, after checking carefully to make sure there is no real physical ailment, will tell the child, "Yes, I understand that your stomach doesn't feel right, but you walk straight along to school, breathe a lot of good fresh air, and when you get there and get busy with your work, you may find that your stomach feels better." Mature people apply the same rule to themselves. They learn that they cannot always avoid such feelings as shortness of breath or weak knees when they have to make a speech, or a stomachache or a headache when they are faced with an uncertainty or challenge. But they do not allow those feelings to dictate their actions. A fifteen-year-old said, "Every time I have to give a report before the class, I get a lump in my stomach, but my stomach might as well learn that I probably will have to keep on giving reports anyway."

So we learn to apply common sense to our aches and pains, just as we learn to cope with fears. We can well ask ourselves, "Is this ache or pain just too convenient? Is it getting me out of a tight situation, helping me to escape a challenge that I should go ahead to meet?"

Steps involved in meeting problems constructively:

1. *Recognize whether or not a real problem exists.*
2. *Face the problem.* Just what is my problem? Sometimes, we shy away from a thing that bothers us; we feel that it is big and unsolvable, when perhaps we would find that it is not so bad if we faced it squarely.
3. *Seek the cause.* Exactly what has created the difficulty? Is it something I have done or am doing that I can change, or is it something beyond my control?
4. *Decide upon a goal or course of action.* What steps can I take either to change myself or to become better able to cope with the circumstances that I cannot control? Do I need help from a qualified counselor?
5. *Begin working in a positive way to carry out the plan for solving the problem.* Even if the plan should not be the best possible one, we get along better when we are doing something constructive rather than just letting our problems weigh us down.

Medical doctors talk of psychosomatic medicine, *psycho* from the Greek word for "mind," and *somatic* from the Greek word for "body." They recognize that many illnesses are neither entirely mental nor physical in origin, but that the mind and body are interdependent in their responsibility for illnesses.

We can cultivate both mental and physical health by facing problems or failures honestly and by being masters of ourselves rather than the victims of fears or aches and pains.

MEETING PROBLEMS, AND PERSONALITY GROWTH

As you look ahead, you hope to have a personality that is an advantage to you in all your associations. Those with such personalities feel generous toward others. They have few feelings of inferiority, or they have

Positive action in meeting problems takes effort. Often with the help of others, seemingly insurmountable odds can be overcome.

learned to recognize and cope with such feelings. They know their own strong and weak points, and they can be fairly realistic in setting goals for themselves. They have a feeling of physical and mental well-being and are willing to work patiently to achieve their goals. Most of all, they have ways to meet life's problems.

In order to make progress in personality growth, it is necessary to look at yourself realistically. Are you pursuing a desirable course of action in meeting problems? If you are compensating, is it a type of compensation that is constructive?

It is necessary that you be able to evaluate yourself before you can evaluate others well enough to choose your friends and associates wisely. This ability to be objective about one's own personality and to recognize a satisfactorily functioning personality in others is of the most fundamental importance to people who intend eventually to marry happily.

FOCUS ON YOU

Some people habitually act in specific ways when they feel frustrated or angry, without thinking about the effects of their actions on themselves and others. Below are some situations that might cause feelings of frustration or anger if they happened to you. Try to think how you might react to each of the circumstances. Can you see a habitual pattern in your reactions? After you have thought through these experiences, perhaps you can deliberately choose more constructive ways of responding, if change is needed.

Here's how you can evaluate yourself. Arrange a page in your notebook, numbering lines from 1 to 11 down the left side of the page. Divide the right-hand part of the page lengthwise into two columns with headings "Desirable" and "Undesirable." Rate your reactions accordingly, and observe the profile of your responses.

1. You want to be good in a certain sport, but so far you have not made the team.
2. Your best friend has grown four inches this year and is now much taller than you. It looks as if you'll be shorter than you want to be.
3. Your mother said to you this morning, "Why can't you be like your sister? She always puts her things away instead of scattering them around." It seems to you that your parents are always unfairly comparing you with your sister.
4. You received a low grade in a class in which you thought you were doing well. It seems to you that the teacher was unfair or at least made a mistake in grading.
5. You received two driving citations since you got your driving license last month.
6. A friend got the after-school job you had also applied for.
7. After what seemed a very pleasant and successful date with a certain person, you were turned down when you asked for a second date.
8. You want to try out for a part in a school or class play. Quite a few people are trying out for the parts, and some of them have had more acting experience than you.
9. You want a new jacket for school, but you do not have the money, and your parents say that they don't think you need it and that they can't buy it for you.
10. You want to watch your favorite program, but your parents insist on watching a program of their choice.
11. You feel that you are in love with a certain person, but he or she suddenly breaks off the relationship and refuses to see you.

QUESTIONS FOR REVIEW

1. Why is it important for you to analyze how you meet your problems?
2. What connection exists between how you meet your problems and your success in friendships? In an occupation? In marriage?
3. What do you understand the term *frustration* to mean? Can you describe feelings of frustration?
4. Distinguish between desirable and undesirable compensation. Give illustrations of behavior representing each.
5. What personality traits arise from fears that are not faced and coped with? Give examples in small children; in people your age; in adults.

6. What is the difference between "giving up" and "retreat," as discussed in the text?
7. What are some common forms of regressive behavior?
8. Why do people like to daydream? Under what circumstances may daydreaming serve a useful purpose?
9. "Fear is a useful emotion." Explain.
10. List some fears that are logical and serve a useful purpose. List some that are useless and handicapping in their effect.
11. What do you understand by "psychosomatic" ailments?

ACTIVITIES AND PROJECTS

1. From your own experience or your observation of others, be prepared to tell the class about examples of compensation, retreat, giving up. Do not identify any person. Make your examples anonymous.
2. Can you recall a situation in which you overcame an obstacle by the method of direct attack? Can you recall one in which you unwisely attempted a direct attack when your purpose might better have been accomplished some other way?
3. What are some rationalizations that are commonly heard in your school?
4. Write anonymously your two most common daydreams. Have a committee tabulate the results of all the students' reports according to subject. Do you find agreement on what young people daydream about?
5. Repeat Exercise 4, but this time, list your most common fears.
6. Determine the origin of and report to the class on a fear that you have.
7. Make a list of any physical symptoms you noticed in yourself when you asked for a first date; had to give a speech; faced an athletic contest.
8. Write a short essay describing a person who has developed a well-balanced personality. Cite examples to show why you assess the person as you do.

WORDS AND CONCEPTS

alibi
behavior pattern
compensation
delinquency
evaluate
frustration
inadequacy

inferiority
objective
psychosomatic
rational
rationalization
realistic
regression

4 Getting Along With Others

After studying this chapter, you will be able to

1. List those personality characteristics that are a hindrance to getting along with others.
2. Describe those habits or personality traits that are valued most by others.
3. Distinguish between flattering and complimenting, and discuss how complimenting others on their good points contributes to one's own personality growth.
4. Give reasons why people may gossip, be jealous, be sarcastic.

In Chapter 3, we considered some of the emotional reactions and the behavior patterns with which people meet their individual problems. Now let us look at some habits and traits that affect the way we get along with others. What are some of the things that determine whether one is sought out or avoided? Whether or not people can figure out why they behave as they do, everyone can follow some objective rules for behavior among others. As you practice behaving in acceptable ways, the responses you get from associates will be rewarding, and it becomes easier to form permanent habits that will help you to live more comfortably with your feelings about yourself and with other people. Your life within your family and in school situations can be a valuable, practical "laboratory" experience to this end.

IMPORTANT PERSONALITY TRAITS

Studies have been made among high school students and adults to learn what specific characteristics people value in friends or in husbands or wives, and also what traits are most disliked.

Young people and adults agree upon a few characteristics that they dislike. Bad temper, jealousy, selfishness, or lack of consideration for the feelings of others, moodiness, being overly critical, and attempts to dominate are handicaps in all relationships. Those traits are likely to lose friends for anyone. They also make for unhappiness and friction in family life.

Young people and adults also agree on traits that are most important and desirable. They like people who are cooperative, who can take criticism without becoming angry, who are cheerful and not moody, whose word can be depended upon, and who are generous in their judgment of others.

It might seem surprising that good looks were not listed as among the most important desirable characteristics in friends or dates. Girls gave good looks eleventh place among traits they liked in boys, and boys gave looks third place in importance. Even when a high rating is given to good looks, the assessment depends on the behavior of the person. "Good looking" is a subjective term. We rate as good looking the people we like. Consider your most valued friends. Why do you like them?

SOME HABITS THAT HINDER

Holding grudges

The person who holds a grudge tends to keep looking for more wrongs—and will find them. We find what we look for. Those who hold grudges often imagine slights where none exist, and they make themselves and others unhappy without cause. An acquaintance of such a person once said, "Why not just forget it? As long as one holds a grudge, one will go around always looking mad about something."

"But," you say, "if someone does a mean thing to me, I certainly can't feel the same toward that person." That is true. But one who holds grudges tends to exaggerate the meanness of what may have been done. Such a person fails to make allowances for mistakes or misunderstandings. Usually, there is an explanation for "dirty tricks," if we are open-minded and withhold judgment. You know that at home many things happen that family members could hold against one another. But the only way that home can be a pleasant place is for all to work at forgetting and overlooking offenses instead of holding grudges. To remember wrongs only enlarges or prolongs conflicts.

Of course, you may be really disappointed in a friend; he or she does something that does end your friendship. What can you do? Losing a friend is painful, but it is possible to get something constructive out of it if you can be realistic in assessing your part in the difficulty. Were there failures or mistakes on both sides? There may be things you can learn from the unpleasant experience that will help you avoid such failures in future friendships. Even if you can't see any way that the problem was partly your fault, to harbor unpleasant thoughts about someone else can only make you unhappy. It is better to fill your time and mind with other interests that crowd out grudges and resentments.

Gossiping

Psychologists have pointed out that people gossip because of a feeling of weakness in themselves; they hope to build themselves up by tearing someone else down. Many people do not realize that that is their reason for gossiping. In a few cases, that may not be a basic cause of the gossiping. The gossipers may just have drifted into a habit of repeating unpleasant things about other people, without realizing that they have the

GETTING ALONG WITH OTHERS

habit. Whatever the reason, the habit of gossiping is unpleasant, unattractive, and destructive. Even those who listen with enthusiastic interest learn to avoid giving any of their own confidences to the gossiper.

There is only one way to be free of the habit of gossiping. That is to refrain from passing on the morsels of gossip that come along. *Things unsaid will not be repeated.* Sometimes, when people begin to practice this rule, they are amazed at how many times in a day they have to restrain themselves; they find that they had fallen into the habit of doing far more gossiping than they realized.

Jealousy

Jealousy is a complicated emotion. Its elements are resentment, suspicion, envy, fear of rivalry, and, perhaps most of all, insecurity. It is usually hard to identify jealousy for what it is, when the jealousy is

Jealousy and antagonisms keep us from being our best selves.

in oneself. You may feel antagonistic toward a certain person, see faults and weaknesses, and have a strong urge to point these faults out to others. Such feelings must always be suspected of being based in jealousy. True, you can observe faults in another; but if you feel emotional, if it makes you boil to see how that person gets by with them, the emotion is probably jealousy. Identifying the emotion for what it is, is the first step toward overcoming it.

It pays to examine any antagonistic feeling or strong urge to be critical of some person, and to decide whether or not you are letting some problem or pressure within yourself make you covet what that person has. When you can identify jealousy, you can see the situation more nearly as it is, rather than an emotionally distorted picture. You can then try to overlook the faults and try to develop an appreciation for the other person. A generous attitude attracts people, but jealousy drives friends away.

The jealous person is seldom happy, and has a poison working emotionally that will affect his or her relationships with others. Actions dictated by jealousy are never reasonable or constructive; they baffle one's friends and destroy pleasant relationships. A jealous husband or wife is likely to create serious marital problems. If your boy friend or girl friend is jealous, this does not mean that he or she loves you. It should rather be a warning signal of rough times ahead.

Laughing at or making fun of others

It takes all kinds of people to make a world. In every school and community, there are some people who are not just like everyone else, or who stand out because of their ways, their dress, or their background.

Those who must make fun of people who are different are showing a lack of confidence in their own standing in the world. In effect, by their actions, they are saying, "Look at how different they are from me! Approve of me and downgrade them."

Sometimes, people even get into the habit of making fun of or ridiculing the ideas of their friends; they are quick to laugh at someone else, but would deeply resent being laughed at. It is important to show sympathy for other people, to respect their ideas, and to accept them as having the same problems and struggles that you have. Maybe their problems are much greater than yours. People are repelled by the one who ridicules the ideas of others or laughs at their mistakes.

Boasting and bragging

We all find it easier to appreciate the good qualities of those who do not do much talking about their own good points. We tend to look for weaknesses in those who boast. No real reason exists not to brag, except that in our society it is not looked upon with favor. Among some other peoples, the opposite is true. For instance, in certain primitive tribes, the successful hunter, coming home with his kill, might call friends together to listen to him tell of the courage and skill with which he brought down the game. He might even make a chant or song in which he repeats over and over such phrases as "I, only I alone, accomplished this feat." The tribesmen listen respectfully and join in occasionally with praise.

But because this is not the custom in our society, one must learn to exhibit skills and charms in a more subtle way. Boasting of possessions is especially boring to others. One who talks about possessions or what parents or relatives own is not likely to win friends.

Arguing and contradicting others

All of us find the person irritating who interrupts with such statements as, "No, it wasn't that big. I saw it, too." Healthy differences of opinion among friends are good. They help us to think more clearly and to be more sure of our ideas, or to see that we may be mistaken. But we can learn to raise a question tactfully about doubtful statements others are making. It is better to ignore minor points of disagreement than to contradict people on matters that are insignificant. Contradicting or challenging trivial points is simply bad manners. It usually reflects upon the one who does it more than on the person to whom it is directed.

Sarcastic and cutting remarks

Sarcasm almost always hurts feelings and drives friends away. Sometimes, people fall into the habit of using sarcasm in misguided attempts at cleverness. Others may use it in a deliberate attempt to hurt. It never pays to damage the feelings of others unnecessarily. No person is of so little account that you can afford to make an enemy instead of a friend, if you can help it. People who refrain from sarcastic and cutting remarks and who cultivate the habit of kindness and friendliness in their speech will attract others to their company. They give others a feeling of worth.

SOME HABITS WORTH CULTIVATING

Dependability

All through life, the person who is dependable has an advantage over the one who is capricious and unreliable. In any job, this person will be preferred over others and is worth more to an employer or to friends. There are some specific ways to establish the habit of being dependable:

1. *By being punctual.* A promise to meet someone at a certain time and place is as serious an obligation as is any other promise. No one likes to stand around wondering whether or not an appointment is going to be kept. One who is habitually late gives the impression that no one else's interests and time are as important to consider as one's own. To be late and keep others waiting is evidence of self-centeredness and indifference to the rights of others.
2. *By borrowing only when necessary and being careful to return what is borrowed.* People soon learn to be wary of the person who borrows pens or pencils and then walks away with them, or who is always out of small change and borrows a dime for the coin machine and then never thinks of it again. The actual money or inconvenience that this costs or imposes on friends may not be great, but such a person becomes known for these inconsiderate ways. People appreciate those who are careful about their obligations no matter how small or great an amount is involved.
3. *By keeping your word.* If Jane says she will help on a certain evening with the decorations for the party, her friends know she will do it, even if a more interesting attraction comes up. If Jim agrees a week ahead of time to substitute for Tom in his job because Tom has a dental appointment, and if Jim then forgets and goes to a game instead, Tom will not have much confidence in Jim in the future. A person who agrees to keep something in strictest confidence but then repeats it will lose standing as a dependable friend.

Carefulness in these and other matters adds up to dependability. One can develop this quality if one works at it.

A good combo is made up of dependable people who can work as a group. By giving pleasure to chronic care patients in a hospital, aren't these girls reaping joy and satisfaction for themselves?

Cheerfulness

Cheerfulness is one of the most attractive traits of all. "Laugh and the world laughs with you" are not idle words. It is not enough to be cheerful only when everything is going your way. Cheerfulness can become a habit that is quite independent of the daily happenings of life. In every school are some girls or boys who are constantly the center of interesting groups. True, they usually have other attractive personality traits, but they are almost never the moody type; they are cheerful and usually good-natured; they have an active sense of humor about their own life and about situations involving others.

Giving honest compliments

All of us know the feeling of warm pleasure and appreciation when someone gives us an honest compliment. We begin to feel expansive toward the world in general, but especially toward the person who was thoughtful enough to give the compliment. We think this person has good judgment.

If, then, you see something good about another person, it pays to form the habit of saying so. It helps you to develop the habit of looking for the good in others; you become more generous and outgoing in your attitudes—traits that make you much more successful in all your relationships.

Cheerfulness can be a habit, and this is one habit well worth cultivating.

Honest compliments are not flattery. Most people can recognize flattery, and they resent it. Flattery is not sincere; it assumes that the person is too dull to know that the compliment is false. It is a rather transparent device to gain favor with people who are not really respected. If we respected them and ourselves, we would not stoop to flattery.

But some people who would not resort to flattery refrain also from giving compliments. If you are careful to compliment people only on things that you honestly believe to be true, your compliments will be received in the manner given.

In daily association with others, you will observe many commendable actions or traits. You may see one friend meet sarcasm with calmness and good humor, another friend handle a tense situation with tact. Why not praise them for what they have done? Everyone likes to hear that he or she has done a job well.

Compliments on actions or behavior usually are worth more than compliments on looks or appearance. They show recognition of what the person is. But most people also like to be told if they look attractive or are wearing good-looking clothes.

Occasionally, people use seemingly complimentary remarks in a two-edged fashion that damages the feelings of the other person. For example, the girl who says, "You look so much better since you had your hair cut, I wondered why you didn't do it sooner," is not really complimenting her friend. She is in a subtle way making her friend feel that up to now she must have been going around looking awful. Numerous examples of such "compliments" could be given. They are used by insecure people who wish to undermine the self-confidence of others.

Insincere, or two-edged, compliments are destructive in relationships. But everyone can cultivate the habit of giving honest compliments, as often as possible. It will make friends for us and better people of us. If you have the habit of expressing your complimentary reactions toward others, you will have a great advantage later when it comes to building a happy relationship in your marriage. In marriage and family living, it is of greatest importance to build each other up and give positive emotional support.

Good sportsmanship

Sportsmanship implies recognition by the individual of the importance of the group. The good sport will pass the basketball to a teammate when that can be effective, instead of always trying to make the spectacular long shots. In games, sportsmanship, or its absence, is quite readily apparent. Sometimes, however, people fail to apply the same principles in their daily life. They are quick to take every advantage in all circumstances. They cannot stand back and let someone else have the limelight. They cannot fit into situations in ways that are supportive instead of competitive toward other people.

A good sport can take criticism or defeat in a fairly objective manner, knowing that one cannot always win. Some disappointments are inevitable, but still one should not mope about them.

Many married people say that a quality they appreciate above many others in their wives or husbands is the quality of "give and take." That is another way of being a good sport.

Consideration for the rights of others

A girl went into a bakery during the noon hour to get some doughnuts. Several people were waiting while the one clerk hurried to fill their orders. The girl went directly up to the counter as if it were her turn to be waited on, and the clerk, too busy to notice, sold the girl her doughnuts while others continued to wait. She appeared to be entirely unconscious of the other customers. If she was aware at all, she may have thought that her action was justified because she was soon due to be in class and so had no time to waste waiting. But what of the others? They also had other obligations and did not like to wait.

Can you ever really hate someone who comes to your aid? Giving a helping hand always wins friends.

To go ahead of one's turn may seem a small thing. But consideration for the rights and feelings of others, or lack of such consideration, becomes an established habit. The person who pushes ahead of others in a line probably also takes the most comfortable chair no matter who else is present, walks carelessly through doors ahead of others, appropriates the belongings of others when it is convenient, and takes the biggest piece of cake. Such actions may be appropriate to a child of preschool age. But even at that age, most children are trying to learn to share and think of the wants and needs of others. The person achieving the tasks of growing up through the teen years and into adulthood can make consideration such a routine part of behavior that it will be almost automatic to do the right thing in situations involving other people. As often as necessary, the considerate person stops to think, "How would I feel if I were in the other person's place? What would I want the other person to do if our positions were reversed?" Life is far smoother for everyone in a family or a group if the members have learned to be considerate of the rights and needs of others.

Being prepared

Some people are never ready for the usual things that come up in a day's routine. They haven't sharpened a pencil, or they are just out of paper when they come to take a test at school. They bring the wrong book to class and are inconvenienced or cause inconvenience to someone else. The successful person uses forethought as much as possible, plans time well, and streamlines routine so that there is more time and energy for enjoying life.

GETTING ALONG WITH OTHERS

In this chapter, we have been looking at some of the things people do and fail to do that handicap or help in getting along with other people. You can, no doubt, add many more in your class discussion. A helpful plan is to list the things you like in people who are desirable as friends or dates; and also list the habits or ways that are unattractive or repelling. You can then apply those standards to yourself. If the result is not very satisfactory, that is no reason to be discouraged. The important thing is to begin a constructive habit-forming program that is sure to show results as time passes.

FOCUS ON YOU

Everyone has behaved in one or more of the negative ways discussed in this chapter. At this stage in your life, you can assess your behavior and evaluate your progress toward becoming effective in getting along with other people. It is important to know why you tend to act and react as you do in your relationships. Below are listed a series of situations. How do you habitually respond to such situations? As you consider your responses, evaluate them as constructive or negative. Set up your answers as you did for page 44.

1. A friend invited all your friends to a party, but failed to invite you.
2. Your teacher reprimanded you in an embarrassing manner for being late to class.
3. You overslept in the morning and so were late for class. You thought someone should have wakened you.
4. You were driving to school in a hurry and were given a ticket for failing to come to a complete stop at a stop sign.
5. You and your best friend both tried for the basketball team. Your friend made the first team, and you only made the third team.
6. Your sibling always makes better grades than you do.
7. You have had several dates with John (Mary), who always talks about interesting dates with other girls (boys).
8. You have been dating John (Mary) when he (she) suddenly begins dating your best friend.
9. You told your parents you would have the car home by 11 P.M., but you got home at 1 A.M. Your parents are waiting up when you come in.
10. You promised to help a friend with some extra work on Saturday morning, but after being out late Friday night, you decided to sleep instead. Your friend phoned you after waiting an hour.
11. As you were going to class, you saw a teacher whom you do not like slip and fall.
12. You approach a group of your friends who are talking and laughing. They stop laughing when you approach.

13. Your teacher says something with which you disagree; in fact, you know the teacher is wrong.

14. You approach the checkout counter in the grocery with one little purchase of a package of cookies. All others in the line have carts loaded with groceries.

QUESTIONS FOR REVIEW

1. What can all of us do to insure that we make a good first impression?
2. Do you agree that the person who holds grudges is not liked? Discuss.
3. What is one basic reason why people gossip? If you gossip at times, is this the reason?
4. How can you identify jealousy in yourself? Why is it sometimes difficult to identify?
5. Give some suggestions for getting over feelings of jealousy.
6. List three questions you might ask yourself when trying to evaluate your own dependability.
7. Why do some people seem to enjoy using sarcasm?
8. "Cheerfulness can become a habit." Discuss.
9. What is the basic reason why some people laugh at or make fun of others?
10. Distinguish between flattering and complimenting.
11. How does complimenting people on their good points contribute also to one's own personality growth?
12. Why are we often more conscious of being a good sport in playing a game than in daily relationships?

ACTIVITIES AND PROJECTS

1. Make a list of traits that you find most attractive among the people you date or would like to date.
2. For one day, make a list of specific behavior in others that would make them liked or not liked. Be ready to report in class without mentioning names or giving facts that would identify any person.
3. It has been said that some very pretty girls may have less attractive personalities than girls who are not as pretty. If this is ever true, what might the reason be?

WORDS AND CONCEPTS

antagonistic
capricious
commendable

ridicule
subjective
subtle

SUGGESTED READINGS FOR THE UNIT

Fitzsimmons, Cleo. *Consumer Buying for Better Living.* New York: John Wiley and Sons, 1961.

Fleck, Henrietta, and E. Munves. *Introduction to Nutrition.* New York: The Macmillan Company, 1971.

Handbook of Food Preparation. Washington, D. C.: American Home Economics Association.

Menninger, William C. *Understanding Yourself.* Chicago: Science Research Associates, Inc.

Peterson, Eleanor M. *Successful Living.* Boston: Allyn and Bacon, Inc., 1968. Chaps. 1–17.

Pickos, Penelope S., John A. Spargo, and Felix P. Heald. "Nutrition Guidelines for Teenagers." *Nutrition Today,* 2(March 1967), 1:22–27.

Rhodes, Kathleen, and Merna A. Samples. *Your Life in the Family.* Philadelphia: J. B. Lippincott Company, 1964. Unit 3, Chaps. 6–15.

Scheinfeld, Amram. *Heredity in Humans.* Philadelphia: J. B. Lippincott Company, 1972.

———.*Your Heredity and Environment.* Philadelphia: J. B. Lippincott Company, 1965.

Sorenson, Herbert, and Marguerite Malm. *Psychology for Living.* New York: McGraw-Hill Book Company, Inc., 1971. Chaps. 1–10.

Stevenson, Gladys T., and C. Miller. *Introduction to Foods and Nutrition.* New York: John Wiley and Sons, 1960.

White, Ruth B. *You and Your Food,* Fourth Edition. Englewood Cliffs, N.J.: Prentice-Hall, Inc., 1975.

Your Food—Chance or Choice? Chicago: National Dairy Council, 111 N.Canal Street, 60606.

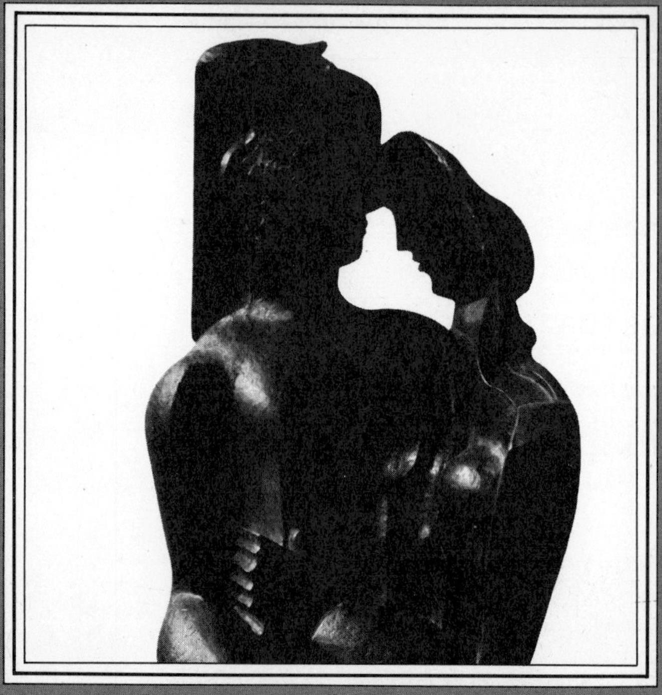

part two

SOCIAL LIFE AND DATING

The needle's eye
That doth supply
The thread that runs so true.
A-many a beau
Have I let go
Because I wanted—you!

American "play party" folk song

5 Dating

After studying this chapter, you will be able to

1. List uncertainties and worries parents may have when their children begin to date, and explain why some of these may result in misunderstanding and conflict.
2. Discuss rules to follow in asking for, accepting, and refusing dates that help smooth the dating process.
3. Describe some of the most common dating problems among high school students.
4. Explain several steps one can take to be more successful in dating.
5. Evaluate your assets and liabilities as a date.

For some people, the first date stands out, marking a turning point in the social experience. Others may have mingled quite freely with friends of both sexes during the preadolescent years so that they drift naturally into group dating and pairing off as couples. They would find it hard to name any one occasion as the first date.

For a great many high school students, dating has not yet begun. Just as there is a very wide range in normal physical development and in emotional and intellectual growth, great differences exist in the age at which different people become interested in dating. Moreover, many people who are interested in beginning to date may still actually have few dates or none at all. It can be difficult to enter this new phase of social activity. For even the most confident young people, the first dating experiences usually bring some uncertainties.

UNCERTAINTIES IN THE DATING PERIOD

Dating begins at a time in life when one is undertaking a great many new and different experiences. At this time, among other things, people are in the process of establishing a greater independence from parents. This process usually involves a certain amount of maneuvering, if not conflict. Parents are not sure how much freedom their children should have, and the young people feel the need for more independence than they have been allowed. Both you and your parents may have a hard time agreeing, or even being sure, about the rights, privileges, and obligations of a person of senior high school age. You want your parents to be available if you need their help, but not standing over you with too many attempts to help or control. On their part, they want to meet their obligations to you, to do whatever they can to help during these years of special choices and decisions in your life; yet they may find it extremely difficult to know where the line should be drawn between their responsibility and yours. They may worry and feel guilty, fearing that they are abdicating too soon, or they may try so hard to help that they seem determined to dominate your life.

Each new step you take away from your parents' supervision is a step into adult responsibility for yourself and adult obligation to society. It is logical that you have uncertainties. Such questions arise as: How much and what kind of social life do I want? How much of what I do want am I able to achieve? Can I be successful at it? If I can achieve what I want socially, how far can I go without interference from my parents, or conflict with them? Will they give me their backing if I confide in them? Do they know enough about my world and my feelings so that I can get help from their counsel, or must I reject their ideas and learn for myself? To find answers to these questions is challenging and sometimes difficult.

When it comes specifically to dating, you may have no trouble deciding whom you would like to date, but many people are not sure how to get the dates they want and how to make the dates successful. Many of you have been dating for some time, and it has been no problem. Even so, as we progress in this course, you may find new ideas about dating, and may look at its functions for your special needs in a new way.

Table 2 gives results of a national study among high school students. It summarizes the special dating problems that cause worry. Those of you who have dated extensively may be surprised to know that nationally almost a third of high school seniors say it bothers them that they seldom have dates and do not have a boy friend or girl friend. The number of those who do not date is higher among juniors, and much higher among sophomores and freshmen. Those of you who are juniors or seniors in high school and not yet dating as much as you might wish are having the same experience that many other people of your age are having.

Table 2 DATING PROBLEMS OF HIGH SCHOOL STUDENTS

Boys Percent		Girls Percent	
48	I seldom have dates.	39	I seldom have dates.
41	I don't have a girl friend.	36	How do I refuse a date politely?
34	I'm bashful about asking girls for dates.	33	I don't know how to keep boys interested in me.
26	I don't know how to ask for a date.	30	I don't have a boyfriend.
25	I don't know how to keep girls interested in me.	29	Is it all right to accept "blind dates"?
23	Is there anything wrong with going places "stag"?	23	I'm not popular with boys.
20	I don't know what to do on a date.	21	How can I keep boys from taking me for granted?
17	What are good manners on a date?	20	Should I kiss my date the first time we go out together?

A summary of statements of high school students from *Purdue Opinion Panel.*

SOME RULES THAT HELP IN DATING

When it comes to getting dates, there are procedures that smooth the process. If you are a boy, you can use the direct approach and ask a girl to go out with you, although that may not be as easy as it sounds. You may feel confident that all the girls like you, that all you have to do is give the nod. Even so, there are useful rules, and knowing the rules will help.

First, be definite. Don't say, "What are you doing Friday night?" and expect her to agree to a date before she knows what you have in mind. You might say, "I have tickets for the play Friday night. Would you like to go with me?" or "Bill, Jim, and I are going skating Friday night. They are asking Helen and Sue. Would you like to go?"

This rule is to your advantage just as much as it is to hers. She can know what the evening has to offer before she commits herself. If she accepts, she will feel enthusiastic about the plans. If she can't skate or doesn't like the company of Helen and Sue, she can refuse, and you are free to ask a girl who will fit into your plans more happily. It helps all the way around if you are definite when asking for a date.

Second, whether this is the only time you will ever ask this girl for a date, or whether you will want to go out with her again, it is an advantage to have her parents for you rather than against you. Parents

Your date and your date's family will like you better if you observe good manners by not monopolizing their telephone.

are likely to be more favorable toward boys who follow certain rules. If you telephone, make it a habit to say, "This is Jack Brown. May I talk to Mary?" Then don't prolong the conversation unduly, even if Mary seems willing. Some parents get angry if the family telephone is monopolized.

If you come in a car, don't announce your arrival by honking at the curb. Call for her courteously at the door. Your date will feel less conspicuous, and her family will like you better.

When the evening is over, take your share of responsibility for seeing that your date gets home at an acceptable hour.

If you happen to be a boy who is not sure that all the girls like you and are anxious to date you, you have much company. Many boys feel the same way. You have the advantage over your self-confident friend in that you know that you need to follow the rules; he may try to skip them. In time, you may be far more successful than he, because you work at being good company rather than depend upon your irresistible charm to carry you through.

If you are a girl, perhaps your problem is to make a choice of the boys crowding around wanting dates. However, comparatively few girls have that problem. Whether dates are few or many, a girl needs to know the rules, for a crowd can melt away amazingly fast if a few boys get to feeling that they have been used as bait for some other boy or as evidence of a conquest to flaunt before friends.

No girl can afford to be rude or ungracious in refusing a date, no matter who the boy may be. She can drive all boys away if she makes fun of a boy who has asked her for a date, either in speaking to her girl friends or to another boy. Also, it is only fair to give a straight answer of "yes" or "no."

It is possible to refuse a date in such a way that the boy will not feel snubbed. He has paid you a compliment by asking you; courtesy demands that you let him know that you appreciate the compliment even if you do not accept.

If you accept, never let him feel that you did so because someone better failed to turn up. And once you accept a date, keep it. It is not fair to break it because a more attractive opportunity arises. If you do that, it becomes known and is a handicap to you.

The problem of standing off a crowd does not bother most people in high school. Almost everyone goes through a time of doubting her or his attractiveness, of wondering whether she or he will have a date for that important occasion when all will be going as couples. It is natural for one to feel that she or he alone has this problem. It would be easier if one realized that this is a universal experience.

WHO ASKS?

In general, boys of senior high school age like to do most of the asking. The most successful girls will show interest in boys in subtle ways and not appear to be doing the pursuing. Not many years ago, a girl who wished to rate with either girls or boys would never telephone a boy and ask him for a date. Today, it is different. In some communities, girls are quite free to telephone and suggest plans. In other communities, it is much less acceptable. Much depends upon the girl's general personality. If she is friendly to everyone and quick to make friendly overtures to girls as well as to boys, boys will be inclined to respond on the same basis. If, however, a girl just singles out one boy and pursues him by telephone and in other ways, the boy may be more embarrassed than flattered by such pursuit and may become resistant.

Girls will be more successful if they observe the customs in their school and community. If other girls customarily wait for the boys to take the initiative, it is usually wise for a girl to go carefully rather than aggressively in trying to set a new precedent.

WHO PAYS?

When people start to date in junior high school, it is sometimes the custom for girls to pay their own way. If the dating is on a group basis, it may be more convenient and practical for each to pay his or her own way to the movie and for the soda or hamburger afterward.

Dating can be expensive for the boy. A girl should not expect to have expensive dates except on very special occasions.

However, in senior high school, many boys feel that it is their place to pay the bills. Again, people in different communities have different standards. In some communities, it is acceptable to share expenses. In communities where expenses are never shared, some boys will ask for fewer dates because they cannot afford to date frequently. Girls can have more dates with these boys if they are considerate in helping to make plans. Study dates, evenings at home, or going to events at school are among the ways a couple can spend time together without spending money.

BLIND DATES

It is usually better to accept dates only when you have become acquainted at school or have met through the normal channels of friends and family. People who accept blind dates may get into situations that may be beyond their control. Much depends upon just how the blind date is arranged. The blind date may be a good idea if arranged by a friend whose judgment of people can be depended upon. Such a friend should know both people involved in order to recommend them to each other. However, there is an obvious advantage to the girl who accepts dates after being asked in person or by telephone by a boy whom she knows.

Positive and friendly attitudes will always be greater social assets than "looks." A quick, friendly smile is worth much more than photogenic features.

Simply wishing will not attract anyone. Try becoming involved in others' interests and you will become interesting to them.

TO BE MORE SUCCESSFUL IN DATING

No one should ever give way to a defeatist attitude about his or her chances for successful dating. It is well to take stock of one's assets. Appearance is not of utmost importance, but it helps. The successful girl or woman usually knows her own type. She knows at least whether her face is square or round and looks better with long or short hair. She knows which colors and what kind of clothes seem to help her appearance. She knows the importance of cleanliness and of clothes that are suitable to the occasion. Whatever one's type, however, the wise person will not waste time wishing he or she looked different, or trying to copy the appearance of someone else. Positive and friendly attitudes will always be greater social assets than "looks." Sometimes, people give much thought to their appearance and fail to realize that they have other assets that are far more valuable. The happy, cheerful person has a big advantage. A quick, friendly smile is worth much more than photogenic features.

Centuries ago, a wise man who had a lot of experience said, "A merry heart doeth good like a medicine." That is still true. Cheerfulness does not depend upon circumstances. We all have problems, but being moody and downcast will not relieve or solve them. No matter what one's inclination, it is possible to build deliberately the habit of cheerfulness. Even when one does not feel very cheerful, it is better to remember that only a selfish person or a very young child imposes individual moods upon others, and that it pays to present a pleasant face to the world.

Another asset is a friendly interest in other people. If we make it a habit to show an interest in others, to listen when they want to talk rather than to wait breathlessly for them to pause so that we can take the conversation back to our own interests, we will discover that they really are interesting. Others are attracted to the person who is not self-centered, but is interested in other people.

Next, it is good to consider what you have to offer as a date. Perhaps you are good in conversation, and others seem to enjoy talking with you. Sometimes, what rates one as a wonderful conversationalist is the ability to listen to others.

What interests do you have that make you a more interesting date? Can you enjoy Ping Pong, handball, darts, swimming, bowling, or other things that people like to do for fun or exercise? Life is more interesting and dating is easier for those who work at learning to do at least a few things well.

Those who are not athletic can collect some good records, read up on movie, television, or sports personalities, or participate in any one of many possible activities that don't require physical prowess. It does not matter so much what the interests are, the point is that everyone needs to have some kind of activity that really matters to him or her, an activity that is enjoyable, even if it has to be done alone. It will not be hard to find someone else who can enjoy it, too.

No one will learn how to mingle with people if he or she sits at home alone. Make an effort to associate with others.

A step toward successful dating is to evaluate your assets and then to work improving your personality and ways. It is also important to know what your standards are, what you believe in, and then to stick by these rather than to change just to please others whose standards may differ from yours. Even if you don't date at all, this self-awareness and self-improvement is an important part of growth.

Next, one limits his or her dating progress if he or she sits at home and fails to mingle with other young people when there are opportunities. Go to games, church parties, or community events and school functions. It is easier to have dates when you know many people well. Girls can do more than just be available. Many schools recognize the problem of getting dates in the early years of dating, and student organizations provide occasions when it is "girls' choice," and girls are expected to ask boys for dates. If both girls and boys enter wholeheartedly into these occasions, the dating process is smoother for all.

Once they have a date, some people make the mistake of being too anxious to please. Certainly, you want the occasion to be a success. And it is important that each try to make the date enjoyable for the other person. Giving the impression of having a good time helps one's date to feel appreciated. It is just as important to know and act upon your own standards as it is to please your date. You want to be the most effective self you are capable of being. You learn by experience. However, for both boys and girls, a point that is important to remember is that you are in a learning process, and mistakes or failures are not fatal. This is not the last date you are going to have, nor is it the most important one. You can enjoy it while learning much that will be useful all the way through your dating years.

FOCUS ON YOU

Which of the following statements apply to you on dates? Think of specific dates and situations, and try to assess your behavior as objectively as someone watching or hearing you might. Rate the behavior as desirable or undesirable, as if you were judging someone else.

1. I try to draw the other person out to talk about his or her interests.
2. I talk about the good times I've had on dates with other people.
3. I think my date should be as interested in my successes and accomplishments as I am in hers or his.
4. I work at cultivating the ability to listen to the other person talk.
5. I talk mostly about my own special interests.
6. (Boys.) I ask for dates well ahead of time.
7. I try to cooperate on plans so the other person will enjoy the date.

8. I talk about the things my parents and my family own.
9. I object to double or group dates; I want my date to myself.
10. I never break a date without a very good reason.
11. I get jealous of my date's other friends.
12. I pretend to agree with my date no matter what I really think.
13. I belittle my date's opinions if we disagree.
14. I try to be friendly and courteous to my date's family and friends.
15. I respect the other person's moral standards.
16. I try to plan in advance for interesting activities.
17. I insist upon my own way about drinking or petting on dates.
18. If I've had a bad day or things have gone wrong for me, I quarrel with my date.

QUESTIONS FOR REVIEW

1. List several uncertainties and worries parents usually have when their children are beginning to date. Which of these may result in misunderstanding and conflict between parents and their teenaged children?
2. What does the national study of high school youth show about the most common dating problems? Do you think these would apply to your school?
3. List the rules to follow in asking for a date.
4. What rules should girls follow in accepting and in refusing dates?
5. Does Table 2 give a clue as to why girls are sometimes rude in the way they refuse dates? Explain.
6. Who should ask for the dates? Why? Are there exceptions? Discuss.
7. Discuss the sharing of expenses on dates.
8. What are several steps that insure more successful dating?
9. What do some people overlook in attempting to become good conversationalists?
10. Do you agree with the statement that other personal traits are greater assets than looks? What traits do you consider most attractive?

ACTIVITIES AND PROJECTS

1. List the three most serious dating problems you have encountered. Let a committee summarize the lists given by class members. How do the problem areas given by your class compare with the national study presented in Table 2?

DATING

2. (Panel discussion.) Three boys and three girls discuss dating problems in your community.

3. (Debates.) *Resolved:* That boys and girls should share expenses fifty-fifty when they go on dates.
Resolved: That it should be as much the right of the girl as of the boy to take the initiative in making dates.

4. (Survey.) Three students make a survey of a certain number of students to see what they think on such dating issues as sharing expenses, who asks for the date, what is a good date, and so forth. Summarize and report to the class.

5. What provisions are there in your community for young people to engage in social activities, either "stag" or in couples or groups? What might the school or community do to improve social life for young people?

6. List your assets and liabilities as a date.

7. Could the problem of what to do on dates be partially solved by planning more activities and parties in homes?

8. Make a list of the characteristics you like in a person you date. Compare and discuss the lists in class.

WORDS AND CONCEPTS

abdicating
defeatist
initiative
monopolize
photogenic

preadolescent
precedent
prowess
self-centered
standards

6 Functions of Dating

After studying this chapter, you will be able to

1. Describe and analyze some specific functions of dating.
2. Define "looking-glass self." Indicate ways in which dating contributes to the individual's development of self-concept.
3. Tell why getting acquainted with other families is an important part of preparation for marriage.
4. Point out both positive and negative effects of dating steadily.
5. Explain the meaning of danger signals in relationships and give some specific examples.

Because some problems arise when one dates actively, one might ask: why date at all in high school? Why not postpone all that until later when one is through with school and ready to marry?

It is true that dating sometimes does become so important that people neglect other tasks and obligations and so handicap their development in other lines. A problem of these years is the necessity to keep the different parts of life in balance, to make the most of the wide variety of opportunities for growth and experience without letting one special interest crowd out too many other equally important interests. The person who is aware of this problem and considers ways in which time and energy are used can allow dating experience to serve constructive functions.

Perhaps most obviously, dating provides opportunities for learning social competence at a time when others are learning the same skills.

You have opportunities to see other people in social situations and to observe what is acceptable and unacceptable behavior. Social mistakes made now are not terribly serious because many of your associates are making the same kinds of mistakes; you are all learning together.

Most people dating in high school have no intention of marrying for some years yet. They date for the fun and sociability of it. But dating does serve an important function as a step in development necessary before one is ready for marriage. In some ways, dating is like other activities that become interesting at certain ages. There is a time to play marbles, to fly a kite, to go fishing, or to learn to cook. However, dating is different from earlier activities in some specific ways. It requires cooperation between two people of the opposite sex. It cannot be a solitary, individual interest as fishing can be. A new dimension of interaction is required to cultivate a relationship with someone of the other sex.

No matter what one's conscious or unconscious motivations are for beginning to date, a realistic view is that the dating years are a preparation for, and a prediction of, the kind of marriage one will have. In our country, 93 percent of all people do marry. The quality of your preparation will inevitably have an effect on how happy and successful your marriage will be.

Specifically, dating can test and assess the concepts and relationships gained from other kinds of observation and experience. One who is aware of the basic functions that dating can serve may increase the probability of becoming able to choose a mate well and to build a good, permanently successful marriage. In this respect, then, it is clear that dating, which we begin primarily for fun and sociability, becomes an especially important stage in our development.

Thus, the *general* functions of dating are learning social skills needed for all of life, gaining experience in cooperative interaction with someone of the other sex, and testing and assessing one's interaction with others and one's concepts of what relationships are and should be. To explore some of the more specific functions of dating, we may think in terms of discovery and growth.

DISCOVERING ONESELF

As you grow through childhood into adolescence, you have, through family association, come to think of yourself as a certain kind of person. You may see yourself as the oldest and most responsible one, or as careless, or as helpful; as the organized one who takes care of your belongings; as a source of joy to your parents or as a problem and burden to them. Sociologists have used the term "looking-glass self" to illustrate the way one sees oneself as a reflection of what others see in one. Thus, as young children, we formed our feelings about ourselves in part as a result of the attitudes and expectations of our parents. The person who

At every age we try to establish our own image, which is often imposed upon us by the attitudes of others.

in childhood is given an entirely positive and satisfactory self-conception is fortunate and rare.

Parents, without being aware of it, may assess the child in terms of their own hopes or preconceived ideas of what their child should be, their ideas having little relationship to the real characteristics and potentialities of the child. As a result, the child may feel the parents' disappointment.

It is natural then, that the average person enters the teens with some doubts and uncertainties. Having dates with people who see you not as your family sees you, whether that is positive or negative, but as a peer, a date, a partner in social life, and a friend, allows you to begin to see yourself in new ways. Thus, *a function of dating is to provide a framework for beginning either to grow away from or to reinforce some of the concepts of oneself developed in childhood.*

When you begin dating, you may have the motivation and the opportunity to look at yourself in a fresh light and to discover and determine what kind of personality you really have. Thus, many young people gradually see themselves in a more positive and favorable light after they have had some experience in dating. To create meaningful friendships with people whom one dates is a challenge and an achievement contributing to positive growth.

BECOMING REALISTIC ABOUT THE OTHER SEX

Dating often provides the first opportunity to become well acquainted with someone of the other sex outside one's own family. As a child, a girl may stereotype boys and men on the basis of what her brother is like, or on what she has seen of the interaction between her father and mother. If she has no brothers, her ideas about boys and how they think or behave may be entirely romantic and unrealistic. The same is true of boys; the tendency is to have a stereotype that may not fit the facts about girls. The first opportunity people have to get acquainted with how members of the other sex think and feel is through dating.

It is even more important to perceive the great differences among people of the same sex. One can begin to discover this as he or she dates different people. Different kinds of personality characteristics can be recognized when some members of the other sex are kind, thoughtful, considerate, and use good judgment, while others are almost the opposite. Some people of both sexes will be found to be thoughtless and inconsiderate, unkind in their attitudes and actions, childish in their behavior, and with little understanding of other people.

"Gee, you're lots of fun. Are you sure you're a girl?"

Such traits in other people or in oneself may not be easily recognized. During the first experiences in dating, the tendency is to be interested and excited and to view dates in a romantic light. "Having a date" may be more important than the person dated, who may be viewed only as a symbol of social or physical achievement. If that attitude persists for too long, an important function of dating is not accomplished. Such dating may even, in the long view, be destructive, in that immature attitudes toward the other sex become fixed and can handicap relationships in marriage and family living.

The one who understands the functions of dating can consciously assess others' attitudes and can try also to perceive one's own attitudes. Dating can thus be a process of sorting and assessing as one makes progress toward making a choice for a permanent relationship. People who never date until they are at an age for marrying may fail to discover some important truths about people and personalities and about ways of interacting. This kind of discovery, earlier, can be an advantage in choosing a marriage partner when the time comes for that.

DISCOVERING FAMILIES

Just as one is likely to go into the teens with stereotyped ideas about members of the other sex, so the individual's idea of a family and what family life is like is based on experiences in one's own family. The child from a happy family whose members meet each other's needs may think of home as a happy place in which one finds security and response. This person may assume that when married, that is the way home and family life will be. Conversely, one who has been growing up in a home that is full of conflict and tension may either block off giving any thought to the kind of family one will have or fatalistically assume that conflict and tension are part of married life. Such a person may take it for granted that after falling in love, one will probably marry and can only hope for the best.

During dating, people have an opportunity to get acquainted with other kinds of families. According to dating customs in many parts of the United States, two people dating are likely to be in and out of each other's homes. If parents cooperate, dating couples may spend a great deal of time in each other's homes. The alert person soon observes that other families are not necessarily like one's own. He or she discovers that in some families the father makes the decisions, handles the money, decides on matters like vacations, and generally dominates the family. In other families, decisions are made by the father and mother, or by the entire family, with each member's ideas receiving consideration. In still other families, the mother may be the dominant one who controls everything.

Families have different ways and attitudes. Dating helps us learn of those unlike our own.

Some families are habitually kind and friendly toward each other and seem to enjoy each other's company. Other families cut each other down, are competitive, and give the impression that they dislike each other or at best tolerate each other for convenience. Some families openly express their warm loving feelings, while others do not show affection.

Some families always eat together, while others seldom sit together to have a meal. To some families, home is a place to spend time only if there is no place else to go; to some other families, home is a place where one relaxes and finds great enjoyment, and also a place to find strength and the perspective that helps in relationships in the larger world.

There are also families made up of widowed, divorced, and separated parents. The interaction in this type of family may be quite new to the person with both parents at home. As one dates and gets acquainted with other families, one also can observe that great differences exist in what things families value and in their goals in life. Some families value material things, the new car, new furniture, and new clothes, more highly than anything else. Other families may value most highly saving for a family vacation or for the children's education.

Religion is important in some families, going to services together, saying grace at meals, and taking part in the activities of their religion. Another family may seem to have no interest in religion, but to have their chief interest centered around the parents' work or the family business.

Thus, there are innumerable ways in which families differ. Surprises may come to the person who observes and tries to understand the families of the people he or she dates. For this reason, it is an advantage to date people from different families before settling down to date one person. But more than observation is needed. The thoughtful person will try to understand why family members behave as they do, and to reach some conclusions about what kind of a family and household one hopes to have after marriage.

During the dating years, the choices are wide open about what kind of a marriage and family one will have. Patterns set in one's own family need not necessarily be repeated. But they will not be changed *accidentally.* To be able to create a new and better pattern in one's own marriage means that the functions of dating have to be accomplished. One must learn to know oneself, to understand people of the other sex, to assess kinds of family life, and to formulate ideas of what kind of family life one wants in the future, for that eventual crucial choice. Very good marriages are more probable when both people have approached marriage in a cautious and realistic way.

DISCOVERING AND UNDERSTANDING THE NEED FOR LOVE

In many families, love that was freely expressed with words and caresses for babies and very small children tends to be less freely shown as children grow into the preadolescent years. At the very time when one is moving into a larger world and may be assailed by doubts and uncertainties and needs reassurance, one may receive less expressed love and emotional support at home.

Yet the need for love and support is strong at this age, as it is at all ages. All through life, loving support is among the most basic of our human needs. One is never too old or too young to thrive without love.

Dating begins at a time when one is moving toward an adult status separate from family, and through dating one begins to find understanding and affection from someone outside the family. Up to this age, perhaps one has never given much conscious thought to a need for love, or thought much about love itself. An understanding of mature love that can grow into a lasting relationship is not suddenly gained. It comes only with growth and experience.

Dating provides experiences that can contribute to an appreciation of love. How these experiences affect any one person is influenced by past experiences with love as a child. One who has not felt loved enough may demand excessive love and devotion in a boy-girl relationship. The

Every person needs love. That which we receive when we are children can have a positive or negative effect on our feelings and actions when dating.

individual who has grown up feeling secure and loved may find it easy to express love for others and may be less demanding in dating relationships. A baby learns to express love by being loved. The person who has not known enough love may be able only to demand, not to give freely. However, wide individual differences exist in ways in which people react to childhood experiences. Some will be affected more negatively (or more positively) than others by similar childhood situations.

A later chapter will discuss love in a broader context. Here we would emphasize the complexity of the concept of love and note that a part of the function of dating is to contribute to an understanding of this concept. One can gradually perceive a need for love and affection, and appreciate the way this need motivates and influences the attitudes and actions of all individuals.

One learns, if one is perceptive, that love has many meanings not easily classified. In dating, some people say, "If you love me, you will do as I wish." They conceive of love as a weapon or a bargaining factor. Others see jealousy as proof of love, which it is not, but rather it is indicative of a lack of self-confidence on the part of the one who is jealous.

An important lesson to be learned in dating is that being in love does not necessarily mean that this love could be the foundation for marriage. All of the people who get divorced believed that they were in love when they married, but the feeling they had did not survive. If you are in love now, you may outgrow this particular love. If that happens, you probably will have gained some understanding of love and its different levels and meanings. It is through these experiences that one can gradually understand the many components of love.

RECOGNIZING DANGER SIGNALS IN A RELATIONSHIP

The person who develops self-understanding, a perception of the personalities of others, insight into varieties of family life, and some understanding of love, should gradually recognize any danger signals in a dating relationship. Many unhappily married or divorced couples might have avoided their failure if they had been aware that even though two people are in love, there may be reasons why they should not marry. They would never have married if they had been alert to signs warning them of elements in their personalities or their relationship that would create increasing problems for them. What are some of these danger signals?

What do you think this couple is quarreling about? How frequently do you suppose they will quarrel before they see this pattern as a danger signal in their relationship?

Quarreling

If you have quarrels with a friend of your own sex, you are not likely to continue that friendship for very long. You drift away from each other and associate with people with whom you get along better. Friendships characterized by quarreling are not meeting your needs; if the relationship were happy and congenial, there would be no need to quarrel. What few misunderstandings occurred could be resolved without angry feelings. But for some reason, people who recognize this in their same-sex friendships may fail to see it in their dating relationships. They may repeatedly quarrel and make up, holding the mistaken idea that lovers' quarrels are natural or even romantic. However, a quarreling relationship will probably not lead to a happy marriage. It is better if that is known early in the dating years.

If you assess the quarrels that occur with friends or with dates, you will probably discover a pattern and determine what the quarrels are telling you about your personalities or about the friendship. Does one of you habitually become quarrelsome when tired or when some outside defeat or disappointment has occurred? To live with a person who reacts that way is very difficult in marriage or in a family. Do the quarrels represent important basic differences in your beliefs or standards? Quarrels that occur because one is trying to dominate and control the other, or persuade the other into actions that the partner does not feel right or comfortable with, are a warning that your differences could destroy harmony in a permanent relationship.

Some couples go through a series of quarrels, breakups, and makeups. One or both may have doubts and uncertainties, or outright unhappiness about their relationship, and yet they find it hard to make a final break. They allow the elements of attraction and habit to keep them together in spite of the factors that are driving them apart, factors that should be acknowledged as serious. Such persisting in bad relationships is partly due to mistaken ideas of love and courtship. In fiction, movies, and television, we are accustomed to stories of stormy love affairs that end happily. To be realistic, we need to recognize that such stories are escapes into fantasy. That is not the way it works with real people. "Lovers' quarrels" between unmarried people are likely to mean that marriage between these two would be characterized by ugly family fights.

Studies of engaged couples show that many people do recognize danger signals and break their relationships before it is too late. We studied 240 men and 570 women who had broken engagements, asking them to report on the reasons why they had done so. Table 3 summarizes the danger signals reported by these people. In another study, married people reported on how confident they had been that their marriage would be a happy one. It will be observed in Graph 1 that it was those who had been very confident who did have the happiest marriages.

Table 3 CAUSES OF CONFLICT DURING ENGAGEMENTS THAT WERE BROKEN

Cause of Conflict	Men	Women
	Percent	
Possessiveness	21	31
Jealousy	22	25
Disagreement about future	20	24
How far to go in sex	15	26
Conflict of personalities	18	18
Quarreling about many things	16	15
Irritability	10	11
Criticism	9	11
Dominance	10	11
Dislike of each other's friends	10	7

As reported by 240 men and 570 women in 18 colleges and universities in 1967.

Those who reported doubts and uncertainty were more likely to be unhappily married. Satisfying and lasting relationships are characterized by confidence and security, not turbulence and uncertainty.

Whether or not you are seriously considering marrying anyone you are dating now, it will be valuable to your future happiness if you learn to recognize the meaning of quarreling and to avoid any permanent commitment to a relationship characterized by quarreling.

Some subjects cannot be discussed

With some people you date, you may avoid certain subjects, because these subjects if discussed would cause misunderstandings. Or you may just feel less confident and comfortable when some things are discussed. It is important to learn which differences represented by nondiscussable subjects are only small matters of opinion and which indicate real contrasts in philosophies and purposes.

It is not likely you will ever know anyone with whom you agree completely. Dating couples who think they "agree on everything" have not recognized and explored their differences. However, in permanent relationships like marriage, the happy couples are those who actually have very few important differences. And the ones they do have, they are able to discuss honestly and with respect for each other's viewpoint, and come to mutually acceptable compromises. Both members of happy marriages probably ended some relationships that had too many or too serious differences, and waited to marry until they found someone with whom there were very few subjects that had to be avoided for the sake

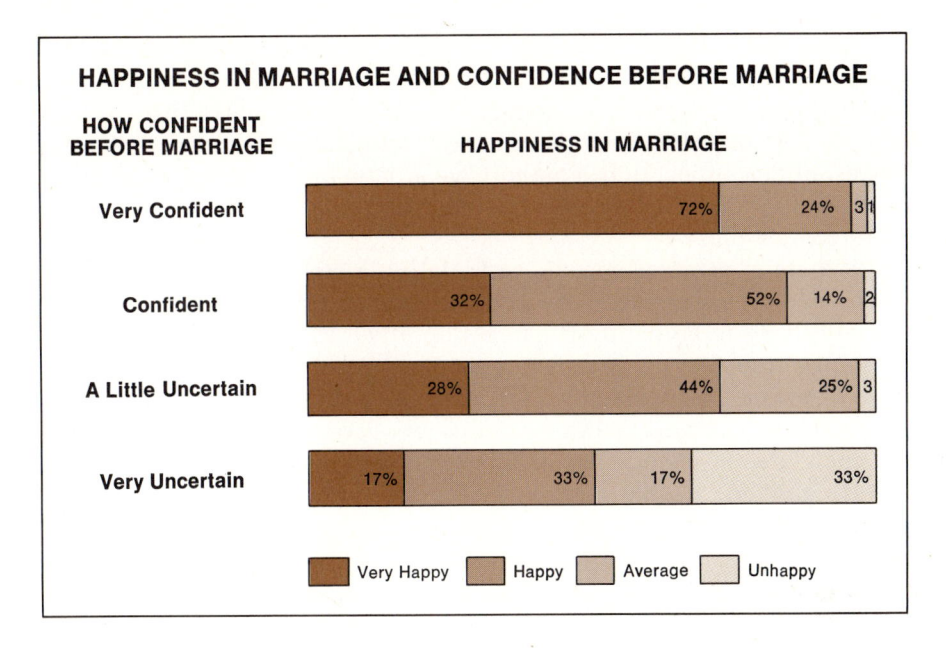

HAPPINESS IN MARRIAGE AND CONFIDENCE BEFORE MARRIAGE

HOW CONFIDENT BEFORE MARRIAGE	HAPPINESS IN MARRIAGE
Very Confident	72% / 24% / 3 / 1
Confident	32% / 52% / 14% / 2
A Little Uncertain	28% / 44% / 25% / 3
Very Uncertain	17% / 33% / 17% / 33%

Legend: Very Happy — Happy — Average — Unhappy

Graph 1. As reported by 581 husbands and wives.

of peace. In our research with married couples, we have found evidence that couples with the fewest real points of disagreement are by far the happiest and, further, that among the most unhappy couples are those who cannot discuss whatever differences they do have.

During the dating years, it is profitable to study the pattern that develops in a relationship to see how any disagreements are handled. Do discussions always result in the same person giving in and the other getting the advantage? Are compromise solutions found with which both can be comfortable? If you are the one who always gives in, could you live happily with this kind of interaction? How desirable do the patterns you see among older married couples seem to you? Which kinds of interaction could you live with happily? If subjects must be avoided for the sake of peace, or if discussing differences does not result in solutions acceptable to both, a danger signal is evident in a relationship.

Dislike for the other person's family

Dislike for the other person's friends or family may mean that there are contrasts in their basic values and attitudes. When the person one is dating is attractive, and both are emotionally involved, it is easy to tell oneself that the date is not like friends or family, that there is something wrong with them, but not with the date. The explanation is probably that the person one is dating is not being viewed realistically.

The reason dislike for a date's friends or family is a danger signal is not that such dislike necessarily means that there is anything wrong with the other person or that person's family. It does mean that the two may not be congenial enough in background (which includes interests, values, philosophies) to be able to have a permanently satisfactory companionship. It would be better for them to find other partners who are more compatible.

If there is parental opposition to dating a certain person, it may be considered a danger signal, because research has found that a marriage is more likely to be happy if parents approve. Parents may not be able to point out all the danger signals in a bad relationship, but if they do have objections, the person might learn from the situation by trying to figure out why parents feel the way they do. Parents are not always right, but their greater experience in relationships should be considered by maturing, young people.

If you are not your best self

If, after dating someone, you seem to be less responsible or less dependable, or if your other relationships seem to be in turmoil, there is reason to question the relationship. In a good relationship, both tend to have good feelings about themselves as well as about the other person.

People who do not quarrel, who tend to agree generally, who can compromise and reach solutions to the few differences they do have, and who respect each other, tend to feel comfortable and good about the relationship. Dating that is fairly free of danger signals tends to bring out the best in us so that we tend to get along better with ourselves, our families, and with others. It is surprising how many couples continue to date and actually marry even though the relationship brings out the worst in their personalities. They may have doubts and uncertainties about each other and about themselves and their past values, and yet they continue dating this particular person.

The approach to marriage

The various ways of approaching marriage differ between those who make successful and unsuccessful marriages. We did research among a large group of married people most of whom were happy, a group of couples who were unhappy and having counseling, and a group of divorced people to see what their courtship histories had been. The courtship histories of the three groups are summarized in Table 4. There are many sharp contrasts observed between the happily married group and the other two groups. The happily married had more traditional approaches to marriage than had the unhappy or divorced groups in that they were likely to have been acquainted longer, to have had informal

Table 4 APPROACH TO MARRIAGE

Approach to Marriage	Married Group	Counseling Group	Divorced Group
	Percent		
Knew partner less than 1 year	16	48	41
Had "understanding" engagement	63	42	64
Had formal engagement	88	37	57
Contemplated breaking engagement	29	44	50
Broke engagement temporarily	9	26	22
Felt confident marriage would be happy	90	83	71
Both parents approved of marriage	84	58	58
Had premarital sexual relations with spouse	38	73	58
Wife was pregnant at time of marriage	5	23	11
Married in church wedding	84	41	55

As reported by 1162 married people, 155 unhappily married people seeking help through marriage counseling, and 164 divorced people.

and formal engagements, to have had fewer conflicts, and so forth. This research may be helpful in pointing out danger signals in how one approaches marriage. Those who were failing or had failed in their marriages seem to have had warnings of failure before they married.

A later chapter will explore some of the reasons why people may fail to recognize signs available to warn them against certain relationships, this failure impelling them into marriages doomed to unhappiness. It is important during your dating years that you become aware that such signs are available in some friendships and that you work toward being objective in assessing the meanings underlying your interaction with people you date. If you can achieve such objectivity and insight, your dating years will be serving one of their most fundamental functions. You will enhance your chances for a happy marriage and family life when that time comes.

CONTRIBUTION OF DATING STEADILY

A large percentage of senior high school students do not date often and have never dated steadily or exclusively. However, going with one person exclusively is a stage of dating that people who date are likely to go through at least once before they leave high school. You will probably have dates with some individuals with whom you are not congenial. You don't particularly like each other after a date or two, or your dates are not interesting or pleasant enough for you to want to continue dating. You don't need to bother about danger signals in these casual encounters. Some other dates are with people congenial enough so that you continue dating and become attached to each other. The relationship may meet enough needs for both so that you settle into steady, exclusive dating. In these relationships, awareness of the possibility of warning signs can be more significant.

Among the positive aspects of dating steadily is your opportunity to become well enough acquainted that you can assess your interaction more and more accurately. Most danger signals discussed in this chapter do not become apparent until two people have associated over a period of time and under a variety of circumstances. Thus, a steady relationship can make a valuable contribution to growth, in addition to meeting the emotional need for closeness with another person.

There are also some aspects of going with one person exclusively that need to be recognized in order that they do not negate the positive results.

SOME NEGATIVE ASPECTS

Many people settle into a steady association chiefly because of the feeling of security that comes with having a steady boy friend or girl friend. It is comfortable to know that the problem of getting dates is settled. However, two people dating exclusively may miss the opportunity to associate with different types of people and to gain a wider knowledge and understanding of people. Two who date steadily when they are freshmen or sophomores are likely to put their dating security above all other considerations. They have not known enough people and families well enough to learn what others their age are learning. The longer some of these couples date, the more limited their learning becomes. You probably have among your acquaintances couples who have gone together for so long that they cannot break off their dating, even though they have lost their early enthusiasm, and even though all their friends can see danger signals for them.

A college girl said, "I dated Jim all through high school. Because I have no brothers, Jim is the only boy I have ever known very well. I realize now that Jim and I really haven't much in common, but going together has gotten to be such a habit that sometimes I think it would be better if I just went home and married him."

Some of those who date exclusively in high school become dependent upon each other and do go ahead and marry, only to find that they would have chosen a different mate if they had known more people well and were more sure about their own needs and relations with other types of personalities. Therefore, to begin too soon to date one person exclusively may defeat some of the functions of dating.

Many people settle into a steady association chiefly because of the feeling of security that comes with having a steady boy friend or girl friend.

In other cases, two people dating exclusively become deeply attached; in many ways, they do meet each other's emotional needs. But to keep all parts of life balanced and not allow their devotion to be disorganizing or negative can be too great a problem for some people. Many college students have told us that they feel that their steady relationships in high school were not constructive because they were not ready for the emotional involvement. They believe that if emotional involvement is great between a steady couple in high school, inevitably "someone gets hurt."

IN SUMMARY

The one who is aware of the various functions of dating can learn much that will help pave the way for happier and more effective living as a married partner and a parent. Your dating gives you the opportunity to compare your goals and values with those of others, and to know which are a permanent part of your makeup. You can get some idea of the kind of person you can or cannot get along with in a close association. You can formulate an idea of the kind of marriage you want to have eventually, and become perceptive about recognizing signs warning you against trying to make permanent relationships that would prove unworkable. You can test and evaluate your own maturity or immaturity. These things can be accomplished in dating if one is alert and interested in making all the growth that is possible.

All your experiences in dating have important implications for your development, helping you create a good marriage eventually.

FOCUS ON YOU

Assess your social life to see how well it is serving its functions. Think through the answers to the questions below. If you are not satisfied with all phases of progress, you can decide how better to apply new concepts you have gained.

1. Am I learning the social skills necessary in order to avoid offending others, and so that I can make a contribution to their enjoyment?
2. Have I established satisfactory ways of balancing my dating, my work, and my studies?
3. Do I understand myself better than I did before I began dating? What special traits or inclinations have I discovered that affect my relationships? Think of specific examples.
4. With my understanding of myself and others, am I developing more self-confidence?
5. What specific things have I discovered about the way other people seem to react to me? Does it give me insight into them as well as into myself?
6. Am I gaining new insights into ways in which other families function? Am I becoming able to evaluate relationships in families without being harshly critical of those whose ways I would not wish to repeat?
7. Am I becoming objective about my own contribution to the kind of family I want to have? Am I realistic enough about relationships so that I can eventually choose a marriage partner wisely?
8. If I am dating one person steadily, am I too dependent upon this relationship, or am I successful at allowing it to contribute constructively toward achieving necessary growth tasks?

QUESTIONS FOR REVIEW

1. Would it be better if people did not date until they were old enough to marry? Discuss.
2. What are the general functions of dating?
3. What percentage of people eventually marry?
4. What is meant by the phrase "looking-glass self"?
5. How can one discover oneself through dating?
6. How can dating help one grow toward maturity in understanding others?
7. Discuss the statement that "having a date" may sometimes assume more importance than the personality of the person dated.
8. What are some of the contrasts in families that may be observed as one gets acquainted with families?
9. Because families differ in their ways of doing things, does it mean that they are any better or any worse than your own family? Discuss.

FUNCTIONS OF DATING

10. Why is getting acquainted with other families important in preparing for marriage?
11. How do small children learn to express love?
12. What are some motivations for settling into a steady relationship? Compare reasons that girls and boys may have.
13. Discuss positive and negative effects of dating steadily.
14. Explain what is meant by "danger signals" in relationships.
15. Why do some people tend to accept quarreling in love relationships as normal rather than seeing it as a danger signal?
16. In what ways may the necessity to avoid some topics be a danger signal in a relationship?
17. Explain why a dislike for the friends or family of a friend might be a danger signal.
18. Which of the functions of dating do you consider most important?

ACTIVITIES AND PROJECTS

1. Use the main headings of this chapter as an outline, and write a paper discussing what your dating experiences have taught you about yourself, members of the other sex, and other families. If you have never dated, base your discussion on your association with friends and families.
2. Write an anonymous description of yourself as you see yourself reflected in the attitudes of other people.
3. What specific things have you observed in families that you think you want in your own family after you marry? Be prepared to discuss these orally or in writing.
4. Be prepared to write about danger signals you observed in some past relationship, your own or a friend's.

WORDS AND CONCEPTS

compatible	peer
component	perceptive
compromise	perspective
conversely	potentialities
crucial choice	preconceived ideas
dominant	sociologists
interaction	tolerate
looking-glass self	unconscious motivation

7 Decisions About Premarital Standards

After studying this chapter, you will be able to

1. Point out the advantages of deciding upon personal standards of sexual behavior before one is dating steadily.
2. Discuss the subject of premarital sexual behavior within the framework of the kinds of responsibility that life places upon one during adolescence.
3. Indicate in what ways motivation for and meaning of premarital intercourse may differ for boys and girls.
4. List some of the negative aspects of premarital intercourse.

A discussion of premarital sexual relationships is theoretical for many people during the high school years. They are not going to have to make specific decisions for some time yet. For some other people, however, the question is already immediate. They are dating steadily and perhaps in love. For them, how far to go and where to draw the line is a question regularly confronted.

Even though many high school people seldom or never date, have not dated steadily with one person, and have not yet considered themselves in love, the subject of premarital sexual standards is relevant for any young person during the dating years. One can think more objectively about one's standards before one is deeply involved in a relationship. It is easier to consider all factors relating to a decision when there is no special emotional pressure to take any specific action. When faced with immediate decisions, the person has an advantage who has thought about moral standards and has reasons for decisions about personal behavior.

Where does one look for guidelines in deciding what is right or wrong, wise or unwise?

Parents seem to have certain standards for their children; churches may have the same or other norms; friends and associates may live by still different standards. Even law enforcement agencies have something to say about your decisions. Is the best test of a policy whether any one of these groups believes certain actions are all right, or whether "everyone else does it," or whether society defines it as moral or immoral? No one of those factors can provide an entirely satisfactory answer. In this book, we can only raise some questions for you to think about; we can suggest a frame of reference that may be useful as you make your own decisions.

RESPONSIBILITY PARALLELS GROWTH—INTO FREEDOM

In Chapter 1, it was noted that while the requirements life makes upon us are not greatly different at any age in life, there are shifts in emphasis as one grows through the different ages. One of the shifts is in the area of *responsibility*. The baby or small child has almost no responsibility;

A child must trust others for guidance and support. As you mature, your experiences and inner resources will help you establish personal standards and self-reliance.

someone else is responsible even for food and rest. Nor does a child have the freedom to make independent choices. People in their thirties and forties have very great responsibilities, not just for themselves. There are others who depend upon them for food and clothing and love, among other things. More than at any other time, people in the middle years of life must think of others far ahead of themselves. They are, in many ways, not free to think of their own wants or needs.

At your age, you are leaving childhood dependency and moving into responsibility, the first phase of which is that you are responsible for yourself. Others' responsibility for you is decreasing, but you do not yet have to undertake responsibility for others that you will have in your thirties and forties. Not far behind your responsibility for yourself comes the necessity to begin to meet a succession of wider responsibilities: toward the boy or girl whom you date; the person you might some day want to marry; your family; and beyond that, the wider society in which you live. These are not responsibilities assigned to you by someone else; they are automatically yours. They are the other face of your new freedoms; the freedoms cannot be separated from the responsibilities attached to them.

Let us then explore the subject of premarital sexual behavior within the framework of the responsibility that life places upon you during the teens. Our thinking about this subject may be more productive if we consider just what we are talking about when we speak of moral standards and of a personal moral code. We might make a distinction between those two, although for many people they coincide.

MORAL DEFINITIONS

Society's moral norm has grown out of social history. That is, behavior is defined as wrong or right, moral or immoral, depending upon what its effect on the social fabric throughout history seems to have been. Behavior defined as moral in one society might not necessarily be so defined in another society. Thus, morality has come to be defined as related to patterns of conduct considered acceptable in a particular society.

Your personal definition of right or wrong is likely to be more internalized than society's standards. That is, we find it easier, as far as our feelings are concerned, to live according to personal convictions than to adhere to a moral standard that might seem to be an arbitrarily established norm. For example, each person has a definition of what is "honest." In one high school class, you might find a specific act defined as honest by some people and as dishonest by others, even though all might readily agree that in our society to be honest is morally acceptable and to be dishonest is not. But each feels more inclined in a specific situation to act according to his or her own definition.

Many pressures confront today's teenagers. These pressures, which include their physical urges, demand a personal code thought out in advance with an awareness of long-term implications.

One's personal moral definitions arise in childhood from parents, family, and environment. A time comes when one's code becomes more independently personal. You now are at an age when you evaluate attitudes and concepts that you gave no thought to or took for granted when you were younger. Your own conclusions about what standard is right, based upon the end results, now becomes most significant. It is necessary to consider the kinds of responsibility involved in your choices about premarital sexual behavior, because your decisions inevitably have long-term effects upon your own life and the lives of others.

RESPONSIBILITY TO SELF

The great advantage you have at your age is that almost unlimited choices are open to you in the kind of education you can get, marriage you will have, work you will do, person you will be, and home and family you will have. Your advantage can be consolidated if these wide choices remain open long enough. Doors need not be closed so that future opportunities would be cut off at a handicapping level.

High school love affairs that involve sexual intercourse present two major risks, either of which would probably limit future opportunities. The first, and perhaps the greatest, is the risk of too-early marriage. Next is the risk of an unplanned pregnancy that would limit the future whether or not the two marry.

Marrying too soon

If a couple becomes so emotionally involved that they decide to marry, in most cases it means their education cannot continue as it could otherwise. College may be out of the question for both, which means their choices of lifetime occupations are narrowed. They cannot hope to enter some fields of work that they might later wish to choose. Early marriage means taking on responsibility for the life of another before one has had a chance to explore one's own potential and determine one's own future goals.

Marriage counselors are familiar with the experience of young people having trouble in their marriages because they were not ready for the load they must carry. One reason the load does become heavy is that one who marries at an early age under the pressure of sexual involvement has not had the chance to know what kind of a lifetime mate one really wants. Sex is a very vital part of a good marriage, but many other elements in personality, and circumstances in life, are equally important. The mate chosen in the teens may not be the one who would be chosen four or five years later. Ideas about qualities desired in a husband or wife, and about what kind of person is most lovable and congenial, often change as the individual passes the teen years, finishes school, and continues to learn about kinds of personalities. That this is not mere theory but fact is evident from the statistical records of marriage failure; the lower the age at marriage, the higher the eventual divorce rate.

Involvement in premarital sex could cause a young person's education to come to an abrupt end. In how many ways would this affect the rest of his or her life?

Harold Christensen of Purdue University has for many years studied records of marriages, births of first children, and divorces, in different regions. He has found that the marriages with the highest divorce rate have three characteristics. They are marriages made at very young ages, usually during the teens; marriages with a premarital pregnancy; and marriages in which the first pregnancy occurred very soon after marriage. Looking at these facts in another way, we see that marriages most likely to succeed are those in which couples are at least in their twenties, had no premarital pregnancy, and waited until they were well adjusted in marriage before starting families. The odds in favor of successful and happy marriage increase rapidly for people who have a few years of freedom to live independently as growing young adults before they marry.

When there is serious emotional involvement associated with a sexual relationship between a high school couple, the urge becomes strong to make sure of the permanence of their commitment by marrying. It is very hard to believe at such a time that this love could ever fade. However, the high school couples who marry because of emotional involvement alone when no pregnancy is involved are in the minority. Studies of high school marriages, quoted later in this chapter, show that a large percentage of high school girls are pregnant when they marry. All of the couples who marry because of a pregnancy have had their freedom of mate choice cut off early by the pregnancy. In the cases in which a couple definitely would have married anyway, and the marriage was not actually forced by a pregnancy, their marriage still has a handicap, according to Christensen's findings. There still is a child arriving in the marriage before they have had a chance to build a good foundation for a lasting marriage.

RESPONSIBILITY FOR THE OTHER PERSON

The reflected side of responsibility to one's self and one's future is the responsibility for the life of the partner in premarital sexual intercourse. Because sexual intercourse is a pair experience, when one decides for oneself that one will go ahead, all the considerations regarding one's own life and future apply also to the other person. Just as most of us during the teens are not yet ready to undertake the emotional and financial support of others that marriage involves, so few people having intercourse at this age can think about the implications for the partner's life.

For the boy, responsibility raises such questions as: What about the girl's standing with her friends and her relationship with her family? Is her emotional commitment greater than his so that she will experience emotional trauma if the love affair breaks up? What would a pregnancy mean in her life? For the girl, responsibility raises many of the same questions. One must weigh these questions against the need for a close relationship and the satisfaction and pleasure one may experience during the time that a relationship seems to have the potential for permanent happiness.

MOTIVATIONS FOR PREMARITAL SEXUAL INTERCOURSE

Our discussion may seem to assume that the choice to engage in premarital sexual intercourse is a mutual decision between two people who think they have the same motives and feelings. But such is not likely to be the case, no matter what a couple's age. Their motives may be very different, and a chasm may exist between their degree of commitment. Because of physical and social developmental differences between boys and girls in our culture, motivations may be in contrast, not only regarding dating but also relative to petting and lovemaking. In general, boys tend to want to go further in lovemaking than girls. There is no way of knowing how much of this difference is actually physical and how much is due to expectations or cultural conditioning in our society. The general assumption is made that boys have a stronger sexual drive and a more difficult time controlling their sexual urges. Such cultural assumptions may influence some people in their actions, whether or not the assumption is valid for the individual.

With some couples, it is the girl who leads on and is willing to engage in lovemaking, sometimes because of emotional drives or for other reasons such as the hope that a sexual relationship will make their commitment permanent.

NEGATIVE ASPECTS OF PREMARITAL SEX

Aggressively demanding attitudes

It should be said that if a wide difference exists between a boy and girl over how far to go in lovemaking, and if one partner persists aggressively against the wishes of the other, a danger signal is evident; the implications go beyond lovemaking and moral standards. An aggressive or demanding attitude about lovemaking means that the persistent one is selfishly determined to have his or her own way at any cost. The selfish person puts wishes or urges ahead of considering the feelings of another or the results of personal actions. This trait will show up not only in sex activity but also in many other areas of life. Marriage to such a person would require more difficult adjustments than to someone able to think beyond his or her own needs and feelings.

In any individual case, whether it is the boy or the girl who initiates sexual intercourse, a serious responsibility is being taken for the other's life. The girl who encourages the boy in extreme petting leading to intercourse may end his educational and vocational plans. An unplanned pregnancy for her, or an intense emotional involvement for them both, may impel them into an early marriage before either has had a chance to prepare adequately for the future each might have. Their future life achievements can be restricted by the early sexual involvement.

Differences in the meaning of sexual intercourse

In sexual intercourse, the girl has more to lose than the boy, in several different ways. Even if no pregnancy occurs, girls tend to be more emotionally committed than boys before they will have sexual intercourse. Girls tend not to engage in sexual intercourse unless they believe that the boy really loves them and that the relationship is a meaningful one. For a boy, sexual intercourse may be an end in itself, not dependent upon any commitment to a particular girl. This difference in their approach can be extremely damaging to a girl's conception of herself when she later realizes that this is the case. She is hurt when sex represents a meaningful love relationship to her, but she finds that to him it does not have that implication. This is especially destructive because many girls who have premarital sexual intercourse have a special need and desire for a rewarding and supportive relationship with someone outside their families. Our studies of thousands of young people who do and do not engage in premarital sexual intercourse show that girls from unhappy families with serious problems are much more likely to have premarital sexual intercourse than are girls from happy families. The secure girl who has received emotional support and nurture at home is better able to take the long view and to think of the potential effect on her own and the boy's future if they should become too deeply involved too early. Thus, unfortunately, the girl who most needs a good permanent relationship is the one most likely to suffer the trauma of the disillusioning conclusion that she has been used or exploited by someone for whom she cared.

Further, research studies show that the girl who has sexual intercourse in one love affair tends to follow the same pattern with a different boy. Although, in each affair, a girl may believe that this time it is truly love and that they are equally committed, still her pattern of behavior tends to become promiscuous. She may, after a while, have the fatalistic feeling that because she is no longer a virgin it does not matter.

Venereal disease

Premarital sex bears with it the possibility of venereal disease. Acquired through intimate personal contact, syphilis and gonorrhea cause physical and mental suffering, and may have long-term destructive effects.

Gonorrhea, the most prevalent, can cause sterility by infecting the reproductive organs. Syphilis may have a latent stage that lasts months or years, only to flare up again. If untreated, it causes degeneration of the heart and nervous system, including the brain and spinal column, which can result in crippling, blindness, mental deterioration, and death.

A syphilitic mother can transmit the disease to the fetus, which may be stillborn, deformed, mentally damaged, or blind. State laws have been established in order to reduce the number of cases of congenital syphilis; that is, the disease contracted by the baby from the mother before its birth. The Wassermann test conclusively determines from a blood sample if syphilitic infection is present. By requiring a couple to have this examination before granting a marriage license, the states substantially reduce the incidence of the disease. Legal precautions are, however, obviously of no value where premarital sexual intercourse is involved.

A strong public health program brought the number of new cases of syphilis to a low of 6400 in 1956. The discovery of antibiotics provided an effective cure. In the following decade, however, syphilis increased fourfold, and gonorrhea zoomed from about 40,000 cases in 1956 to more than 718,000 cases in 1972. Over one-half of these new reported cases involved persons fifteen to twenty-four years of age. Unreported cases are estimated to be at least double this figure.

Guilt feelings

Because most families try to rear their children to accept society's definition of acceptable and unacceptable premarital behavior, comparatively few young people can engage in premarital sexual intercourse without some feelings of guilt and regret. For some people, these guilt feelings become a seriously disturbing factor in their adjustment to life. Some other people who have been brought up with less clearly defined ideas about acceptable and unacceptable moral behavior may have few feelings of guilt or regret. But because such wide differences exist in the way people feel about what is right and wrong, the one who leads or persuades the other is taking a special kind of responsibility for the emotional development of the other person. An important part of becoming a mature person is becoming capable of considering the effect of one's actions upon the lives of others, and then acting in ways that will be positive in their results rather than destructive.

RESPONSIBILITY TO SELF VERSUS RESPONSIBILITY FOR ANOTHER PERSON

In a way, this aspect, the effect of premarital sexual intercourse upon the partner's life, is an essential part of one's obligation to self. To be so soon responsible for another person can be a heavy burden. The conscientious person cannot help being aware of the responsibility when another person's life becomes closely tied to one's own. There are too many other requirements now in terms of one's own growing up. Most people who recognize this responsibility to a sexual partner know that they are not ready for it in their teens.

This matter of responsibility for another person poses a problem, somewhat of a dilemma, which each person must face and think out to some acceptable conclusion. Dating relationships and close friendships with someone of the other sex are constructive; they can meet urgent needs for response, and they help toward understanding oneself and others. The problem is to accomplish the growth task of creating good relationships with those of the opposite sex, and yet to keep involvements at a level that does not have negative effects or hinder achieving one's purposes in life.

To one who considers all the different ways in which responsibility is inherent in lovemaking situations, it becomes clear that decisions about premarital behavior have broad implications. Sometimes, a young person may honestly believe that petting or lovemaking is strictly a private matter and that, "What I do is my own business and nobody else's." But that view is unrealistic.

PREMARITAL PREGNANCY

Even today, premarital sexual intercourse involves the possibility that a child may be conceived. That it may be possible to prevent unplanned conceptions is a matter of general public knowledge. You know about contraceptive pills and other methods for preventing unwanted pregnancies. From discussions in the news media and elsewhere, the implication seems to be that no couple ever need conceive a child except by intention; or in other words, that because birth control is a fact in our society, people of any age may have sexual intercourse without an unplanned pregnancy occurring. But the facts are different.

First, in spite of public knowledge about contraceptives and their availability, large numbers of unplanned and undesired pregnancies continue to occur. To space their children as they wish is a problem for many married couples under the most advantageous conditions; under the circumstances in which the young unmarried couples have intercourse, unwanted pregnancies are certainly more frequent. In 1968, some 300,000 babies were born to unmarried mothers in the United States. This year, many thousands of children will be born to unmarried parents, and many thousands more will be born to married couples whose marriages will break up or whose wedding would never have taken place if a premarital pregnancy had not occurred. Our study of

1425 marriages of high school students in seventy-five California schools revealed that between 44 and 56 percent of the marriages followed discovery that the girl was pregnant. A study by Lee Burchinal of marriages in Iowa found that eight out of ten high school marriages took place because of pregnancy. In our California study, the findings showed that of the high school marriages that had taken place as long as three years before the study, one in five had already ended in divorce, annulment, or separation. Vital statistics in California showed that of couples applying for divorce with children, approximately one-third of the women who had married in their teens were pregnant before marriage.

These statistics show that unplanned pregnancies do continue to occur with a high statistical frequency in the population. Even if the couples go ahead to marry, their chances for permanent happiness are low compared with those of the average couple in the population. The significance of the records is that decisions about premarital sexual intercourse have implications far beyond the two individuals.

RESPONSIBILITY TO A CHILD AND TO SOCIETY

The moment that a conception occurs, other responsibilities have been undertaken, ready or not. Someone might suggest here that a premarital pregnancy might be medically terminated. Society now recognizes that some premarital pregnancies should end in abortion, and in 1971, the California Supreme Court ruled that unmarried pregnant women under twenty-one years of age could have abortions without consulting their parents. In 1973, the U.S. Supreme Court overruled all state laws that restrict or prohibit a woman's right to an abortion during the first three months of pregnancy, but ruled that states could still regulate abortions later in pregnancy. With the legalization of abortions, and their being done under approved conditions, they are safer physically, but there are far-reaching emotional, psychological, and ethical implications. For you to think of abortion as a realistic alternative to restraint from sexual intercourse would have no logic. It would be like suggesting that to try to choose the best possible marriage partner is unimportant because one can get a divorce if the marriage turns out to be a mistake. At this point in life, one would not want to decide about behavior in light of such traumatic "solutions."

With conception, responsibilities must be undertaken for the child and to society. These cannot be separated.

More than anything else, a child needs to be loved and cared for by two people who are ready for parenthood. It is true that many children are born to older couples who, if judged only by age, should be mature, good parents, but who are irresponsible, immature, and unable

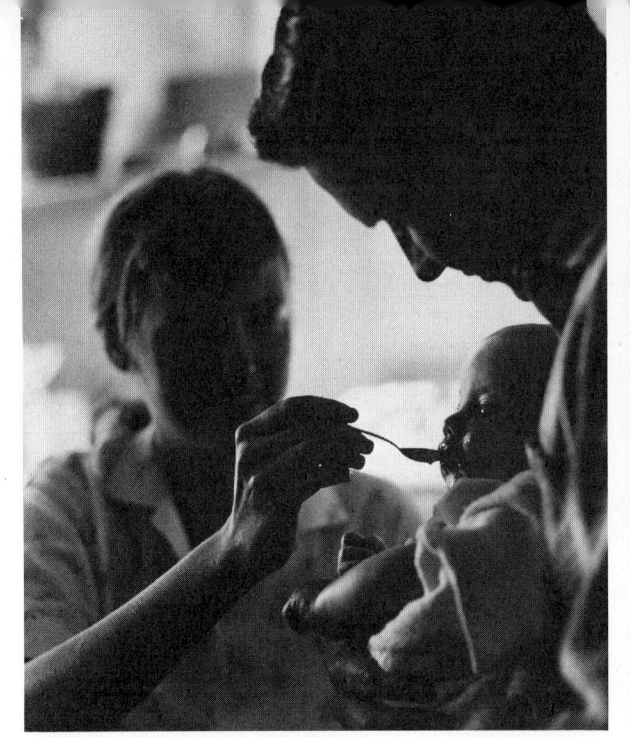

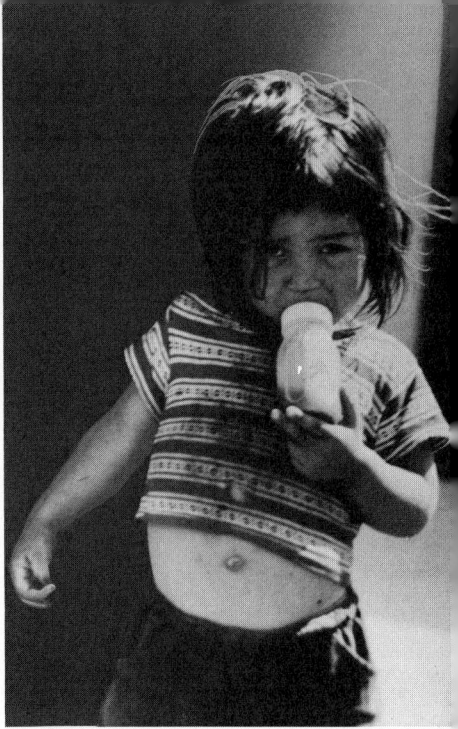

(Left) A child deserves responsible parents. If parents face their mutual task maturely, parenthood brings joy and produces healthy, happy children.
(Right) If parents fail to care for a child's essential needs, the public must take up the task. Such a child may easily develop antisocial tendencies and become a problem to himself or herself and to society for the rest of his or her life.

to cope with the requirements of parenthood. Records concerning mental illness, emotional problems, dependency, and delinquency offer evidence of this. However, for children born to unmarried couples, couples who marry because of pregnancy, and couples who are very young when their first child is born, statistical chances of a good start in life are much below average. In today's complex world, individual personal problems become the problems of society.

To illustrate: Accepted as a part of the bill of rights for children is that they have a right to food, shelter, loving care, medical attention, and schooling. If parents cannot meet these responsibilities, the federal and state governments step in and try to provide for the children through a program of federal aid to dependent children. Governments cannot meet emotional needs, but our government tries to meet the other needs through tremendous expenditures of dollars. In 1971, approximately ten and one-half million people were supported by the Aid to Families with Dependent Children program. Most of the children were born either to unmarried mothers or to young parents whose marriages ended in separation or divorce. A smaller percentage of the dependent children are from other categories of failing families. The cost of the total program to the taxpayers in that year was about five hundred and fifty million dollars.

As heavy as the tax burden may be, an even greater burden to society is poor mental health, crime and delinquency, suicide, alcoholism, and other social problems. These problems are all closely related to what happens early in the individual's life. If parents cannot or do not assume responsibility for their children, the likelihood of such problems is far greater than in well-established homes.

Thus, the social effects of each person's premarital decisions do matter. More than in any previous time, your generation shows concern about the problems in our society. You have been questioning some of the values that have become dominant in national decisions and policies. Your concern has compelled the older generation to do some new and realistic thinking in the area of individual and public responsibility.

As we all become more sophisticated in our philosophy regarding the relative rights of different groups and the individual's obligation to these groups, the question of responsibility in the area of sexual behavior comes into somewhat better focus. We become able to see the meaning in the concept that no one is an island, and that every choice we make, even in such a personal matter as lovemaking, affects the lives of others and of the whole society. What I do or what you do can never be only my or your own business.

LIVING ACCORDING TO PERSONAL STANDARDS

Both boys and girls sometimes have doubts about whether or not they can act according to their own standards of behavior and still be accepted by schoolmates. Boys may fear that they will be thought slow if they do not go as far as a girl will allow, and girls may fear that they may be considered naive or prudish if they firmly draw the line.

Studies among high school and college students show that such fears are unnecessary. Friendships are based on traits of personality that make a person desirable as a friend; standards of conduct reached after thoughtful assessment are not a handicap. In most schools, people who are well-liked are those who are independent and self-confident enough to have personal standards that they arrived at through serious reasoning. They know their reasons for their own conduct and can show unbiased attitudes toward others whose ethical norms may be different.

Some people are overly uneasy about maintaining standards of behavior because they believe that they stand alone, and that they are in the minority if they want to maintain premarital virginity. In casual talk, and in the public press, many irresponsible statements are made about the sexual revolution, the implication being that all moral standards have become obsolete. Thus, one may get to thinking, with regard to any activity, that "everyone else" is doing it and that to be different is futile or peculiar. Perhaps, in fact, if you feel that you stand alone you may find that many of your associates feel the same.

When one can thoughtfully choose one's standards instead of acting on emotional impulses, one becomes a confident, self-possessed individual.

Many people have a self-conception that requires certain behavior, and they are determined to meet the different responsibilities that they recognize. They are not likely to do much talking about it. Much more is heard from those who are aggressive about what is sometimes called individual sexual freedom.

Such a term as sexual freedom has little relevance for the majority of people accomplishing the growth tasks of these years, making decisions thoughtfully, and planning for life. As people achieve increasing levels of maturity, sexual intercourse can be appreciated as among the deepest and most meaningful of human experiences. With true maturity, there is less tendency to begin sexual intercourse for superficial reasons, such as to gain status with peers, or as an experiment, or to prove something. To grow up emotionally stable and healthy, one must value sexuality and its contribution to personality. For all of us, sexuality is one of the special endowments in our nature and personality. Admittedly, to make decisions about premarital sexual intercourse poses some problems at a time when so many puzzling choices have to be made. Decisions now become easier when we keep a wide perspective on all of life.

Strong physical urges, the need for a close relationship, needs for status and recognition, fears of being different from others, all these can be kept in balance by the person who is equally aware of the importance of vocational choice and education, of having a good marriage that will last for a lifetime, of being a good parent and a responsible member of society.

QUESTIONS FOR REVIEW

1. Why is it desirable to consider personal standards of sex behavior before one is dating steadily or is in love?
2. In what ways may the high school student safeguard the future by refraining from premarital sexual intercourse? How does this apply to both boys and girls?
3. What has Harold Christensen found through his studies of records of marriage, childbirth, and divorce?
4. In what ways may the motivation for premarital intercourse differ between boys and girls?
5. Is it always the boy who takes advantage of the girl and handicaps her future? Discuss.
6. How may premarital sexual intercourse be more traumatic for the girl than for the boy?
7. Discuss some kinds of responsibility each person takes for the other when premarital intercourse occurs.
8. What do statistics show about the prevalence of premarital pregnancy? About premarital pregnancy and divorce?
9. How can marriage during the teens be as serious a handicap as premarital pregnancy? Can it be even more serious?
10. Discuss the harm done by a premarital pregnancy to the boy; the girl; the baby; the parents of the young couple; the taxpayers.

ACTIVITIES AND PROJECTS

1. What examples can you cite from your school or community to show that high school people recognize their responsibility for others?
2. Guest speaker. Ask a representative from the local office of the federal program of Aid to Families with Dependent Children to talk to the class. Ask the speaker about the numbers of children and unmarried mothers being supported by the program in your area, about what types of families and children are being supported, and the costs of the program.
3. Ask someone from the local mental health program to discuss mental and emotional costs of failing families as these costs are seen by workers in the mental health program.
4. If you have a home for unmarried mothers in your community, ask the director to discuss their program and the problems of unmarried mothers and their children.
5. From files in your school or public library find copies of *Life* magazine for June 14 and June 21, 1968. Read the series by Richard Meryman entitled "Adoption." Part I gives insight into the experience of a young couple whose romance

resulted in a pregnancy and the birth of a child. Report on the response to the situation by the boy, the parents of the boy, the parents of the girl, the girl, and others involved in trying to help solve the problems.

WORDS AND CONCEPTS

abortion
contraceptives
dilemma
ethical norms
frame of reference
gonorrhea
intercourse

moral standards
promiscuous
relevance
syphilis
traumatic
venereal disease

8 More Decisions: Alcohol, Smoking, Drugs

After studying this chapter, you will be able to

1. List the findings of the alcohol research studies, and discuss their implications.
2. Discuss recent findings on the effects of smoking on health.
3. Explain the meaning of the statement, "Ours is a drug-oriented society."
4. Illustrate in what ways drug use may be related to personal problems.
5. Discuss the similarity and difference between dependence upon drugs and addiction to a drug.

Inevitably during your high school years, you will have to decide upon your personal policy regarding such practices as drinking alcohol, smoking, and using drugs. In our society, these decisions are being made by people in all age groups. Because social drinking, smoking, and using drugs are so widespread, the tendency may be to accept them all as a part of the culture without stopping to consider the implications of each for you personally.

You are making many decisions now: setting your standards of conduct, choosing the types of people you want for friends, weighing your acts and the acts of others to decide what seems desirable or wise, deciding about the type of person you want to date and perhaps marry, and considering kinds of work that you might want to make your vocation.

All decisions have implications for your life now and in the future even though some choices seem to depend merely upon the circumstances of a moment. How fast you drive, how you spend money, how far you go in lovemaking, whom you trust, what you tell or refrain from telling, whether you drink or smoke—each one of these choices contributes to widening your opportunities or to closing off your freedom of choice in some parts of life.

ALCOHOL

Early in this century, a constitutional amendment was passed (the Eighteenth Amendment) prohibiting the sale of alcohol in the United States. Enforcement proved to be impossible, and after fourteen years in which feelings about the subject became extremely intense, the amendment was repealed. For some years after repeal, the approach to alcohol continued to be emotional rather than rational, and many people still hold confused ideas and misunderstandings about its uses and effects.

It is legal in almost all states for adults to buy alcoholic drinks. About 80 million Americans drink and of these about 6 million are alcoholics. Evidence suggests that an increase in social drinking, problem drinking, and alcoholism can be expected in the future. Since 1949, Purdue University has been studying drinking among high school students from all sections of the country. Their studies have found a general pattern toward greater acceptance of the use of alcohol. A larger percentage of parents use alcohol today than in 1949; a larger percentage of students use alcohol, and a larger percentage of students are less critical of the use of alcohol among their peers. There is little doubt that drinking will remain a part of our social fabric even though serious problems are associated with alcohol. These problems have focused attention on the need for exact knowledge of alcohol and its effects. A number of universities have research institutes in which scientists study its effects and use, attempting to discover all significant facts. Much remains to be known; however, so much has been learned and published that you may set your policy about drinking based on knowledge and reason rather than upon emotion or misinformation.

RESEARCH FINDINGS ABOUT ALCOHOL

Alcohol as a depressant drug

Alcohol is a drug having a depressant effect on the brain and nervous system similar to the effects of ether and other anesthetics. It is not a stimulant. Its effect may seem to be stimulating because it acts first upon the higher centers of the nervous system, those that control judgment, the sense of responsibility, and critical thinking. Because the centers controlling emotional responses are not so quickly affected, the drinker may feel excited or emotional, more impulsive, and less inhibited. He may feel that he is "stimulated." Most states rule that a blood alcohol concentration of only 0.15 percent indicates that a driver's judgment is so affected that he is beyond the limits of operating a vehicle safely.

Tests in the Alcohol Studies Section of the Laboratory of Applied Physiology at Yale University showed that students accustomed to typing increased their errors by 40 percent after taking alcohol, but lost only 3 percent of their speed. The researchers reported that the students usually believed that they were doing better than before they had the drink. Their judgment and ability to evaluate their work was dulled, or partially anesthetized. They were surprised to find that the tests showed their efficiency had been impaired.

When the narcotic effect of alcohol increases, after more is taken, the dulling of judgment becomes more pronounced. Later, the centers controlling muscular coordination are affected. If enough alcohol is taken, the drinker shows clearly the anesthetic effects: he goes into a stupor, or "sleeps." Before other anesthetics were developed, alcohol had been used to prepare patients for operations.

Alcohol as a "food"

Alcohol is sometimes called a food because it contains calories, the units of energy found in food. However, it does not provide any of the important elements needed for good health and growth. Yet, because alcohol is higher in calories than sugar, excessive users of alcohol are likely to be overweight and to suffer from malnutrition.

Some people who struggle against being too fat cut out candy and other sweets, but increase their drinking. Instead of eating, they may have a drink when they feel tired or hungry, not realizing that they are substituting empty calories for needed nourishment.

Moreover, alcohol taken without food is absorbed into the bloodstream much more quickly than if used with or following foods, and thus a small amount may have a more intoxicating effect than if used at meals as an accompaniment to food.

Some mistaken ideas contradicted by research studies

Mistaken ideas have long been held about the immediate and long-term effects of alcohol. Research studies have found the following statements to be true:

1. Moderate amounts of alcohol taken slowly with food may not be physically harmful to a healthy, well-fed person. For some people, especially the aged who suffer from certain diseases, alcohol may act as a mild sedative and may be medically useful.

MORE DECISIONS: ALCOHOL, SMOKING, DRUGS

2. Alcohol can irritate and inflame the digestive systems of even healthy people, and continued excessive drinking is likely to damage the heart and liver, and shorten life.
3. Rapid drinking of more than a pint of alcohol may be fatal. The effect is similar to the effects of an overdose of an anesthetic.
4. The body can burn up alcohol at a steady rate; for a person of average size, the rate is about one-half ounce an hour, no faster. There is no way to "sober up" in a hurry if one has had too much to drink; beliefs about drinking strong coffee or taking a cold plunge are folklore.
5. The effects of drinking depend on the actual alcoholic content of a drink. Any person who is going to drink socially should know that most vodkas, gins, whiskies, and rums contain about one-half ounce of pure alcohol for each ounce of the liquor (50 percent alcohol); table wines contain from one-tenth to one-fifth of an ounce of alcohol per ounce of wine (10 to 20 percent); most American-made beers contain about 4 percent alcohol. One does drink excessively, whether he drinks beer, wine, or other drinks, if his consumption adds up to enough pure alcohol.

Alcohol can create serious problems not only for individuals but also for their families. The person who takes a social drink seldom thinks of this aspect, but social drinking can lead to alcoholism in all too many cases.

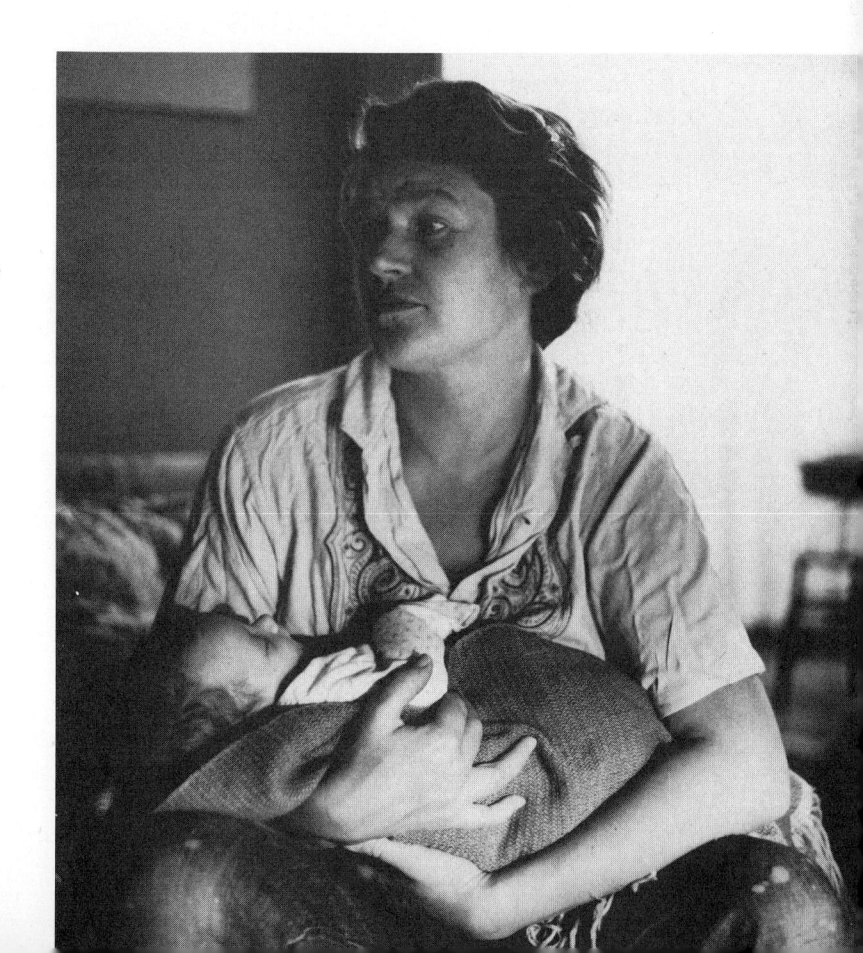

6. Alcohol affects judgment and muscular coordination much sooner and more potently than many people believe. Evidence of this was shown by specific before-and-after tests to check drivers' reaction times, the time it takes a driver to put on the brakes after a red light is flashed. The average time to put on the brakes before alcohol was taken was one-fifth of a second. A short time after the drivers had had the equivalent of two glasses of beer, their reaction time was three times as slow. A car traveling at 60 miles an hour covers 88 feet in a second; thus, if the driver's reaction is slowed by three-fifths of a second to one second, it means that in an emergency, he cannot possibly stop in time to avoid an accident. According to the National Safety Council, such tests indicate that in a dangerous road situation, a driver who has had as much as two glasses of beer is 55 times more likely to have an accident than one who has had no alcohol.
7. Slightly more than 7 percent of the people who drink become alcoholics. An alcoholic is a person who is dominated by drinking; the inability to control drinking may destroy marriage, family life, or work, and sooner or later, health.

Few people are instant alcoholics; it usually takes some years for a drinker to become an alcoholic. Most people believe they will never be problem drinkers, but many who believe themselves to be social drinkers do not or cannot control their drinking and are already suffering from alcoholism. Studies show that there are usually symptoms that could help one realize personal danger if the symptoms were recognized early enough.

Some of the danger signs are:

1. Any increase; more frequent drinking or drinking larger amounts than formerly.
2. Drinking because of a "need" for a drink, or as an escape or relief from emotional problems.
3. Drinking alone or in the morning.
4. Drinking on the sly because friends or relatives are worried about one's drinking.
5. A "blackout" from drinking. A blackout is a temporary loss of memory and is *always* a danger signal.

IMPLICATIONS OF THE FACTS ABOUT ALCOHOL AND ALCOHOLISM

You will want to think about all the facts concerning alcohol and its effects as you decide on your personal policy. In all situations, you need to be at your best physically and mentally so that you can act according to decisions you have made thoughtfully and for sound reasons. If, after studying the subject, you can discuss the matter with your parents, it will probably be of help. Whether or not you talk it over with them, the attitudes of your family and their practices will certainly influence you, and it is better if you can exchange ideas with them.

If you decide to drink, it is necessary that you set limits and adhere to them. Whom you drink with, when, under what circumstances, how much, and why, are basic questions. It is necessary to be aware of certain dangers; you risk making unwise decisions because of the effects of drinking. There is also the fact that drinking during the teens under present laws usually means obtaining alcohol illegally or being a party to illegal acts unless states have modified the age allowed for drinking since passage of the Twenty-sixth Amendment. For many young people, that factor weighs heavily in decisions about drinking.

During the teen years, you reach the age for learning driving skills and obtaining a driver's license. Most people enjoy driving and being able to take friends with them; and in our society, dating often involves driving. The facts about the alcoholic content of drinks and the length of time necessary for the body to burn up even small amounts clearly prove that to drink and drive is to invite disaster. The person who decides to drink must choose to be a passenger, not a driver, because it is not possible to be a safe, expert driver if one drinks.

One who decides to drink during the teens must be realistic about the risks involved. Many young people conclude that life is complicated enough without adding the risks associated with drinking.

If you decide not to drink, you will want a plan of action that will help you carry out your decision comfortably. It is important that you know why you don't drink. You have good reasons for your choice. You don't have to explain your reasons; to say "No, thank you," is enough. If you happen not to be a turnip eater or a coffee drinker, you probably don't bother to explain why or to apologize when you say, "No, thank you." You expect your friends to respect your preferences. The same kind of refusal is appropriate about drinking. It is *your* decision. The person who questions it or tries to pressure you into changing your mind may be either insecure and uncertain on the matter and is seeking reassurance, or is simply ill-mannered.

It is not necessary to be conspicuous or to create embarrassment for yourself or others. There is always something else to drink at a party, even if it is a tall glass of water on ice.

You must also respect the preferences of your friends. But at the same time, you have no obligation to risk dangers resulting from the decisions that some of your friends may make. You may prefer not to date a person who uses bad judgment about drinking. In every school, there are many boys and girls who do not drink and many others who may accept a drink on occasion but who have found appropriate answers to the questions of when, where, why, with whom, and how much a responsible person might drink.

SMOKING

For many years, cigarette smoking was accepted in our society with less serious questioning or objection than was directed at drinking. Many people who knew about personal and family problems associated with excessive drinking, and did not wish to take these risks, saw no reason at all why they should not smoke. True, as long as sixty years ago, there was some talk of cigarettes being "coffin nails," and in some circles, smoking was considered to be dirty or sinful. But there were no proposals to make smoking illegal for adults, as was attempted with alcohol by the Eighteenth Amendment. Among the general public, smoking became more and more widely practiced. Tobacco growing and selling became a billion-dollar business in the United States, and many people have had the attitude that there could not be anything seriously wrong with a habit that is legal, that is socially accepted, and that is highly advertised as desirable.

However, attitudes about smoking are changing. Almost no one proposes making smoking illegal for adults, but attempts are being made to let the public know the facts that years of continuous research have discovered about the effects of smoking on health. Efforts are also being made to control or prohibit advertising that misleads people into believing that smoking is a key to popularity and happiness.

The picture at left shows normal lung tissue. The air sacs are too fine to be visible. In the picture at the right, we see how heavy smoking has greatly enlarged the air sacs.

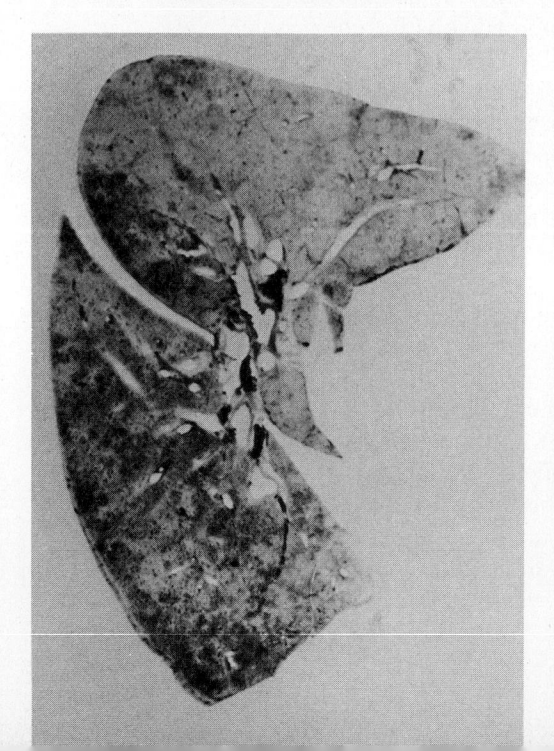

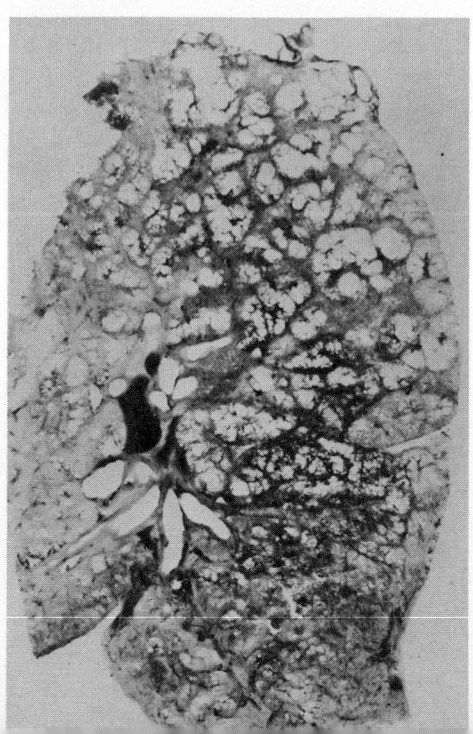

Effects of smoking.

It was not until recent years that the relationship between smoking and early death was clearly established. It is now known that cigarette smoking is a direct cause of lung cancer and of emphysema (inability of the lungs to absorb oxygen because of destruction of the lung tissue). Research has discovered that smokers are more subject than nonsmokers to heart attacks and to other diseases of the circulatory system.

Because statistical records show that smokers have a shorter life expectancy than nonsmokers, some life insurance companies have begun to insure nonsmokers at lower rates than smokers.

Even after some of the effects of smoking were discovered, some people felt that the findings were not relevant for them, because it was assumed that the effects of smoking would not be felt until many years later. Middle age may seem far away when one is in the teens, so it is easy to feel that what may happen then does not particularly matter now. However, significant for young people is the discovery that the heavy smoker not only has his life shortened but all the way through life is more susceptible to handicapping disease. Smoking destroys the cilia of the lungs, which serve to sweep out dust, dirt, and germs, and as a result smokers suffer from pneumonia, bronchitis, and other infectious diseases more than nonsmokers do.

Research that studied people of college age, smokers, and nonsmokers, found that smokers suffer from far more illnesses associated with the lungs than nonsmokers. In general, they have less endurance and energy. This and similar research findings have led to the conclusion that it is not just a question of life being shortened, it is a matter of a whole lifetime of being handicapped by health limitations. A great many smokers who may never die of heart disease or lung cancer will be limited in their ability to function fully at work and to have the fullest enjoyment of life. Their smoking will handicap them while they are still young.

WHY PEOPLE START OR STOP SMOKING

For years, many young people have tried smoking once or a few times just to see what it is like or because others do it. Many of these never become habitual smokers. Probably the most common reason for becoming a smoker is that people tend to follow the example of their parents and others. Purdue University, through its study of high school students, found that more children with smoking parents than with nonsmoking parents were opposed to laws that would ban cigarette advertising, and a larger percentage of these children approved of smoking among their peers. Some people associate smoking with being an adult, and their

Miss American Teen-Ager for 1970, Rose Marie Klespitz, works with the American Cancer Society urging people not to smoke. If you have already started, the next best tip is to stop now before the habit becomes too strong.

smoking is a striving for the appearance of maturity. Another influencing factor is the advertising that promotes smoking as pleasurable, romantic, relaxing, and the thing to do. Since 1972, positive action has been taken to encourage people not to start smoking. All advertising of cigarettes on television has been banned. There is also action being taken to protect the health of nonsmokers from those who smoke. Airlines and many other forms of public transportation must provide separate sections for smokers or may prohibit smoking altogether. Smoking in public buildings and in offices where people work or congregate is often prohibited. Probably every smoker today has noticed that some of his nonsmoking friends are no longer as gracious about providing an ash tray.

Actually, most people do not find smoking pleasant at first, but rather distasteful. Only later, they become psychologically dependent upon smoking and physically addicted to nicotine. The psychological dependence is upon smoking as a "prop." The person may feel a little less ill at ease in some situations if he can occupy himself with a cigarette or pipe. The physical addiction is that the body becomes habituated to the repeated effects of the tobacco's elements and reacts with unpleasant nervous and physical symptoms if smoking is discontinued.

Many young people who try smoking a few times, do not become addicted. Some decide it is really not pleasant enough to make it worth the trouble and expense. Others resist developing a habit that they recognize as a potential handicap. Some have a strong resistance to becoming dominated or controlled by a habit about which they had a choice in the beginning. Among people who are habitual smokers, increasing numbers now are trying to break the habit. Women seem to find it harder to quit than men. Of women and men smoking in 1966, 25 percent of the women and 39 percent of the men had quit by 1970. Lung cancer is the leading killer among all types of cancer. It is increasing as a cause of death among women as the number of women who smoke increases. In recent years, there has been a more rapid percentage increase of smoking among teenage girls than among teenage boys. Less than half the adult population smokes today, but this group is smoking more heavily, having increased the number of cigarettes per person.

Publication of research findings helps some people to realize the valid reasons for not smoking. Until fairly recently, it was the policy not to publicly name cancer as a cause of death. A change from this taboo has also had an effect. The lung cancer deaths of prominent people are regularly reported in the press now.

Members of the medical profession also are having an influence with the public. Many doctors who smoke have tried repeatedly to break the habit, but their addiction is too well established. They admit their helplessness, but continue to urge their patients not to smoke. Others succeed in stopping. It is estimated that among doctors less than 30 percent smoke, while ten years ago more than half were smokers.

The informational campaign of the American Cancer Society, radio and television spot commercials to counteract the commercial advertisements of cigarettes, and more general public information have all had some effect in decisions not to smoke or to stop before becoming addicted. Many children who have seen their parents unsuccessfully try again and again to stop smoking, decide they would rather not repeat their parents' experience with addiction.

At present, there is available more information about tobacco and its effects than about any of the other addicting drugs. The information indicates that while alcohol has always had certain medicinal uses, and most of the other addicting drugs have been developed in response to specific medical needs, smoking has no known benefits or medicinal uses to justify it.

LIVING IN A DRUG-ORIENTED SOCIETY

Throughout history, people have sought drugs or aids of some type to help them ease physical pain, to relieve them of psychological anxiety, and to produce feelings of euphoria, or well-being.

During the past thirty years, a great advance has been made in discovering or creating drugs for most of the ills of mankind. We speak of the "miracle drugs" and what they will do. Antibiotics such as penicillin and sulfa have enormously reduced deaths from some infectious diseases. In most cases, high blood pressure and migraine headaches can now be controlled. Because of the relief of misery and the lifesaving effects provided by many of the new drugs, there has developed an almost blind acceptance of the "magic" of drugs. In the past fifteen or twenty years, we have become a pill society. Many hard-working, law-abiding, middle-aged people who cannot bear the pressures of life depend on pills to sleep, to stay awake, to calm down, and to have energy to work.

USE AND ABUSE OF DRUGS

In the face of this widespread use, one authority, Roland Berg, says, "Essentially, all drugs are harmful. Even when used medically, they do their good deeds by unnaturally altering the functioning or chemical structure of various organs of the body. A physician must weigh carefully potential harm against potential good. The nonmedical, unsupervised use of drugs holds no safeguards, only dangers."

Over a period of time, some people of all ages have become drug dependent without realizing that there are dangers. They have read or heard of the magic effects of some pills, and their doctors quite readily have prescribed the pills for them. In fact, for some years after the great

Many drugs, such as the oral polio vaccine this girl is taking, are important in disease prevention. Addictive drugs, however, cause trouble.

expansion in developing new drugs and new combinations of drugs, there was little recognition even in the medical profession that the negative effects of some of the drugs might outweigh the positive effects. Gradually, the evidence of "side effects" became more clear, and doctors became more cautious about prescribing.

The thalidomide cases in 1963 to 1964 focused attention on the kinds of unpredictable disasters that may result from drugs that seem to be helpful. In the thalidomide cases, doctors freely prescribed the drug for pregnant women who needed tranquilizers in order to relax and rest. Only later, after an unprecedented number of babies were born deformed, armless, or with undeveloped arms or legs, intensive research and study of records began to reveal ways in which the *useful* and *seemingly harmless drug* worked to cause deformities in unborn babies.

Studies of the effects of drugs, and of how their effects are brought about, continue. It is known that some drugs alter the functioning of the central nervous system and some alter the chromosomes, but there is still uncertainty about exactly how others work.

YOUR POLICY ABOUT THE USE OF DRUGS

Whether or not and how to use drugs becomes a part of one's life philosophy. At every stage of life, one needs to be at one's best physically and mentally in order to meet life's challenges. During the teen years, you have a free choice about most courses of action, including drugs. Some young people, who have been given pills for as long as they can remember, may in the teens have few if any inhibitions about experimenting. However, resistance is developing toward indiscriminate use of drugs. With more and more facts coming to light, increasing numbers of people resist taking any more drugs than are absolutely necessary. They have observed or experienced the unpleasant and terrifying effects of some drugs.

You are in the best position to know the facts about drugs and to make decisions that will avoid unnecessary handicaps. For older people, many choices no longer remain open. For them, there may be enough benefits to balance the damage done by some of the drugs they may use. Grandfather may be addicted to alcohol or nicotine or barbituates and may wish to be free from the addiction. In addition, he may be suffering from insufficient blood supply to the heart muscles, and because of pain, he may be addicted to a pain-killing drug. Such a person's condition is sad, but for many people, it is a part of the process of aging. For young people, experimenting with drugs can only invite effects that would not need to be faced for many years, if ever.

There is no good reason to experience the problems associated with drug abuse during the time of life when you have as a natural endowment good health and few physical limitations. Your generation did not start the overuse and abuse of drugs in our society. But as with many of the other social ills that you would like to change, yours can be the generation to bring the problem under control. A beginning is your own individual decision to avoid all drugs except as prescribed by a doctor in case of illness.

PERSONAL PROBLEMS AND DRUGS

Some young people experiment with drugs out of curiosity because they lack sufficient knowledge of the dangers. They hear about what others are doing, or they are offered opportunities to try drugs, and they participate without really making a thoughtful decision.

Some others try drugs because they feel they need help in coping with life. Earlier chapters of this book considered the kinds of growth requirements that challenge you now. As you know, most people have some defeats, problems, and feelings of unhappiness or disappointment as they attempt to accomplish their tasks in growing to maturity.

Some young people have anxieties of a more serious nature than this, but turning to harmful habitual practices offers no solution.

For some of these, drugs appear to be a means of possible help or escape. Some people with serious personal problems may experience a temporary escape through drugs, but inevitably, the escape is not permanent, and the problems will be intensified by the attempted remedy and may cause permanent damage.

In addition to physical effects, drug use snowballs problems in life because depressants, stimulants, tranquilizers, and hallucinatory drugs used without medical prescription are illegal. Severe penalties are being risked by the person using or possessing such drugs, and even more severe penalties loom for anyone who sells or supplies them to others. If there were no other reason for avoiding illegal involvement with drugs, the danger of having one's life disrupted and permanently damaged by punishment for lawbreaking is reason enough.

A high school senior, discussing former use of drugs, said, "Having lived outside the law for a while, I can personally say that living within the law has more future in it. To live outside the law is to be just constantly afraid of being caught and locked up. I don't want to spend my time behind somebody's bars. Actually, living within the law is much easier, and it takes a whole lot of worries off my mind."

Perhaps some of the laws will be changed. But even if laws were changed, the fact remains that most of the drugs experimented with do not help with problems, but rather they do create or increase physical and emotional problems.

One who cannot face problems, and finds temporary escape or relief through drugs, tends to turn to drugs again and again rather than to find real solutions. This person may become physically addicted by using certain drugs and psychologically addicted or dependent by using some others.

CONFUSION ABOUT ADDICTING AND NONADDICTING DRUGS

Today, people may be confused by what they hear about addictive and nonaddictive drugs. They may oversimplify the matter and believe that physical addiction or nonaddiction is the only crucial factor to consider in deciding about drug use. The truth is that one can become dependent upon drugs that are not physically addicting. The person develops a drug dependence on a psychological and emotional level; this dependence may be as difficult to end as a physical addiction. For example, marijuana is usually placed in the nonaddictive category. Nevertheless, the one who receives pleasure through using marijuana accepts the concept of drug use to achieve euphoria, and may become dependent upon other drugs; this dependence which may dictate decisions and dominate actions. Whether or not one goes on to addictive drugs, one has made a decision and entered the world of illegal drug users. It does not matter whether we call a drug's effects dependence or addiction. The results in one's life are likely to be equally handicapping.

Moreover, although marijuana may be considered by some to be nonaddictive, there are many unanswered questions about its effects. Present knowledge about marijuana is similar to the limited knowledge available about effects of cigarettes a generation ago. At that time, many people believed that objections to cigarettes were mere "scare talk." Many years of research have finally established the truth, too late to be of much help to people who began smoking twenty-five years ago. It remains to be seen what more extensive research will reveal about the various effects of marijuana. Certainly, any drug that creates recognizable reactions is also altering the functioning or the structure of some of the body's components. Exactly what these alterations are remains to be discovered.

IN CONCLUSION

In this chapter, we have not given you arbitrary and precise rules for action concerning drinking, smoking, or using drugs. You will make your own decisions. We have attempted to offer a sound viewpoint based on information from available scientific research. We have tried to present these matters within a framework that allows you to view them from a reasonable perspective. The key thing to remember is to rationally make your own decisions, think ahead, and set your own policies. Don't just drift unthinkingly along and let things happen you may regret later.

QUESTIONS FOR REVIEW

1. How does the scientific approach to the study of alcohol differ from the emotional approach?
2. How did the passage and repeal of the Eighteenth Amendment affect attitudes toward use of alcohol?
3. Describe the narcotic effect of alcohol. Why is it sometimes thought that alcohol is a stimulant rather than a depressant?
4. Summarize the effect of alcohol on judgment and coordination.
5. What is the significance of the order in which alcohol affects the functions of the brain and nervous system?
6. Why do some life insurance companies offer lower rates to nonsmokers than to smokers?
7. What specific illnesses afflict higher percentages of smokers than nonsmokers? Why does smoking have that effect?
8. When do these effects become evident? Explain.

MORE DECISIONS: ALCOHOL, SMOKING, DRUGS

9. What are some reasons why people begin to smoke? Have you observed smoking that seems to be so motivated?
10. What leads some people to refrain from smoking or to try to break their habit?
11. What is meant by the term "drug-oriented society"?
12. Explain the statement quoted that "all drugs are harmful."
13. In what ways may the use of unprescribed drugs create and increase personal problems?
14. Discuss dependence upon and addiction to drugs. What is the difference? In what ways may they be similar in their eventual effect?

ACTIVITIES AND PROJECTS

1. The most successful organization treating alcoholics, Alcoholics Anonymous, believes that alcoholism cannot be cured in the individual, but can be controlled. Ask a representative of Alcoholics Anonymous to talk to the class about their program for helping alcoholics.
2. (Report.) Consult a police officer who serves on the night force about the effect of the extensive use of alcohol upon family life. Report to the class or ask the officer to talk to the class on the subject.
3. Report on the Eighteenth Amendment, its passage and repeal.
4. Prepare a display of advertisements from current magazines that include erroneous or misleading implications about alcohol, smoking, or drugs.
5. Report on the thalidomide tragedies. Include how the Food and Drug Administration works and the role it played in these and other cases.
6. Prepare a report on some research findings about alcohol use.
7. Ask someone from the narcotics squad, your district attorney's office, or some other agency to discuss laws and penalties regarding illegal drugs.

WORDS AND CONCEPTS

addiction
aggressive
anesthetic
critical thinking
dependence
depressant
impediment

inhibited
muscular coordination
narcotic
reaction time
social situation
stimulant
susceptible

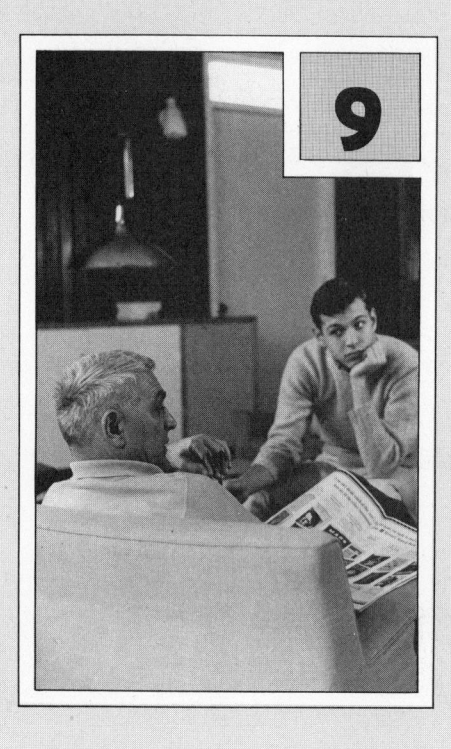

9 Family Understanding During the Dating Years

After studying this chapter, you will be able to

1. Explain in what ways both parents and children are in a stage of transition when children reach adolescence.
2. List some of the basic causes of conflict between parents and children during the dating years.
3. Examine the term "generation gap" from the point of view of both parents and children.
4. Analyze and discuss the meaning of communication between parents and children.

In many families, conflicts between the parents and children begin to develop at about the time that the children enter adolescence. Some of the conflicts become intense during the years in which the young people are dating. Some parents complain that the children become self-assertive and demand rights and privileges that the parents are not ready to grant. Their children may think that the parents have become excessively critical, irritable, and hard to get along with. Many people, after they become adults, regret that so much conflict during adolescence occurred. Yet if these people do not understand the real causes of the conflicts, the same course of events may be repeated between them and their own children.

Why may such situations develop in families at this point? Is it possible for parents and young people to get a good enough understanding of each other's viewpoint so that they could avoid friction and enjoy these years together?

BASIC CAUSES OF CONFLICT

Underlying at least some of the difficulty is the fact that both parents and children are in a stage of transition. Both have especially challenging growth tasks to accomplish at this time; their growth tasks are related to each other, but in some ways are antagonistic. The teenage person who is making growth suitable to that age must achieve an increasing independence in thinking and actions; the parents must gradually relinquish authority without abdicating their responsibilities. The teenaged person's world is becoming centered in groups outside the family. Friends and associates now seem to have more influence than do home and parents. Parents may find it hard to accept that fact. They may have difficulty seeing their child as an individual separate from themselves. If they see their son or daughter make a decision that they feel is unwise, they can hardly refrain from interfering and trying to change that decision. How far they go in their attempts to control their children's choices, to what extent they react emotionally rather than rationally, and how well the young person is maturing will have much to do with how much conflict occurs.

A great many parents, perhaps the majority, recognize their children's right to grow up: they want only to help in any way they can; they have no wish to interfere or dominate. But how to play that role satisfactorily may baffle them. They find it hard to know when to advise, when to criticize, when not to criticize, when to make suggestions, and when to keep silent and let events take their course. It requires special perceptiveness and sensitivity for parents to know whether they are being too rigid and directive or standing aside so much that they seem to be uninvolved and not available to help when children would like their counsel about difficult matters.

Many parents are sensitive and shaken because they have heard so much about the "generation gap." They realize that things do not look the same to their children as to them, and they would like to understand the viewpoint of the younger generation. But if a good level of communication was not established with their children earlier, their attempts to communicate now may seem to be a prying into matters their children consider private.

Sometimes, parents who feel misunderstood and misjudged may be uncertaic in their actions, wavering between seeming too aggressive in trying to control or restraining themselves so much that they seem indifferent. In such situations, neither parents nor children know what to expect from each other.

WHAT OF THE YOUNG PEOPLE?

The teenaged person who prefers to spend all his or her time with the parents at home, and who is willing to let the parents make all decisions, is not showing the healthy growth and development suitable to the teens. However, the young person who is growing toward responsible maturity does not feel that parental restraint and influence must suddenly be ignored; parental interest is valued. This young person is not unreasonably aggressive in asserting the right to independence and tries to understand why parents behave as they do, and to profit by associating with them.

There are some good shortcuts toward establishing the fact that one is becoming an adult who can handle one's own affairs, without as much parental supervision. Showing responsibility in some relatively routine matters can be useful in establishing increased independence. Even such things as hanging up clothes, rather than dropping them in a heap to be picked up by some "adult" who is conscious of cleaning and pressing bills, helps to make a point. One can show initiative by taking responsibility for doing family shopping, or doing things about the house without being asked. Keeping one's own room or part of a room in order before anyone has a chance to push and prod about it, or being a driver who does not get traffic citations, can make a point. Parents recognize a person's mature status more readily when their teenager shows the kinds of habits that are characteristic of a responsible person. The young person who does show these characteristics is in a better tactical position to insist on the right to more independence.

PARENTS AND DATING

Parent-child disagreements may arise over such matters as when the son or daughter is old enough to date, dating steadily, use of the family car for dates, hours for coming in after dates.

Good reasons exist for differences in some of these areas. Customs have changed since your parents were in their teens. People begin to date at an earlier age now, mingling socially with more freedom and less supervision than was the custom twenty years ago. It may take time for parents to recognize and accept that such changes have actually taken place. They are also aware of some special problems associated with too early dating.

Parents often oppose dating steadily because they know that constant dating with one person leads to greater physical intimacy and the possibility of premarital sexual intercourse, which might handicap their child's future.

Lend a hand to younger brothers and sisters without being asked. Help to care for your own clothes. Help with household chores. Your parents will see you as a cooperative, maturing person and will be more willing to consider your requests.

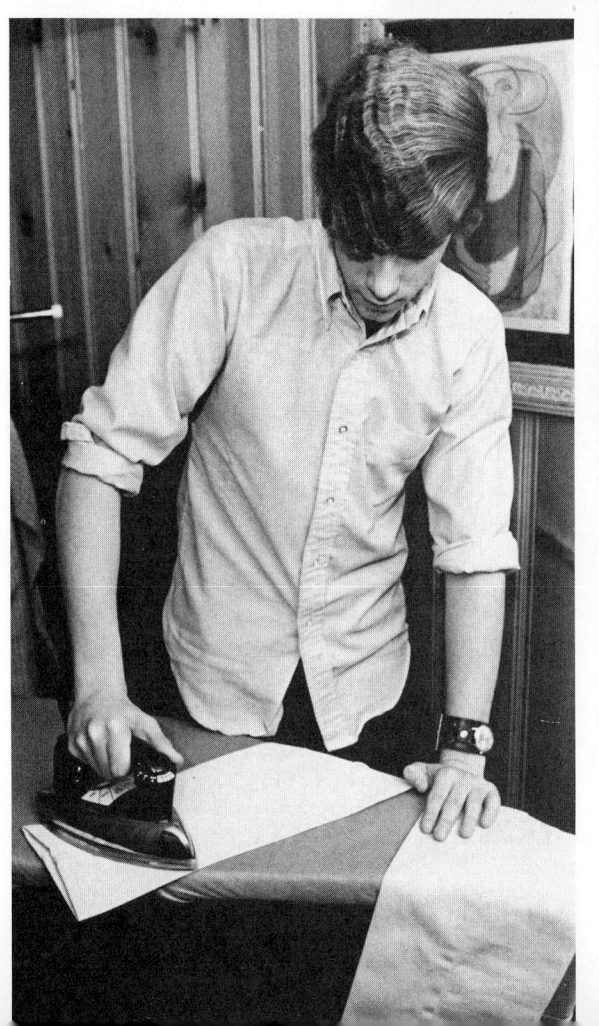

THE FAMILY CAR

When it comes to the question of using the family car on dates, serious problems sometimes arise. One father said to a friend as he left the office to go home, "I just wish I didn't have to go home tonight. I know Tom will be wanting the car. Every night this week, we've had an argument about that. Tom is sixteen and has just received his driver's license. I would trust him alone with the car; but when he has it, there are usually at least three couples loaded in at once—and I don't think any driver can be responsible for his driving with all the talking and laughing and confusion that go with that many people in one car. I worry every time Tom is out with the car. Besides, it seems he always wants the car on the same evenings that his mother and I want it, and we have a hard time deciding where to draw the line between what we owe to ourselves and to him."

In some families, frequent use of the car by the children represents a financial burden that the family cannot afford. Even if the son and daughter buy gasoline out of their own earnings or allowance, there are many other expenses in upkeep that may strain the family budget.

Whether or not we like it, statistics show that teenage drivers have more accidents per mile driven than older drivers. Automobile insurance rates, which are based on actual accident records, are more than three times as high for unmarried men under the age of twenty-five as for men twenty-five and over. The parents know they have to pay the bills and are in danger of being sued if the children wreck the car or do damage to others. That knowledge may make them resistant toward letting the children use the car freely.

One teenager, in attempting to ease the parents' minds before driving away, said, "Don't worry about reckless driving and an accident—we won't drive much of the time—we'll park."

That hardly relieved the parents' minds. Many parents feel that the hazards of parked cars are almost as great as the risk of accidents. But many parents will not express that thought to their children because they fear that their children may think the parents do not trust them.

Having the family car is no problem if you have your own car. If you do, however, you are in the minority of high school people. Of a large group of high school seniors polled, it was found that only 22 percent owned their own car, 59 percent used the family car, and 19 percent did not drive.

Families need to talk frankly about their different ways of thinking. Sometimes, a discussion will bring out facts and considerations of which parents have been unaware, and they may therefore be able to change some of their viewpoints. Also, it will become much easier for you to cooperate with your parents when you can understand why they feel as they do.

HOURS TO BE IN

In some communities, groups of parents and children have found a satisfactory solution to the question of how late to stay out on dates. Community clubs or organizations such as the Parent-Teachers Association have provided opportunities for parents and children to discuss the question of hours and reach an agreement or a compromise that most of the group use as a standard. This makes it much easier for people who want to cooperate with the standards of their families but who do not like to be singled out by their friends as different or restricted.

However, if the rule in a family requires the members to be in at a certain hour—even if the hour seems too early—it is possible for a young person who has poise and self-confidence to conform without embarrassing himself or herself or friends.

If one is good company, the fact that the date has to end at a certain hour will not be a handicap in getting future dates. People usually find that their friends show understanding and are willing to cooperate. Friends know that family backing is valuable, and most of them accept the fact that with backing there are also obligations.

Some parents "preach" because their sons or daughters date at an earlier age than they did and they find it hard to adjust to this.

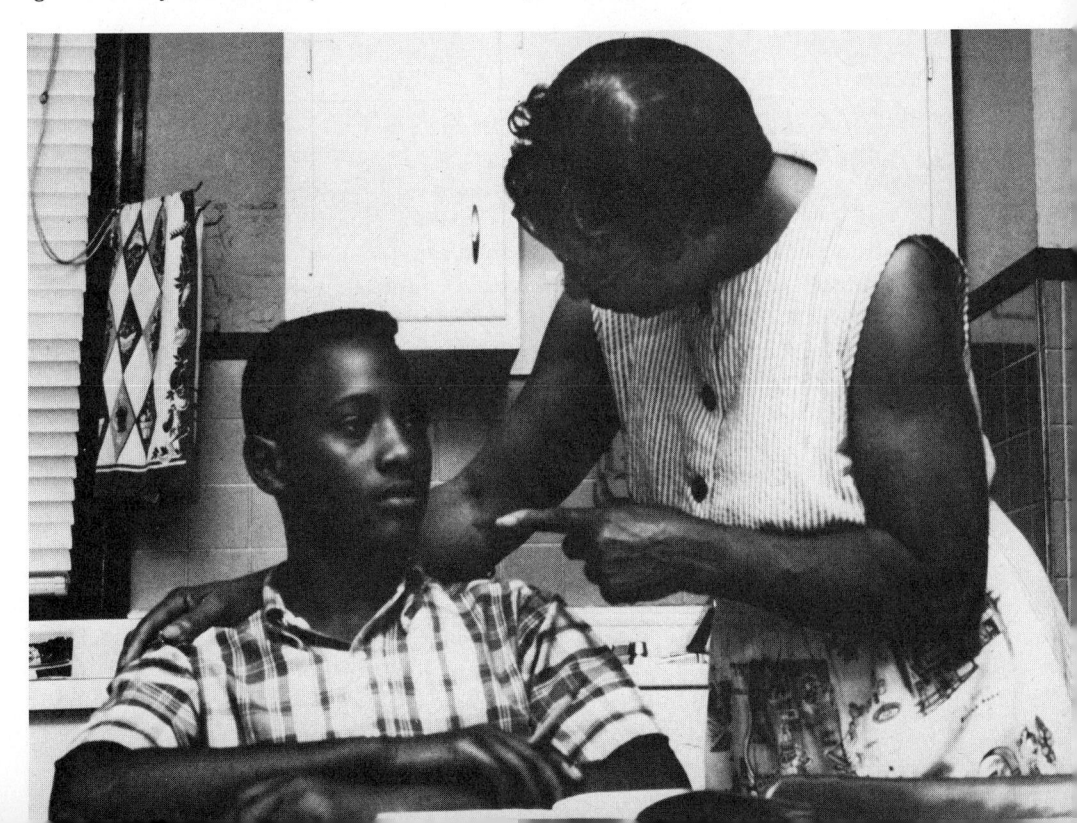

Many teenagers who live at home do have to be in at a set hour. They say that although it is not always convenient to get in on time, still they feel that it is better to have a definite time to be in. They feel more cared for and looked after than if their parents were indifferent about the hours they keep. One person said resentfully, "My parents just go to bed and to sleep, and don't know or care when I get in. I envy my friends whose parents are interested enough to care what goes on."

Many parents cannot relax until they know that their children are safely in at night, and they may lose sleep and become irritable when the hour for coming in is set very late. They may have to be up and about their business early the next morning and unable to sleep late, as might a son or daughter who has been out the night before.

Some families have been able to avoid friction over hours by working out a compromise. They agree upon a reasonable hour at which the son or daughter will either be in or will telephone. Thus, on a special occasion when the party lasts somewhat later than usual, some leeway is allowed. If a half-hour longer will really mean a far more pleasant evening, it then takes only a minute to telephone home so that the parents can go to sleep without worrying and wondering where the son or daughter is. It sometimes seems ridiculous to young people that their parents should worry over such matters, but parents do; they always have and always will. When you become a parent, you will probably worry over these same matters, just as your parents now worry over you.

DISAGREEMENT OVER YOUR CLOTHES AND HAIR

Perhaps you and your parents disagree about the way you dress or the way you wear your hair. Some families have so much conflict about these points that other relationships are damaged. Some of the emotional conflict could be avoided if each would make every effort to understand how the matter looks to the other.

Ideas about what is appropriate or inappropriate to wear to school have changed greatly in some parts of the United States since your parents were in school. Even within states, standards vary among different schools and communities. Naturally, you feel that the way you dress, or how long or short your hair is, should be your own decision and not a subject for dispute. At the same time, your parents are aware of what their generation thinks about suitable or unsuitable appearance, and they have their own ideas about how their children should look when they go out in public. It is hard for them not to make an issue of it if they feel defensive about the way you dress; they may find themselves reacting emotionally even if in theory they accept the idea of your increasing independence.

To talk things over takes cooperative effort to bridge the generation gap, but it is worthwhile for both parents and children when they can maintain such a relationship.

As with other controversial subjects, it will help if you can manage to talk the subject over peaceably. You may be able to interpret your feelings about it to them so that they can become more flexible. By demonstrating your good judgment in other matters, you may be able to show that you are responsible and mature enough to determine for yourself how you are going to dress and what kind of an appearance you will make at school or in public.

In turn, you may be able to understand their viewpoint. If they are buying your clothes and you are impulsive about following fads that change rapidly, their expense is greater and financial pressures may increase their critical attitudes toward your appearance. Moreover, it is true that their pride is involved where you are concerned, and that makes it harder for them to be sure just where their responsibility for you ends and your own begins.

PARENTS CANNOT ALWAYS DISCUSS THEIR WORRIES

Parents want their children to date, have friends, and eventually marry successfully. Yet because of their own past experience, their observation of people whose lives have been unwisely wrecked, and their interest in their children, they are often tense about the activities of their sons and daughters. Because they are so concerned, they may focus on the pitfalls and dangers about you rather than seeing the important social and emotional growth you are making and should make. So they appear to be unusually negative.

Another factor that makes for parents' uneasiness and tenseness is that they may not have had any communication with their children about the emotional side of sex development. These parents are troubled because they cannot discuss sex behavior and problems with their children. Because they cannot talk about these things, they become more anxious about the children's behavior than they would be if they could discuss their feelings freely. They might, however, be encouraged by the views that their children have. As long as there is no open communication, parents may appear to be touchy or critical—obstructive rather than cooperative.

You may see your parents as people who pry into your affairs, criticize your friends, and seem not to trust you. All of us would like to enjoy a feeling of family solidarity. It will help you to get along with your parents, and will help them to get along with you, if each of you can try to understand the other. All of us, young and old, have our own reasons for thinking as we do. An exchange of ideas will be useful toward clarifying and modifying viewpoints of both young people and parents. The responsibility here is not solely on the parents. It may be less difficult for you to bring up matters that need to be talked over. Many parents are more inhibited than their children in talking about things—although that may surprise you.

SOME YOUNG PEOPLE DEMAND TOO MUCH

A complaint sometimes made by parents is that their teenaged children want many things that are beyond the parents' means to provide. Some people demand possessions that "all the others have" and put so much pressure on their parents that family happiness is marred. Almost all parents would like to give their children every possible gift and advantage. Parents who think first of their own wants are in the minority. Parents are more likely to deprive themselves in order to do things for their children.

The average family cannot give all family members every desired material thing. The parents may have to pass up the remodeling they had hoped to begin this year. But the sixteen-year-old may insist on having a certain popular record album. If the parents say an insurance premium must be paid, the sixteen-year-old may mope and complain and be irritable toward the entire family until the parents manage to juggle family finances and get the desired object.

Perhaps the parents have made the mistake of failing to discuss family finances. The children may have no idea what a struggle it sometimes takes to make the dollars stretch to cover all family needs. Many parents would have less reason to criticize their children for demanding too much if they would be democratic in handling family finances. And many sons and daughters could help initiate democracy if they would take an interest in family financial problems and in the needs of all of the members of the family. This would be invaluable experience when they establish their own households.

It is true that we see many things we might like to have. We are susceptible to advertising, and we want to own some of the articles that look so attractive when advertised. We are also subject to suggestion; when we see others owning and apparently enjoying certain things, we think those things are necessary to our happiness.

Many people who are not satisfied with their success in human relationships fix their minds and desires upon material possessions in an attempt to gain satisfactions that are lacking in their lives. Often the girl and boy who have few friends and few skills will be especially demanding of things from their family. The attitude will be, "If I only had this or that—" inferring that possessions could make up for other failures.

If you look about you, you will find some people who have few material possessions, but who are successful and happy. In every school are some students who are liked by everyone, but who have inexpensive clothes and no other impressive possessions. Some others will have everything anyone could want, but will be unhappy and full of complaints about how the world treats them. The person who has plenty of spending money is not always the one who is happy and successful in his social relationships.

Some families simply cannot afford many things that young people feel are important. Perhaps there are several children in the family. How do parents set priorities to meet each one's needs?

Parents with limited incomes sometimes seem to their children to be lacking in sympathy because they do not provide some desirable things. Perhaps some parents are not so adept at managing family finances as they should be; with better management, the money would go farther. But they are probably doing their best, just as you are with the money you have to spend. The need is for family understanding. In some families, all members make an effort to understand and appreciate the desires of the others, and all are willing to forego some of their own wishes in favor of the interests of the whole family.

ESTABLISHING AND MAINTAINING GOOD COMMUNICATION

Whether the point of friction with parents is possessions, the kinds of clothes you wear, hours to be in, friends of yours, or any other matter, there is always value in trying to keep lines of communication open. In fact, the key to avoiding or solving many problems lies in establishing and maintaining good communications. This is as much your responsibility as theirs. Their habits are likely to be more set than yours, and it may be harder for them to discuss some subjects than it would be for you. Their reticence may give you the impression that they are not willing to talk matters over or do not want to hear your ideas. It will be worth something to make the effort. They do care about what happens to you, and they have had some experiences that may have given them some insights that can help in your own thinking. If open communication is possible among members of the family, it is mutually beneficial.

FOCUS ON YOU

Your answers to the following questions may help you decide whether or not there is anything you can do to improve or maintain family understanding during your dating years.

1. Do your parents lose sleep because of the hours you keep?
2. If you leave a social event earlier than others do, which explanations are satisfactory?
    "I need my sleep."
    "My parents will scold me if I'm not in by midnight."
    "My parents will be angry if I stay out any latar."
    "The invitations said eight to eleven-thirty, and it is after eleven."
    "If I go now, I won't risk missing the last bus home."
    "I agreed to be home before twelve, and I can make it if I leave now."

3. If both you and your parents get emotional when you try to discuss dating hours, have you figured out just why? Could you do anything to bring about better understanding?

4. Have you demonstrated that you are responsible in the use of the family car by:
    helping to keep it clean and in running order?
    observing traffic rules carefully?
    refusing to race or to play games with the car?
    taking driving lessons and passing an examination for a driver's license?
    showing consideration for other family members who need the car?
    willingly doing some family errands when you have the car?
    not leaving the gas tank empty for the next person?

5. Do you help ease your parents' minds by:
    telling them with whom you are going out?
    telling them where you will be?
    telling them approximately when you expect to be home?

6. Do you demonstrate to your parents that you are no longer a child by:
    willingly sharing home responsibilities?
    showing judgment in the use of money?
    controlling your temper?
    recognizing the rights of other family members?
    trying to explain your viewpoint rather than just having unpleasant clashes?

7. If your parents are critical of your appearance, have you talked it over with them? Have you tried to demonstrate that you are mature and responsible in all your obligations so that they need not feel responsible for the way you dress? Have you thought carefully about whether the way you want to dress might possibly be motivated by a need to shock them or make them concede that your appearance is your own business?

8. Are you trying your best to keep open lines of communication with your parents? To give up and conclude that they are not interested in your feelings or don't want to hear your views is probably a mistake. Parents usually are interested; they would like to understand how things look to you. If they and you keep trying, you can probably find a way to achieve understanding helpful to all of you.

QUESTIONS FOR REVIEW

1. In what respects are both the parents and children in a stage of transition when the children reach their teens?

2. What are some of the basic causes of misunderstanding between parents and children during the teen years?

3. List several problems that may arise between parents and children during the dating years.

4. How do you interpret the term "generation gap"?

5. What are some problems that center around the use of the family car? Are parents justified in their anxieties when children are out with the car?
6. How might parents and children in a community arrive at a better understanding of each other's point of view? Has this been attempted in your community?
7. Why are parents especially anxious when their children are out late on dates? Do you think they are justified in their anxiety?
8. Is it better to have parents strict and concerned or permissive and indifferent?
9. Why are parents concerned about their children's clothes and hairstyles?
10. If a young person is especially demanding in wanting everything others have, what may it indicate?
11. Does possession of a car or having a large allowance attract friends? Discuss.
12. Discuss "communication" between parents and children.

ACTIVITIES AND PROJECTS

1. Select three boys and three girls from the class to hold a panel discussion on parent-child frictions over dating, hours to be in, use of the family car, clothes, and haircuts. If possible, have some parents attend and participate in the panel.

2. (a) Consult the *Reader's Guide* for magazine articles discussing accident rates by age of drivers. Report to the class.

    (b) Consult some automobile insurance agents on this subject, and report. Find out what special insurance regulations apply if a car or truck is to be driven by people of certain ages.

3. Companies direct some of their advertising to the special wants of teenagers. Collect and evaluate some advertisements. What effect may this have upon parent-child relationships?

4. Do you know parents who deny themselves too much in order to meet the wants of their children? Parents who seem to think more of their own needs than of their children's needs? Have a panel discussion of ways to resolve conflicting needs of parents and children.

5. Have four or more students discuss with the class ways to develop and maintain good communication with parents.

SOCIODRAMA

Present a scene in which two students play the parts of parents. They are discussing some problems with a sixteen-year-old son or daughter and trying to decide on solutions. Choose a specific problem to be considered.

WORDS AND CONCEPTS

adolescence
controversial
family solidarity
generation gap

reticence
suggestible
tactical position
transition

SUGGESTED READINGS FOR THE UNIT

Albrecht, Margaret, *Parents and Teen-agers Getting Through to Each Other.* 1972. New York: Parents' Magazine Press.

Berg, Roland H., "Why Americans Hide Behind a Drug Curtain," *Look,* August 18, 1967.

Blakeslee, Alton L., *Alcoholism—A Sickness That Can Be Beaten.* 1966. New York: Public Affairs Committee, Inc.

———, *What You Should Know About Drugs and Narcotics.* New York: Association Press.

Bowman, Henry A., *Marriage for Moderns.* 1974. New York: McGraw-Hill Book Company, Inc.

Consumers Reports. Go through their issues and find the latest reports on smoking.

Duvall, Evelyn M., *Love and the Facts of Life.* 1963. New York: Association Press.

———, *Why Wait Till Marriage?* 1965. New York: Association Press.

———, and Joy D. Johnson, *The Art of Dating.* 1967. New York: Association Press.

Gmur, Ben C., and J. T. Fodor, L. H. Glass, and J. Langan, *Making Health Decisions.* 1975. Englewood Cliffs, N. J.: Prentice-Hall, Inc.

Johns, Edward B., W. C. Sutton, and L. E. Webster, *Health for Effective Living.* 1970. New York: McGraw-Hill Book Company, Inc.

Landis, Judson T., and Mary G. Landis, *Building a Successful Marriage,* Fifth Edition. 1973. Englewood Cliffs, N. J.: Prentice-Hall, Inc.

Neisser, Ruth G., *Mothers and Daughters: A Lifelong Relationship.* 1973. New York: Harper & Row, Publishers.

Nelson, Jack, *Teen-agers and Sex: Revolution or Reaction?* 1970. Englewood Cliffs, N. J.: Prentice-Hall, Inc.

Paolucci, Beatrice, Theodora Faiola, and Patricia Thompson, *Personal Perspective: A Guide to Decision Making.* 1973. New York: Webster Division of McGraw-Hill Book Company, Inc.

Schneider, Robert E., *The Venereal Diseases.* 1968. Boston: Allyn and Bacon.

Smoking, Tobacco, and Health. 1969. Washington, D. C.: U. S. Department of Health, Education, and Welfare. Public Health Service.

Thinking About Drinking. Washington, D. C.: Superintendent of Documents, U. S. Government Printing Office. Ask for Children's Bureau Publication No. 456 and include 20 cents.

Vermes, Jean C., *Pot Is Rot.* New York: Association Press.

Way, Walter L., M.D., *The Drug Scene: Help or Hangup?* 1970. Englewood Cliffs, N. J.: Prentice-Hall, Inc.

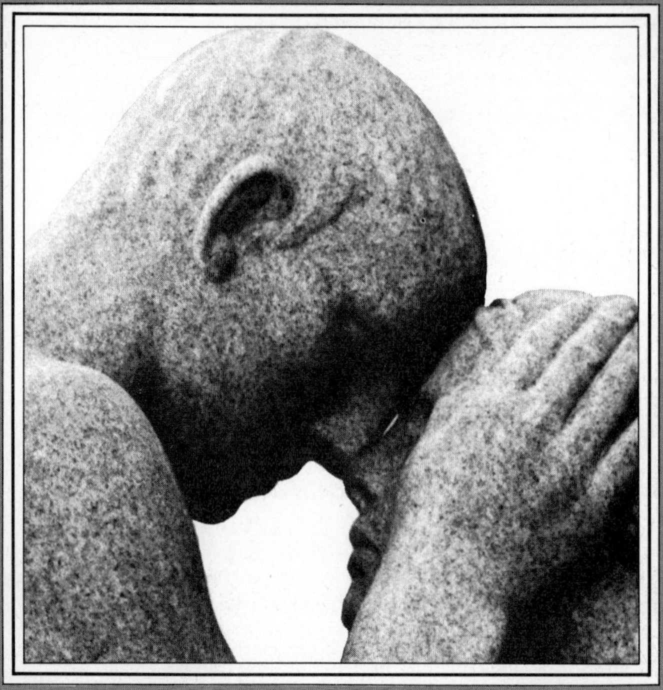

part three

LOOKING TOWARD MARRIAGE

What really counts is that love which is able
to say yes to the other,
to accept the other,
to reveal to the other one's own humanity,
one's own personhood;
that love which is for the other
a principle of strength,
of inner growth,
of grace.

Father John Catoir and José de Vinck

10 Dating Becomes Mate Selection

After studying this chapter, you will be able to

1. Describe the distinction between dating and courtship.
2. Discuss in detail how family background affects marriage.
3. List the traits and characteristics that tend to increase one's chances of a happy marriage.
4. Determine differences between individuals that make for difficult adjustments in marriage.

Up to now we have been discussing ways in which we develop through our relations with members of our family and with those whom we have been meeting socially. Dating has required new adjustments. We have been using this time to establish our standards so as to make the many decisions life demands. Sometime during the teen years or early twenties, dating gradually progresses into courtship. We begin to look upon the people we date as a possible wife or husband. Now let us think about factors to consider before one is ready to go into serious courtship leading to marriage.

FAMILY BACKGROUND AFFECTS MARRIAGE

Marriage is the merging of two family lines. Studies of families in the United States have found that happiness tends to run in families. After studying many marriages, researchers have concluded that an important factor in predicting the success of a young couple is the happiness or unhappiness of their parents' marriages. A larger percentage of happy marriages occur among people whose parents remain married than among those whose parents divorce or separate. In a study in which we had the cooperation of one group of married people and one group of divorced people, we compared the family backgrounds and found a clear picture of differences. A summary of this research may be found in Table 5.

Table 5 FAMILY BACKGROUND FACTORS

Family Background	Married Group*	Divorced Group*
	Percentage	
Parents' marriage happy or very happy	55	39
Childhood happy or very happy	66	41
Adolescence happy or very happy	55	36
Relationship with father to age fifteen close or very close	42	23
Relationship with mother to age fifteen close or very close	63	44
Doubts about having a successful marriage	24	42

* As reported by 1162 married people and 164 divorced people.

You will see that other situations are important also, such as childhood and adolescent feelings of happiness, relationships with both parents, and feelings of doubt or confidence about one's own future marriage. Additional factors that have been shown by research to be predictive of happiness are

Lack of conflict with mother,
Home discipline that was firm but not harsh,
Parental frankness about matters of sex.

These are situations more characteristic of happy than of unhappy homes, and for logical reasons. Just as happiness tends to run in families, so divorce runs in families. Two thousand of our college students

PATTERN OF DIVORCE IN TWO GENERATIONS

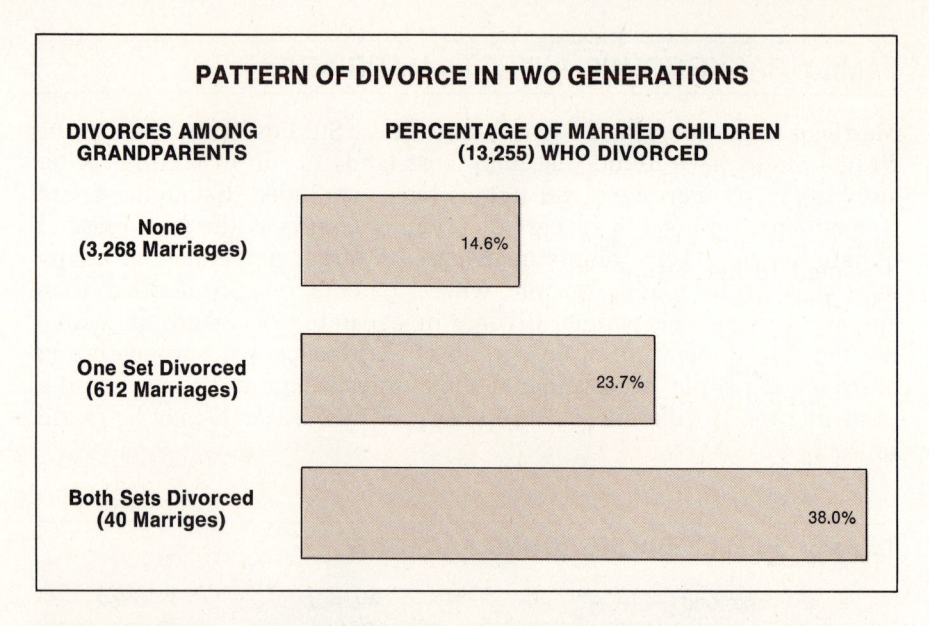

DIVORCES AMONG GRANDPARENTS	PERCENTAGE OF MARRIED CHILDREN (13,255) WHO DIVORCED
None (3,268 Marriages)	14.6%
One Set Divorced (612 Marriages)	23.7%
Both Sets Divorced (40 Marriages)	38.0%

Graph 2. Of 1977 college students, this shows the percentage of parents, aunts, and uncles who had divorced, and the marital status of the grandparents.

reported anonymously on the divorce histories of their grandparents, parents, aunts, and uncles. If the grandparents had divorced, there were many more divorces among their parents and aunts and uncles. If both sets of grandparents had divorced, there was an even higher divorce rate among the parents and aunts and uncles. Results of the research with college students is summarized in Graph 2.

Many people are not aware that their family background affects qualifications for marriage. The evidence suggests that the person should take a careful look at the family of the one being dated. Before marrying into a family in which there have been unhappiness and divorces, one should carefully weigh the chances of success.

Certainly, we do not mean to imply that all children from unhappy homes are going to be unhappy when they marry. We know that some young people who have lived with unhappily married parents are determined that when they marry they will establish a happier home than that in which they grew up. They will try to assess the ways in which their childhood situations have influenced their attitudes and ways of interacting with other people, and they will be determined to overcome whatever handicaps they have.

An unhappy home background may cause some people to be more cautious in mate choice and to work harder at building a good marriage. People who recognize their unhappy family background as a handicap to be overcome, and who approach marriage intelligently, may succeed in building happy relationships in their own marriages.

One girl of nineteen said to a counselor, "My family is a mess. Grandmother divorced grandfather; mother divorced father and is now unhappily married to my stepfather. My two aunts have been married twice each and still aren't happy. I couldn't stand it if my children had to grow up in the kind of family I've had."

Perhaps it seems cruel that she had to speak in such a way of her family, but this girl was trying to face her background objectively, as it related to her future. She went on to say, "I'm not going to marry until I'm sure I understand myself, and until I've known the man for a long time and understand him, too. I've decided that I'm going to be the one to break the chain of unhappiness in my family."

There is some evidence that people who have courses in preparation for marriage and parenthood tend to become able to overcome some handicapping factors in their backgrounds. Several studies of students who have had courses in preparation for marriage show that those students, when married, felt that the courses had helped them to be more realistic about marriage, and so to do better at solving marital problems. In our 1967 study of 581 couples, one or both of whom had had a college course in preparation for marriage, those couples had much more successful marriages than their parents had had. They had a much lower divorce rate and were happier in their marriages than they believed their parents had been. If these couples had continued the pattern predictable by their parents' divorce rate, many more of them would have been unhappy or divorced than actually were.

Similar educational backgrounds, particularly when both have had courses in family living, serve as good foundations for marriage.

In either case—whether you are from a happy family or an unhappy one—preparation for marriage is desirable. Sometimes, people from very happy families may take marriage happiness for granted, thinking it will come automatically, without special effort on their part. On the other hand, those from unhappy families may be discouraged and believe they have little chance for happiness. Neither view is sound. Whatever your background, you can work to build a good marriage. A happy background will not insure success, nor need an unhappy background be a fatal handicap.

The important thing is for people to be able to consider family background objectively and to recognize ways in which this background has affected personal attitudes toward the other sex and marriage.

Lack of parent-child conflict

Researchers have found that, if there has been a lack of conflict and a good understanding between parent and child, the chances for a happy marriage are greater. People who complain about and have frequent conflicts with their parents are not as likely to be good husbands or wives as those who are generous in judgment and willing to allow parents their faults.

Physical and mental health

Is the family into which one might marry physically healthy and emotionally stable? Marriage requires two people who are physically, mentally, and emotionally strong. Bearing and rearing children, running a home, supporting a family, and making the adjustments that are necessary throughout life require all the abilities of two healthy, emotionally balanced people.

Just as good or poor physical health may run in families, so also may good or poor mental health. Mental health shows up in the way problems are met. In Part 1 of this book, ways of meeting life's problems were discussed. You know that some people try to "block off" problems, by refusing to face them. Others try escapes such as sickness or alcohol or drugs. Some people blame others for every difficulty and refuse to take any responsibility for their own actions. Some retreat to childish behavior such as sulking or having temper tantrums. On the other hand, many people have learned to face life squarely and to cope with problems in constructive ways.

In your dating, it is well to think about these habits and ways that are indications of good or poor mental health. Before you are seriously committed to anyone, you can be more objective in analyzing what the future with such a person might be like.

It is also necessary to look at one's own habits and ways. Mental health is even more important than physical health as a factor in marriage success. Consider the question: What patterns of mental health

The marriageable personality develops through parent-child relationships. Deep affection within a happy family produces people who will carry this pattern into their own marriage.

have I learned from my family? To answer that, you will need to think about what you and others in your family do when any serious problem or crisis occurs. Do some of you blame others for the trouble instead of joining forces to meet the crisis cooperatively? Does the family pattern include brooding or retaliation against each other or escape such as alcohol or illness? Has your family the policy of facing problems as well as they can and, when escapes are needed, using desirable escapes such as hobbies or productive work? You will also want to observe and think about these factors in the family of any person you date.

Good mental health does not grow in a day. All of us have to preserve it year after year. It is important to know that and to be alert to habits or traits that would contribute to poor mental health and would be handicaps in marriage.

WHAT TRAITS DO YOU CONSIDER MOST DESIRABLE IN A MATE?

The Purdue Opinion Panel asked high school students in all parts of the country to rate traits from "very desirable" to "undesirable" for a future mate. In Table 6 on page 146, we have ranked the traits that boys and girls considered very desirable. The study was first made in 1950 and was repeated in 1961; there was little difference in the way students ranked the traits in the two periods. Do you think your generation would rank the traits in the same order?

Table 6 TRAITS STUDENTS CONSIDER DESIRABLE IN A MATE

Trait Ranking	Boys	Girls	Total
	Percentage		
Is dependable, can be trusted	92	96	94
Is considerate of me and others	84	95	90
Takes pride in personal appearance and manners	87	90	89
Shows affection	84	85	85
Acts own age, is not childish	77	87	82
Desires normal family life with children	77	87	82
Has pleasant disposition	77	84	81
Is clean in speech and action	72	82	77
Knows how to budget	62	75	69
Approved of by my parents	56	74	65

MARRIAGEABILITY

It takes two marriageable people to make a good marriage. It is important to look at your own marriageability as well as at the traits of the possible mate.

Research shows that there are a series of personality traits that are likely to be found in those who make a success of marriage. In general, marriage does not change basic personality traits. One is the same after marriage, except that many people are less likely to put their best foot forward after marriage.

Some years ago, Lewis Terman's studies of marriages revealed many of the traits of marriageable and unmarriageable people. Summarized opposite are some of the traits more often found in happily married men and women and traits more often found in unhappily married people. You can see how these could affect marriage and why certain traits would make trouble in any marriage, and in other relationships. Of course, if both persons agreed on a given point, the marriage might be successful even though to someone else that trait would indicate trouble ahead.

In marriage, a very important personality trait is *adaptability* or *flexibility*. No matter how well acquainted people are before they marry, or how deeply in love, the many adjustments required after marriage call for great flexibility. Both must be able to give in gracefully, to compromise, to learn new ways of looking at life, to see the other person's point of view. People who are rigid and inflexible will have problems.

Marriageable people also are able to identify with others. This kind of *identification* is the quality that enables us to try to put ourselves

HAPPY

Men

1. Emotionally even and stable.
2. Are cooperative.
3. Equalitarian attitudes toward woman.
4. Benevolent toward inferiors or underprivileged.
5. Not self-conscious or too introverted.
6. Show initiative.
7. Take responsibility.
8. Saving and cautious about money.
9. Favorable to religion.
10. Uphold sex standards and social conventions.

Women

1. Not easily offended.
2. Not competitive in social situtations.
3. Are cooperative.
4. Not annoyed by advice.
5. Like activities that give others pleasure.
6. Careful about money.
7. Conventional in religion and morals.
8. Optimistic in outlook.

UNHAPPY

Men

1. Inclined to be moody.
2. Have inferiority feelings.
3. Compensate by being domineering.
4. Enjoy commanding others.
5. Withdraw from competing with superiors.
6. Compensate by daydreams and dreams of power.
7. Irregular in work habits.
8. Dislike saving money.
9. Express irreligious attitudes.
10. Inclined to be radical in sex morals.

Women

1. Are emotionally tense.
2. Have ups and downs in moods.
3. Are aggressive because of inferiority feelings.
4. Inclined to be irritable or dictatorial.
5. Would rather be important than liked.
6. Interested only in activities that offer personal rewards.
7. Tend to be impatient workers.
8. Dislike cautious or careful people.
9. Dislike work that requires careful effort.
10. Inclined to be radical in ideas and beliefs.

in the place of others and to try to feel as they feel. It is the basis of cooperation, sympathy, and most of the deeper understandings in all close personal relationships. Some people never know how the other person feels; they are aware only of "me-ism," of how they themselves feel.

You can accomplish much if you work to develop the personality traits that are especially characteristic of marriageable people. At this point in your life, the important question is, "Am I *becoming* a marriageable person?" From now on, much of your personality growth is in your own hands.

DO YOUR PERSONALITIES FIT?

Sometimes, two marriageable people wed, but find adjusting difficult because they do not meet each other's personality needs. All of us have certain needs that must be met if we are to be happy. It is important to be marriageable, but a matching of personalities is also important. Let us illustrate.

Ellen came from a family of serious-minded New Englanders who were thrifty and studious. Her father never joked. He was dignified and intellectual, extremely punctual, and careful about details. To Ellen, he represented the manly qualities that were important in the head of a family. She also was careful of details and in many other ways was like her father.

She married John, who was in every way her opposite. He was carefree and full of fun. He spent money as fast as he earned it; but he earned it easily so that he supported his family without serious difficulty. He was seldom on time for appointments, but managed to overcome that handicap by being such good company that people were inclined to overlook this. He liked to spend his time with people rather than reading quietly at home, and he would make jokes about the "highbrow books" that Ellen enjoyed. He was rather hasty in his speech and would speak sharply when annoyed with Ellen. He was always sorry immediately and would apologize.

This couple never once considered divorce. But their marriage involved many rather constant irritations and misunderstandings. In all their years of married life, Ellen was never able really to understand John. She had to struggle not to criticize his easygoing ways. She hoped, in spite of herself, that their children would not be like him, and she tried to influence them not to be.

John, on the other hand, could not understand Ellen. After many years of marriage, he once said, "If only she would lose her temper and shout at me just once! I get so tired of always being the one who makes the mistake and does the wrong thing."

Tolerance and understanding are required in all relationships and can help to make a marriage successful no matter how opposite the two personalities are; but if people choose wisely, they can marry someone with whom they can adjust more easily.

The person who considers financial security of the most fundamental importance should not marry one who is careless and wasteful in the use of money. One who is very sensitive to friction or quarreling among others should not marry one who is quarrelsome and does not mind friction.

One girl broke her engagement because, as she said, "He has some speech habits that annoy me so I can hardly stand it. I know that if I married him, I would never get used to the way he talks." Perhaps she was just not ready for marriage, or if she was, this was not the right man for her. Although speech habits may seem a small thing to criticize, the girl's critical feelings meant she really could not accept her fiance as he was. If they had married, their marriage would have been destructive to them both.

There is no benefit in marrying someone with faults that we know we cannot tolerate; we cannot change the other person. The point is to try to be realistic before you choose a mate about which traits are irritating and which are endurable. This means, of course, that two people need to take plenty of time to know each other well before they make a decision to marry.

WHAT ABOUT RECREATIONAL INTERESTS?

Recreational interests do not change greatly from youth to old age. In general, the things that interest us when we are young are the things that interest us as we grow older. Research on marriage adjustment shows that the more parts of life in which a couple are in agreement, the better are their chances for happiness; the more areas in which they are not together, the poorer will be their chances.

Marriage is similar to other associations. You enjoy being with those who have the same interests that you have, and who like to do the same things you like to do. Good friendships are based on this principle. The same is true of marriage.

Sometimes, people enjoy dating those whose interests are widely different. The difference represents novelty; so an element of adventure is present; but in order to enjoy each other's company permanently, they must be companionable in as many ways as possible. That is what Robert Louis Stevenson meant when he said, "A certain sort of talent is indispensable for people who would spend years together and not bore themselves to death—a while together by the fire happens more frequently in marriage than the presence of a distinguished foreigner to dinner—that people should laugh over the same sort of jests and have many an old joke between them that time cannot wither nor custom stale, is a better preparation for life, by your leave, than many other things higher and better sounding in the world's ear—to find your wife

Friendships are more satisfactory with those who have the same interests that we have. The same is also true of marriage.

laughing when you had tears in your eyes or staring when you were in a fit of laughter would go some way towards dissolution of the marriage."*

You may know some married couples who are bored in each other's company. They have little to talk about. When they were dating, their conversation was about themselves or, specifically, about their date or marriage plans. But after people are married, the time comes when there is little left to say about themselves, and their day-to-day plans have settled into a routine that requires little or no discussion. Some couples discover then that they have very little in common. One of them may like to read, but the other can think of nothing so boring as an evening at home with a book. If they care for music at all, they may differ in the kinds of music they enjoy. If one offers an opinion on a subject, the other may respond only with a contradiction, or may not be interested enough to reply at all. It is better to discover such lack of real companionship during dating. Surely, such uncongenial couples had no better basis of companionship before they married; but they were too interested in getting married and too busy planning the wedding to notice that they did not share the kinds of interests that provide a permanent basis for friendly companionship in their marriage.

* *Virginibus Puerisque.*

WHAT ABOUT FRIENDS AND SOCIAL INTERESTS?

Preferences for certain types of people will not change much with marriage. If you cannot stand the friends your girl friend or boy friend has now, you would not find them any easier to tolerate later. But if two who marry enjoy the same kinds of friends before marriage, it will be an advantage.

Before they marry, people need to get well acquainted with each other's friends and family. Sometimes during serious dating, two may find each other so interesting and absorbing that they tend to eliminate other people from their company. People who do this are failing to carry out one of the purposes of the courtship period. They need to become acquainted with the way the partner interacts with others. If one alienates friends and makes enemies easily, it should warn the other that he or she may be hard to live with as a permanent partner.

Couples must become well aquainted over a long period of time before they can know whether or not they meet each other's personality needs.

In your view, what constitutes "a good time"? How do you prefer to spend time, energy, or money? Would you rather

Stay at home	or	Be on the go
Read	or	Go to a show
Listen to good music	or	Watch a football game on television
Go to a concert	or	Go to a ball game
Make new friends	or	Stick to established associations
Spend evenings with groups such as a church organization	or	Spend evenings at movies or watching television
Spend vacations in the out-of-doors, mountains, or a lake	or	Spend vacations in a city or resort
Travel	or	Stay near home
Participate in church activities on Sunday	or	Go to a movie or for a long drive on Sunday
Spend quiet weekends at home	or	Use weekends for parties and entertaining
Discuss politics, religion, and ideas	or	Talk about people and current happenings in your neighborhood or school
Save for the future	or	Spend it today
Have a new car that you pay for over a two-year period	or	Buy a used car for less and pay cash

Think about the contrasts suggested by the list above. Decide which items tend to characterize your preferences and those of your family. Try to assess people you date and their families in the same way. Such assessment may help toward choosing a mate with whom a high level of companionship can be permanent.

PARENTAL APPROVAL

Often young people have to face the problem of parental disapproval of their marriage. Some people tend to think they are marrying only each other and not the families involved. They may believe that no reason exists why they should care about the respective families' approval or disapproval. However, marriages that parents approve are more likely to succeed than those in which parental approval is lacking.

Sometimes, parents oppose a marriage for no very good reason. They may only be resisting their child's inevitable growing away from them, but they may give other more acceptable reasons. Such parents, however, are rare. Most parents want their children to find good mates and be happily married. When parents' disapproval is unjustified and emotional, the young people may eventually be able to convince them otherwise. To do this, the couple must be sure that they are right in their choice. It is often worthwhile to wait and try to win parental approval, meanwhile examining the relationship to be sure that there is no real basis for the parental opposition.

Some parents have good reasons for opposing a marriage. These parents then face a hard question in knowing how far to go in their opposition.

Margaret, an attractive nineteen-year-old girl, became involved in a love affair with a man of whom her parents disapproved. Tom was only a few years older than she, but he had been married and divorced twice. He explained both failures by saying that the marriages had been unhappy mistakes: the two former wives had been selfish and inconsiderate, and had not understood him. He also blamed the in-laws, who, he said, had interfered in both his former marriages.

Margaret's parents, however, felt that the young man was extremely selfish. He was striking in appearance and could be unusually charming when things were going his way, but would sulk and be unpleasant when his wishes were opposed. He seldom had occasion to sulk with Margaret, for she was devoted to him and tried to please him as much as possible. To her, he seemed entirely desirable, and she felt that she could never be as happy with any other man.

The parents did not openly oppose the marriage. The couple seemed to be so much in love that the parents feared Margaret would marry secretly if opposed; therefore, they asked only that she wait a few months. In the meantime, they made Tom welcome in their home. He was with Margaret daily, so that she had time to become well acquainted with him. As time passed, she began to feel the strain of trying to keep him happy when he never thought of anyone but himself. She began to see him as he really was, and after a few months, she broke with him.

One reason, then, that parental disapproval is a strike against a marriage is that in many cases good reasons do exist for the opposition. Another reason is that, if parental opposition exists, whether or not it is justified, the young couple can hardly be unconscious of it, no matter how independent they are. When adjustments later have to be made, as happens in all marriages, the knowledge that the parents disapproved may bolster any unwillingness to make the necessary compromises. The son or daughter may think, "It is probably as bad a marriage as my parents think it is; there is not much use trying." Or one may regress by turning to the parents for support against the mate. On the other

Two people who have similar interests and similar backgrounds feel at ease with each other and have a good chance for happiness in marriage.

hand, if everyone concerned believed the marriage to be a good one, the couple would make a greater effort to work their way through the problems.

Parental cooperation and approval is a valuable asset, and the lack of it is a danger signal.

HOMOGAMY IN MATE CHOICE

People tend to marry someone who is quite similar to themselves in age, stature, intelligence, temperament, race, religion, education, socio-economic class, and nationality. People also tend to marry those with the same drinking and smoking habits and the same leisure-time interests. This is called *homogamy,* meaning the mating of like with like.

However, the average couple will probably not be alike in every one of the items just listed, and no two people will be just the same in all the elements of their personality makeup or their background. Some specific differences in characteristics or in background are not important, but some other differences are more basic, and these make for disharmony and require special adjustability if the marriage is to be happy.

DIFFERENCES MAY OR MAY NOT MATTER

Physical differences such as being tall or short, fair or dark, stout or slim, have no significant effect on the happiness of a married couple. Studies have been made to learn whether or not a difference in age matters, but there is no evidence that this has any effect on happiness in marriage. Most young people will say that they think the husband should be two or three years older than the wife. Because people feel that way, most men in our society do marry women two or three years younger. However, the young man who is not bothered by the fact that the woman he dates is older can marry her and have a very happy marriage. A few years' difference is not important except in the minds of those who believe it to matter.

As for education, in most cases, small differences in years of schooling are not important. The kind of difference that matters is if two people come from families with entirely different educational backgrounds and attitudes. For example, one family might put high value on study and learning, and believe in sacrificing in order that the family members receive good educations; while the other family might not be concerned with education or might believe that schooling or college training is a waste of time or money. Such opposite viewpoints represent serious contrasts. A couple from two such families would probably have many other contrasts in their backgrounds that could handicap their happiness in marriage.

Contrasts in economic or social status may or may not represent important differences. Two who marry from widely different socioeconomic backgrounds might have different types of friends, different recreational interests, and possibly different standards of behavior. The families of the two young people might not be very congenial. In many such marriages, it develops that the wife is more or less separated from her family and friends in favor of mingling in the social class to which her husband belongs, whether his status is higher or lower than hers. However, much depends upon the life circumstances and the ages of the couple. If they are mature and independent, and the circumstances of their married life do not require them to live and associate too closely with their families, a contrast in socioeconomic background need not matter.

MIXED MARRIAGES

Marriages in which the two people come from backgrounds with many contrasts, especially contrasts that society considers unusual, are called *mixed marriages*. A marriage with so many contrasts that it is truly "mixed" has all the usual marital problems and, in addition, may have problems related to differences in background.

In our country, even though it is recognized that certain types of combinations in marriage will tend to have more problems, laws no longer restrict whom one can marry except in certain cases. At one time, states had laws prohibiting interracial marriages, but the Supreme Court in 1967 ruled those laws unconstitutional because they interfered with the rights of individuals as guaranteed by the Constitution. The removal of the laws against interracial marriages did not result in any significant increase in such marriages.

There has been a fairly continuous increase in international marriages, some of which are in fact, interracial, ever since World War II. It has been estimated that approximately one hundred thousand war brides from all parts of the world returned with servicemen after World War II. Because of the Korean war, the Vietnam war, and the thousands of military personnel that are stationed in bases all over the world, there is a steady increase in the number of international and interracial marriages. The expansion of American business into foreign countries, the Peace Corps, aid programs to other countries, and the student exchange programs have all resulted in a greater mingling of United States citizens with people of other nationalities. And an increase in mixed marriages can be expected to continue.

Whether or not national and racial differences have an influence upon the success or failure of a marriage will depend to a great extent upon the community in which the people live, and upon the contrasts in religion, language, or customs of the two people marrying. Some such marriages include circumstances that require many more adjustments than do others. Two cases illustrate this.

A young American businessman who, while in the army, was stationed in England married a British girl who had lived in London all her life. At the end of his service, they returned to the United States and settled in New York City, where the man continued in the exporting business. The girl liked life in New York City as well as she had in London. Her husband's business sent him to England occasionally, which made it possible for her to return for brief visits with her family. In this marriage, the nationality difference was not important.

Another American boy from a farm in one of the poorer rural sections of a midwestern state also married a girl from London while he was overseas. After the war, they settled on a small rented farm near the boy's home. The girl found the quiet rural life intolerable. She hated the hot, dry summers and the drudgery involved in trying to make a living from the poor soil. She longed for some of the sights and sounds of a city, but their poverty did not permit trips to a city. She became homesick for a visit with her people, but there was no money for the trip. After two years, she left her husband and went to a city, where she worked in a factory and saved enough money for her passage back to England. She insisted that she still loved her husband, but could not stand the life that marriage with him involved.

It is readily seen that more adjustments were required of the second girl, for she married into a way of life entirely different from her accustomed one. Personality traits, such as an unwillingness or inability to adjust, no doubt played a part, because personality traits have more to do with success or failure in marriage than do circumstances. However, in general, fewer handicaps are involved in marriages in which few serious differences and many similarities are to be found in the background of the couple.

If people intend to marry across lines of difference, they should consider carefully whether or not they both have the qualities that will enable them to make all the adjustments required. They should know, before they marry, that their mixed marriage will probably require them to work for success with more intelligence, understanding, and determination than are required of those who marry people with similar backgrounds. Especially, they will need to be the kind of people who can accept differences, who can give respect and emotional support to a mate whose ways or beliefs may be in contrast to their own.

The most common type of mixed marriage in our country is marriage across religious lines. Many young people who know that they differ in religious beliefs still want to marry, believing that they can somehow harmonize their differences or that the difference will not affect their marriage. Mixed religious marriages will be considered more extensively in Chapter 14.

DATING, MATE CHOICE, AND MARRIAGE SUCCESS

As we think of the subjects discussed in this chapter, it becomes clear that whatever a person's reasons may be for wanting to date, dating does become mate choice. And to choose a mate wisely is a necessary basis for a happy marriage. One must be aware of personality traits, family background, and interests that lead to a lasting companionship.

If two people, who have many personality defects and who come from unhappy homes, have personality traits that do not meet each other's needs, or have values and attitudes that conflict, they do not have a good chance for happiness in marriage. It is possible, even easy, to fall in love with someone who is quite opposite from you and whose personality you would find extremely hard or impossible to live with. Love is not some mysterious force that guides people into wise marriages. Love is a relationship that develops and continues to grow and mature if the two people meet each other's personality needs and have a basis for lasting companionship.

So, when you think about life—the future as well as the present—you should try to be realistic during the years when dating is likely to lead to serious courtship and marriage. You should consider the personality traits of those whom you date, and the factors that are important in family background, in your own family as well as in the other person's. It is not realistic to continue to date a person with whom marriage would not have a good chance for success and happiness.

QUESTIONS FOR REVIEW

1. What distinction is made between dating and courtship?
2. How can happiness "run in families"? Is it inheritable? Explain and illustrate.
3. Does coming from an unhappy home doom one to an unhappy marriage? Explain.
4. How is problem solving related to mental health?
5. What do you understand the term "marriageability" to mean? List certain traits or characteristics that would tend to increase marriageability.
6. What is the best guarantee that a couple will enjoy their leisure-time activities together after they marry?
7. Do you think Margaret's parents were wise in their attitude toward their daughter's love affair with Tom?
8. In what characteristics do marriages tend to be homogamous?
9. What do studies of age differences between husbands and wives reveal?
10. Under what conditions may differences in education make for misunderstanding in marriage?
11. What problems might arise in marriage if the two were from widely different economic levels?
12. What is your understanding of the term "mixed marriage"? Illustrate.
13. How may problems in mixed marriages differ from the problems in other marriages?
14. What social changes have led to an increase in international marriages?
15. What factors other than the difference in nationality may affect the happiness of some international marriages?
16. Love is more likely to last after marriage if what factors are present?

ACTIVITIES AND PROJECTS

1. Write an anonymous essay entitled "My Family Tree," in which you evaluate the marriages in your immediate family. How have these marriages influenced your personality development, and what effect have they had in conditioning you for marriage? If there have been any unhappy marriages in your family, have you profited by the failures of others? What are you going to have to work on if you are to have a good marriage?

2. Be prepared to discuss a marriage that faced parental opposition. Had the parents good cause to oppose the marriage? How has it worked out?

3. Make a list of the personality traits that you would hope to find in the person you marry. Are these the same traits you would have considered important a year ago?

4. If everyone refrained from marrying those from unhappy families and those with poor health, many people would be left unmarried. How can you justify the statement that we should marry those from healthy, happy families?

5. Women live an average of five years longer than men. Men tend to marry women who are about three years younger. Can you see any good reasons why it might be better for women to marry men who are younger than they?

6. What mixed marriages are accepted without question in your community? Are attitudes becoming more accepting?

7. (Report.) Describe an international marriage you know. How has the couple coped with differences that may exist?

SOCIODRAMA

Write and present two skits that illustrate what may happen if personalities do or do not meet each other's needs in marriage. Have two different couples act the parts of husbands and wives: in one skit, they agree on recreation, social activities, and friends; in the other, they have few things in common.

WORDS AND CONCEPTS

adaptability
cultural characteristics
equalitarian
homogamy
impelling
indispensable
marriageability

mixed marriage
panacea
retaliation
significance
socioeconomic
statistical
status

11 Maturity for Marriage

After studying this chapter, you will be able to

1. List criteria to use in judging whether one is mature enough for marriage.
2. Identify and analyze the problems that often go with youthful marriages.
3. Examine and explain the relationship between age at marriage and the divorce rate.
4. Discuss the importance of long-range goals when considering marriage.

Many people ask: How old is "old enough to marry?" Why does it matter at what age people marry? If they find the right person, is there any good reason why people should not marry at seventeen? The early chapters of this book explored the various growth tasks that challenge you now. In your class discussions of these tasks, you probably concluded that these growth tasks take time and that although chronological age alone does not determine whether or not one is old enough to marry, there actually is not time enough before the age of seventeen or eighteen for most people to accomplish all the maturing that needs to be achieved to be ready for the greater challenges that will come after marrying.

MATURITY FOR MARRIAGE

"Maturity" is a word that often implies that each person can be definitely labeled as mature or immature. Such use overlooks the fact that in the same person there may be several different "ages" or levels of maturity, and that different kinds of maturity may develop at different rates in the same person. Thus, one person at fifteen may be almost fully mature physically but immature emotionally. One may have the mental age of an adult and yet be at the twelve-year-old level in social maturity. People who are making good progress toward the maturity that will enable them to make a success of marriage and parenthood will gradually achieve consistent levels of maturity in all phases of their development. Especially, their emotional maturity will be consistent with their chronological age and their physical development. At each age in life, there are certain levels of maturity satisfactory *for that age.* It requires maturity to be able, at sixteen or seventeen or eighteen, to look objectively at traits of character and personality and to decide not to date seriously someone who would not be a good marriage partner. It requires a valuable kind of maturity to examine one's own background and personality,

A young person who has plans or ambitions for the future may need to put vocational preparation ahead of immediate marriage.

to resolve to overcome handicaps, and to work consistently at the task. It also takes a high level of maturity for two young people who are in love not to rush ahead with marriage plans, but to take time to find out whether or not they really have enough shared interests so that their companionship could lead to a permanently happy marriage. There are many other tests for maturity.

Few people of any age show all the characteristics of maturity or of immaturity listed here. Most people have to work throughout life to overcome some immature tendencies. But the person who is old enough to marry will show a fairly general pattern of progress toward maturity. The person who has too many of the traits of the immature person, as on the second list, still has a lot of growing up to do before having the qualities of a good marriage partner.

One who has the maturity for marriage has learned and practices certain techniques or policies:

1. One is not dominated by moods, and has learned constructive ways for working off feelings. One does not "take out one's feelings" on others.
2. One is cooperative. One does not have to dominate others.
3. One has overcome tendencies to be jealous.
4. One is not easily hurt.
5. One can be generous in judgments of others and give them the benefit of the doubt.
6. One works to be adaptable and is able to adjust to differences or to changes that life brings.
7. One has grown up to the point that one holds positive and wholesome attitudes about sex in life.
8. One is reasonably cautious about making decisions, and does not make major choices on impulse, or act first and think later.
9. One has learned good ways for meeting problems and does not turn to unhealthy or destructive escapes when under pressure.
10. One is realistic about what can be expected from life and what must be given in return. One does not live in a dreamworld.
11. One has a fairly clear idea of what kind of person one is and hopes to be. One knows something of one's own philosophy and direction.
12. One can discipline oneself to meet responsibilities and obligations.
13. One has learned to use good judgment in earning and spending money, and can plan finances and stick to the plan.
14. One is reasonably independent of one's parents, yet not childishly rebellious.
15. One can sacrifice personal preferences for the good of others. One works to overcome selfishness and self-centeredness.

The one who is still too childish for marriage, no matter how old, shows rather opposite characteristics:

1. One is inclined to be erratic and moody, and is likely to impose moods upon others.
2. One is competitive and aggressive in trying to have one's own way.
3. One tends to "cut down" or belittle others.
4. One is jealous and easily hurt.
5. One is rigid, cannot admit mistakes and try to change, but must always be right and others wrong.
6. One cannot change places and understand how another person feels or thinks.
7. One does not face problems constructively. Rather, one blames others for whatever happens and uses escapes such as temper spells, sulking, reckless driving, or drinking when things are upsetting.
8. One makes snap judgments and impulsive decisions without getting all the facts needed for making a wise decision.
9. One cannot look ahead, but thinks only of what is desired at the moment.
10. One is generally self-centered. One's own wants and needs are more important than the wishes or needs of anyone else. In relationships with others, one does not adjust, but expects others to adjust.

As we think of all these different evidences of maturity or immaturity, it becomes clearer why it is difficult to say that any one specific age is the best age at which to marry. At the same time, it would be unrealistic not to say that in average cases, chronological age does have some relation to whether or not one ought to marry.

While keeping in mind the discussion of maturity for marriage, let us look at some of the things that are closely tied to age and are important to consider.

SOME PROBLEMS THAT GO WITH AGE AT MARRIAGE

The fact that a person is young may not imply immaturity. Some people in their forties or fifties are less mature than some teenagers. Nevertheless, to marry while very young may cause some problems that do not arise if the person marries when older. For example, often parents do not feel that the teenager is ready for marriage. Because parents feel this way, they are more likely to interfere, thinking that they must continue to guide and control their child's life. They may also question whether or not their child knows how to care for the children that are born.

In fact, they almost *have* to be involved in various ways, because few teenagers are prepared to carry the financial and other responsibilities of running a household.

Couples who marry young are more likely to have to live with the parents until they can support themselves, and in-law friction occurs more often if couples live with parents than if they can live alone.

People are more likely to be emotionally dependent upon their parents and continue to seek advice from their parents after marriage if they marry young. This pattern of close parent-child interaction is apt to cause in-law trouble.

If children marry at a later age, when their parents can see that they are old enough to take on the responsibilities of marriage, the parents will more readily accept their children's marriage. There will be less need for their help, and they will be less apt to interfere. In-law friction will be less likely or less intense. Financial pressures are a more serious problem for teenage couples than for older couples.

Studies have revealed that the happiness or unhappiness of men, more than of women, seems to be affected by age at marriage. At first, that seems surprising, but it probably has a logical basis. Most men feel responsible for supporting themselves and their wives. Sometimes, a young man is working and making a fairly good income that is adequate for his needs. Then he marries and finds that the income that was adequate for him alone is not enough for two, or possibly three. Sometimes, the financial pressures during the early years of marriage, in addition to the new responsibilities that come with youthful parenthood, become a heavy burden.

"Slick, isn't it? I got it by throwing a tantrum in the toy department." If you are old enough to consider marriage, you are old enough to leave behind childish characteristics.

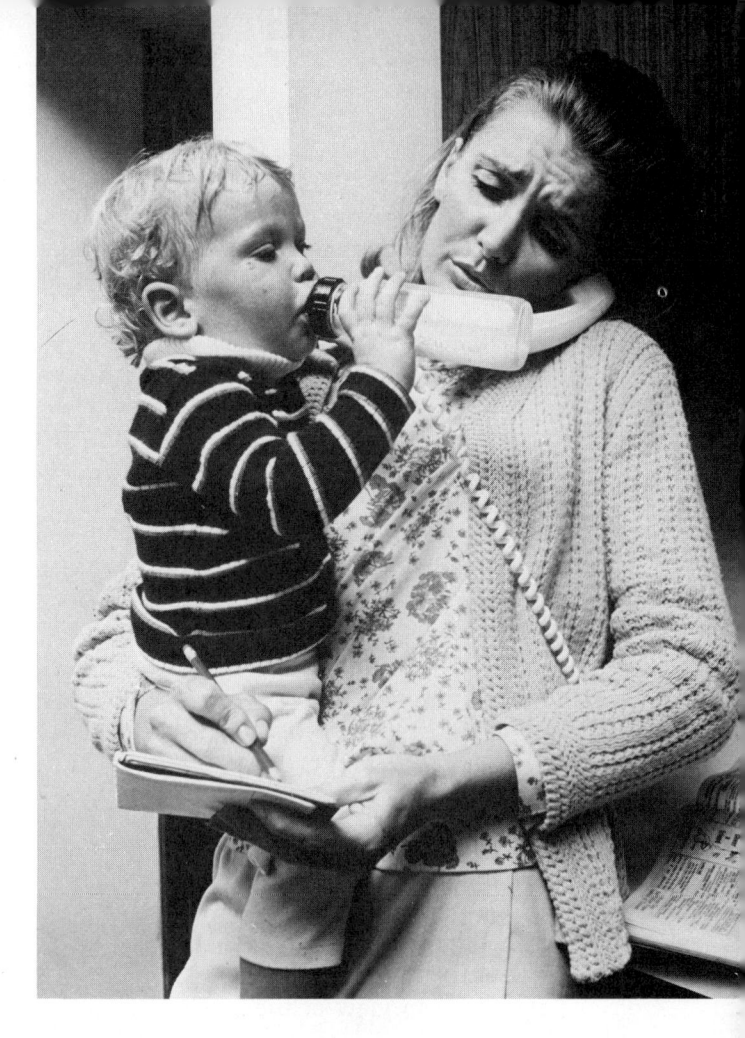

Some who marry too young never seem able to adjust to life's demands. This affects the children as well as the marriage.

Financial pressures are often part of marriage at any age. But in marriages that take place when people are very young, financial problems are likely to be worse, because if education was interrupted, earning ability is thereby impaired. Labor records show that most high school graduates earn as much by the time they are twenty-five as the average drop-out is able to earn at forty-five. Chances for steady employment and for high incomes improve with each year of education completed. Couples who marry very young are likely to have a limit set on future income.

Young people, both boys and girls, have a vocation to think about other than their role as husband or wife. They usually want to finish their education, job training, or military service before they marry. Although they may feel that they are ready for marriage, many are more confident about their future if they complete their education and start a job or profession before they marry. They recognize that early marriage might mean the end of their education or training, thus creating the necessity of accepting a lifework that would be their second or third choice rather than the one they would have preferred.

A girl who married at sixteen said, "Bill and I married instead of waiting, because we got tired of not having any freedom. Our folks were always fussing about what time we got in, where we'd been, or what we'd been doing. We decided to get married and have a place of our own. We thought we'd go on and finish school together. But it cost us so much to live that pretty soon Bill had to quit school to work full time and then as soon as we knew the baby was coming, I quit school too. It just isn't working out the way we planned. Maybe we'll make it, but most of the time, I'm awfully worried about everything."

This is not meant to give a pessimistic view of marriage, but rather a realistic one. Marriage at any age means responsibility and work, and the necessity to outgrow some of the fun and pleasure one has formerly enjoyed. In exchange, one receives rewards that are basic to life's happiness. Nevertheless, work, responsibility, and sacrifice are a fact of life in marriage, and the person who is thinking of marrying needs to consider thoughtfully whether he or she is ready for it. Those who undertake it too soon miss many special advantages and enjoyments that others of their age are having.

AGE OF MARRIAGE AND DIVORCE

Several research studies of marriage happiness and unhappiness and divorce have found the same thing: in general, more unhappy marriages and more divorces have been found among men and women who married under twenty than among those who married later. This is understandable in view of the special problems that go with very early marriage.

A far-reaching study by the Bureau of the Census found a close relationship between early marriage and a high divorce rate. The census findings show that divorced or separated women married for the first time about two years younger (at an average age of nineteen) than women who remained married to the first husband. The once-married women married at an average age of twenty-one. The census findings show that the relationship between early marriage and a high divorce rate has not changed for the past thirty-five years; this means that the factors handicapping youthful marriages are not a recent development. When we analyzed the relationship between the age at which over three thousand couples were married and the divorce rate, we found that those who married in their teens had a divorce rate several times higher than that for those who married later. The divorce rate gradually decreased as the age at marriage increased. You will see the exact percentages of increase in Graph 3.

We know that many people who marry during their teens have good marriages. But the evidence indicates that the problems do prove insurmountable for large numbers of these couples. Research findings do not support the idea that to marry young and grow up together is easier

AGE AT MARRIAGE AND DIVORCE RATE

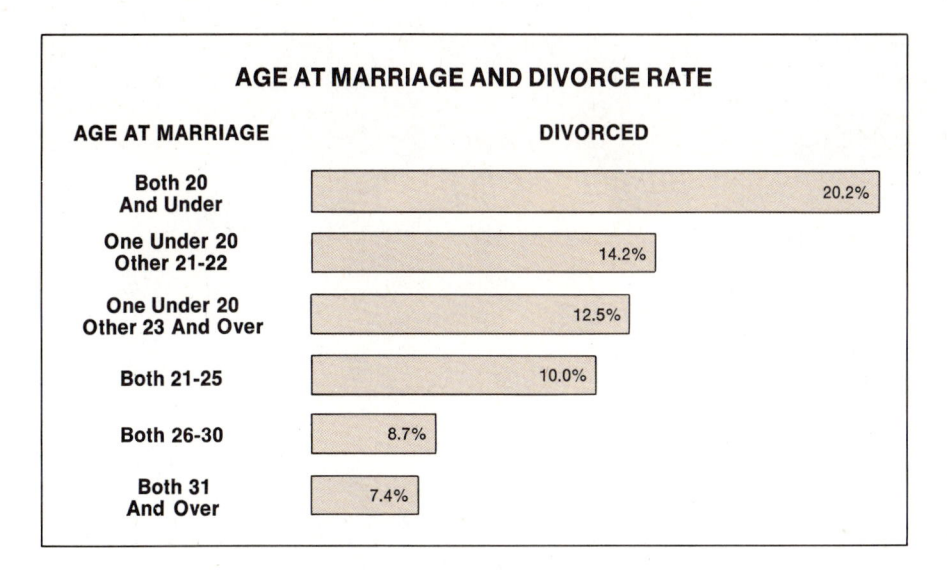

AGE AT MARRIAGE	DIVORCED
Both 20 And Under	20.2%
One Under 20 Other 21-22	14.2%
One Under 20 Other 23 And Over	12.5%
Both 21-25	10.0%
Both 26-30	8.7%
Both 31 And Over	7.4%

Graph 3. The divorce rate decreases as couples' age at marriage increases (a study of 3000 marriages).

than to marry when older. In a study of people who had been successfully married for some years, we found that even among these couples it had taken longer for those who married under twenty than for those married later to satisfactorily adjust to living together.

The special areas in which the younger couples had most difficulty adjusting were sexual relations, handling money, associating with friends, in-law relationships, and social activities or recreation. These are problems that must be coped with in all marriages, but they are especially difficult for people who marry in their teens, because it is in these very areas (except for in-laws) that the single teenager is trying to determine what goals, standards, or policies to choose. The developmental tasks of these are far more complicated if two must meet the responsibilities of marriage while they are separately trying to solve their individual problems associated with growing up. With more maturity should come more understanding of oneself and of others, so that consequently one can become more tolerant and flexible.

Being "set" in one's ways is often an indication of insecurity, and is not necessarily related to age. As one becomes more secure, one can more readily accept others, compromise over differences, and work smoothly with others. True maturity makes for flexibility, not rigidity.

There are other factors that explain the greater unhappiness and higher divorce rates of teenage marriages. Many people who marry very early do so because they want to escape an unhappy home. Marriage may seem to offer a way out of an immediate problem, but it usually does not provide solutions to such problems. Because marriage means the abrupt assumption of great responsibilities, it is more likely to bring difficult new problems for the person who has not yet solved old ones.

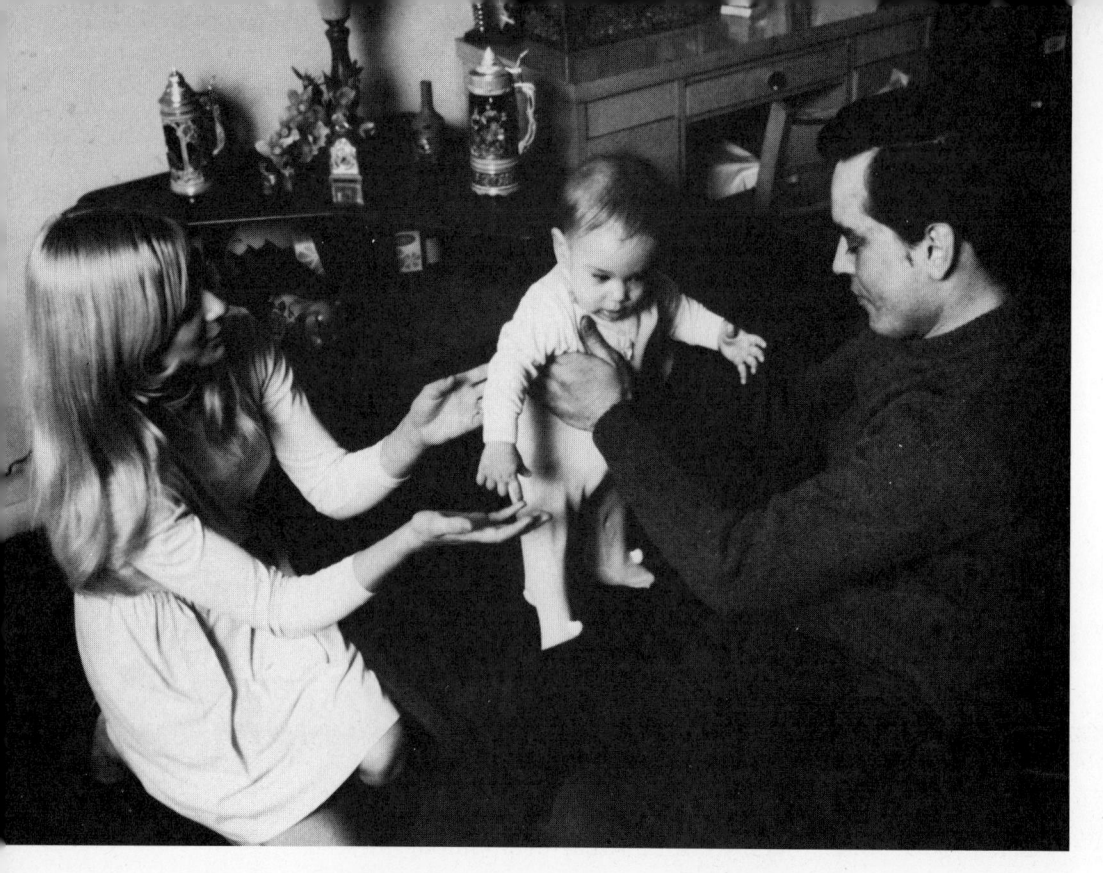

People with sound values and a desire to make marriage work will find parenthood among the most fulfilling aspects of life.

SCHOOL POLICIES TOWARD HIGH SCHOOL MARRIAGES

In the past, most high schools had policies that in effect excluded married students from school. Officials began to recognize, however, that people who marry at young ages need all the education and training they can get.

A study of school policy related to motherhood, pregnancy, and marriage in high schools in all parts of the United States found that a receptive attitude is developing toward the attendance of married students, pregnant students, and married mothers. Large city schools are more likely to encourage attendance by married students than are those in small towns, and schools in west coast states are less restrictive toward such students than are those in the southeastern states. But schools are not as willing to accept pregnant girls, married or single, and often require that they attend adult evening classes rather than day classes.

Another study of high school marriages, in California, found that although school policies are not restrictive toward married students, such students tend to drop out before graduation. Whether the reason for dropping out is school policy or other pressures, to leave school before graduation is a handicap to a young married person.

YOUR LONG-RANGE GOALS

In marrying at any age, it is important to consider long-range goals. Most people hope to be happily married and to have some degree of financial security. As you try to achieve your goals, at times you have to postpone things for the long-term view. You may care a great deal for someone when you are eighteen, but you may also wish to continue your education and training so that you will have greater financial security throughout life. No matter how much you care for your friend, you may have some doubts about your ability to make a wise marriage choice at your present age; your parents may frown upon early marriage, or you may know that at this point you could not possibly finance a household. As you consider everything, your affection may fall into a different perspective, and you may make the difficult decision to postpone thoughts of marriage.

During the late teens, people tend to change many of their ideas, especially about whom they would like to marry. It pays to take a little time to think it over. A good marriage is worth waiting, working, and preparing for.

Talking things over with an understanding counselor may help one assess one's own maturity and put matters in their proper perspective.

MARRYING TO AVOID SEPARATION

Sometimes, high school couples who have been dating steadily or who may be engaged consider getting married sooner than they had planned because they face a separation. This may be brought about by only one going to college, by each going to a different college, by one going into military service, or by each taking jobs miles from one another. The couple may feel that being apart will put too much of a strain on their relationship and that they may not marry unless they do so prior to separation. By marrying at this time, they hope to guarantee that each will be waiting for the other.

In reality, many young couples who think they want to marry eventually will decide not to marry after they have been separated. Our study of engaged couples who broke their engagements found that they had done so because of a separation. This may be fortunate rather than unfortunate. As people get older, more mature, and date others, they may see that the earlier relationship would not have resulted in a happy marriage. A period of separation before marriage for the very young may serve as a safeguard against making an unwise marriage. Certainly, it is unwise to attempt to cement a relationship by marrying before a forced separation. Often, it is better for the two to go to separate colleges or to take jobs in different communities so that they can assess their relationship, make new friends, and perhaps date others. As they mature, they may be more sure of their choice and decide to marry each other. On the other hand, during the separation, there may be an unequal maturing of partners and one or both may choose an entirely different type of person, and as a result, make a better marriage.

FOCUS ON YOU

How will you know when you are old enough to marry? Think through the answers to the following questions. What other criteria for maturity should be added to the list? If you are dating someone seriously, think these points through together. Do most of your answers show a similar pattern?

1. Am I relatively independent of my parents?
2. Do I make decisions on the basis of carefully gathered facts, or do I tend to jump to conclusions and make impulsive decisions?
3. Have I outgrown rebellion as a motive for choices? That is, can I be sure my decisions are based upon careful conclusions about the wisest course of action rather than motivated by a wish to show that I can do as I please?
4. Have I completed my education?
5. Has my judgment stabilized as to the type of marriage partner I want? How long has it been since I considered someone very desirable who would not suit me now?

6. Marriage at an early age usually means a larger family. Do I have enough education and work skills to support a family?

7. How well can I support myself now with no outside help?

8. How well do I manage the money I earn? Do I run out of money and find that I don't know what happened to it? Or can I make and follow a budget?

9. Have I found job security? How long have I held the same position?

10. Am I old enough to undertake the responsibilities and obligations of being a husband (or a wife) and a parent? Particularly, can I consistently sacrifice my own pleasures and wishes for the sake of others?

11. Am I ready to take on the regular routine of a permanent job? Of housework? Cooking three meals a day? Caring for babies or children?

12. If things go wrong, must I find someone else to blame or can I accept responsibility for my mistakes and do the best I can?

13. Am I sufficiently flexible to make the adjustments that marriage requires? Can I include others in my plans and make satisfying compromises with in-laws and children as well as with my spouse?

14. If I qualify on all these important points, am I sure I am ready to settle down? Or do I still need time to be free to run around with my friends?

QUESTIONS FOR REVIEW

1. Why can't we use chronological age as an absolute measure of maturity for marriage?

2. What are some of the measures of mature behavior? Some measures of immature behavior?

3. What are some of the problems that often go with youthful marriages?

4. Give an illustration to show why those who marry in their teens might have more difficulty with in-law relationships.

5. How do you explain the fact that the happiness of men, more than of women, seems to be affected by age at marriage?

6. What do studies show about age at marriage and the chances for happiness? About age at marriage and the divorce rate? What were the findings of the Bureau of the Census on age at first marriage and divorce?

7. What are some school policies in dealing with those who marry while in high school? What do you think is the right policy?

8. Why is it important for young people to think of long-range goals when they are dating?

9. Give several questions that a person might consider in an effort to decide whether or not one is old enough for marriage.

10. Why might "love not survive a separation"?

ACTIVITIES AND PROJECTS

1. Be ready to give examples of immaturity that you have noticed among adults or young people.//

2. Can you illustrate exceedingly mature behavior that you have observed among children?

3. What is the policy in your community toward the education of married high school students?

WORDS AND CONCEPTS

chronological age
emotional maturity
erratic
long-range goals

Engagement   12

After studying this chapter, you will be able to

1. Describe and explain the relationship between length of courtship and adjustment in marriage.
2. Articulate the relationship between adjustment during engagement and adjustment in marriage.
3. Discuss the real purpose of engagement.
4. List some danger signals that might show up during engagement.
5. Cite reasons why some people marry in spite of danger signals.

Couples who are engaged or dating seriously, whose association is harmonious and happy, hope and expect that their marriage will be equally happy. Many couples whose courtship is characterized by unevenness, by makeups and breakups, also hope and believe that their marriage will be harmonious and free from serious problems. People studying marriage and family life have attempted to discover to what extent the pattern of relationships during courtship may predict the quality of the marriage.

A study of one thousand engaged couples was made by sociologists Burgess and Wallin. Their follow-up studies of the same couples for some years after they had been married, revealed that those couples whose engagement had certain characteristics were the happiest.

According to the Burgess and Wallin findings, if the couple enjoy the same type of social activities and recreation, if they like each other's parents, if they have never regretted their engagement, if they have not contemplated breaking up, and if quarrels have not threatened their relationship, they have a good chance for happiness.

The smoother the courtship and engagement, the better the chances are for the married couple's happiness. If they have quarrels and emotional explosions during engagement, they should hesitate to marry, for they have no good basis for believing that they will get along any better after marriage.

LENGTH OF COURTSHIP AND ADJUSTMENT IN MARRIAGE

Several studies were done to measure the relationship between how long a couple had known each other and how happy their marriage turned out to be. This evidence indicates that short acquaintance and hasty marriage tend to go with unhappiness or hasty divorce; the longer people are acquainted, the better are their chances for happiness after marriage. Graph 4, adapted from a study by Burgess and Cottrell of the relationship between the length of courtship and marital adjustment, shows that of those who had been acquainted for as long as five years many more were happy than of those who had been acquainted for less than six months.

Our study of the approach to marriage by two groups of people, one group of married people and another of divorced people, found that those who were unhappily married or divorced had had short acquaintances and fewer of them had had an engagement stage in their courtship than was true of the happily married group.

Why do short acquaintances and short engagements tend to be predictive of marital unhappiness? One reason is that the short period of

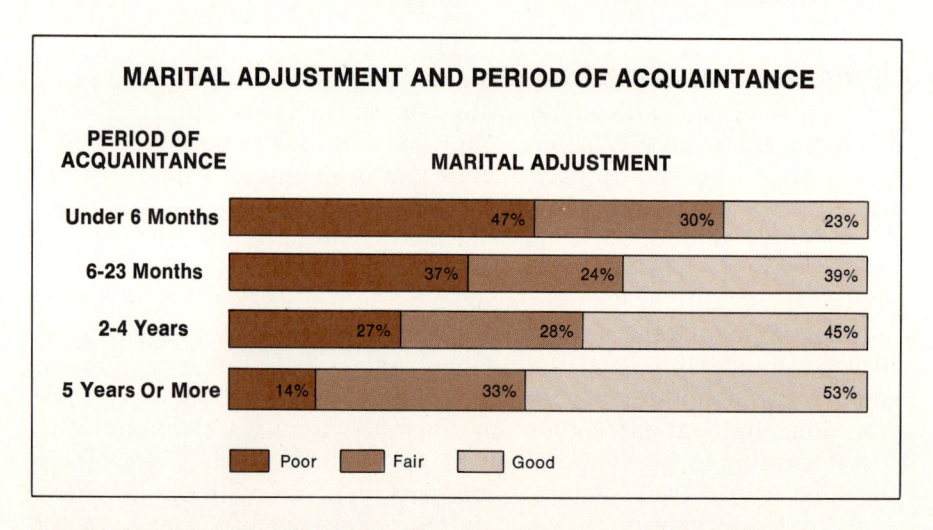

MARITAL ADJUSTMENT AND PERIOD OF ACQUAINTANCE

PERIOD OF ACQUAINTANCE	Poor	Fair	Good
Under 6 Months	47%	30%	23%
6-23 Months	37%	24%	39%
2-4 Years	27%	28%	45%
5 Years Or More	14%	33%	53%

Graph 4. The longer the acquaintance, the better chance of a happy marriage.
(Adapted from E. W. Burgess and L. S. Cottrell, "Predicting Success or Failure in Marriage." Englewood Cliffs, N. J.: Prentice-Hall, Inc.)

time does not give people a chance to assess their relationship accurately or to recognize and evaluate danger signals that might warn them against the intended marriage.

Today, marriages are held together by mutual attraction, companionship, affection, and common interests. If people do not find that they have these bonds, there is a good chance that they will not continue to live together.

In generations past, once couples were married, they remained married whether they wanted to or not. Attitudes toward divorce were different. Churches and communities disapproved, and divorced couples were subjects of gossip much more than they are now. Today, the greater ease in getting a divorce and the removal of some of the social stigma means that couples are less likely to remain married if they are not happy.

A strong attraction can draw two people together. They may become engaged and marry after a short acquaintance. Such couples really have no opportunity before marriage to find out whether or not they are companionable. After marriage, they may discover that their only mutual interest was a strong physical attraction, that actually they have few similar interests, and that they disagree on many important things. Such couples will be unhappy, and many of them will divorce.

A hasty marriage may indicate that in other respects a person is impulsive in making judgments. The sudden decision to marry may fit one's usual pattern for making decisions; and this general lack of good judgment is as basic in marriage failure as are the short acquaintance and engagement.

Similarly, we might reach certain conclusions about the couple willing to date for a year and then be engaged for six months to year or more. The couple who take long enough to do their courting may also possess other traits that indicate stability and a willingness to work through to the solutions of problems. These traits will be an asset to them after they are married.

BEING WELL ENOUGH ACQUAINTED, A CRUCIAL FACTOR

It is true that we differ in our ability to get acquainted with others. Some couples get as well acquainted in one year as others do in two. How much time a couple spends together and how they spend that time affect how well they actually know each other. Each needs a chance to learn how the other functions under pressure, in work situations as well as in other circumstances.

A difficulty is that almost all couples think they are well acquainted even though they have gone together for a very short time. The remark is often made, "We have written to each other or talked on the telephone

While engaged, corresponding is a poor substitute for being together and learning each others' moods and values and ways of coping.

every day for three months, so we have gotten to know all about each other," or "We have only known each other three months, but that is enough, because we have been together almost constantly." Other people who know the couple may see that they have not even begun to know each other's personalities. Each may be seeing in the other an idealized version that has little relationship to the actual person. People who make the best marriages are able to realize that "until death" may be a long time and that it is worthwhile to take longer than a few weeks or months in order to become well acquainted before engagement or marriage.

AGREEMENT DURING ENGAGEMENT AND AGREEMENT IN MARRIAGE

In one study of engaged, married, and unhappily married couples having counseling, we asked the different couples to rank their degree of agreement in different areas of living. The study then compared their agreement on such matters as how to use money, how to train children, how they felt about their in-laws, how well they thought they understood each other when they discussed problems. The interesting finding was that in all areas of living, a far larger percentage of the engaged couples than married couples thought they were in perfect agreement. See Graph 5 for a summary of the agreement in four areas of living. This does not mean that married people who agree during engagement

DEGREE OF AGREEMENT IN AREAS OF LIVING

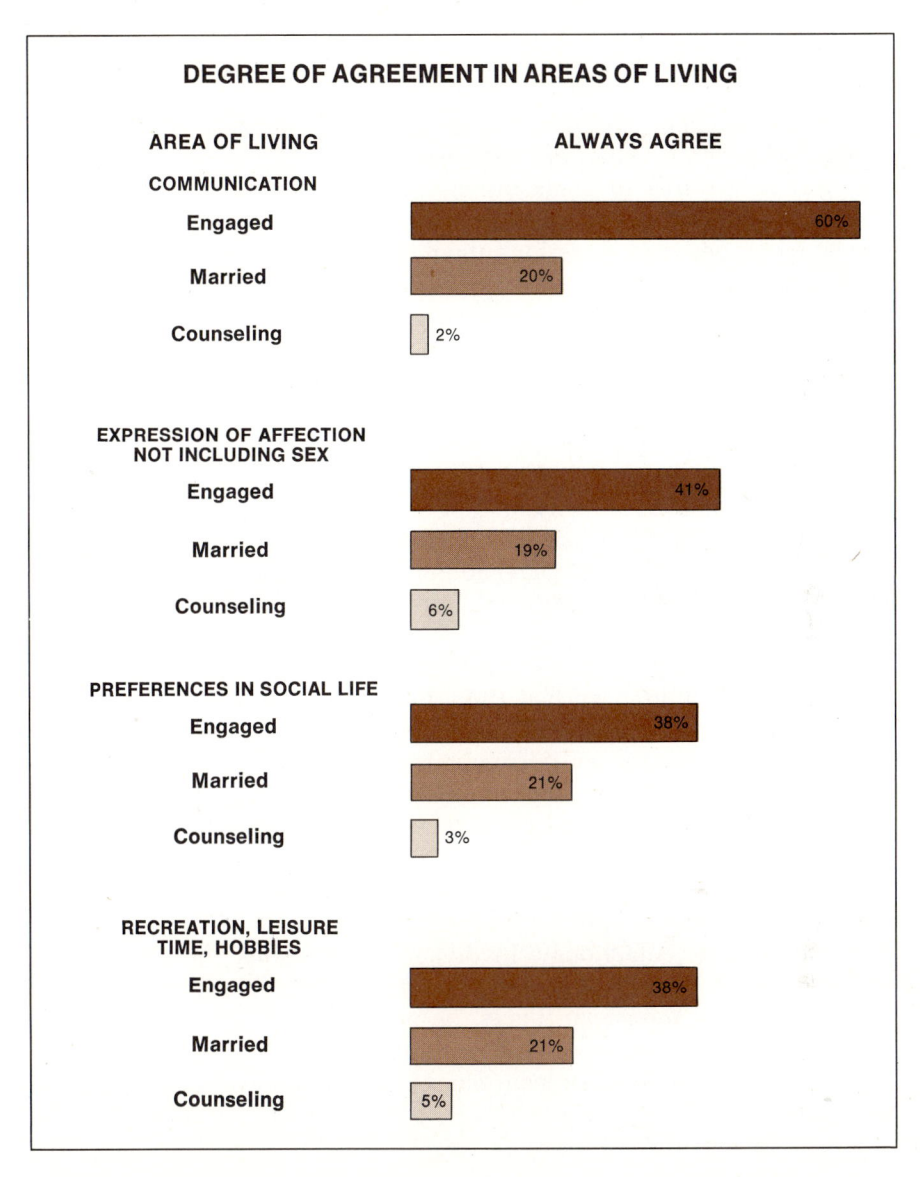

AREA OF LIVING	ALWAYS AGREE
COMMUNICATION	
Engaged	60%
Married	20%
Counseling	2%
EXPRESSION OF AFFECTION NOT INCLUDING SEX	
Engaged	41%
Married	19%
Counseling	6%
PREFERENCES IN SOCIAL LIFE	
Engaged	38%
Married	21%
Counseling	3%
RECREATION, LEISURE TIME, HOBBIES	
Engaged	38%
Married	21%
Counseling	5%

Graph 5. Engaged couples are more confident of agreement in areas of living than are married couples or those seeking counseling. As reported by 122 engaged couples, 581 married couples, and 155 people seeking marriage counseling.

start disagreeing after marriage. It means that during engagement many people do not know enough about each other to judge accurately their degree of agreement in vital areas of living. They assume agreement where it may not exist. Longer acquaintances and longer engagements would weed out many of those who have large areas of disagreement that will appear after marriage and damage their relationship.

READINESS FOR ENGAGEMENT

A college freshman, eighteen years old, is engaged to a boy who is a college sophomore. They became engaged after six months of dating. The girl now wants to break the engagement. She still wants to date him, however, but she wants to be free to date others. She feels that she is not yet ready to be serious about marriage. She wants to complete her college education, and she enjoys living in a dormitory with other girls.

Although the young man is only a sophomore, he is twenty-four years old, was in military service for two years, and feels that he is ready to marry. Most of his friends are married and going to school or working. He opposes breaking the engagement because he feels certain that this is the girl he wants to marry.

The girl can think of a number of reasons why she is doubtful about marrying him. She fears that he has traits that do not fit her ideal. She wonders if he would ever make enough money to support her. She says that she keeps finding more and more kinds of interests that they do not share.

It is apparent that if this couple had married soon after they became engaged they would have had little chance for happiness. The girl is not yet ready for marriage, and this is not the man she will choose when she is ready. True, the engagement itself was a mistake; she was not ready for that either. But a broken engagement is better than a bad marriage. If this couple had dated for a few more months without becoming engaged, they would probably have broken up much less painfully.

Today, people begin to date earlier than ever before. With early dating, especially steady dating, people become involved emotionally at very young ages. Affectionate involvement with someone of the other sex is a constructive part of growing up, but to believe one is in love at this time does not mean this is the person to become engaged to or marry. Because teenagers are maturing and changing so rapidly, one's idea of an ideal mate at sixteen changes considerably by the time one is twenty-one.

PURPOSE OF THE ENGAGEMENT

The engagement is a period of serious courtship, a time during which the couple can make a careful check to see whether or not they have chosen someone with whom they can live for the next forty years or more.

It used to be that during the engagement period the couple thought only of getting ready for the wedding. The girl prepared her trousseau and made definite plans for marriage. It was assumed that a wedding

Engagement is not simply a time for having fun—although enjoying the same interests is one strong bond for a happy marriage. What are some others?

would certainly follow; in fact, the promise to marry was considered a legal contract. If either party broke the contract, it was cause for legal action, called a "breach of promise" suit. It was usually the girl who sued the man when he would not carry out his promise to marry her.

Today, people do not feel that they have made a legal contract when they become engaged. Some states have outlawed breach of promise suits so that it is impossible for either party to sue when an engagement is broken. Thus, the law recognizes the engagement as a period of serious courtship, a time during which the couple can take a last careful look before they enter the uncertainties of marriage, but not a binding legal agreement as marriage is.

DANGER SIGNALS DURING ENGAGEMENT

The experiences of many engaged and married couples who have come to the writers for counseling have led us to the conclusion that in engagements that would lead to unworkable marriages, there are usually danger signals flashing along the way. Some couples become aware of these warnings and break the engagement. Others fail to recognize the signals for what they are, or they are determined to marry in spite of everything that suggests caution. They marry, then break up the marriage over matters they had recognized during engagement.

You may wish to read again the discussion of danger signals in Chapter 6. Danger signals that might not seem serious during dating become particularly significant during engagement.

Quarrels during engagement should raise serious doubts about whether or not a couple should marry; it is especially important if people find there is a *pattern* to their quarrels. Are there certain kinds of situations that seem especially provocative? Does the pattern suggest basic differences in values or in feelings about moral or ethical standards? Do the quarrels represent deep conflicts in their personality makeups? For example, both may have strong urges to dominate, or one may be very dominating and the other very resistant. One may be very insecure, and quarrels may result from the insecure one's excessive need for reassurance. One or both may be extremely selfish, and this thoughtless lack of consideration may cause friction or irritation. If there is a basic pattern, it is likely to last throughout marriage. More situations arise in engagements than in dating that allow conflicts to come to the surface.

"I don't know whether I can stand a long engagement . . . sometimes I can barely keep from correcting some of Wilbur's faults . . . ."

A few quarrels may only mean that the two are in the process of working out their relationship by trial and error; they may reach the place where there will be no more quarrels. But any quarrels should provoke a thoughtful evaluation of the relationship. If they do represent serious differences, it is safe to assume that the condition would not be improved by marriage, but only worsened. The engagement had better be broken.

Another consideration is *one's general sense of well-being or happiness during engagement.* One girl whose wedding day was only a few weeks away came to the counselor in tears. She minimized her reason for coming. She said, "It isn't anything serious. We are very much in love. It's just that I seem to get so upset over some of our quarrels. I know the quarrels must be all my own fault, because if I try hard enough, we get along beautifully. Most of the time, I do try awfully hard, but then I get under a strain because it's not natural for me to be so careful of what I say and do." She commented further, "I've always been a happy person. I guess I've done more crying during my engagement than in all my life before, but don't you think that's natural when one is in love and feeling emotional?"

It was clear that warning signals were flashing for this girl, but she had not understood or realistically interpreted her feelings and her reactions to her engagement. If she married this fiance, she would find herself boxed into a situation in which she could not possibly live.

FAILURE TO RECOGNIZE DANGER SIGNALS

There are specific reasons why some couples go ahead to marry in spite of all signs warning them against marrying each other.

Ignoring the quarreling pattern

Some individuals have never experienced harmonious relationships in their family, or outside, and they have no standard for assessing relationships. Children who grow up in homes where constant conflict between mother and father and among brothers and sisters is the rule may accept conflict rather than harmony as normal. These people, therefore, do not look beyond quarrels and conflict to see what the conflicts may indicate about basic differences that warn against marrying. Some others fail to recognize the meaning of quarreling during engagement because of the folklore that says that true love does not run smoothly. The contemporary implication of the folk belief is that two who are in love and deeply involved emotionally will express the emotion aggressively in negative as well as positive ways, that is, that there will be wide emotional swings in their relationship, each quarrel being followed by a deeper love. People who do not question that idea may see no significance in quarrels.

Pregnancy

For a young couple marrying because the girl is pregnant, many danger signals may be apparent, but they may feel that no other choice is open to them. Marriages forced by pregnancy are mentioned here because the records show that a larger percentage of marriages among teenaged couples are of this type than of marriages at older ages. When pregnancy is a factor in the decision to marry, the couple has a very high rate of unhappiness and divorce.

If there had not been a premarital pregnancy, many of these bad marriages would never have taken place. One or the other would have recognized the danger signals when it was still possible to end the relationship.

Lack of experience in dating

It takes some experience in dating and considerable maturity to be able to understand oneself and others and the complicated interaction that goes on between two people who meet each other's needs.

Romantic lovers' quarrels are the theme of many a ballad, but in real life they are a danger signal in a relationship and should be heeded.

People who never date until they are ready for marriage may have no standard of comparison in relationships. They may become serious fairly soon and no matter what the interaction pattern may be, may believe simply that this is the way man-woman relationships are.

Although there are some hazards and problems involved in extensive dating through the high school years, part of the important function of dating is to enable one to become fairly objective about people and relationships. If this function of dating has been accomplished, the individual is better prepared to recognize danger signals during engagement.

Mistaken idea of love

Many people hold a conception of love gained from songs, movies, television, and folk beliefs. It takes time and experience to reach some understanding of the nature of love and the kind of love that grows in a good marriage.

There is a tendency to see love simply as a strong, all-powerful emotion, and to believe that this feeling will overcome all difficulties. People with an immature conception of love believe that if they are really in love, this one overpowering element in a relationship becomes the crucial test. Unrealistic conceptions of love are not characteristic of young people only; such ideas cause people of all ages to ignore or rationalize the meaning of danger signals and marry in spite of them.

Problems or crises in life

Some people, because of an immediate problem or crisis, fail to recognize, or ignore, danger signals. Problems such as one's parents' extreme unhappiness or a parental divorce may cause a young person to marry in order to get away from home. If there has been a divorce and remarriage and the teenager is now living with a stepparent, he or she may decide that marriage will be an escape from an unpleasant situation.

Some high school students conflicting with their parents see marriage as a chance to be on their own and out from under parental dominance or control.

When people are frustrated by the pressure of difficult circumstances, they are not likely to recognize danger signals in a relationship. They focus on what they want to get away from, and do not consider whether or not the marriage might get them into a situation equally as difficult and much harder to escape.

Sometimes, high school students, perhaps girls more often than boys, who are not doing well and are unhappy in school, see marriage as a way out. Or they are nearing graduation and face the problem of what to do next, if college is not in their future. Perhaps they are dissatisfied with living at home, and not prepared to hold a good job. Marriage at this point seems a solution, so if a girl is seriously dating or engaged, she may make her goal getting married rather than having a good, lifelong marriage. In such circumstances, one may refuse to see danger signals in a relationship.

Pressure of social attitudes about singleness

The emphasis in our society on marriage puts pressure on everyone, which leads many to ignore danger signals in relationships. People fear that they might be permanently single, so they settle for relationships that are not really satisfactory and that do not meet their needs. Social attitudes need to change more in the direction of recognizing that singleness is a perfectly normal and satisfactory way of life for some people and that even though singleness may include some problems, a bad marriage is a tragedy not limited just to the two who marry.

Overemphasis on the wedding

Another reason why some couples fail to recognize danger signals is that after too short an acquaintance they have a short engagement that is consumed in making wedding plans. Planning the wedding, choosing attendants, choosing a silverwear or china pattern, and planning the honeymoon can become so absorbing that the real functions of the engagement period are not achieved. Sometimes, people who are anxious to marry seem almost deliberately to involve themselves in complicated plans and preparations. Their preoccupation with plans enables them to avoid facing the unsatisfactory facets of their association with each other.

A girl who was to be graduated from college in mid-June became engaged early in May to a boy whom she had known six weeks. She planned to be married in her home church five hundred miles away, on the day after graduation. During her short engagement, while she was taking final examinations and completing the requirements for graduation, she prepared for a large wedding. She asked friends to be attendants, arranged for their dresses, collected an extensive trousseau, attended two or three bridal showers given by her attendants, made decisions about patterns in china and glassware and registered her preferences in stores. She was determined to have in every detail the kind of wedding she had daydreamed about for years before she ever met the man she was to marry.

By the week before her wedding, she was nervous, tense, and physically exhausted, and she was having a hard time suppressing her anger and irritation with her fiance. To a close friend, she said, "I wish Dick would just stay away until the wedding! That would be a help. I don't expect him to help me with the shopping I must do, or with the other extras in getting ready for the wedding. But he wants to be with me

Even the perfect wedding lasts only a day; a good marriage lasts for years. Where should the emphasis be?

constantly; he doesn't seem to realize how much I've got to do. He comes every evening and stays so late that I almost fall asleep; then I drink coffee to stay awake so I can study after he leaves. Just because his workday ends at five o'clock, he seems to think mine should. He sulks and complains about it every time we are together. That seems to be all we talk about lately. I'll be so glad when we are married and things settle down the way they were when we first met."

There is little possibility that things would ever again be, for this couple, "the way they were when we first met." They had not made any realistic assessment of their relationship and interaction. The first test of their ability to cooperate toward a common goal was the approach to the wedding, and they appeared to be failing that test. Almost all of the danger signals discussed in this chapter were evident if they had not been too busy getting married to pay attention.

QUESTIONS FOR REVIEW

1. What is the relationship between adjustment during engagement and adjustment in marriage?
2. What is known about the relationship between length of acquaintance and happiness in marriage? Length of engagement and happiness in marriage? Length of engagement and divorce?
3. Give several factors that explain why those who are engaged a longer period of time have more successful marriages.
4. What social changes have made it more necessary for young people to choose carefully if they are to remain married?
5. Was it fair to the boy, in the case given in the text, for the college freshman girl to insist on breaking their engagement? Explain your reasons.
6. What are some factors that cause couples to get engaged too soon?
7. What is the real purpose of the engagement? How does this differ from its purpose in previous generations?
8. Name some danger signals that may become evident during engagement.
9. List several reasons why some people marry in spite of danger signals. Which of these reasons are due to circumstances within the life of the individual? Which ones are partly due to circumstances beyond the control of the individual? Which ones are due to attitudes and beliefs in our society?

ACTIVITIES AND PROJECTS

1. Can you think of some commonly accepted or often heard statements that are unreliable when analyzed? Examples are "The course of true love never runs smoothly"; "Gentlemen prefer blondes."
2. Ask your parents how long they dated and how long they were engaged. Have a class committee summarize the results to see what the average length of dating and engagement were among the parents. It might prove interesting to get the same information from your grandparents and compare that with the average among your parents.
3. Talk to your grandparents about the meaning and purpose of engagement when they were young.

WORDS AND CONCEPTS

breach of promise
extricate
facets
predictive

preoccupation
provocative
social stigma
trousseau

Engagement (continued) 13

After studying this chapter, you will be able to

1. Cite some of the main reasons for broken engagements.
2. Describe some of the common reactions one has to a broken engagement.
3. List the issues that should be discussed during engagement.
4. Explain how the engagement period can serve as preparation for marriage in a definite way.

Most of us have known engaged couples who did not marry. Many engaged couples do recognize warning signs in their relationship and break their engagements. In a study of 3184 college students, we found that one-fourth of both the men and the women had already had one or more broken engagements, and 15 percent later broke the current engagement.

A broken engagement usually represents heartbreak. Nevertheless, it is certainly better for young people to find out they are not suited for each other during the engagement than to marry and later regret it. Although a broken engagement is better than a broken marriage, much emotional misery could be avoided if couples dated longer and approached engagement more cautiously.

BREAKING ENGAGEMENTS

Some couples can become aware of danger signals only after being engaged and associating together in a relationship more complicated than dating. If, as time passes, one has serious doubts about whether an engagement can lead to a good marriage, it is better to break the engagement or at least postpone marriage for long enough to determine whether or not a mistake is being made.

Nancy, twenty-one, a junior in college, was engaged to Henry, twenty-two, who was in the Marine Corps. Nancy was taking a course in preparation for marriage, and the more she read, the more she doubted she should marry Henry. Henry would never go to Nancy's house because he said her folks did not like him. He disliked many of her friends, and on different occasions had threatened to fight boys with whom she was friendly. She wanted to get a college degree and teach music, but he insisted that a wife didn't need a degree. Nancy finally decided to break the engagement; but when she told Henry, he would not listen to her. He appealed to her sympathy, telling her no one had ever cared for or understood him. He also made threats that he would do her harm, or tell things that would damage her reputation. Nancy was afraid of what Henry might do, and she felt sorry for him. She was much troubled about how to get out of the engagement.

Such problems sometimes arise when one person has decided it would be a mistake for marriage plans to be carried out, but the other is still in love and thinks it would be a mistake for them not to marry. The one who is more involved emotionally has a hard time being reconciled to the fact that the partner does not want to marry.

Some people who are hurt by a broken love affair attempt to get even with the one they loved, and prove they are not hurt, by quickly falling in love and marrying someone else. This is marriage on the rebound and is more of a gamble than the usual marriage. If a love relationship has just ended, one should be doubly cautious about becoming deeply involved with another person too soon. In rebound love affairs, one is not in any state of mind to see things that warn against the new relationship. If one is looking only for escape from emotional pressures regarding a past relationship, or is trying to prove something, there is no safe basis for the new relationship.

BROKEN HEARTS DO HEAL

The emotional readjustment that must take place after a divorce is far more severe than the emotional readjustment after an engagement has been broken, hard as a broken engagement may seem at the time.

With maturity comes the ability to readjust after experiences of disappointment or grief. We shall face many crises as we go through life.

A joyous, carefree time, engagement is also a serious period in which to examine personalities and goals. Are these compatible, or would it be better to find someone else with whom one would mesh more harmoniously?

A broken heart may be one. Bereavement that comes with the death of a loved one is another.

These hard emotional experiences are comparable to physical ailments. In times of illness, you may have felt sick enough to die, but a gradual recovery took place, and you finally felt like yourself again. The same thing happens during an emotional crisis. One may feel that life is not worth living. However, as time goes by, it is possible to make a new adjustment and to be happy again. When you have survived such an experience, you are better prepared to understand and accept with some equanimity the hard realities that life offers.

Our research studies among college students have found that the majority of people do recover quite quickly from the effects of a broken engagement. More than half say that they recovered from the emotional involvement of a broken love relationship within two months, and another one-fourth say they recovered by the end of six months. If both members of a couple recognize danger signals before they break up, their feelings may be more nearly relief than despair. The problems come when one decides to break an engagement and the other cannot see any reason for the break, and resists.

Nearly two thousand students who had had serious loves described their emotional reactions and their behavior after the relationship ended. Table 7 summarizes the percentages of men and women reporting different reactions. You will see that most of the students reported reactions that were quite logical and not extreme or neurotic. However, one person in ten, of both men and women, reported thinking about how to get even or even of suicide.

Table 7 ADJUSTMENT REACTIONS WHEN LOVE AFFAIR ENDED

Reaction	Men	Women
	Percentage*	
Remembered pleasant association	70	75
Got dates with others	62	68
Daydreamed about partner	40	37
Preserved keepsakes	21	41
Avoided meeting him (her)	30	33
Read over old letters	23	31
Attempted to meet him (her)	25	21
Remembered unpleasant association	21	32
Frequented places of common association	22	20
Liked or disliked people because of resemblance	12	14
Daydreamed	11	12
Avoided places of common association	17	19
Resolved to get even	5	5
Thought of suicide	5	5

* Percentages of 1894 students (624 men, 1270 women) from eighteen colleges in 1967. These were reactions when their most serious love affair ended.

To want to get even by doing harm to someone at such a time is evidence of extreme immaturity. A part of growing up is becoming able to handle frustrating situations. Chapter 3 discussed ways in which one who is growing toward maturity copes with disappointments or blocking of wishes. No matter how difficult being rejected by a loved one may be, the individual who is growing toward maturity will try to see that to cling to a relationship that is not mutual could only be a continuing disappointment and frustration. There is little the one breaking the engagement can do to help the other at this point, except to be as considerate as possible. To weaken and make up, only to have another breakup later, will not help; it will only prolong unhappiness.

Although there may be a world of differences to overcome before a couple decides on engagement, the two should find themselves able to discuss matters openly with each other. What are some of these matters?

ISSUES TO BE DISCUSSED DURING ENGAGEMENT

Engaged couples need to give serious thought to whether or not they are together on all possible matters. They need to discuss the subject of money and how they can handle it as a married couple.

If theirs is a mixed engagement with respect to religion, race, or nationality, it is important that they be aware of the special problems that may arise and they should attempt to solve some of these problems before they marry.

They need also to become acquainted with each other's feelings and attitudes about having and rearing children. Marriage usually implies parenthood.

People who are considering marrying while one or both are still in school need to consider practical matters such as where they will live. Some couples consider living with one of the parent families. That plan seldom works. It would seem better to postpone the marriage, if necessary, until the couple can live alone. Discussion may help them understand each other's feelings on this subject.

Present-day couples need to discuss their views on the roles of men and women in marriage. Does the man think that a wife's place is in the home, or does he think she should hold a job outside? Does he think her role is to help him succeed in business? What does she see as her role? Do they agree? Have they both lived long enough and had enough varied experience to *know* how they really feel about this? Some couples may view marriage romantically and think that "of course" he will be the wage earner and she the housewife, but may change this view later. Some good discussions during the engagement may help both to clarify their ideas and to understand each other's point of view if they differ. It is possible that they may find such a wide difference in their viewpoints that they will decide not to marry. If their ideas and attitudes conflict, it is a good thing to find it out before marriage. In general, the engagement is a time when people need to be realistic about their marriage and the circumstances peculiar to their case.

ENGAGEMENT AS PREPARATION FOR MARRIAGE

Some problems are easier to solve before marriage than after. It is probably true that couples who are willing to discuss their differences frankly and with good humor are also the type of people who can face their problems in marriage more realistically and work out successful adjustments.

Even more important than discussing potential areas of disagreement is that engaged couples establish in their day-to-day association successful patterns that will serve to make marriage adjustment easier.

Patterns of communication

Engaged couples could do much to prepare themselves for marriage if they learned to understand each other through better communication. Communicating not only involves discussing subjects; it is understanding. Someone expresses ideas and your ears hear what is said, but you interpret what you hear according to your own life experiences. Actually, there may be little relationship between what the speaker means and what the listener hears. For example: Max and Jane discussed the subject of money and how they would handle their finances. They both said that their families had always had a fifty-fifty arrangement in money matters. They agreed that this had worked satisfactorily and that they would follow the same policy. They were happy to find that they agreed perfectly about this subject.

After they were married, Jane discovered that Max's idea of fifty-fifty was that he would consult her, but he would actually make all final decisions and handle most of the expenditures. He gave her an allowance for household expenses, food, and clothing. Jane objected to this arrangement. She felt that Max had either deceived her or had changed.

LEVEL OF AGREEMENT IN LEVEL OF COMMUNICATION

TYPE OF COUPLE — **ALWAYS AGREE**

- Engaged Couples: 60%
- Married Couples: 20%

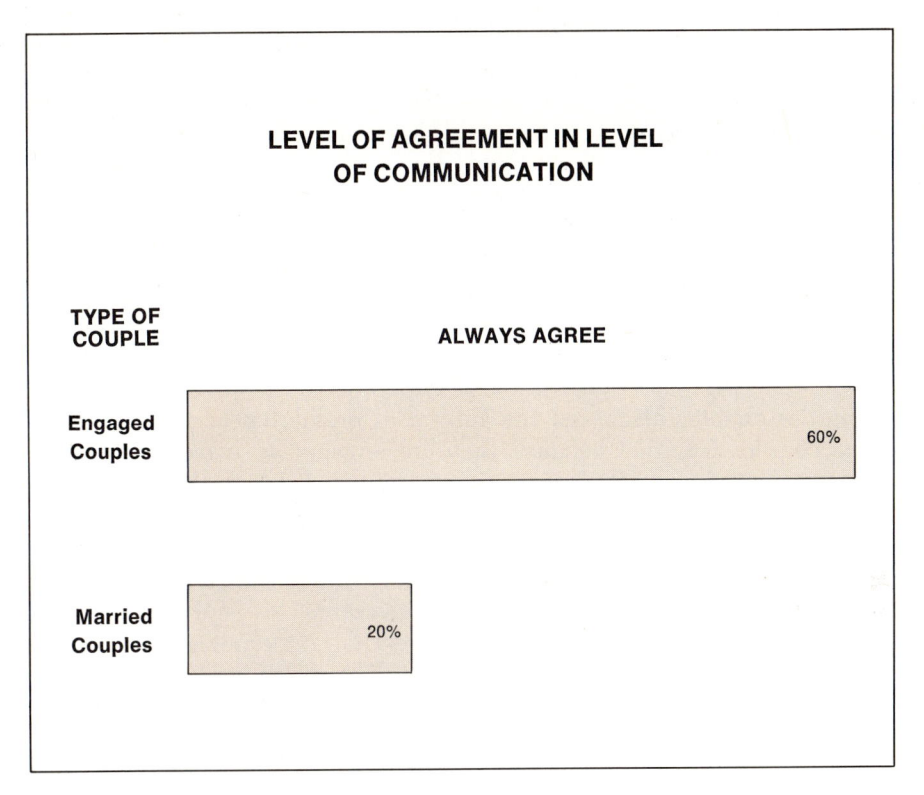

Graph 6. Of 122 engaged couples, 60 percent reported that they always agree or almost always agree on their level of communication with each other. Only 20 percent of 581 married couples report this to be the case.

The trouble was that in their prewedding conversation they had been talking but not communicating. Each had in mind a different idea of what fifty-fifty meant. It had not occurred to them to explore the other's real meaning. When Jane talked about a fifty-fifty pattern of financial responsibility, she thought of the way it worked with her parents, who had always had a joint checking account from which both were free to write checks. They had always made final decisions together about expenditures; they used charge accounts, and the bills were paid by whichever one had time for that task. Usually, it was her mother who actually spent the money and paid the bills. For Max to hand her an allowance for household expenses made her feel as if she were a child still on an allowance.

If Max and Jane had developed a more effective pattern of communication during engagement, they would not have been content with letting a term like fifty-fifty prevent them from trying to perceive each other's real understanding of and feelings about the meaning and value of equality in marriage.

Graph 6 summarizes findings from a study comparing reports of engaged people and of happily married people on how well they agree about their level of communication. You will see that 60 percent of the engaged couples think their communication is always or almost always good, while only 20 percent of the married couples report this much agreement. These findings do not mean that couples change after they marry; they show that many couples, like Max and Jane, talk to each other without perceiving the underlying meanings and feelings that words may not reveal.

Sexual behavior during engagement

An earlier chapter discussed the subject of premarital sexual behavior. Some couples feel that because they are engaged to marry, no reason exists for maintaining their previous standards. Because they are going to marry, and there may be some delay, they may see no reason for refraining from intercourse. The figures given earlier in this chapter on broken engagements have logical implications for behavior during engagement. A sizable percentage of engagements will not end in marriage. Engaged couples who have premarital intercourse may defeat some of the purposes of the engagement. They may miss their chance to evaluate their relationship while they still have time to change their minds. Many young people, because of their background, feel a compulsion to marry a person with whom they have had sexual intercourse, and so will go into an unwise marriage even if an undesired pregnancy does not force such action.

During the courtship and engagement periods, most people should pursue a course that will guarantee the greatest chance for success and happiness throughout their lifetime. One factor in this program is to make sure sexual intercourse does not distort the approach to marriage.

IN SUMMARY

There are a number of ways in which people may prepare for marriage. Reading will be a help to some people; excellent books are available that present a realistic picture of what is required of people who build successful and happy marriages. Other people can prepare by visiting a qualified premarital counselor, if they live in cities where such counselors are available. However, most important of all is to try to approach marriage with realistic attitudes. It is necessary to think through, *together and separately,* some important questions. If every couple intending to marry had complete and honest agreement on the answers to the questions below, this would not necessarily insure that they would be happy. But it would be an excellent foundation for a relationship that has a good chance of success.

Reading is one way of trying to prepare for marriage. What are some others? What kinds of books would one read? Would you include fiction?

1. When we marry, what are we signing up for?
2. What are the special responsibilities and the tasks that we are undertaking?
3. Are we close enough in our attitudes and purposes that we can work together, and help and encourage each other, no matter what comes up?
4. Are we both comfortable and happy about the way we spend our time now? The things we talk about? The way we use money?
5. Have we thought about what makes a home happy, and are we ready to do whatever is necessary to make ours a happy home for each other and the children we may have?

QUESTIONS FOR REVIEW

1. What are some of the chief reasons for breaking engagements?
2. What things did Henry do that indicated that he was immature?

3. What are some common reactions of the person who has been rejected in a love affair?
4. Analyze the statement that a broken engagement is better than a bad marriage. What are some considerations involved in a broken engagement? In a bad marriage?
5. How is getting over a broken engagement somewhat similar to getting over an illness?
6. What issues should be discussed during the engagement?
7. How may discussing a matter and communicating differ?
8. How can the engagement serve in a definite way as preparation for marriage?
9. What are some reasons for maintaining preengagement sexual standards during engagement?

ACTIVITIES AND PROJECTS

1. Does your community have a premarital counseling service? If so, visit it and report to the class on the type of available services. Perhaps one of the workers at the counseling service would talk to your class.
2. Write the "case history" of a broken engagement of which you know. On the basis of what you have learned from Chapters 12 and 13, try to decide whether or not the reason for the breakup was that either or both parties recognized danger signals.

WORDS AND CONCEPTS

bereavement
communication
compulsion
equanimity

marriage on the rebound
neurotic
reconcile
reputation

Religion and Marriage

14

After studying this chapter, you will be able to

1. Discuss the ways in which religion is related to marital success or failure.
2. Name some of the functions of religion.
3. Interpret findings of research on mixed religious marriages.
4. Describe common ways of resolving differences in mixed religious marriages.

Well over half the people in the United States are members of some religious denomination. Among these are to be found all types of beliefs. Some people look upon religion as the mental acceptance of certain creeds; others think of it chiefly as ritual. For some, religion is an emotional or a spiritual experience that may influence their behavior. For some people religion is a commitment to certain basic values relating to all mankind. Still others define religion in terms of patriotism or of nationalism. There are others whose religion emphasizes the negative; they try to live by a list of prohibitions. They define being religious as refraining from certain specified actions.

The kind of religion to which one subscribes depends on many things: the individual's family background, socioeconomic level, personality makeup, among other factors.

In this chapter, we are concerned primarily with raising questions that can help people to be aware that religion is related to marital success and failure. A religious faith, or the lack of it, the conception of religion that one holds, and agreement or disagreement on these matters will have implications for marriage and future family living.

Sociologists have found that in the United States people with a religious faith have, statistically, a better chance to have successful marriages and happy homes than people with no faith. For example, people who are church members report their marriages to be happier than do those who have nothing to do with religion.

The divorce rate is not so high among couples who were married in churches as among those married by civil authorities. In our own study of marriages among three groups of people—a successfully married group, unhappy group having marriage counseling, and a divorced group—a comparison between the successful couples and the unhappy couples showed that 84 percent of the happy and 41 percent of the unhappy couples had had a church wedding. Four percent of the happy and 41 percent of the unhappy had been married by a justice of the peace. This does not mean that having a church wedding will guarantee a happy marriage. The research merely reveals that there was a different approach to marriage and probably a different religious orientation between the couples who did and did not make a success of their marriages.

RELIGION AND RELATIONSHIPS WITHIN THE FAMILY

In a recent study, over three thousand college students reported on how religious their families were and on other relationships within the family. The responses of the main religious groups, Catholics, Protestants, and Jews, and those of people who professed no faith were analyzed. The responses from all four groups found a high association between religious devoutness and successful family living. The divorce rate had been four times higher in nonreligious families than in devout families. The happiness of the parents' marriage increased in direct relationship to their devoutness. Further, the students from devout homes, in contrast to those from nonreligious homes, reported being closer to their parents and having a higher conception of self as measured by such factors as their appraisals of their personalities, their ease in making friends with the other sex, and their confidence that they would be able to have a successful marriage themselves. A larger percentage of those from more devout families reported that they had adhered to a standard of premarital chastity.

Of the four groups, the group having no faith reported the largest percentage of divorced parents, and the largest percentage of unhappily married parents.

There are probably many logical reasons why the religious families seem to be more successful in their relationships. For one, doing things together as a family is important to most children. Families that are religious have an additional part of their lives they can enjoy together. Children from devout families tend to be devout themselves and thus to make religion a part of their family life when they marry.

There seem also to be factors inherent in religion and its application to life that have an impact on marriage and family living. A psychiatrist has said, "Throughout the ages, religion has been the psychiatry of mankind." By this is meant that many people, through their religion, are able to gain a better perspective of themselves and the world. Their religious faith enables them to believe that certain values outweigh other considerations and are worth making a needed sacrifice. Thus, they can more readily accept the fact that their own interests and wishes are not necessarily the final end and aim of life; the needs and interests of others are also important.

For many people, a religious faith is a source of inner confidence. Because they put their trust in a power greater than themselves, they are not easily hurt by shifts in circumstances or by problems. They know that possessions, success, or favor with other people can be lost easily and suddenly, but their religious faith is not dependent upon these things. Therefore, they can be content regardless of changing circumstances in life.

When we think of the ways religion may affect the individual, we can understand why religious faith should contribute to success in marriage and family life. Psychologists know that the person who is hard to live with because of being aggressive toward others, or suspicious of their motives, is often one who has no inner security. Because of feeling inadequate, the actions and motives of others cannot be accepted. The inner security of a religious faith may help one to be more understanding and perceptive of the needs of others.

Further, religion requires self-discipline. You know that if you are from a religious family, regardless of denomination or faith, you probably go to services quite regularly and do other things your religion requires whether or not you always feel so inclined. You give to the support of your church or synagogue, even if it means self-denial. In other words, in many ways you exercise self-discipline.

In family life, self-discipline is important. In any home, there are times when life is much happier if each family member can be depended upon to think of the needs of others and do whatever is required for the well-being of all, rather than to think only of personal feelings and act according to selfish desires.

RELIGION AND FAMILY BACKGROUND

We have said that religious attitudes and beliefs depend somewhat upon family background. Children are usually taught to accept their parents' religion. It has been found that about four-fifths of young people who are affiliated with some church have accepted the religion of their parents. Few young people adopt a religious belief entirely different from that of either of their parents. If parents have no religious faith, children will tend to grow up with less religious orientation than those from homes in which religion is important.

Young people are often more tolerant than are their elders of the beliefs of others. They may have friends of all faiths, or friends of no religion. Associating only with one's group can make for narrowness, lack of understanding, and prejudice. In considering marriage, however, it has been found that agreement on religion is a significant factor for happiness.

Some young people who might decry religion still instinctively react in a religious way to things that move them deeply. We usually accept the religion of our family.

RELIGION AND MARRIAGE

AGREEMENT ON RELIGION

The individual who hopes to be happily married should choose someone with whom he or she can agree on religion. This is important—just as it is important that a married couple be able to agree about spending money and the use of leisure time. If one person has a religious faith and is accustomed to organizing life in relation to values that harmonize with that faith, it will be disappointing not to be able to share this important part of life with the married partner.

Sometimes, young people not yet married underrate the importance of their religion. During adolescence, most people begin to evaluate their religious beliefs and to decide what they can honestly accept among those things that they have been taught. Up to this time, they may have had little reason to dissociate their religious attitudes from those of their parents and to decide how much their religious faith is a part of their personal philosophy. If they are not yet sure how much their religion means to them, they may believe that it is of no importance whether or not they marry someone who values religion and whose religious faith agrees with theirs.

It is important that two who are thinking of marrying look at their attitudes to see whether their religious beliefs will help hold their marriage together or their differences will be a disruptive force after they are married and settled into the business of living.

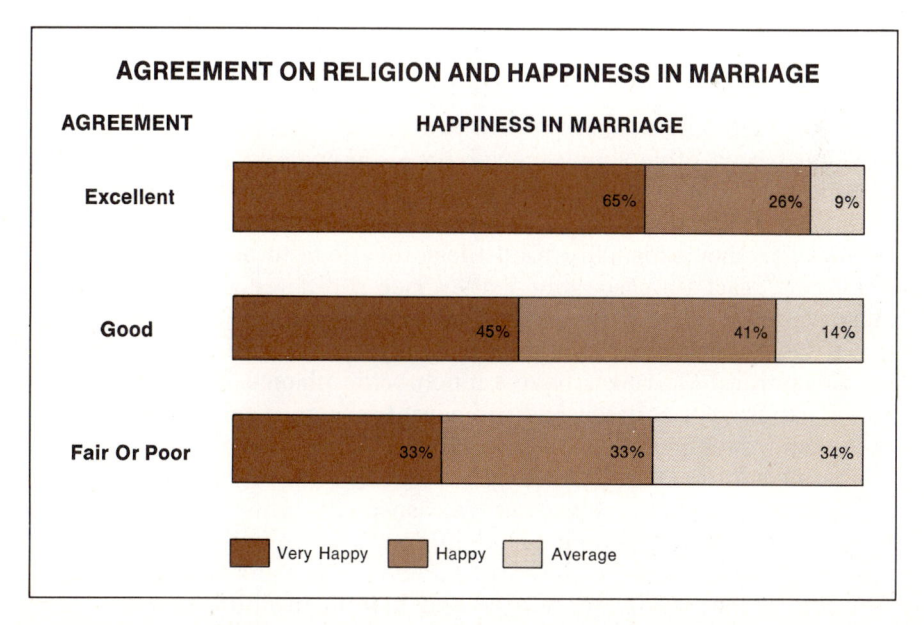

AGREEMENT ON RELIGION AND HAPPINESS IN MARRIAGE

AGREEMENT	HAPPINESS IN MARRIAGE
Excellent	Very Happy 65% / Happy 26% / Average 9%
Good	Very Happy 45% / Happy 41% / Average 14%
Fair Or Poor	Very Happy 33% / Happy 33% / Average 34%

Graph 7. A study of 409 couples showed that those who agreed on religion were happier in their marriage than those who did not.

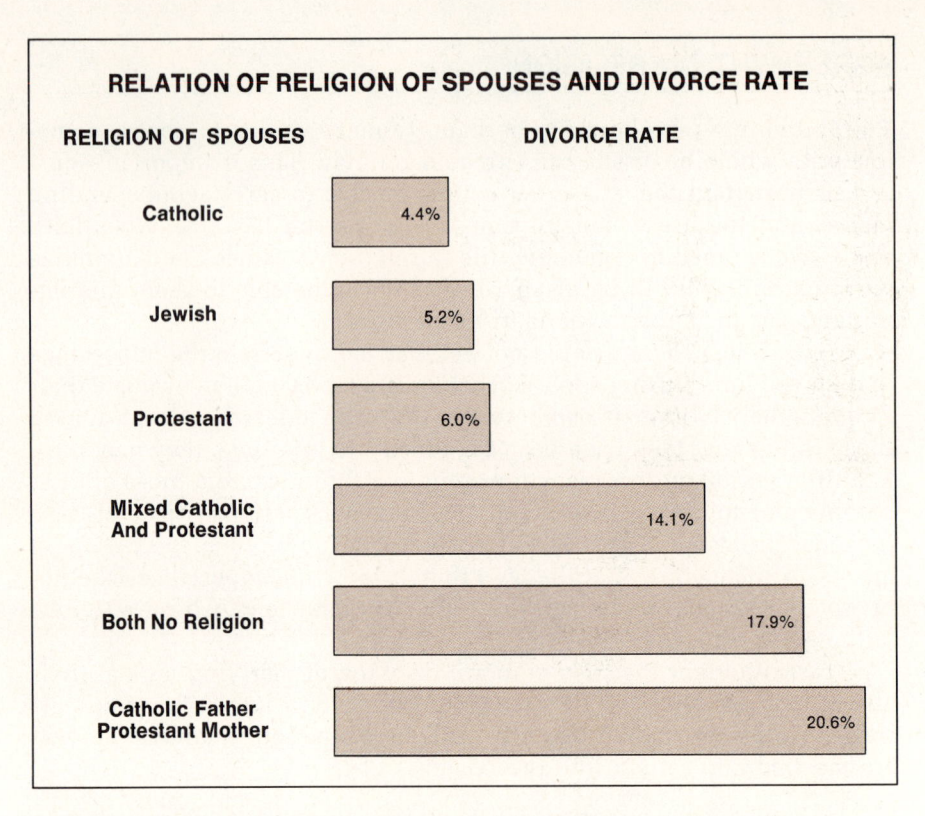

RELATION OF RELIGION OF SPOUSES AND DIVORCE RATE

Religion of Spouses	Divorce Rate
Catholic	4.4%
Jewish	5.2%
Protestant	6.0%
Mixed Catholic And Protestant	14.1%
Both No Religion	17.9%
Catholic Father Protestant Mother	20.6%

Graph 8. The divorce rate is higher when people have no religious belief or when two people are from different religious faiths.

If both are religious, but of widely different faiths, they must be able to respect each other's religion, or the difference will be a roadblock to happiness. But because many people identify all their religious faith with a particular sect or creed, and tend to feel that only that creed can be effective, they especially want those they love to believe as they do. They may react unreasonably if they face a difference in beliefs after marriage.

A factor affecting all types of marriage is the attitudes of the two in-law families. Marriages have a much better chance for success when parents approve the match and can accept wholeheartedly the new son-in-law and daughter-in-law. Any extreme difference between the families is an additional hurdle for a newly married couple to overcome. Some parents will actively interfere, especially when it comes to the religious upbringing of their grandchildren. Others will try not to interfere, but their feelings may be apparent enough to exert pressure. Parents may find it hard to be supportive and helpful to children who marry outside the family's faith, and the child-in-law may interpret their attitude as a rejection of him or her individually.

MARRIAGES OF PEOPLE OF DIFFERENT RELIGIOUS FAITHS

Catholic, Protestant, and Jewish church officials urge young people not to marry outside their faith.

Sociologists have become interested in mixed marriages, not because of the religious implication, but because they are interested in knowing how well such marriages work out from the viewpoint of success and happiness for the couples who make such marriages.

Studies of religiously mixed marriages, which included approximately 25,000 couples living in three widely separated sections of the country, have been made by sociologists. These studies considered the

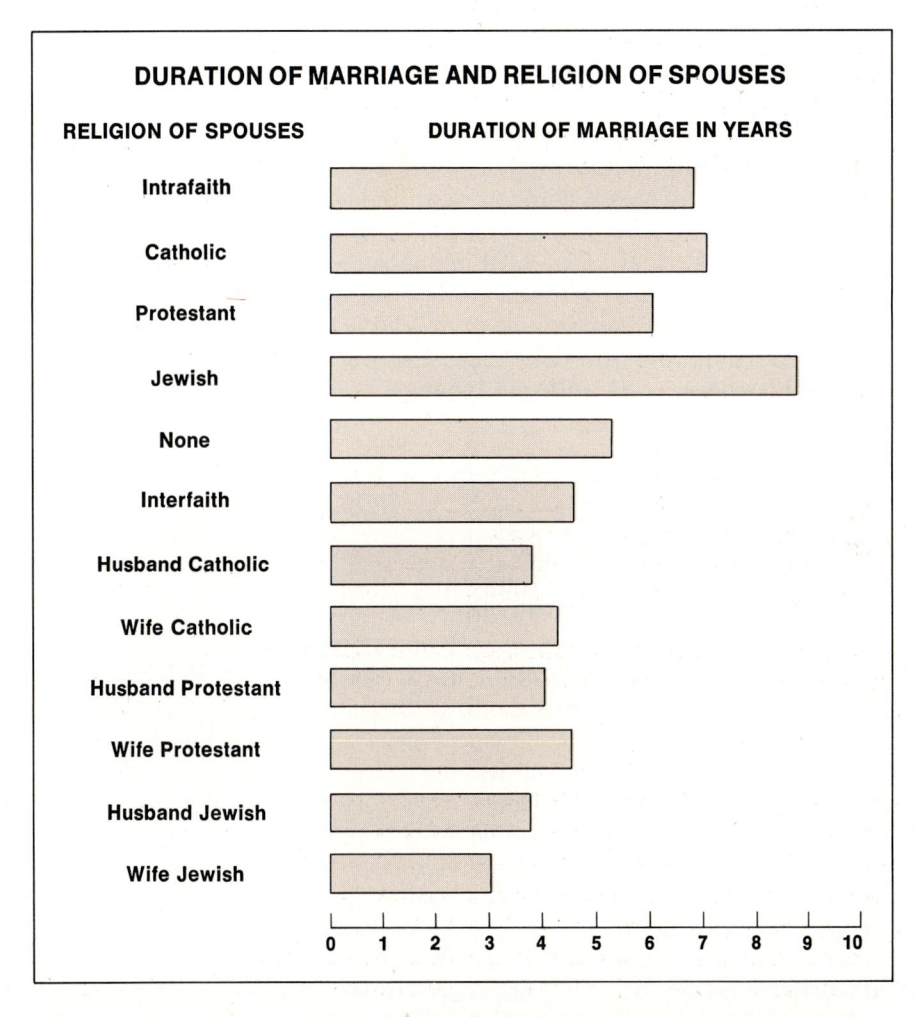

DURATION OF MARRIAGE AND RELIGION OF SPOUSES

RELIGION OF SPOUSES	DURATION OF MARRIAGE IN YEARS
Intrafaith	
Catholic	
Protestant	
Jewish	
None	
Interfaith	
Husband Catholic	
Wife Catholic	
Husband Protestant	
Wife Protestant	
Husband Jewish	
Wife Jewish	

Graph 9. Among 105, 167 marriages in California, the median duration of the marriage until time of separation is shown by type of marriage and religion of husband and wife.

religious background of couples and the percentage of the marriages that ended in divorce or separation. Graph 8 summarizes a study of 4100 marriages in which there were children. It will be observed that if a Catholic had married a Catholic, slightly over 4 out of 100 marriages had ended in divorce or separation. If Jew had married Jew, approximately 5 out of 100 marriages led to divorce or separation; if Protestant had married Protestant, 6 out of 100. If a Catholic had married a Protestant, however, 14 out of 100 marriages ended in divorce or separation; when the man was Catholic and the woman Protestant, approximately 21 of 100 of those marriages had ended in divorce or separation, the highest rate of all.

It is interesting to note that if both members of a couple had no religion the divorce rate was higher than all others except the Catholic man–Protestant woman combinations: approximately 18 out of 100 of the no-religion marriages had ended in divorce or separation.

Statistical data now available on over 100,000 couples show that among marriages that end for any reason, those that are interfaith have trouble sooner; the length of time from the wedding to separation is shorter than in the nonmixed marriages. Data on 105,167 couples applying for divorce or separation in California are summarized in Graph 9.

All intrafaith marriages (within the same faith) had lasted longer before separation than had interfaith (mixed) marriages. Jewish marriages lasted longer than any other intrafaith marriages; but when Jews married outside the faith, their marriages lasted a shorter time than interfaith marriages of any other religions.

FOCUS OF PROBLEMS

Our study of religiously mixed marriages led to the conclusion that disagreement over the religious training of children is a factor about which difficulty centers. Although a couple may decide before marriage that each will go his or her own way as far as religion is concerned, and that the children will be brought up in the faith of one or the other, it is not always possible to live up to this agreement without conflict. Because it is impossible for the young people to project themselves into the future and know how they will feel as parents, agreements that are made during the engagement often have to be remade after the children are born.

Our study of 192 mixed Catholic-Protestant marriages, in which there were 392 children, found that half of the children had been reared in the Protestant faith and half in the Catholic faith. What really happened in these marriages was that the children were brought up in the faith of the mother. If the mother was Catholic, the children were reared Catholic; if the mother was Protestant, the children were reared Protestant. Approximately 75 percent of the children followed the faith of the mother and only 25 percent followed the faith of the father.

Until recently, couples in Catholic-Protestant marriages had to sign a prenuptial agreement promising four things, one of which was that the children would be reared and educated in the Catholic faith. It was surprising to find that, although such an agreement had been made, the children tended to follow the faith of the mother. In recent years, the Catholic Church has been liberalizing its policy on marriages involving mixed faiths. The formal prenuptial agreement signed by both parties is no longer required, although a Catholic must still promise that all children will be baptized and educated in the Catholic faith.

KINDS OF SOLUTIONS

Studies show that couples faced with problems associated with their mixed religious backgrounds have a tendency to react in certain typical ways.

One or both may drop all religious practices. The husband more often is the one who gives up, either for the sake of peace or because religion is not a common bond of interest. Or each may hold to his or her own religion, and they live with divided loyalties as far as religion is concerned. In other cases, one gives up his or her religion and accepts the religion of the other. If one can sincerely do this, it solves many of the problems of a mixed marriage. In effect, it is no longer a mixed marriage.

Our study of mixed Catholic-Protestant marriages revealed a lower divorce rate when potential conflict had been avoided by one's changing to the faith of the other. However, it is impossible for some people to take that step and be permanently satisfied with their decision. As we said earlier in our discussion, by the time one is an adult, religious attitudes are likely to have become rather deeply ingrained, and it is difficult to change those beliefs.

JEWISH-GENTILE MARRIAGES

In general, the potential problems in Jewish-Gentile marriages are similar to those in Catholic-Protestant marriages. A Jewish-Gentile couple may find it hard to agree about the religious training of the children. One is disappointed or hurt if children are brought up to accept the other's religion. Differences in holidays and feast days, or contrasts in cultural background, may also be more of a complication than in the average marriage within either faith.

Difficulties in Jewish-Gentile marriages will tend to differ by devoutness and by whether the Jew is Orthodox, Conservative, or Reform. Orthodox Jews follow all the ancient commandments and customs of the faith. Conservative Jews hold to the Torah (the first five books of the Old Testament) as being God-inspired, but they will accept some

FAMILY ACCEPTANCE AND REJECTION IN JEWISH-GENTILE MARRIAGES

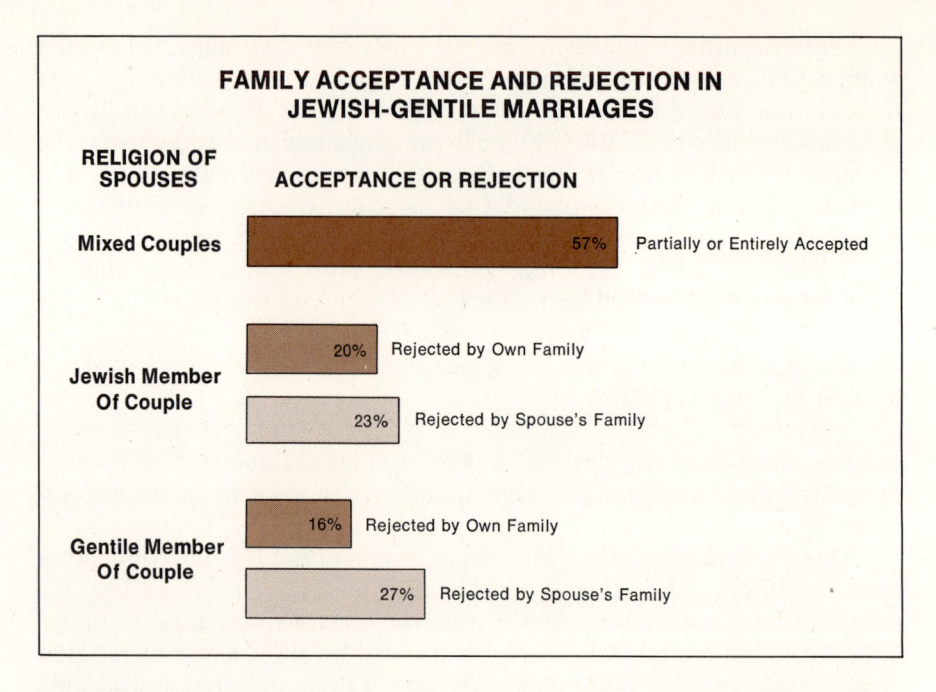

Religion of Spouses	Acceptance or Rejection	
Mixed Couples	57%	Partially or Entirely Accepted
Jewish Member Of Couple	20%	Rejected by Own Family
	23%	Rejected by Spouse's Family
Gentile Member Of Couple	16%	Rejected by Own Family
	27%	Rejected by Spouse's Family

Graph 10. Partners in Jewish-Gentile intermarriages face the problem of rejection by the families of both sides.

changes in practices. Because Reform Jews do not follow so many of the traditional rituals, there might be fewer potential conflicts between a Reform Jew and a Gentile. Most rabbis do not accept mixed marriages and will refuse to officiate. All rabbis, however, will perform marriages between Jews and converted Gentiles.

Marriage outside one's faith is more prevalent in areas of the country where one's particular faith is in the minority. Where there are very few Jews in the population, more Jews make mixed marriages. This is also true of other groups; if there are few of one's own faith, one finds a mate among the people available.

CONCLUSION

All the evidence seems to indicate the following two important facts: first, a religious faith is valuable to individual personality development and in family living; second, young people should marry those with whom they can agree in religious faith.

People should see to it that their religious faith is a bond that will contribute to happiness and success in their marriages. Couples should examine their attitudes before marriage to be sure that they understand and accept each other's feelings and beliefs in the area of religion.

QUESTIONS FOR REVIEW

1. What are some of the contrasts in the religious beliefs of different faiths and of different denominations?
2. How does family background affect our religious beliefs?
3. What are some functions of religion?
4. What do you understand by the statement, "Throughout the ages, religion has been the psychiatry of mankind"?
5. Why should a religious faith give a person perspective?
6. How may religion give security to the individual?
7. What facts have been learned from studies of mixed religious marriages?
8. What seems to be a major source of conflict in mixed Catholic-Protestant marriages?
9. Is it possible for people to settle all the possible causes for conflict in mixed religious marriages before they marry? Explain.
10. In what faith are children of mixed Catholic-Protestant marriages more likely to be reared? How do you explain this?
11. What prenuptial promise does a Catholic make?
12. What are three common ways of resolving religious differences in mixed marriages?
13. What are some of the contrasts in Jewish-Gentile marriages that may cause misunderstandings?

ACTIVITIES AND PROJECTS

1. Write an account of the growth of your own religious attitudes from as far back as you can recall.
2. Is it conceivable that the time will come when differences in religious creeds and points of view will be eliminated? Why would or why would not the elimination of such differences be desirable? Defend your answer.
3. Can you analyze just what religion means to you personally, apart from your family?
4. Analyze a religiously mixed marriage that you know. What factors seem to have contributed to its success or failure?
5. Tell of a family you know well, showing how harmony in religious beliefs has contributed to the general happiness of the family.
6. Ask representatives from the Protestant, Catholic, and Jewish faiths to come before your class and discuss the mixed religious marriage from their respective points of view.

WORDS AND CONCEPTS

cognizance
commitment
creed
denomination
disruptive
dissociate
inherent

inner security
intrafaith
orientation
psychiatry
sense of proportion
supportive

IS IT LOVE? 15

After studying this chapter, you will be able to

1. Define the basic components of love.
2. Name some of the basic personality needs that must be met for permanent love to develop.
3. Discuss the purpose served by early love experiences.
4. List questions that those in love might ask themselves when considering whether their love is likely to last.

Millions of words have been written about love. Falling in love is advertised as one of life's greatest happenings. People of all ages find themselves experiencing emotional reactions in response to others. Some of them begin to wonder, "Am I in love?" Others do not stop to wonder. They marry without taking time to think. Probably most of you have already had feelings for someone you have met or have been dating that have caused you to ask, "Is this love?" or to conclude, "This is love."

Because the question of love is in the minds of so many people, it might seem that in a book such as this, love should have been the first subject discussed. However, it is necessary to have a perspective on many important elements before one can possibly begin to define the nature of love. In earlier chapters, concepts have been explored that should lead toward developing an understanding and a definition of love. Some of the concepts in this chapter may be a review of conclusions you have already reached.

COMPONENTS OF LOVE

Love is not just an emotion, but rather it is a complex relationship having many components. True, love includes emotion. It also includes mutuality giving and receiving by two people. It includes the satisfying of personality needs of both who love each other. Love includes physical attraction; it includes unselfish sharing. Love also includes sacrifice of personal preferences or wishes, and cooperation instead of competition. Without these elements, the emotion one feels for someone else is not love. Let us examine more carefully some of these integral parts of love.

PHYSICAL ATTRACTION

We begin with physical attraction because it is the element we notice at the beginning of attachments. It is also the thing most commonly mistaken for love. A girl says, "I like John. He is a lot of fun to be with. He is dependable, too, and is considerate and thoughtful. But I am in love with Jim. He is terribly attractive, and all the other girls envy me when they see me with him." Is it love?

A married woman says, "I have a husband with whom I have been happy, and two children. But I met a man who is so completely attractive that I fell in love with him the day we met." Such a woman is confusing physical attraction with love.

Physical attraction is a strong force that impels men and women, boys and girls, toward an interest in each other. It enhances all associations between the sexes. One reason why people begin to wish to date and spend more time with those of the other sex at adolescence is that they are maturing sexually, and they enjoy attracting and being attracted to others. It is an exhilarating and enjoyable experience.

At the same time, many young people when they first experience a strong response to someone whom they date become confused. The feeling is relatively new to them, and they believe it can only be love. Some of these make hasty marriages.

Physical attraction usually happens suddenly; one may feel it at first sight. Love does not happen that way. When people speak of falling in love at first sight, they are mixing terms. For one does not fall into love as one might fall over the edge of a cliff; one can only grow into love. But one can "fall" into physical attraction in the sense that one may feel that it struck suddenly.

When we get clearly in mind the difference between love and physical attraction—without minimizing physical attraction as a factor in love—we are then ready to begin to understand more clearly what love is.

A girl who was proudly showing an engagement ring to friends said, "Oh, I'm so in love with Jerry. He's the most wonderful person I've ever met. I've been thrilled every minute since I met him two weeks ago!" Do you think she—or he—could know so soon whether or not the feeling they had for each other could grow into love?

SATISFACTION OF PERSONALITY NEEDS

People who are attracted to each other seek out each other's company. If their association becomes friendship that can develop into love, they must feel more than physical attraction. Each must find in the other, and give to the other, satisfaction of certain basic needs.

A large number of young people were asked to list the needs they felt to be important. Among those listed were: someone to understand me; to respect my ideals; to appreciate what I wish to achieve; to understand my moods; to help me make decisions; to stimulate my ambition; to give me self-confidence; to look up to me; to back me in difficulties; to appreciate me just as I am; to admire me; to relieve my loneliness.*

* Ernest W. Burgess, Harvey J. Locke, Mary Margaret Thomes, *The Family: From Institution to Companionship,* 3rd ed., New York: American Book Company, 1963.

Do you want his class ring or later his engagement ring to give you status among your friends, or can it really be love that will last for the rest of your lives?

Can you name others? Those people whose relationship goes on to develop into love find fulfillment of whichever of these or other needs are present in their personality. An important point, however, is that *both* must find satisfaction. If the relationship is one-sided, in that one seeks appreciation, understanding, and an ego boost but is not able to give the equivalent in exchange, real love does not result. In other words, there must be mutuality.

SHARING

The Archbishop of York said at the marriage of Queen Elizabeth II and Philip of England, "Love must always be unselfish, and unselfishness is the true secret of a happy married life. It must show itself not only in a great moment of heroic self-sacrifice but continually in all small problems and incidents of everyday life. It means patience, ready sympathy, and forbearance, talking over and sharing together the special interests and cares which each of you will have."

This kind of sharing means the ability to laugh at and to believe in some of the same things. Such sharing cannot happen to people at first sight, nor can they "fall into" it suddenly. Two people learn to cooperate, to exchange understanding and appreciation, and to enjoy working or playing together over a period of time, and so love grows.

We asked 122 engaged couples to describe the progress of love in their relationship from their first date to the time of our study. These couples were approaching marriage slowly. On the average, they had dated casually for five months, dated steadily for eight months, had had an "understanding" engagement for eight months, had been "formally" engaged for six months, and they would not be married for seven months. Notice that few of these people fell in love at first sight (see Table 8). For most of the men and women, it was a gradual growing into love as they continued seeing each other.

Table 8 PROGRESS OF LOVE UP TO ENGAGEMENT

Progress of Love	Men	Women
	Percentage*	
We both fell in love at first sight	4	4
I fell in love at first sight	1	3
Fiance(e) fell in love at first sight	0	1
One fell in love first, the other later	33	30
It was a gradual falling in love for both	62	62

* Percentage of 122 engaged couples.

It is necessary that common interests and enjoyment of some of the same kinds of activities be present, for these will outlast physical attraction.

If people really love each other, they will willingly share work and responsibility as well as pleasure and good times. It is said that certain German peasants require a young couple who are thinking of marriage to perform the following experiment. They are brought together and given a two-handled saw. In the presence of their neighbors, they have to saw a log. It is a test that can reveal many things. If one wishes to take the lead and do everything alone, the rhythm is lost. If they tug against each other, the job takes twice as long and uses twice as much energy. If one leaves the work for the other, the saw wobbles and the cut is uneven. Such an experiment tells the observing neighbors something about how well the love of a couple is going to wear.

WE LOOK AT OUR RELATIONSHIPS WITH OTHERS

If some of the necessarycomponents of love are kept in mind, it is easier to classify our relationships. For some people, we feel a physical attraction. Other people meet some of our personality needs. During the high school years, this is especially true of some friendships. Because we feel the need for security—for knowing there is someone we can depend upon for dates and flattering attentions—we may cling to those who give it to us. But as we become older and more confident, needs may change. The present relationships will have served their purpose: they may never include components that would enable them to grow into a lasting love. On page 211, reread the various needs people listed as important. In some relationships, *some* of these needs may be met. But in a love relationship that can survive years, *many* or *most* of them must be mutually met.

Jane, sixteen, says, "I know I did love Tom. We agreed about everything. We liked to do all the same things. We studied together and played tennis together. We were proud to be seen together, and we were attractive to each other. But while I was away for a year with my parents, Tom began dating someone else. Now that I am back, he says he only wants to be friends—that he loves Sally just as he did me. At first, I felt terrible about it, but now I have started dating some other boys, and I am surprised to find that Fred suits me as well as Tom did—in some ways, even better. He is more responsible, although it never really bothered me while we were dating that Tom was so irresponsible. I didn't think, then, that it mattered."

Jane's experience is normal and evidence that both she and Tom are growing toward maturity. They met each other's needs during adolescence, but their needs are changing. While their love did not survive their growing maturity, it served its purpose.

VALUE OF LOVE EXPERIENCES

It is a good thing to have such love experiences, for they help one learn to evaluate relationships thoughtfully. You have learned an important thing when you realize that it is not necessary to marry the first person you love. Those who love early, before they are ready for marriage, can let that love be an enriching experience that contributes to their capacity for a wise and lasting love in the future.

Sometimes, people speak laughingly of "puppy love." But there is nothing funny about puppy love. It is an important part of development.

The twelve-year-old may love the girl who sits beside him at school. He is just becoming aware of girls, and this one seems to be completely charming, clever, and exciting. She makes him feel comfortable and appreciated when he might feel awkward and ill at ease. Almost as soon as he begins thinking about dating, and while he is still timid and uncertain about whether or how he should go about getting dates, she asks him! It does good things for his self-confidence. The world is wonderful. He spends hours standing around talking to her, and more hours thinking of her and planning to see her. For a while, they suit each other completely. They are in love; it makes no difference that it is "puppy love." Normally, they will outgrow it, but both will have benefited from the experience.

When love occurs during the later teen years, it is past the puppy-love stage. It may begin to have aspects of the mature love that leads to marriage. People then need to evaluate their relationships even more carefully. Emotions are stronger now. There is more freedom from parental restraint and more of a tendency either to plunge into marriage or to become so involved emotionally that it may be a handicap when the time does come to marry.

Now is the time when people must look at their love rationally because they are reaching the age when marriage is more apt to be considered seriously. The most important question is not, "Is this love?" but "Is it the kind of love that could last and grow for the next forty or fifty years?" A very old lady said, "John and I have been married for sixty years. His love and consideration have made my whole life happy." Such people could teach us much about what love really is and how it grows.

We suggest some questions that can be applied to any relationship. They can help you to decide whether or not the love you may feel for someone is the kind that can grow and last in marriage.

1. *Are we both mature enough so that our personality needs will not greatly change in the next few years?* Between the years of seventeen and twenty-four most people change greatly. The person one loves at seventeen might not be suitable five years later.

How do we know it's love? Answer honestly. If we marry, is this feeling and relationship likely to last and to grow? Does it include mutual respect and kindness and a cherishing feeling one for the other?

2. *How many important interests do we have in common?* Do we both genuinely enjoy the same kind of music, people, books, and activities or sports? Or is one of us bored by many of the things that seem enjoyable to the other? Do we see humor in the same situations? Or is one of us serious and intense about something that seems funny to the other?
3. *Are our backgrounds similar enough so that we could understand each other readily in marriage?*
4. *What about the family of the person I love?* Are they a happy, congenial family? If he (she) comes from an unhappy family, has it marred his (her) personality?
5. *What do my family and friends think of him (her)?* If he (she) embarrasses me around them, is it because I am overly sensitive, or is it that he (she) really does not fit in with the other people for whom I care?
6. *Do we quarrel?* A few quarrels may occur in almost all courtships, but many quarrels mean that there will be many quarrels in marriage.
7. *Am I comfortable around this person?* That is, can I be my real self or do I feel that I must work hard to live up to some of the expectations he (she) has for me? Do I feel that I must try to appear to be different from what I am?

"What's the matter with him, lady? Is he sick?"

8. *How well do we agree on roles of men and women?* Does one of us believe in equality and the other in the male-superior and female-inferior pattern in life? That kind of a difference does not help love to grow.
9. *Have we been acquainted long enough to know how well we agree on important matters,* or have we been so busy being in love that we just assume that we agree on everything?
10. *How much do we confide in each other?* People who confide in each other are establishing a good pattern for their future happiness.
11. *Would I want to change this person if I married him (her)?* It probably cannot be done.
12. *Do I respect his (her) judgment?* Are there many occasions when it seems that he (she) makes the wrong decision or choice?
13. *How mature are we both?* Have we learned the difference between love and physical attraction? Can we look at marriage objectively, or are we basing our ideas and expectations upon romantic stories or movies?
14. *Do we have the same goals in life?* Are we going in the same direction, so we can happily strive for the same things?

IS IT LOVE?

Those who can ask themselves these and other such questions, and answer them honestly, may get help in determining whether or not their feeling is a love that can last and grow.

It never hurts love to look at it reasonably. Rather, the love that passes the tests of reason becomes solidly entrenched. It is worth sacrificing for, and worth working to maintain. It will enrich all of life and will be a strong force holding a marriage together.

QUESTIONS FOR REVIEW

1. Why should a chapter on love be delayed until this point?
2. Give some of the components of love.
3. Why do people often confuse physical attraction with love?
4. What do people mean when they say it was "love at first sight"?
5. Name some of the basic personality needs that must be met if two people are to develop a permanent love.
6. What phases of love did the Archbishop of York stress when he married Elizabeth and Philip of England?
7. When German peasants required the two young people to perform the ceremony of sawing a log, what were they trying to make the young couple realize about marriage?
8. Do our personality needs remain the same as we mature? Illustrate.
9. Give your understanding of "puppy love." Does it serve a useful purpose? Explain.
10. What are several questions that couples might ask to determine whether or not their love is likely to last?
11. If two people are in love, do you think it would be possible for them to be objective in answering the questions at the end of this chapter? Discuss.

ACTIVITIES AND PROJECTS

1. Evaluate the type of love presented in a movie. Did the relationship of the hero and heroine include the elements necessary to a lasting love? What elements were emphasized and which ones were lacking?
2. Evaluate magazine stories that presented unrealistic pictures of falling in love and of marriage.
3. Give an account of a couple who are in love, but have little chance for a lasting love in marriage because certain essentials are lacking.
4. "Love will carry a couple through all their difficulties." Discuss.

5. Consult many different sources for definitions of love. Make a list of these definitions, and be prepared to evaluate them in class.

6. (Report.) "My first experience with 'puppy love.'" Tell or write about some of the things you did, how you felt, how you got over the experience, and whether it seems to you to have been helpful or harmful as an experience in growing up.

WORDS AND CONCEPTS

ego
enhance
exhilarating

forbearance
mutuality
personality needs

Marriage Customs and Laws

16

After studying this chapter, you will be able to

1. Tell why the state regulates marriage laws.
2. Describe the relationship between legal age for marriage and teenage marriages; tell how the passage of the 26th Amendment will be likely to affect these two.
3. Define marriages of affinity and consanguinity.
4. Explain the differences between void and voidable marriages, between annulment and divorce, and give legal reasons for each.
5. List the usual procedures one must go through to meet legal requirements for marriage, and list some ways these vary by state.

Many different forms of marriage are found in the world. The most common is *monogamy,* the marriage of one man to one woman. Even in countries that do not prohibit a man having many wives, monogamy is still the most common type of marriage.

As life becomes more complicated, marriage customs concern the state more, and laws are passed that attempt to regulate marriages to protect the interests of those who marry and of the children. At one time in our country, two people could, without benefit of license, judge, or minister, just set up housekeeping and be married. This is known as *common-law marriage.*

Common-law marriages are still valid in some states, and other states recognize the validity of common-law marriages if entered into prior to the passage of laws banning common-law marriages. States outlawing common-law marriages recognize their validity if they were legal in the state where contracted. Common-law marriages can result in great confusion for the couple as well as for society. How long does the couple live together before they become husband and wife? Are their children legitimate? Do they go through a divorce if they decide to separate? Who gets custody of the children? Is alimony granted? If one spouse dies, who inherits the property? These questions do not have definite answers in common-law marriages and often have to be settled in the courts. Because of the potential confusion, most people getting married go through certain formalities and meet the legal requirements of the state in which they live.

The regulations governing marriage developed gradually in the different states. The laws tend to be based upon the marriage customs in that section of the country. If laws are passed that are not in harmony with the customs of an area, they tend to be ignored or unenforced.

Some of the laws are conflicting and create confusion for people who move from state to state. This was of little importance formerly when the population was less mobile; but at present, more uniformity in marriage regulations is needed.

PHYSICAL AND MENTAL QUALIFICATIONS FOR MARRIAGE

All states now recognize the necessity for prohibiting the marriage of people who might produce defective offspring. All have laws stating that insane persons, idiots, imbeciles, and the feebleminded may not marry. Some of these regulations are very old and were originally passed because one qualification for making a legal contract was that the person be of sound mind. If one were insane or feebleminded, this person would be automatically disqualified from making any type of contract, including the marriage contract.

The modern reason for prohibiting the marriage of the mentally unfit is that society wishes to prevent the production of offspring who would be defective. Some states permit the feebleminded to make legal marriage contracts if they first submit to a sterilization operation so that they cannot have children.

All but five states have venereal disease laws that require a blood test to determine the absence of syphilis before a marriage license is granted (see Table 9). Some states' tests include all venereal diseases.

Some physical and mental requirements for marriage, other than the ones mentioned above, are those found in North Carolina and North Dakota, which require a certificate from a physician stating that the man and woman are free from tuberculosis in the infectious stage. North Dakota has restrictions regarding alcoholism and Oregon's include both alcoholism and drug addiction.

MARRIAGE CUSTOMS AND LAWS

Table 9 MARRIAGE INFORMATION

Marriageable age, by states, for both males and females with and without consent of parents or guardians. But in most states, the court has authority, in an emergency, to marry young couples below the ordinary age of consent, where due regard for their morals and welfare so requires. In many states, under special circumstances, blood test and waiting period may be waived.

State	With consent Men	With consent Women	Without consent Men	Without consent Women	Blood test Required	Blood test Other state accepted*	Wait for license	Wait after license
Alabama (b)	17	14	21	18	Yes	Yes	None	None
Alaska	18	16	21	18	Yes	No	3 days	None
Arizona	18[2]	16	18	18	Yes	Yes	None	None
Arkansas	18	16	21	18	Yes	No	3 days	None
California	18	16	18	18	Yes	Yes	None	None
Colorado	16	16	21	18	Yes	. . . .	None	None
Connecticut	16	16	18	18	Yes	Yes	4 days	None
Delaware	18	16	19	19	Yes	Yes	None	24 hrs(c)
District of Columbia	18	16	21	18	Yes	Yes	3 days	None
Florida	18	16	21	21	Yes	Yes	3 days	None
Georgia	18	16	19	19	Yes	Yes	None (b)	None (o)
Hawaii	18	16	20	18	Yes	Yes	None	None
Idaho	16	16	18	18	Yes	Yes	None[4]	None
Illinois (a)	16[4]	16	21	18	Yes	Yes	None	None
Indiana	18	16	21	18	Yes	No	3 days	None
Iowa	18	16	21	18	Yes	Yes	3 days	None
Kansas	18	18	21	18	Yes	Yes	3 days	None
Kentucky	18	16	18	18	Yes	No	3 days	None
Louisiana (a)	18	16	18	18	Yes	No	None	72 hrs
Maine	16	16	18	18	No	No	5 days	None
Maryland	18	16	21	18	None	None	48 hrs	None
Massachusetts	18	18	18	18	Yes	Yes	3 days	None
Michigan (a)	18	16	18	18	Yes	No	3 days	None
Minnesota	18	16	21	18	None	. . . .	5 days	None
Mississippi (b)	17	15	21	21	Yes	. . . .	3 days	None
Missouri	15	15	21	18	Yes	Yes	3 days	None
Montana	19[2]	19[2]	19	19	Yes	Yes	5 days	None
Nebraska	18	16	20	20	Yes	Yes	5 days	None
Nevada	18	16	21	18	None	None	None	None
New Hampshire (a)	14(e)	13(e)	20	18	Yes	Yes	5 days	None
New Jersey (a)	18	16	18	18	Yes	Yes	72 hrs	None
New Mexico	16	16	21	21	Yes	Yes	None	None
New York	16	14	18	18	Yes	No	None	24 hrs(h)
North Carolina (a)	16	16	18	18	Yes	Yes	None	None
North Dakota (a)	18	15	18	18	Yes	. . . .	None	None
Ohio (a)	18	16	21	21	Yes	Yes	5 days	None
Oklahoma	18	15	21	18	Yes	. . . .	None (i)	**
Oregon	18(e)	15(e)	21	18	Yes	No	7 days	None
Pennsylvania	16	16	18	18	Yes	Yes	3 days	None
Rhode Island (a) (b)	18	16	21	18	Yes	No	None	None
South Carolina	16	14	18	18	None	None	24 hrs	None
South Dakota	18	16	18	18	Yes	Yes	None	None
Tennessee (b)	16	16	21	21	Yes	Yes	3 days	None
Texas	16	14	19	18	Yes	Yes	None	None
Utah (a)	16	14	21	18	Yes	Yes	None	None
Vermont (a)	18	16	21	18	Yes	. . . .	None	5 days
Virginia	18	16	18	18	Yes	Yes	None	None
Washington	17	17	18	18	(d)	. . . .	3 days	None
West Virginia	18	16	21	21	Yes	No	3 days	None
Wisconsin	18	16	18	18	Yes	Yes	5 days	None
Wyoming	18	16	21	21	Yes	Yes	None	None
Puerto Rico	18	16	21	21	(f)	None	(f)	None
Virgin Islands	16	14	21	18	None	None	8 days	None

Many states have special requirements; contact individual state.
(a) Special laws applicable to non-residents. (b) Special laws applicable to those under 21 years; Alabama; bond required if male is under 21, female under 18. (c) 24 hours if one or both parties resident of state; 96 hours if both parties are non-residents. (d) None, but male must file affidavit. (e) Parental consent plus Court's consent required. (f) None, but a medical certificate is required. (g) Wait for license from time blood test is taken; Arizona, 48 hours. (h) Marriage may not be solemnized within 10 days from date of blood test. (i) If either under 21; Idaho, 3 days; Oklahoma, 72 hrs. (x) May be waived. (1.) 3 days if both applicants are under 18 or female is pregnant. (2.) Statute provides for obtaining license with parental or court consent with no stated minimum age. (3.) If either party is under 18, 3 days. (4.) Under 16, with parental and court consent. (0) All those between 19-21 cannot waive 3 day waiting period.

STATE RANKINGS OF ALL MARRIAGES INVOLVING TEENAGE BRIDES AND GROOMS BY AGE

BRIDES | GROOMS

Percent

Rank	State	Brides %		Grooms %	State	Rank
1	Kentucky	47.4		24.7	Kentucky	1
2	Alabama	46.5		22.5	North Carolina	2
3	North Carolina	45.4		22.5	South Carolina	3
4	South Carolina	44.7		20.3	Missouri	4
5	Arkansas	44.2		20.0	Alabama	5
6	West Virginia	42.3		19.6	Utah	6
7	Utah	42.0		19.5	Arkansas	7
8	Mississippi	40.6		18.6	Tennessee	8
9	Louisiana	40.1		18.3	Mississippi	9
10	Missouri	39.4		18.1	Indiana	10
11	Kansas	39.0		17.8	Texas	11
12	Tennessee	38.9		17.8	West Virginia	12
13	Indiana	38.6		17.7	Louisiana	13
14	Iowa	38.3		17.3	Michigan	14
15	Texas	38.2		17.1	Iowa	15
16	Montana	37.2		16.5	Kansas	16
17	Oregon	37.2		15.3	Oregon	17
18	Maine	36.6		15.1	Georgia	18
19	Maryland	35.5		14.7	Ohio	19
20	Vermont	35.2		14.5	South Dakota	20
21	Michigan	35.1		14.1	Delaware	21
22	North Dakota	35.0		14.0	Maine	22
23	South Dakota	34.0		14.0	Nebraska	23
24	Georgia	33.8		13.7	Idaho	24
25	Nebraska	32.9		13.7	Virginia	25
26	California	32.8		13.6	California	26
27	Wyoming	32.5		13.2	Wyoming	27
28	Virginia	32.4		13.1	Montana	28
29	Idaho	32.3		13.0	Vermont	29
30	Ohio	31.4		12.9	Maryland	30
31	Alaska	31.1		12.1	Pennsylvania	31
32	Delaware	31.1		11.3	Minnesota	32
33	Wisconsin	30.5		11.3	North Dakota	33
34	Minnesota	29.9		11.1	Illinois	34
35	Florida	29.3		11.0	Florida	35
36	Illinois	28.4		11.0	Wisconsin	36
37	New Hampshire	28.3		9.2	Massachusetts	37
38	Pennsylvania	27.3		9.1	Rhode Island	38
39	Hawaii	24.2		9.0	Alaska	39
40	Massachusetts	24.1		9.0	New Hampshire	40
41	Rhode Island	23.5		8.1	Hawaii	41
42	New Jersey	22.9		8.1	New Jersey	42
43	New York	22.7		7.7	New York	43
44	Connecticut	20.6		7.4	Connecticut	44
45	District of Columbia	19.2		6.3	District of Columbia	45

Under 18 Years   18-19 Years   Under 20 Years

Graph 11. As reported by 44 states and the District of Columbia, 1969.

AGE FOR MARRIAGE

In most states, marriage is prohibited before a certain age. The most common age for permitting marriage with consent of the parents or guardians is sixteen for girls and eighteen for boys. States also have laws allowing people to marry without consent when they have reached certain ages, usually eighteen for girls and twenty-one for boys.

Teenage marriages are more common in certain sections of our country. In general, a larger percentage of people marry in their teens if they live in southern states. Graph 11 summarizes the percentages of those in their teens marrying in various states in 1969. For example, of all those marrying in Kentucky, 47 percent of the brides and 25 percent of the grooms were in their teens. In contrast, in Connecticut, only 20 percent of the brides and 7 percent of the grooms were in their teens.

The general pattern seems to be that those states having a higher than average percentage of teenage marriages have a relatively low minimum age for marriage, at least for one partner. When states revise their minimum age either up or down, the percentage of teenage marriages goes up or down accordingly. In Kentucky, the minimum age was lowered for each sex in 1967, and the number of teenage marriages increased 45 percent during the next year. In Idaho, the legal minimum age was raised in 1967 and a three-day waiting period instituted; teenage marriages decreased 60 percent within two years.

In 1972, the passage of the Twenty-sixth Amendment to the United States Constitution, giving the right-to-vote to people of eighteen years and older, will doubtless result in the revision of some marriage laws. The most likely revision will be to lower the minimum age for both men and women to eighteen without parental consent. If this should happen, then there probably will be an increase in teenage marriages in those states changing the law. Many states have already revised their marriage laws to agree with the new amendment. Social conditions also affect the percentage of teenage marriages. Economic recession may make it impossible for young people to marry, although the law says they can. Since 1969, a smaller percentage of teenage girls have married than in the early 1960s.

MARRIAGE OF RELATIVES

All states prohibit marriage between close relatives, but the laws differ on the degree of relationship allowed or prohibited. Brothers and sisters, fathers and daughters, mothers and sons, grandfathers and granddaughters, or grandmothers and grandsons cannot legally marry in any state. About half of the states prohibit the marriage of first cousins and of half-brothers and half-sisters. Only six states prohibit the marriage of second cousins. Many states that prohibit the marriage of first cousins recognize this marriage if they marry in another state where first-cousin marriage is legal.

Many states have laws prohibiting *marriages of affinity*—that is, marriages of those who are related, not by blood, but by marriage. The most common of these laws prohibit stepparents from marrying stepchildren. Some states prohibit the marriage of parents-in-law to sons-in-law and daughters-in-law, and eighteen states say that a man or woman may not marry the granddaughter-in-law or grandson-in-law. Some states go so far as to say that a man may not marry his former wife's grandmother.

Many of the regulations on marriages of affinity seem to have no reasonable basis. There is no more valid reason that a man should not marry his granddaughter-in-law or his former wife's grandmother than that he should not marry any other woman who is much older or much younger than he. Such laws were probably formulated by people who failed to see the difference between relationships based on affinity and relationships of consanguinity.

Consanguineous marriages are those of people who are related by blood. Laws against such marriages have a logical basis, for it is a sound biological fact that close blood relatives are more apt to carry the same genetic defects. If first cousins marry, whatever biological defects they carry have a double chance of being passed on to their children. If an individual marries someone unrelated, there is less chance of a combination of identical hereditary defects.

If they could be certain that both were free from all biological defects, the marriage of first cousins might be a good idea. Among thoroughbred animals, close relatives are often mated to produce an even better strain. However, people can never be entirely sure of all the elements present in the germ plasm; thus, in general, it is better that society prohibit the marriage of close blood relatives.

INTERRACIAL MARRIAGES

At one time, forty states had laws prohibiting interracial marriages. Sixteen states still had such laws in 1967 when the United States Supreme Court ruled unanimously that laws prohibiting marriages between whites and nonwhites are unconstitutional. In California, the State Supreme Court had ruled a law against interracial marriages unconstitutional in 1948. After that year, the most common interracial marriage in California was between black men and white women, and between white men and Japanese and Chinese women.

Viewed on a percentage basis, whites and blacks tend to marry within their own race more than any other racial groups in the United States. American Indians, Japanese, and Chinese marry outside their races much more than whites and blacks. This may be because in numbers they are a small minority; there is more opportunity to marry outside their own groups than within.

Nevertheless, the majority of people tend to marry someone like themselves rather than someone different. This means that individuals are inclined to marry someone of similar education, hobbies and interests, family backgrounds, and someone of their own race.

VOID AND VOIDABLE MARRIAGES

After couples have gone through the formalities of getting married, they may find that they are really not married, because there were legal reasons why the marriage could not take place; therefore, it is void. If either party is married and has not secured a divorce, there cannot be a legal second marriage until the first is dissolved. A second marriage of this type would be void from the beginning, even though the couple may have had a license, a church wedding, and all other formalities of a wedding.

Some marriages prohibited by law stand as legal unless they are declared void by legal action; these are called *voidable* marriages. The legal action taken is called *annulment.* Annulment which differs from divorce in that it operates on the assumption that no valid marriage existed. Property is returned to each individual, and neither is entitled to support or alimony. If there are children, they are considered illegitimate unless state law grants legitimacy to children of annulled marriages.

The grounds recognized in various states for annulling marriages are: being below the legal age, insanity or lack of understanding, force or fraud, bigamy, and impotence. The most common reason given is that one spouse feels the other used fraud in getting married; that is, he or she lied about some circumstances in his or her background. Although bigamy makes it legally impossible to get married (it is a void marriage and a punishable offense), still a charge of bigamy is the second most common reason given for an annulment. There is confusion in the law about whether or not one is married, and people may want to clear up the confusion through legal action even though the legal action may not be necessary if bigamy exists.

Lack of mental or physical capacity is also reason for annulment. The man or woman who cannot complete the sex act is considered impotent, and impotence is an accepted reason for annulling a marriage.

GETTING MARRIED

When the time comes for marriage, people living in states requiring a venereal disease test must first meet that requirement. The examination is good for a period of from ten to forty days, the time varying in different states. If the person does not marry within the specified time, it is necessary to have the test repeated.

After passing the venereal disease test, the couple applies for a marriage license. All states now require that people have a license before

E-Z WEDDING CHAPEL

LAKE TAHOE

COMPLETE WEDDING ARRANGEMENTS
COLOR PHOTOS AND CORSAGES AVAILABLE

OPEN 24 HOURS

NO BLOOD TEST — NO WAITING

COME AS YOU ARE

MOST CREDIT CARDS HONORED

PHONE: **702 871-1120**

Nevada is known for its easy divorce laws. Nevada also extends a helping hand to couples who wish to be wed quickly.

they can marry. However, states usually do not enforce regulations for religious groups that have rules that conflict with those of the state.

After a couple gets a blood test, a waiting period of a few days is necessary in most states before the license can be issued. If you check Table 9, you can learn the regulation on this point in your state.

Before the waiting-period laws were passed, a great many hasty, impulsive, and ill-advised marriages took place. People could decide suddenly that they wanted to marry, hurry to a justice of the peace, and marry. Authorities believe that many potentially unhappy marriages can be prevented if people are forced to hesitate a little before marrying.

A study of couples who applied for marriage licenses in one Wisconsin county found that many couples did not return for the license at the end of the waiting period. Those who did not come back were found to have characteristics that would put them in the category most likely to fail in marriage. That is, they were marrying in haste, pregnancy was involved, or they were trying to evade legal obstacles to marriage in some other state.

Some couples go out of state to avoid the regulations on marriage in their home state. Many Californians, for example, go to Nevada to marry. Requirements for marriage are lenient in Nevada in that there is no waiting period or blood test required. A study of divorce in California shows that if couples divorce, the duration from the wedding to the separation is much shorter among couples who go out of state to be married.

THE MARRIAGE OFFICIANT

Although many different people are qualified to perform marriage ceremonies, a majority of couples are married by a minister, a priest, or a rabbi. In most states, marriages may be performed by a justice of the peace, who represents civil authority.

It is not even necessary to have a marriage officiant. In most states, people of any sect believing in a special way of solemnizing a marriage may be married without an officiant. In the ceremony of the Society of Friends (Quaker), after having secured a marriage license, the couple actually marry themselves. The two simply repeat the marriage ceremony in the presence of witnesses. After they have pledged themselves, all of the people present sign the wedding certificate. Such a wedding is legal, although no officiant is present.

PREMARITAL EXAMINATION

Many couples want to have a more complete premarital examination than the tests required by law. A good consultation includes the following: a complete physical examination, attention to diseases or defects that might be hereditary, and an opportunity to secure reliable medical information about sexual intercourse and contraceptives if that is in accord with the beliefs and wishes of the couple.

If a regular premarital counseling service is available in the community, couples should take advantage of it. Some counseling centers have doctors give the physical part of the premarital examination. This detailed physical examination is desirable because it will give couples information on their physical condition, and it may also lead to the correction of any physical ailments that they may have. The examination will tell the couple what their chances are for having children and whether difficulties might be involved in bearing children.

PLANNING THE WEDDING

Formerly, planning the wedding was largely up to the bride and her family. Today, weddings, like family living, are becoming more democratic. It is still the custom for a bride and her family to pay the expenses of the wedding, except that the bridegroom pays for the wedding officiant, for corsages, and for a few other matters.

The average girl looks forward to her wedding and gives it much thought. Whether the wedding will be large and elaborate or simple and inexpensive will depend upon the economic level of the two families and upon the preferences of the couple. The cost and the plans for most weddings ought to be kept within the means of the family and on a standard comparable to that upon which the young people will live.

Ministers, priests, and rabbis can often give good suggestions to those planning a wedding. Many churches have committees of women who make a speciality of assisting with weddings held in the church. They will attend to all the details of the wedding and reception, after consulting with the couple and their families.

Marriages that are planned, and for which the plans are announced ahead of time, have a better chance for success than marriages that result from elopements. Paul Popenoe made a study of 738 elopements and found that 52 percent did not turn out happily. He found that the most common reason for elopement was that the parents opposed the marriage. This was true in almost half of the 738 elopements. The unhappiness was attributable in part to the fact that the parents were opposed to the marriage.

All Christian couples are enjoined to establish a home according to Christian principles. Couples who marry in a religious service have a statistically better chance for success than those who marry in a civil service.

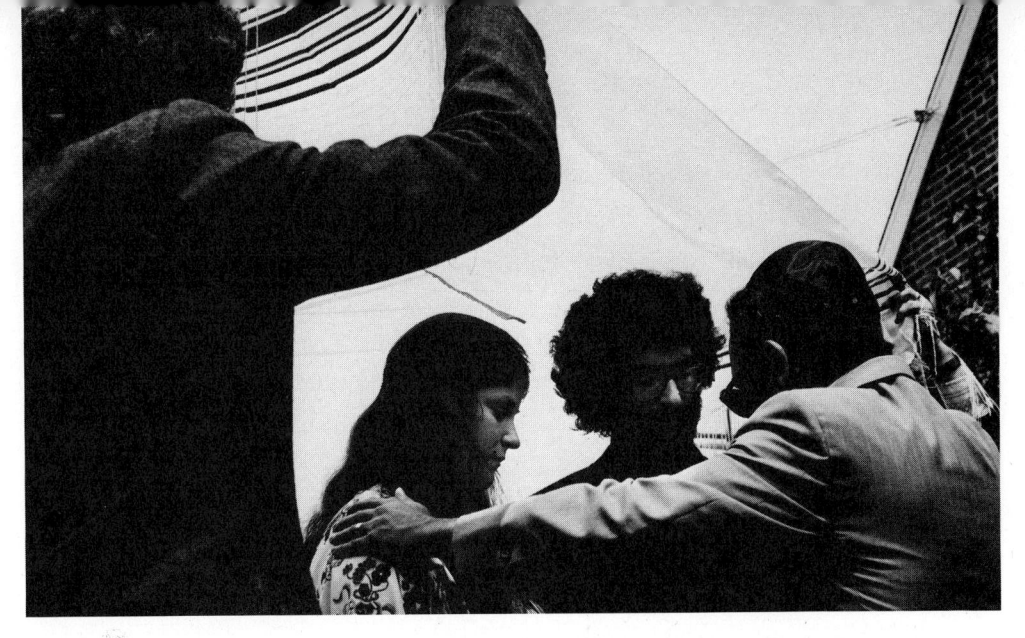

Jews marry beneath a canopy representing the roof of a new family unit. The groom crushes the glass from which the couple has sipped wine to symbolize the uniqueness of each marriage and its frailty unless both cherish one another.

THE HONEYMOON

Most engaged couples look forward to the time when they will be married and begin their honeymoon, whether the honeymoon is to be a journey or simply moving into their own home. The custom of having a honeymoon goes back into a dim past and has a sound basis. It is a good thing for a newly married couple to go away where they can start their married life alone, away from members of either family. Today, the custom of going away for an extended honeymoon of weeks or months is less prevalent than it was in former years. Many couples find it easier to plan for a few days or a weekend.

Whatever the plans, a few principles might be suggested as a guide. First, the honeymoon should not be so expensive that the couple will be burdened with debts afterward; it is possible to have a successful honeymoon without spending lavishly. Second, the honeymoon should be free from the rush and hurry of ordinary living. Its purpose is to give the pair a chance to start married life as advantageously as possible. This purpose is defeated if they undertake such a strenuous travel schedule that they become tired and tense. Third, wherever the honeymoon is spent, it should be in a place that provides complete privacy so that they can establish early the habit of affectionate understanding in their association together, without self-consciousness. Most people prefer to leave all family members and friends out of honeymoon plans. Fourth, if they go away, the couple should go where they can enjoy social and recreational activities that are of mutual interest. If one loves the great out-of-doors while the other prefers the city, they must find a compromise suitable to both.

QUESTIONS FOR REVIEW

1. What is the most common form of marriage in the world today?
2. How do common-law marriages differ from other marriages? Why do most people go through the formalities of getting married?
3. Give reasons why states pass laws regulating marriage. Why do laws differ?
4. Is the percentage of teenage marriages about the same in all states? Explain.
5. How will the passage of the Twenty-sixth Amendment affect the number of teenage marriages? The revision of marriage requirements?
6. What is the most common age at which young people may marry with parental consent? Without consent? What is the legal age in your state?
7. Are there any biological reasons why marriages of affinity should not take place? Consanguineous marriages? Discuss.
8. Are interracial marriages legal in your state? What racial groups tend to marry outside their race most frequently?
9. What is the difference between void and voidable marriages? Give an example of each. What are some of the reasons given for declaring a marriage void?
10. How does annulment differ from divorce?
11. Give the usual steps that one must take to meet the legal requirements for marriage. What are the exact regulations in your state?
12. Cite evidence to show that it is good to require a waiting period between the application for a marriage license and the marriage ceremony.
13. Is it necessary to have a marriage officiant? Why, or why not?
14. What is the purpose of the premarital examination?
15. Do elopements turn out as happily as other marriages?

ACTIVITIES AND PROJECTS

1. (Debate.) *Resolved:* That all applicants for marriage licenses be required to pass tests to determine mental competence.
2. What is the law in your state concerning marriages of relatives by consanguinity and affinity? Consult your county clerk, and report to the class.
3. Is there a premarital counseling service available in your community? If so, report to the class on the type of counseling given.
4. Ask a minister, priest, or rabbi to come to the class and give a talk on the different types of marriage ceremonies performed by different denominations and faiths.
5. If different nationalities are represented in your class, have as many as possible give reports on marriage and wedding customs.

WORDS AND CONCEPTS

affinity
alimony
annulment
common-law marriage
consanguinity
elopement
honeymoon
idiots
illegitimate
imbeciles
impotence
insane
justice of the peace
monogamy
officiant
prevalent
void
voidable

SUGGESTED READINGS FOR THE UNIT

Black, Algernon D., *If I Marry Outside My Religion*. New York: Public Affairs Pamphlet No. 204A.

Bossard, James H. S., and Eleanor Stoker Boll, *One Marriage, Two Faiths*. 1957. New York: The Ronald Press Company.

Bowman, Henry A., *Marriage for Moderns*. 1974. New York: McGraw-Hill Book Company.

Burchinal, Lee G., "Trends and Prospects for Young Marriages in the United States," *Journal of Marriage and the Family*. Vol. 27, No. 2 (May 1965). Pp. 243–254.

Duvall, Evelyn M., *Love and the Facts of Life*. 1963. New York: Association Press.

Fromme, A., *The Ability to Love*. New York: Farrar, Straus, & Giroux, Inc.

Furlong, Robert E., "Youthful Marriage and Parenthood: A Threat to Family Stability," *The Hastings Law Journal*. Vol. 19, No. 1 (November 1967). Pp. 105–145.

Gordon, Albert I., *Intermarriage: Interfaith, Interracial, Interethnic*. 1964. Boston: Beacon Press.

Journal of Marriage and the Family. Vol. 27, No. 2 (May 1965). Whole issue on teenagers and teen marriages.

Landis, Judson T., and Mary G. Landis, *Building a Successful Marriage*, Fifth Edition. 1973. Englewood Cliffs, N. J.: Prentice-Hall, Inc. Chs. 8–10, 12–15.

―――, "High School Student Marriages, School Policy, and Family Life Education in California," *Journal of Marriage and the Family*. Vol. 27, No. 2 (May 1965). Pp. 271–276.

Mayer, John E., *Jewish-Gentile Courtships*. 1961. New York: Free Press of Glencoe.

Peterson, Eleanor M., *Successful Living*. 1968. Boston: Allyn and Bacon, Inc. Chaps. 18–21.

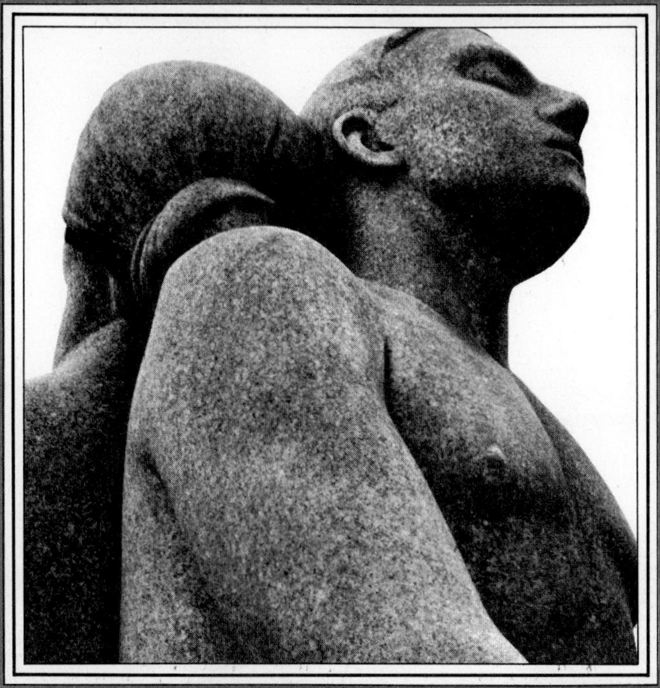

part four

WHEN YOU MARRY

Marriage hath in it less of beauty,
but more of safety
than the single life;
it hath more care, but less danger;
it is more merry, and more sad;
is fuller of sorrows, and fuller of joys;
it lies under more burdens,
but is supported by all the strengths
of love and charity,
and those burdens are delightful.

Jeremy Taylor: Twenty-seven Sermons, XVII, 1651

17 What It Means to Be Married

After studying this chapter, you will be able to

1. Give a realistic picture of marital happiness, based on statistics.
2. List the seven chief areas in which married couples must reach workable agreements; tell which areas take the longest time for adjustment and which the least.
3. Discuss the meaning of the statement, "A happy marriage is an accomplishment."
4. Define the three chief ways of adjusting in marriage.
5. Describe the relationship between length of time to adjust in marriage and marital happiness.

Short stories and movies often end with the final kiss at the wedding and the happy send-off as the newly married couple leave for a honeymoon. We close the book or go home from the movie thinking that the story had the right ending. The hero and heroine are married; now they will live happily ever after. But is that really the end?

In real life, couples who marry find the wedding a beginning, not an ending. If we read the daily papers, we will see reports of divorce and desertion, and even stories of murder arising from marital unhappiness.

The romantic concept of love would lead people to believe that once they marry they are on the threshold of happiness, and that all their problems are over. On the other hand, the newspaper stories of marital disaster might cause people to think that there are few, if any, happy marriages. The truth about marriage is to be found somewhere between these extremes.

MOST MARRIAGES ARE HAPPY

In spite of the publicity given to the failures, the unhappy marriages are still in the minority. It is not easy to measure happiness, but psychologists and sociologists who have studied marriage agree that of the marriages that do not end in divorce or separation, about 65 to 75 percent are happy or very happy.

In one study, Lewis M. Terman asked 792 married people whether they would marry the same person again. Over 80 percent said that they would.

In a Purdue University Opinion Panel, high school students in all parts of the United States were asked to rate their parents' marriages on a happiness scale. Seventy-three percent rated their parents' marriages as happy, 16 percent as neither happy nor unhappy, and 9 percent as unhappy or divorced. In 1967, over three thousand college students in eighteen different colleges rated the happiness of their parents' marriages on a similar scale. Sixty-six percent rated their parents' marriages as happy or very happy, 23 percent as average, and 11 percent as unhappy or very unhappy.

All of these figures show that the spectacularly unhappy marriages that get publicity are not truly representative. It is news when the marriage of a prominent couple breaks up. But it is not sensational, and therefore gets little attention that such a large proportion of the married people are happy or very happy.

BUT ALL MARRIAGES REQUIRE ADJUSTMENT

People have to work at understanding others to be successful in relationships before they marry. Becoming skilled in relationships is one of the major tasks of the growing-up years. As we mature, we learn, sometimes the hard way, that we have to change and adjust if we wish to be liked, but many of us think it will be different when we marry. We would like to think that then it would no longer be necessary to work at keeping relationships and understandings in good order, that they come as a natural result of love. But people who go on that assumption are likely to have to settle for a lower level of marital happiness than are couples more realistic about the challenges of living together and cooperating in all areas of life.

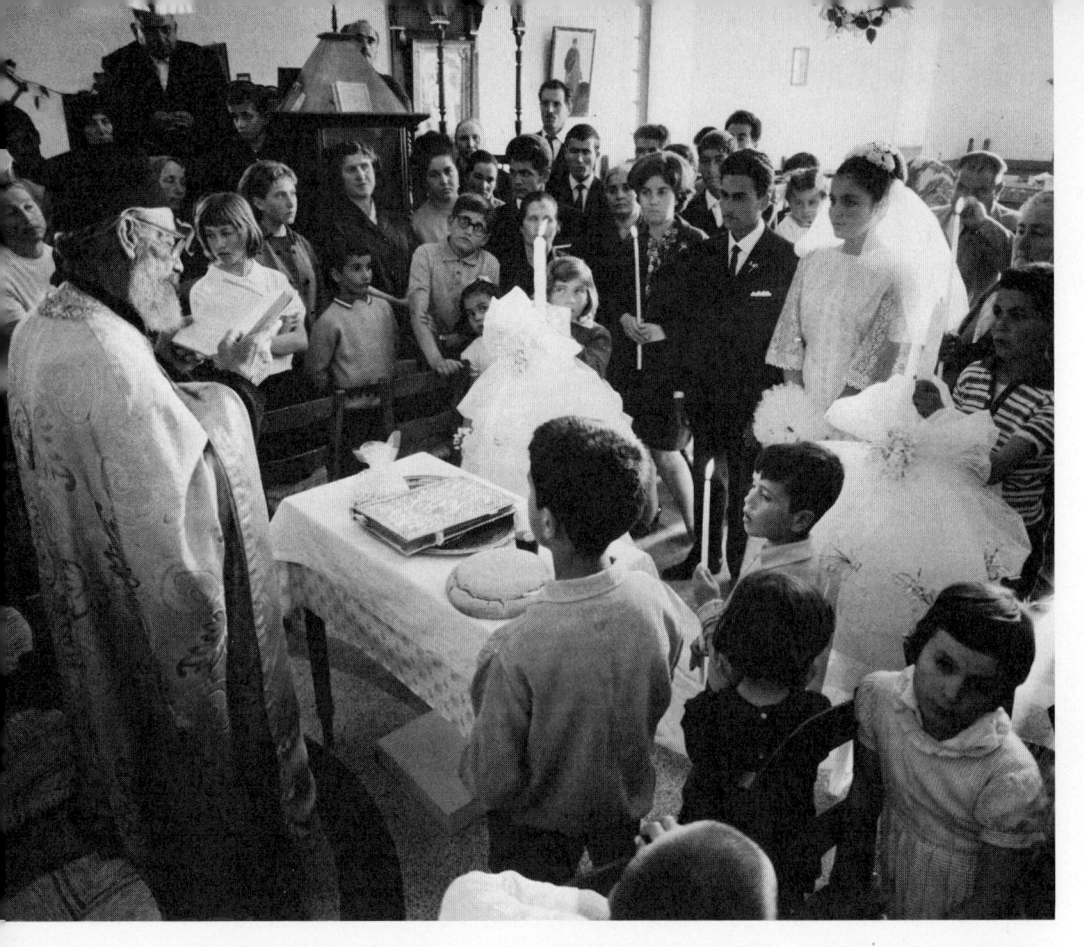

It takes years to build a good marriage. The wedding ceremony is only the beginning.

During the engagement period, the couple is inclined to emphasize the points on which they agree. They enjoy discovering their mutual likes; and if they discover points upon which they disagree, these points can be ignored or dismissed as unimportant. After the couple marries and the honeymoon is over, they gradually settle down to the everyday business of living. As time passes, they become aware of their points of disagreement.

True, some points of disagreement are not important. If one likes seafood and the other hates it, the problem is not very serious unless one tries to impose personal preferences upon the other. Many differences in tastes, attitudes, or feelings require only minor adjustment. If both people are fairly reasonable, they will hardly be conscious that they have adjusted. But there are a few major areas in which married people must work together. They must either agree or they must work to adjust their differences if they are to live happily together. They cannot ignore or bypass such differences.

AREAS REQUIRING ADJUSTABILITY

The economic side of life is one of the *seven chief areas* in which married couples must reach workable agreements. A study of a great many marriages has revealed that, sooner or later, problems arise concerning *money.* The couple must arrive at a feasible arrangement, or they can expect this basic, recurrent matter to cause friction. In order to reach a working agreement, both may have to compromise. Rarely do two people agree perfectly about handling money. If they disagree, the question cannot be settled by one member of the pair completely surrendering his or her approach in favor of the other. That might appear to be a quick and simple solution, but it is usually unworkable. Neither can they ignore differences about the use of money, because it is a practical matter that is bound to arise over and over in daily life.

The other main areas upon which couples must reach agreement are *in-law relationships, sex relationships, social activities and recreation, associating with friends, religious life,* and eventually, in most marriages, *training and disciplining children.*

The couples who are happy have met the problems in these areas. Their marriages are successful because they have accepted the task of adjusting to each other's viewpoints. They have arrived at working arrangements. In later chapters, we shall discuss the different areas further and attempt to point out ways in which couples solve their problems.

ADJUSTMENT TAKES TIME

People who have been happily married for enough years to be qualified to speak of what makes a marriage successful, have given some interesting information about their experiences in making the adjustments required in marriage.

More than four hundred couples supplied us with information anonymously about the areas that caused them the most trouble. One of the most interesting things about their responses was the high rate of agreement on the fact that it took definite lengths of time to reach working arrangements in the different areas of living.

These couples had been married an average of twenty years. Almost without exception, they had met difficulties in at least one of the seven areas. Many married couples, when they first meet problems, are disillusioned and conclude that they are unhappily married and might as well get a divorce and try again with someone else. The 409 couples who responded in our study had all remained married. Most of them had worked out their problems so that after a while they were happier than the average in their marriages. The following outline summarizes what they said about the length of time it took to reach working agreements in the different areas.

1. Husbands and wives agreed it had taken longer to achieve harmony in sexual relationship than in any other area. Approximately half of the couples said that they had had no problems from the beginning. With the exception of 12 percent, the remainder overcame their difficulties during the first year or within an average of six years.
2. Husbands and wives agreed that the second most difficult adjustments were in connection with spending the family income. Slightly more than one-half of the couples said that they had never had any problems here, while the remainder took months or years or had never been able to agree very well. The average time required to reach a workable agreement was seven years if they had not agreed satisfactorily from the beginning.
3. Two out of three couples said that they had had no problems from the beginning in social activities and recreation. There were, however, more who had never arrived at real agreement about social activities than there were in any other area. It had taken the couples an average of six years to reach a good understanding if there had not been agreement from the beginning. The wives were more apt to be conscious of a failure to adjust to differences in this area. Husbands often were not aware of differences.

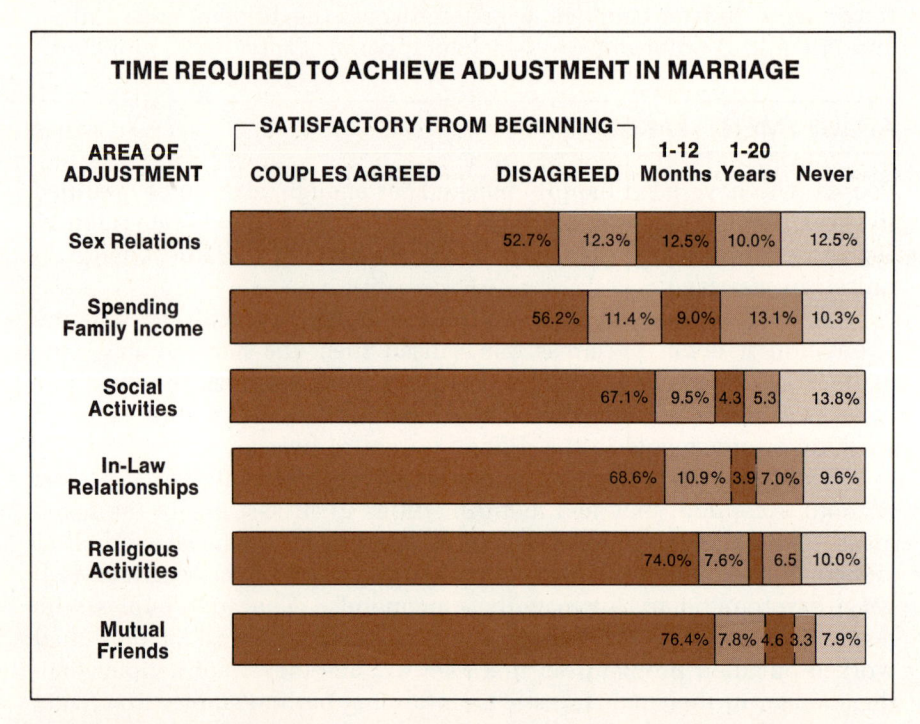

TIME REQUIRED TO ACHIEVE ADJUSTMENT IN MARRIAGE

AREA OF ADJUSTMENT	SATISFACTORY FROM BEGINNING — COUPLES AGREED	DISAGREED	1-12 Months	1-20 Years	Never
Sex Relations	52.7%	12.3%	12.5%	10.0%	12.5%
Spending Family Income	56.2%	11.4%	9.0%	13.1%	10.3%
Social Activities	67.1%	9.5%	4.3	5.3	13.8%
In-Law Relationships	68.6%	10.9%	3.9	7.0%	9.6%
Religious Activities	74.0%	7.6%		6.5	10.0%
Mutual Friends	76.4%	7.8%	4.6	3.3	7.9%

Graph 12. Percentage of 818 spouses reporting periods of time required to achieve adjustment in six areas.

4. Approximately two out of three reported a good understanding from the beginning about relations with the in-laws. Those who had trouble took an average of eight and one-half years to arrive at the place where they understood each other and had a good working arrangement. Again, the wives were apt to feel more keenly the difficulties arising from unsatisfactory in-law relationships.
5. The couples had the least difficulty in agreeing on religion and on associating with friends. Approximately three out of four couples said that they had agreed satisfactorily from the beginning in both of these areas. Again the wives were more likely to be dissatisfied. Graph 12 summarizes this study.

WE NEED TO BE REALISTIC

The chief thing to be learned from the studies of the experiences of successfully married couples is that a happy marriage is never presented as a gift. A happy marriage is an *accomplishment.* It is evidence that two people have cooperated, each giving up some personal preferences and attitudes in favor of mutual understanding and affection.

All couples believe they are in love at the time of marriage, but some face reality and learn to live together in the early years of marriage while others resist accepting and coping with the demands of married living. The latter may find constant difficulty in adjusting to married life.

We bring into marriage the basic habits and personalities that we developed over a period of years; these do not change with the wedding. The person who is habitually considerate will be the same in marriage. Similarly, the one who has grown up feeling that his or her own wants are more important than anything else, and who is apt to sulk or display temper when crossed, will be no different in marriage. The fact that one may be very much in love with the other will not change personality patterns or habits of behavior.

So, fundamentally, people do not change much after marriage. The most disillusioned person is one who thinks, "Of course, I don't like that trait, but I think my spouse will change after we marry!" People who go into marriage with the idea of reforming the mate, or who expect to make changes in the mate's personality are headed for disillusionment.

During courtship, people may appear to alter their personality or may promise to change, but most people will not continue to date those who try to transform them. We enjoy being with those who make us feel appreciated, and we feel uncomfortable with those who are critical. In marriage, people are no different. The one who constantly tries to reform the other is doing damage to the ego of the other and will be more likely to arouse stubborn determination not to change. Any changes that occur in a personality take place only over a long period of time. People gradually grow and reach greater maturity if they can work together patiently for years.

CHIEF TYPES OF ADJUSTMENT

Although personality traits cannot be expected to change with a wedding, people do adjust to each other in a number of ways. Evidence of this is the large percentage of marriages that are successful and happy. The happiest type of adjustment is to be found in marriages in which the couple has been able to understand and sympathize with each other's viewpoints on most important matters. This type of adjustment we may call *agreement.*

Of course, in some marriages, the two individuals are in good agreement on almost everything from the beginning. However, these marriages are the exception. People seldom just happen to agree satisfactorily on everything. Our study of 409 couples showed that the majority agree in some of the seven areas, but find that in other areas they must work to create a good relationship. The satisfactory agreement comes about because they have been adjustable in their attitudes. They have worked at understanding, have analyzed their personal attitudes, and have been willing to change individual viewpoints in some respects. Thus, without any serious sacrifice, they have been able to agree.

Probably the most common adjustment in marriage is a *compromise.* In most marriages, at least one of the important areas of living will require a serious adjustment that can only be a compromise for both. The couple may find that mostly they agree easily; but in some areas, one or the other, more often both, must make serious concessions. Such a compromise may be satisfactory or quite unsatisfactory. If the adjustment is unsatisfactory for both in one or two areas, the marriage may still be successful because of other good agreements. We shall illustrate this form of adjustment.

Mr. and Mrs. Thomas have been married for twenty-five years. Each rates their marriage as happy. Mr. Thomas makes a good income. They have four children. The youngest is still at home and attending high school. The other three have finished high school and are now in college or working. The Thomases always agreed on how to spend money. They are both Protestant and enjoy going to church together. They consider their sex life satisfactory. They like the same type of social activities, recreation, and friends. But they have always had differences over their in-laws.

Mrs. Thomas was very attached to her family and wanted to live in the same town with them. Mr. Thomas felt that her family was always trying to interfere, telling them what to do with their money and how to rear their children. He objected to the many dinners with his wife's family.

WHAT IT MEANS TO BE MARRIED

"Are you sure we're both going on the same vacation?"

Mr. Thomas's family lived about fifteen miles from Mrs. Thomas's hometown. His family was not clannish, did not care to have family functions, and were not very close. Mrs. Thomas liked her husband's family fairly well, but never had much to do with them. Throughout the early part of their marriage, there was frequent conflict over her family, his in-laws.

After ten years of marriage they moved to another state approximately five hundred miles away. For the last fifteen years, Mr. and Mrs. Thomas have had little to do with either family. They visit them seldom and stay for only a short time. This situation is not satisfactory for Mrs. Thomas. She misses her family and finds it hard being away from them. Mr. Thomas has never had any complaint since they moved away. He feels that the adjustment is satisfactory and that suitable "agreement" has been reached.

This case might seem an extreme one, but the solution is a very common type of adjustment. That is, when two people do not find themselves in agreement, they must work out some kind of compromise in order to have a fairly workable arrangement. In this case, Mr. Thomas did little compromising, because his relation to his family was not very close. The sacrifice was largely Mrs. Thomas's, and, in general, she felt it was worthwhile because her adjustment removed a point of friction. In any compromise, the sacrifice can hardly be divided evenly.

In some marriages, the two partners are on some points unable to adjust to differences. They brace themselves in opposition. They simply cannot agree, and they settle into a state of conflict.

If their disagreement happens in only one division of life, as it did with the Thomases, it is possible for them to keep the conflict at a minimum. Still the happiness of the marriage will be somewhat marred. Our studies of large numbers of marriages show that if conflicts exist in more than two chief areas of life, the marriage is average in happiness or actually unhappy.

In few such marriages do the partners continue to live together. The case we just described started out with one conflict that continued for the first ten years. However, the couple finally settled their conflict by a compromise. If they had disagreed in more than one such important matter, it would have been more difficult for them to have a happy marriage. The fact that they had made good adjustments in six of the seven important areas allowed them to have a happy marriage, although one relationship remained quite unsatisfactory to one of them.

A happy marriage is not a wedding present from heaven. Rather, it is evidence of mutual hard work to iron out rough spots amicably. In what area do you think you might have difficulty in making adjustments?

TABLING DIFFERENCES

If we are realistic, we recognize that certain differences between husbands and wives can never be settled satisfactorily. For the sake of the happiness of the two individuals and the general happiness of the home, it will be necessary for married couples to "table" some of their differences. That is, no amount of discussion, quarreling, or conflict will solve some of the opposing viewpoints. They cannot discuss or quarrel indefinitely, and, therefore, they recognize that these differences may continue to exist as long as they live together. They conclude that some differences are not of great importance when viewed in comparison to the whole of their married life. It must be said here that couples can table their differences only if there are *not too many*. On one or two matters, for the sake of their marriage and their happiness, they can learn to step carefully and avoid confrontations. If, however, there are several important areas of living in which they differ, most couples cannot cope, and the marriage fails.

An agreement to disagree is often seen among older couples who have long been married. One such couple had been married for fifty years. During severe weather a neighbor offered to do their grocery shopping. As the seventy-five-year-old wife gave the list to the neighbor, she explained that it called for both rye bread and whole wheat bread. "The whole wheat is for me. The rye is for Henry. Henry believes that rye bread is just as nutritious as whole wheat. I disagree. Therefore, we buy both. Henry eats the rye. I eat the whole wheat."

Such differences are, of course, trivial and require no serious adjustment. They can easily be tabled. Yet some couples battle over even such minor points, each trying to force the other to come to his way of thinking. The happy couples learn to have a sense of proportion about which are important matters and which are not. They agree to disagree on minor matters, then work to adjust on fundamental points.

TIME TO ADJUST AND HAPPINESS IN MARRIAGE

Our study of the 409 married couples has shown that the sooner couples adjust to their differences on important matters, the more likely they are to have happiness. Those who have to struggle with their differences for months or years are not as likely to have a happy marriage. It is important to recognize differences and to work at resolving them early. But it is more important to decide before marriage whether or not disruptive differences exist. If there is disagreement on too many of the areas listed on page 237, the marriage probably should not be undertaken.

Young people should recognize that marriage is new to both of them, that naturally they will encounter some problems as they attempt to live together. To think otherwise would be just as ridiculous as to

MARITAL ADJUSTMENT AND HAPPINESS

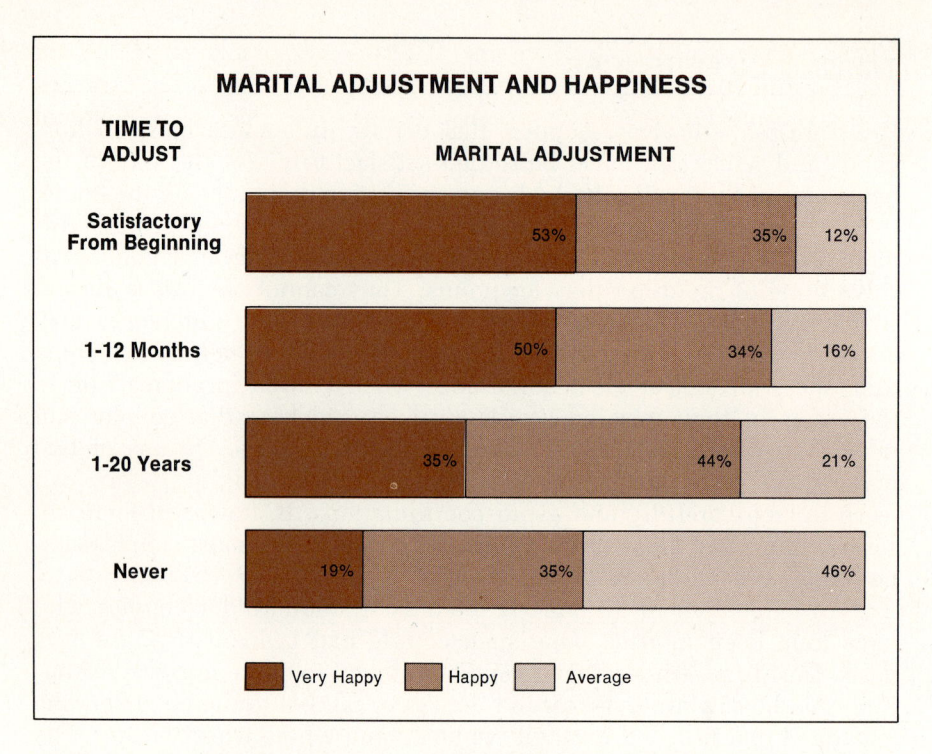

TIME TO ADJUST	MARITAL ADJUSTMENT (Very Happy / Happy / Average)
Satisfactory From Beginning	53% / 35% / 12%
1-12 Months	50% / 34% / 16%
1-20 Years	35% / 44% / 21%
Never	19% / 35% / 46%

Graph 13. A study of 409 couples who had been married for some time showed that those couples were happier who worked out their adjustments early in the marriage.

assume that when a person takes a new job, it would not be necessary to work at overcoming a few puzzling problems. With a new job, one expects to have to take a little time at first to learn new techniques and to understand the ways of the new employer and associates. This should not be a discouragement but a challenge. We expect to work at anything that is worth doing, whether it is learning to drive a car, work a drill press, or live happily in the family.

If it were not for the fact that we have been confused by the fantasy of romance, love, and marriage promoted in our society, we would naturally recognize that it takes time to learn to become good husbands and wives. Having been conditioned to think that happiness in marriage is a sort of magic gift presented ready-made at the time of the wedding, some of us are not prepared to accept reality when it comes to adjusting in marriage.

IMPORTANCE OF ADAPTABILITY

Some children find it necessary to move from one community to another and to enter different schools. For some, it is difficult to make new friends. They dread each move and each adjustment. At the other extreme are people who have learned to adjust quite easily. They are pliable and can get along in any group. They have friends of many different types, and yet they seem to get along well with them all.

It will require a longer time for those who are uncompromising, rigid, and unadaptable to work out good relationships in marriage. It is desirable to work at developing adjustability, because life is a continuous process of adapting to new situations. The more adaptable people are, the more likely they are to find happiness in marriage, on the job, and in social life.

CONCLUSIONS

Each couple has a tendency to think that their marriage will be different; but if we could look in upon all the couples who marry each year, we would find that they must go through the same stages of progress in learning to live together.

Some couples learn readily and achieve a happy marriage within a short time. Others struggle along, decide that love has tricked them into an intolerable marriage, and then divorce. All were in love when they married, but not all realized soon enough that happy marriages are the result of cooperation and a realistic acceptance of responsibility for working to build good relationships.

QUESTIONS FOR REVIEW

1. In what ways are people given a confused picture of courtship and marriage?
2. What do studies of marriage happiness reveal? Why may this seem surprising?
3. What are the chief areas in which husbands and wives must learn to get along?
4. What areas seem to take the longest time for adjustment, and which ones take the least time?
5. "A happy marriage is an accomplishment." Discuss.
6. Should we be surprised to learn that it takes time to work out adjustments in marriage? Explain.
7. Why do people resist being changed after marriage?
8. Give three common types of adjustment in marriage.
9. Do you think that the Thomases could have found some better solution for their problem? Explain.
10. Is it possible to have a happy marriage and continue to conflict in several areas of living?

11. Under what circumstances should a couple solve their disagreements by "tabling their differences"?
12. Do you think happiness has been oversold as something attained when we marry?
13. Why is adaptability an important asset in marriage?

ACTIVITIES AND PROJECTS

1. Getting along with friends and getting along in marriage are similar in several ways. Tell of friendships you have that illustrate the three different patterns of adjustment discussed in this chapter.
2. In friendships, can you think of any that finally dissolved because there were too many points of friction, or possibly because one of you had to do too much of the adjusting?
3. Have you noticed that, upon some things, your parents have never agreed? Have they solved the problem by tabling the differences?

SOCIODRAMA

A domestic scene takes place in the early months of marriage in which both the husband and wife are trying to get each other to change certain habits. Frustration results when neither will change. Act this out.

WORDS AND CONCEPTS

accomplishment
adjustability
agreement
confrontation

disillusioned
feasible
pliable
rigid

What About Quarreling?

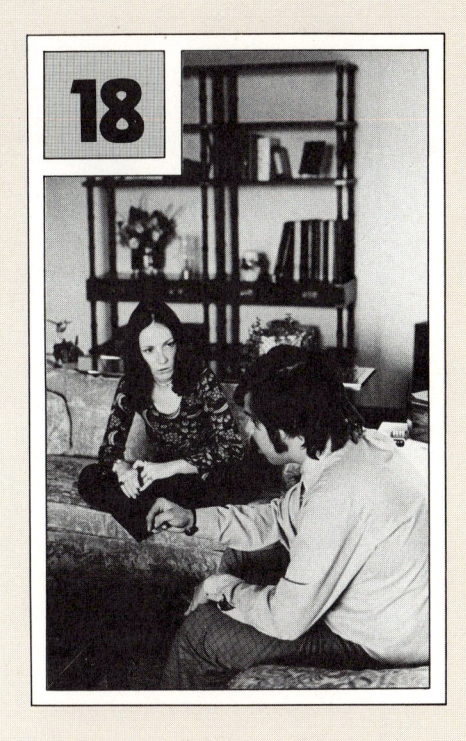

After studying this chapter, you will be able to

1. Point out the differences between quarreling, disagreement, discussion, argument.
2. Indicate what research shows about areas of difference likely to be discovered by couples before marriage, and those likely to be discovered during the first year or later.
3. Discuss quarreling as a pattern of behavior in marriage.
4. List some advantages of the family conference approach to settling differences.

If you have brothers and sisters who are anywhere near your own age, no doubt you have quarreled with them. All that may be in the past—or possibly within the last week or month, you have had some unpleasant or upsetting arguments with a brother or a sister.

If you take time to analyze the reasons behind a quarrel, you will find that some of the quarrels represent serious attempts to establish or define disputed rights. Such a quarrel may settle some points at issue. But often no such basis exists. Some brothers and sisters have just fallen into a habit of bickering and disputing over trifles. With them, it becomes a habitual way of interacting.

Whatever the reasons underlying quarrels, anyone who has had a chance to watch the behavior of young children will concede that quarreling fits into a childish pattern of behavior. "That's mine." "No, it isn't." "He pushed me." "She knocked over my block house." "Leave me alone."

None of it makes much sense; but if you have watched your younger brothers or sisters playing with other children, you have heard such talk, sometimes mingled with crying or scuffling. Parents learn that there is little use in trying to settle childish quarrels with justice, for usually the offenses are quite evenly distributed. Many parents simply separate the children when they seem especially ill-humored; in this way, they can at least bring about temporary peace and quiet.

QUARRELING IN MARRIAGE

Perhaps somewhere there live a husband and wife who have never had a quarrel, but it is safe to say that they have not been married long. Most couples will probably have at least one or two quarrels.

Nevertheless, many couples who have been married several years seldom or never quarrel. Their few quarrels are in the past. They have learned where they must step lightly and where they may be completely open. They have found other, better ways than quarreling for settling differences. Quarreling has no place in the lives of many long-married couples who are happy together.

WHAT IS QUARRELING?

There is a difference between facing a disagreement and quarreling. An open acknowledgment and discussion of differences is not quarreling. Quarreling is usually emotionally charged, often explosive. It tends to include an increasing desire to hurt. The difference between discussion and quarreling is that, *in a good discussion, people attack their problem or their point of disagreement; in a quarrel, they tend to attack each other.* That difference is crucial. Quarrels drive people farther apart, while a frank discussion of differences can serve to bring them nearer. Facing a point of disagreement can create a better understanding of each other's viewpoint.

FUNCTION OF QUARRELING IN EARLY MARRIAGE

In the early months of marriage, most people are cherishing illusions that have little relation to the realities of life. A young wife once said, "We are going to be different from others. We are going to keep our romance alive. We will keep every Friday as an anniversary because it was on a Friday that we had our first date; and we will never quarrel."

WHAT ABOUT QUARRELING?

"Married three weeks this coming Friday."

She had not yet learned that the clock cannot be stopped. People delight in the romance that characterizes the courtship period, and may not yet realize that the depth and security of married love is a different stage of romance; it can be incomparably more satisfying.

Thus, in the early months of marriage when couples are learning to live together, they may look upon a quarrel or even a small disagreement as a major catastrophe. They believe it means that their dreams are shattered—that perhaps they do not love each other. Some of them will go to great lengths to avoid a quarrel. When they discover irritating habits or attitudes in the mate, they suppress their irritation until it has built up to an explosive point.

Then some word or action may set off the explosion, and a quarrel results. Such a quarrel may serve to bring into the open differences that are not hard to resolve. When the blow-up is over, the two may be able to discuss the differences frankly and reach agreement. A happier method would be to discuss differences without first having the quarrel. However, in the early months of married life, people are in the experimental stage of learning to live together, and it takes time to learn to be objective. It is not always easy to discuss problems without becoming emotional. Talking differences over freely is a practice that engaged couples should work to cultivate. If before they marry people have been able to recognize and to face their differences, talk them over calmly, and either make compromises toward agreement or accept without anger or grief the fact that they cannot agree on some matters, it will be much easier for them after marriage. They will already have developed techniques for solving problems without having to quarrel. Because newly married people often hope and try to believe that they have no differences, they may refuse to be objective about those that arise. They try to ignore them until an emotional outburst forces them to face their differences and reckon with them.

DISCOVERING AREAS OF DIFFERENCE

Research has provided the explanation of why a few quarrels may occur early in marriage even among couples who are eventually to be very happy. The research gives insight also into why couples who are unhappy have continuing quarrels as long as they stay together. For a married couple to discover unsuspected differences does come as a shock. Some of the differences or points of disagreement that will be most seriously disruptive, such as over sex and money, are the ones that usually do not show up until after people are married. The shock of discovering that previously unsuspected differences exist is likely to result in emotional clashes. If too many differences come to light and if the couple reacts by quarreling, the marriage will be under severe strain.

In one of our research studies, of 581 married couples, those couples who were having disagreements reported on when they first discovered their differences, whether before the wedding or in some year of their married life. The findings showed that in the most crucial areas of living (child rearing, sexual relations, making and spending the family income, communication, and showing affection) from 6 to 23 percent of the couples were not aware before marriage that they might disagree at all. These are crucial areas of living because they are part of life in which couples *must* come to some working arrangement if they are to live in harmony. Most of the couples tended to discover their differences the first year. This means that early, before they had had time to build good patterns for solving problems together, they had to face seriously conflicting viewpoints or attitudes. Graph 14 on page 251 shows their patterns of becoming aware of differences.

It is probably fortunate that couples do not become aware of all of their differences at one time; they might become so discouraged they would feel their problems were unsolvable. However, a study shows that some of the most serious adjustments do have to be made early, and sometimes several kinds of adjustments at once. The most fortunate couples are those who accomplish the purposes of dating and courtship. They get an accurate assessment of their potential problem areas while they still have a choice about whether or not to marry. If they have enough time before marrying to develop good ways of handling their differences, they can avoid extreme pressure leading to quarrels after they are married.

WHAT ABOUT QUARRELING?

QUARRELING MAY BECOME HABITUAL BEHAVIOR

While quarrels early in marriage may serve to bring differences into the open, people who are working to build a happy marriage should not have to quarrel repeatedly about the same point. If they can analyze the reasons they are emotional about certain matters, they can work toward a solution. They can progress so that in time quarrels will no longer occur. If, however, they simply give expression to their feelings of irritation or anger, then kiss and make up, quickly dropping the subject for fear they may lose their tempers again, they will not solve anything. They may settle into a habit of having quite frequent emotional outbursts and allow quarreling to become the established pattern in their marriage.

AS A TENSION RELIEVER

Those who form the quarreling pattern tend to use quarreling more and more frequently as an outlet for everyday tensions. The spouse who has a job that causes special strain may go home ready to battle over the

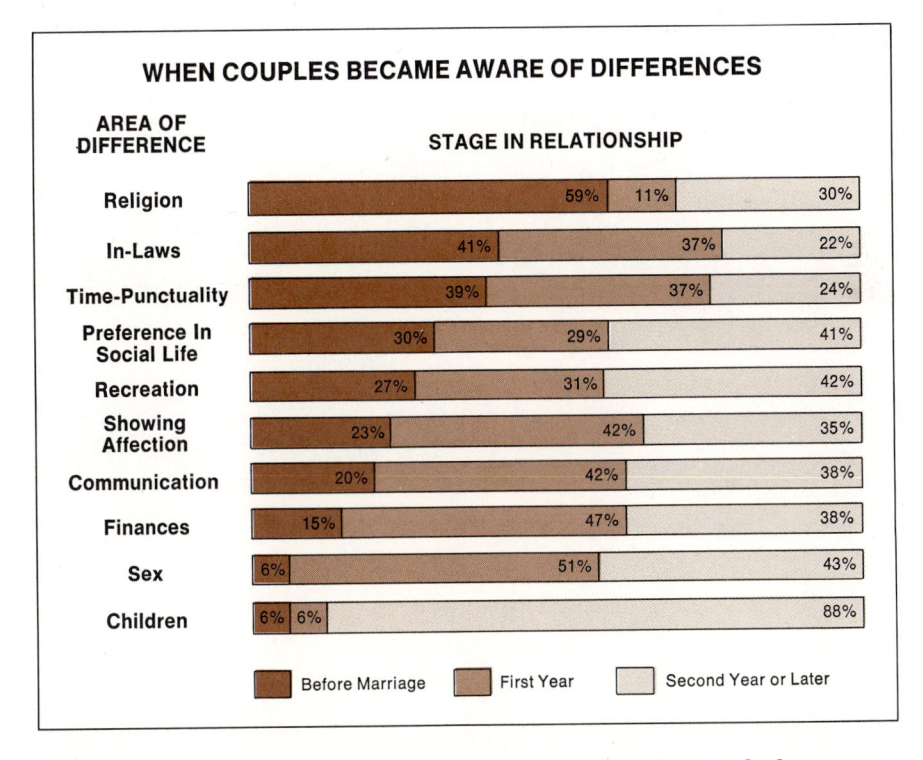

WHEN COUPLES BECAME AWARE OF DIFFERENCES

AREA OF DIFFERENCE	Before Marriage	First Year	Second Year or Later
Religion	59%	11%	30%
In-Laws	41%	37%	22%
Time-Punctuality	39%	37%	24%
Preference In Social Life	30%	29%	41%
Recreation	27%	31%	42%
Showing Affection	23%	42%	35%
Communication	20%	42%	38%
Finances	15%	47%	38%
Sex	6%	51%	43%
Children	6%	6%	88%

Graph 14. Areas of differences and the stage in the relationship when couples became aware of their differences, 581 husbands and wives reporting.

first irritating trifle. All day long self-control was exercised because that is the behavior expected at work, but at home, one may relax control and behave in a childish way.

It is true that the pressures of life would be too much for many of us if we did not have tension relievers. However, other outlets that are more constructive than quarreling are available for this purpose. Any good physical exercise or absorbing creative activity may be useful to those who need relief from emotional pressure.

A sense of humor helps to relieve stress and keeps quarreling at a minimum. Some people find going to a movie, taking a long walk, reading, or listening to music helpful.

Some kinds of disagreements cannot be absolutely resolved, but these are often not important enough to quarrel over. If people can turn their minds to other interests, temporary tensions can be allayed with no harm done.

Taking a walk before a quarrel develops can often relieve tensions and ward off a stormy scene. It can also serve as a release from feelings of regret and hurt that are the results of a quarrel.

CUMULATIVE EFFECT OF QUARRELING

It is worthwhile to make constructive use of quarrels in the early years of marriage, so their occurrence may become less and less frequent. Some quarrels may seem harmless; the couples even seem to enjoy them. Nevertheless, frequent quarrels tend to have a cumulative effect. In each quarrel, things are said that may be hard to forget. If in anger unpleasant truths are told with bitterness, they rankle long after the quarrel is past. In the next quarrel, not only will the new grievances enter into the battle, but the old points that rankle are also likely to come in for their share of attention. The couple may apologize and make peace, but that does not erase the memory of the things that were said. Gradually, their relationship accumulates scars.

Quarrels in marriage are likely to be more damaging than those among friends or acquaintances. This is because married people know one another's weaknesses only too well. It becomes too easy to strike where it will hurt the opponent most—to say things that are most damaging to the mate's ego.

PHYSICAL FACTORS AND QUARRELING

Many mothers have learned that sometimes when small children are quarrelsome little can be accomplished by settling the immediate issue. They know that the child is overtired, hungry, or otherwise not quite at a normal level physically. The same factors affect our dispositions, no matter what our age.

Sometimes, married people bicker over things that are not of any real importance—things that, even if settled one way or another, could not possibly make any permanent difference. Sue may lose her temper at the end of a long day because Jim comes into the kitchen before dinner, gets a drink of milk from the refrigerator, slams the refrigerator door, and stands in the middle of the kitchen to drink the milk. She has to go around him six times on her way back and forth from the stove to the sink. Suddenly, she almost shouts at him, "Can't you possibly stand somewhere else! Do you have to drink that milk this very minute when I am trying to get dinner on?"

If Jim happens to have had a hard day himself, and has come home tired and hungry, he may retort instantly, "Yes, I have to have this milk right now. It's a fine thing if I can't come into my own house once and have a glass of milk—" and so on. Before either knows it, they both feel like exchanging blows. They eat dinner in a sulky silence, both feeling much wronged, misunderstood, and unappreciated.

What was wrong? Really nothing except that they were both tired and hungry, and their particular emotional reactions depend upon their physical well-being. That is true of most of us.

Many couples make the serious mistake of trying to talk over matters that vitally concern their marriage when physically, they are not up to par, with the result that they may do real damage to their relationship. An excellent rule is never to discuss any controversial or emotionally charged questions if either one is ill, overtired, or hungry.

Rather than, "Never let the sun go down on your anger," it is often better to get a good night's sleep. They may find that the anger has faded away, and that what seemed so bad the evening before is good for a laugh. If it is really a serious matter, the time to discuss it is when both are rested and have a little better sense of proportion.

In our study, the 581 couples listed ways in which they reacted to the serious problems or crises in their marriages. They also stated what feelings had been produced by the ways they had reacted. We have grouped these under *positive* or *negative* feelings resulting from behavior under pressure. Study the lists in Table 10 for added insight into effects of quarreling.

THE FAMILY CONFERENCE

One of the best ways to meet differences is to make it a habit to discuss problems that threaten to bring tension and quarreling *before* they build up to the point of an emotional explosion. It is not necessary to meet formally once a week or once a month to talk over problems, although it might be as sensible to do this as it is to have regular policy meetings in other organizations.

Families are like other units in society. Any situation in which two or more people live together requires periodic discussions or conferences in order that the members of the group may live together harmoniously. Students living in dormitories or in other groups meet regularly to discuss matters that concern them. They agree upon general rules for conduct, consider any group expenditures, and formulate plans for improving or changing their living conditions. These are also functions of the family conference.

In marriage, many petty irritations may pile up until these little things appear to be serious handicaps to happiness. Ray Baber called these situations "tremendous trifles." It may be that the husband reads at the table, rattles his coffee cup, or always throws the newspaper on the floor after reading it. "Tremendous trifles" will not become so tremendous and cause explosions if they can be discussed when no one is angry.

One couple decided during their engagement that they would have the family-conference way of settling differences. They were going to live in their hometown, quite close to both families. They knew that it would be easy to have "in-law trouble" because in many ways their two families were very different. By planning ahead to try to talk over

WHAT ABOUT QUARRELING?

Table 10 WAYS IN WHICH COUPLES REACTED TO THEIR DIFFERENCES*

Behavior Resulting in Positive Feelings	Behavior Resulting in Negative Feelings
1. We discuss differences peacefully.	1. We start peaceful discussion, but we get emotional.
2. After discussion, we compromise.	2. I keep differences to myself.
3. After discussion, spouse generally has his (her) way.	3. We argue and quarrel.
4. After discussion, I generally have my way.	4. Spouse brings up problem, but I get emotional.
5. I do something nice for spouse.	5. We avoid any discussion of our differences.
6. I cool off for a time.	6. I bring up problem, but spouse gets emotional.
	7. We do not talk to each other.
	8. I leave the room.
	9. Spouse leaves the room.
	10. I take frustration out on others.
	11. Spouse refuses to have sex relations.
	12. I refuse to have sex relations.
	13. I slam doors.
	14. Spouse slams doors.
	15. I drink when we have differences.
	16. Spouse drinks when we have differences.
	17. Spouse strikes or slaps me.
	18. I strike or slap spouse.
	19. I cry.
	20. Spouse cries.
	21. I get physically ill.
	22. Spouse gets physically ill.

*As reported by 581 husbands and 581 wives.

problems that might arise, this couple remained on good terms with their in-laws and avoided misunderstandings that could have arisen under the circumstances.

Happy families "go into conference" before making any major decision that affects the entire family. Sons and daughters have a right to participate in decisions, and every member needs the happiness and security that comes with being a functioning part of the family organization. Patterns for this must be set by the married pair early, before their lives become more complicated by added members.

Most people tend to be willing to cooperate in carrying out decisions or policies that they have had a part in formulating. Thus, family policies that have been arrived at through open discussion can be carried out more easily than decisions made arbitrarily by one person.

Isn't it better to resolve differences than to have a battle? The discussion pattern between husband and wife can be well established by the time children join the family conference.

Even if not all members agree on the final choices that come out of discussions, families that try to handle problems democratically are most successful. they are using a constructive method to reduce friction and conflict.

In these families, the parents are likely to have met their own differences in positive ways, and early in their relationships had begun to build good patterns of cooperation and understanding.

QUESTIONS FOR REVIEW

1. Define quarrel, disagreement, discussion, argument.
2. How might quarreling serve a good purpose in the early years of marriage?
3. What other ways would be preferable to quarreling, even in the early years of marriage?
4. In what area of relationships are differences likely to be discovered before marriage? In what areas are differences more likely to be discovered during the first year? Two years or more after being married?
5. If couples "kiss and make up" after each quarrel, have they necessarily resolved their difference? Explain.
6. Why do people today seem to need "tension relievers" more than in past generations?

7. Does quarreling relieve tension? Discuss.
8. What effect does a person's physical condition have upon the tendency to quarrel?
9. "Never let the sun go down on your anger." Discuss.
10. What are some advantages of a family conference to settle differences?
11. From your own observations, describe some "tremendous trifles."
12. Discuss the part children may take in a family conference.

ACTIVITIES AND PROJECTS

1. If you have quarreled with someone recently, try to analyze it objectively. How much of it was due to (1) a real difference in viewpoint on an important matter (2) tiredness (3) misunderstanding (4) irritation over something besides the quarrel (5) anything else? Was the effect of the quarrel on your relationship destructive or constructive?

2. Evaluate a family conference (or a similar group) in which you took part. Did anyone show heated emotion? Did you feel that anyone imposed a selfish viewpoint on the rest of the group? Was the outcome of the conference acceptable to everyone? If not, what seemed to be the reason?

3. How do you react to others when you are hungry or tired? Recall an incident in which you recently had difficulty with someone. Was there a physical basis for the difficulty?

SOCIODRAMA

A married couple, Helen and Tom, differ over eating meals out occasionally. Helen frequently suggests that they go to a restaurant for dinner. Tom objects on the basis of expense. How can they reach agreement? Demonstrate two ways of meeting the situation: a quarrel; a conference.

WORDS AND CONCEPTS

allay
arbitrarily
catastrophe
controversial question
cumulative

democratic methods
family conference
rankle
tension reliever
tremendous trifle

19 Sexual Adjustment in Marriage

After studying this chapter, you will be able to

1. Cite what research shows about the degree of agreement in sexual relations as reported by engaged, married, counseling, and divorced people.
2. Discuss the relative importance of sex as part of the total marriage relationship.
3. Analyze the reasons why it is more difficult to arrive at satisfactory sexual adjustment than it is to adjust in some other areas of marriage.
4. List some of the normal problems couples have in sexual adjustment.

In a previous chapter, we quoted our study of the length of time it had taken couples to adjust in various areas of living. The study found that it had taken couples a longer time to work out sexual adjustments than it took in any other area. Other studies of couples coming for marriage counseling support the finding that sexual adjustment may not come soon or easy. Yet couples approaching marriage may think they are in agreement on what their sex life will be.

In our study of four groups of people—engaged couples, happily married couples, couples in marriage counseling, and divorced people—we found the engaged couples to believe themselves in greater agree-

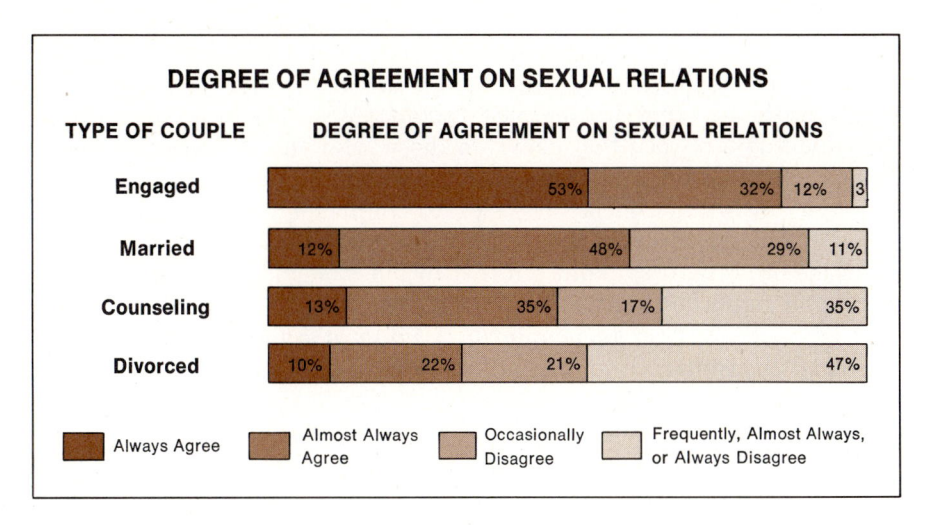

SEXUAL ADJUSTMENT IN MARRIAGE

DEGREE OF AGREEMENT ON SEXUAL RELATIONS

TYPE OF COUPLE	DEGREE OF AGREEMENT ON SEXUAL RELATIONS
Engaged	53% / 32% / 12% / 3
Married	12% / 48% / 29% / 11%
Counseling	13% / 35% / 17% / 35%
Divorced	10% / 22% / 21% / 47%

Legend: Always Agree | Almost Always Agree | Occasionally Disagree | Frequently, Almost Always, or Always Disagree

Graph 15. As reported by 122 engaged couples, 581 married couples, 155 people having marriage counseling, and 164 divorced people.

ment on sex than the other three groups. Over 50 percent of the engaged couples said they were in agreement on sex in contrast to approximately 12 percent of the married or previously married groups. Graph 15 summarizes the research on the four groups studied. Of course, engaged couples cannot know before marriage what some of their agreements or disagreements will be. Until people actually experience their feelings of pleasure, agreement, frustration, and well-being, they have no basis for judging. Pronounced differences in some of the most basic areas do not congeal until after marriage. Study Graph 14 on page 251 in the previous chapter. Notice that in this study of 581 married couples, it was in the first year or later that the couples really became aware of their differences in the areas of finances, sex, and child rearing. Many of the 581 couples had engaged in premarital intercourse at least a few times, and yet this experience did not give them insight into the problems of sexual adjustment in marriage.

SEX AS A PART OF THE TOTAL MARRIAGE RELATIONSHIP

Most studies show a close relationship between a satisfying sexual adjustment and the overall happiness of a marriage. People who are happily married usually enjoy sex with each other. Also, they tend to agree on how to spend money and to rear their children; in general, they agree on most things. It is difficult in research studies to determine how much each phase of agreement contributes to the degree of happiness. Certainly, the satisfaction of sexual needs seems basic to getting along in all areas of marriage. People sexually frustrated often find it difficult to have a sympathetic understanding of the spouse in other areas. The reverse may also be true; if there is conflict over the use of money, for instance, one or both may find it difficult to cooperate in sex. In a way, sexual enjoyment is a reward that comes to those who enjoy themselves in all areas of married life. But it may also be looked upon as the basic element in a relationship that makes it easier for couples to agree in other areas. We will not try to place a specific value on sex as a part of a happy marriage other than to point out that in most marriages sexual satisfaction is an important part of their lives. We will point out some things that might be helpful to people in arriving at a better understanding of sexual adjustment in marriage.

BIOLOGICAL BASIS FOR SEXUAL DRIVE

When couples marry, they find areas in which they do not agree and soon need to start making adjustments and compromises. In the area of sex, adjustments and compromises are complicated and made somewhat more difficult because of the biological basis of sex. Sex glands secrete hormones into the bloodstream; this results in the buildup of sexual tension that seeks periodic release. In marriage, most of this release comes through intercourse; it is the expected and anticipated way to receive sexual satisfaction. Satisfying sexual needs is the most intimate of all husband-wife relationships. Expressing feelings about sex, and being able to discuss innermost thoughts about sex and sexual desires is difficult for many people, even in marriage. Couples do have biological differences in sexual drive, and such differences cannot be ignored or so easily compromised as in some other areas of living. Hunger, for instance, also has a biological basis, so that people need to eat periodically, but eating does not require the same intimate cooperative effort that sex does. Recurring sexual desire does have a strong biological basis; however, it is also surrounded by social conditioning that affects its expression.

SOCIAL CONDITIONING ABOUT SEX

People do not respond to sex drives on a purely biological basis. From the time of our birth, the society in which we live influences our development. Our sexual natures are shaped by what we are taught in the family and what we learn outside the home. There is no standard for what we have been taught. People grow up with a multiplicity of feelings about the place of sex in life, about what is right or wrong and about what is desirable or undesirable in meeting sexual needs. It is very common while growing up and becoming oriented to sex, for people to be confused and in conflict. They are uncertain of their feelings and in need of accurate information.

Further, there are two worlds of social conditioning, one for males and another for females. In general, society conditions boys to be more open in accepting their sexual development. It accepts the idea that "boys will be boys" and find sexual release in many different ways. Families are more open in accepting the developing sexuality of the boy. Parents are more protective of the girls in the family from babyhood, through dating, and until they are married. There tends to be less acceptance of the development of female sexuality in terms of the need for sexual satisfaction. Most girls mature believing that they are the ones to draw the line in physical intimacy on dates, that they are the ones who will suffer most if premarital intercourse is discovered, or if pregnancy occurs. The general conditioning of boys tends toward a positive orientation to sex. In contrast, girls tend to be given a positive orientation to marriage but a negative orientation to sex.

TIME TO ADJUST IN SEX

Studies of the sexual satisfaction of wives during the honeymoon have found that for most, sex was not very satisfying. This should not come as a surprise. As in all areas of married living, satisfying relationships require effort and time, but a satisfactory sexual relationship probably takes the most effort and the longest time. In one of our studies, we asked couples how long it had taken them to work out their sexual adjustment. The study is summarized in Graph 16. Notice first, there is a positive relationship between how long it had taken to arrive at adjustment and the general happiness of the marriage, and second, those who had never arrived at a satisfactory adjustment were more likely to rate their marriage as only average in happiness. Slightly over one-half of these couples reported their sexual adjustment had been satisfactory

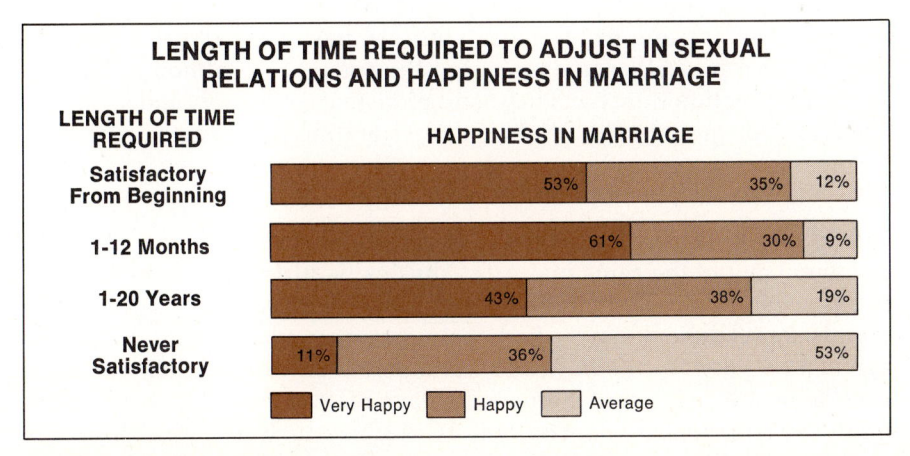

LENGTH OF TIME REQUIRED TO ADJUST IN SEXUAL RELATIONS AND HAPPINESS IN MARRIAGE

LENGTH OF TIME REQUIRED	HAPPINESS IN MARRIAGE
Satisfactory From Beginning	Very Happy 53% / Happy 35% / Average 12%
1-12 Months	Very Happy 61% / Happy 30% / Average 9%
1-20 Years	Very Happy 43% / Happy 38% / Average 19%
Never Satisfactory	Very Happy 11% / Happy 36% / Average 53%

Graph 16. As reported by 409 couples

from the beginning of their marriage. Those remaining had taken months or years to adjust, and in 12 percent of the cases, they had never arrived at a satisfactory adjustment.

It is expected and normal that sexual adjustment will take time, possibly months or even years. This does not mean that couples may not enjoy sex in the beginning of marriage. It means that as they come to a better understanding between themselves their level of sexual satisfaction and enjoyment will reach new levels.

The important thing to remember is that couples should not become discouraged in their early attempts at intercourse. The uncertainty, awkwardness, and excessive sexual tension in first attempts are such that satisfaction may be difficult. Time and familiarity often take care of many of the problems involved in these early attempts toward mutual sexual satisfaction.

SOME SPECIFIC PROBLEMS IN SEXUAL ADJUSTMENT

Varied information and experience

In this section, we will discuss some of the normal problems couples have in learning to understand each other's sexual natures, as well as one's own. People come to marriage with much sex information and misinformation. Their knowledge may be based upon facts as well as learned from friends, from movies, and from reading. Some have developed wholesome acceptance of their sexual desires and feelings while others have developed many negative and false ideas. Some are sexually experienced when they marry and may feel confident that their experience will be of value in helping them with their sexual adjustment in marriage, while in fact it may be detrimental. No two people are alike, and it would be almost impossible for a man and a woman to marry with identical sexual feelings and experiences.

It is important for young couples to recognize that they have had different feelings and experiences with sex before marriage. Their task now is to learn together in developing their sexual adjustment. The variety of information they have learned before marriage may hinder or help them in their progress, but mutual understanding is the important thing.

Physical sexual development at marriage

In addition to having varied feelings and experiences, biological development is not of the same maturity. Physically, girls develop earlier and reach puberty younger than boys. A study of over three thousand young people found that the girls had their first menstruation at an average age of 12.5 years, while boys did not report their first seminal emission until almost a year later, at an average age of 13.3 years. But the mature adult sexual response, *orgasm,* occurs in girls much later than it occurs in boys. In general, orgasm does not occur in women until after marriage, while in boys and men the orgasm response, accompanied by seminal emission, is repeatedly experienced either during night dreams or through masturbation. In discussing orgasm response as well as many other sexual differences, we must remember that there are great individual differences between men and women and among people of the same sex. In general, women are relatively "unawakened," or less developed, in their sexual response to orgasm than are men. But there are some women who are very mature in their orgasm response and have been since they were very young girls.

Over the past forty years, studies of the development of orgasm response in married women have found that one-half experienced orgasm during the honeymoon or the first month of marriage; another one-fourth experienced it during the first year of marriage, and one-fourth after a year, or they never had experienced orgasm. It is not known why some women can never develop orgasm response; some authorities think it has a biological basis, and others think it is due to false teachings that have resulted in extreme inhibitions in sexual expression. However, it must be remembered that there are many levels or degrees of sexual pleasure; orgasm is only one. Some women report complete satisfaction with the loving and tenderness expressed during intercourse when they seldom or never experience orgasm.

Physical changes and sexual desire

Men and women differ in the way their sex glands operate from day to day. In general, the testes secrete hormones into the bloodstream the same way and in the same amounts day after day; there are no hormonal changes that affect a male's physical and emotional well-being. In women, the ovaries function differently in order to secrete hormones that prepare for the possible fertilization of an egg each month. When the egg is not fertilized, menstruation occurs, and the cycle starts over. Because of the hormones secreted, there are accompanying physical and emotional swings in feelings. These often affect a woman's desire or lack of desire for sex, and her ability or lack of ability to get sexually aroused. The glandular changes that take place with pregnancy may completely alter the sexual desire and response of the woman, while the man never experiences the same changes.

Strength of the sexual drive

It is usually believed that the sexual drive is much stronger in men than in women. One explanation is that the male sex hormone secreted by both the testes and the ovaries, *testosterone*, determines sex drive, and the testes secrete more testosterone than do the ovaries. In only a minority of marriages does the wife report greater desire for sex.

Compromise based on understanding, sympathy, and acceptance of differences is required in those marriages in which one has a greater sexual desire than the other. There is no easy answer. A couple may be in agreement in most other areas. To adjust happily to their differences, one may need to suppress sexual desire while at other times the less-interested one may need to participate in sex for the satisfaction of the partner.

In early marriage, especially in teenage marriages, before the wife has become as awakened sexually, there may appear to be a greater difference in the sexual desires. However, this difference may completely change after the couple have been married a few years.

Differences in sexual arousal

In general, men are quick to be aroused sexually and are easily stimulated. They are also quickly satisfied. In contrast, women tend to need a great deal of loving and foreplay before they become sexually excited, and their duration of satisfaction may extend over a longer period of time. Some observed differences may have both biological and social bases. In our culture, it is generally the husband who initiates sex. Because his hormones have built up a certain amount of physical tension desiring release, he may already be aroused when he initiates sex. He is confident he can perform the sex act and may want to do so quickly. On the other hand, his wife may have no thoughts of sex and may not be interested in nor want intercourse. It is to be expected that it may take considerable time before she can equal his excitement and readiness for intercourse. The difference in time for sexual arousal and satisfaction can be explained in terms of the husband usually having a head start. If studies were made of marriages in which the wife was always the one who initiated sex play, then it might be found that it was the husband who was slow to be aroused because he often would not be ready or thinking about sex when she initiated it.

With time and patience, couples can learn the moods and expectations of the other so that they can usually gauge the times when both are in need of sexual satisfaction.

Frequency of sexual satisfaction

No standard can be set for the frequency of sexual intercourse in marriage. Studies show that on the average couples have intercourse two or three times per week, but there is great variation. Some couples have intercourse much more frequently than this, and some couples may not have intercourse more than two or three times per month. The important consideration is not one of frequency but rather that both partners feel content with the frequency they have established. If they cannot agree on frequency, it is important to make a compromise that is relatively satisfactory for both.

Some causes of sexual frustration in marriage

Even in the happiest of marriages, there are difficult times, or times of frustration in the sexual adjustment.

When the first baby arrives, a new stage develops for most couples. There is loss of sleep, extra work, worry if the baby is sick, and many new experiences that occur in the home. Naturally, loss of sleep and added responsibilities are going to affect the ability of the couple to engage in sex. The parent who is taking a turn at getting up for the night feedings and extra diapering will probably lose some enthusiasm for sex.

When there is sickness in the family or when either parent is having personal stress or is working too hard, the sexual life is likely to be affected.

When couples have serious conflict in their marriage, it becomes difficult or impossible to enjoy sex. Sometimes, one, often the husband, can enjoy sex even though there is serious conflict. If she will not participate, he may accuse her of withholding sex to punish him. In conflicts in marriages, either a husband or a wife may at times withhold love, affection, and sex to punish the mate.

SUMMARY

Day-to-day sexual satisfaction is closely related to a general happiness and satisfaction with life. A satisfying sexual relationship is a positive element and contributes to the well-being of a married pair, which in turn contributes to the general happiness in the home.

A satisfying sexual relationship is a positive element and contributes to the well-being of a married pair, which in turn contributes to the general happiness in the home.

In sexual adjustment, as in all areas of married living, people need to strive to keep perspective on the overall adjustment, not what it is during special times of stress. If the sexual adjustment is one that meets the needs of both partners most of the time, then it can be considered highly successful.

QUESTIONS FOR REVIEW

1. What do studies reveal about sexual adjustment in marriage?
2. How do the findings of studies of engaged couples differ from the findings of the studies of married and divorced couples?
3. Why is it difficult to measure the effects of sexual adjustment upon total marriage adjustment?
4. Why is it more difficult to arrive at adjustments in sexual expression than it is in some other areas of marriage?
5. What are some of the variations in social conditioning that affect sexual response?
6. Why is it the norm to take time to adjust in sexual intercourse?
7. Contrast the biological-psychological development of boys and girls in adolescence.
8. What hormonal changes affect sexual response?
9. Name some factors or conditions that may contribute to sex drive.
10. Why may men, in general, seem to be more interested in sexual intercourse than women?
11. Name some day-to-day situations that may contribute to sexual frustration.

WORDS AND CONCEPTS

hormones
masturbation
menstruation
orgasm

seminal emission
sexual arousal
sexual desire
testosterone

You and Your In-laws

20

After studying this chapter, you will be able to

1. Discuss the parent-child dependency pattern and its effect on in-law relationships.
2. Explain the growth tasks required on the part of newly married couples and their parents if satisfactory in-law relationships are to be established.
3. Illustrate the difference between subjective and objective attitudes about in-laws.
4. List some rules to follow that can help one establish good in-law relationships.

"I'm marrying Jack—not his family!" That was Linda's view before her marriage. However, after some months of marriage, it dawned upon her that she had married not only Jack; she had married *into a family*. With Jack, she had acquired a whole set of relatives. Grandparents, aunts, uncles, and cousins, some of whom she had scarcely heard of, now looked upon her as one of their clan. A mother-in-law, a father-in-law, and several sisters-in-law were now interested in her life just as her own parents and brothers and sisters had always been. Many people, like Linda, marry believing that the in-laws will not matter. Others are not even aware that marriage usually means in-laws.

Still others marry with the fatalistic feeling that in-law friction is inevitable. Some marry anticipating with pleasure the happy relationships they will have with their in-laws, and many of these do find much pleasure with them. Sometimes, however, people find that they are sensitive where the in-laws are concerned, and they begin to have a problem. Just where the trouble lies may not be easy to determine.

In some countries, especially in the Orient, patterns of family life are much different from ours. In such cultures, when a girl marries, she accepts without question the fact that she is now in a new family. She moves into the home of her husband's family and gives to her husband's parents the respect that is due them as the family authorities. Her husband also accepts the authority of his parents. The young married couple are not an independent family unit. As years pass and the older members of the family die, the younger members gradually assume more responsibility. The transition from their status as children to that of responsible family heads is not sudden, but gradual.

In the United States, our system is different. No matter how dependent upon their parents two young people have been, the traditional feeling is that when they marry they are out on their own. They are now a new family unit, responsible for their own lives and free to live as they see fit. So strongly established is this attitude that many young married couples, in their attempt to establish their independence, resist aggressively any direct or indirect parental guidance. Interestingly enough, this resistance is usually directed at the family of the spouse, rather than one's own family.

THE FAMILY PATTERN

For approximately twenty years, we live in our parental home and look to our parents for most of our needs. As small children, we depend upon them for guidance and support in all our affairs. As we grow to maturity, we gradually assert our own independence; but if a good parent-child relationship has been developed, we continue to consult with them and to give consideration to their viewpoints. We may not follow their advice on all points, but we do find it helpful to talk some problems over with an interested parent.

Parents are far more interested in their children's lives than their children realize. Many mothers, especially, invest most of their time, thoughts, and energy in the lives of their children. Some mothers are so concerned with the development of their children that they neglect their own individual interests.

Then the children marry and set up housekeeping for themselves. The mother, especially one who has not taken an outside job, is suddenly left with more time than she has had for years. Her habits have become so established that it may be hard for her to find a job or to find

Parents should not interfere in the affairs of their married child's household. Talks should be on a "consultation only" basis.

new interests to occupy her time. The father's life is not so seriously affected, for his daily work continues as usual. He may even be relieved of financial pressures when the children move out.

The mother is as interested as ever in the lives of her children, and she has even more time to think of them. It is entirely natural, then, that she may offer them advice or help when she sees that they need it; and they usually do need it, for we all have much to learn when we marry and assume the responsibilities that come with being married and managing a household.

What of the children? When they marry, they do not suddenly feel perfectly capable of meeting all their problems. If it has been their habit to talk things over with either parent, they will naturally continue the habit.

Dick and Sue, who have not been married very long, are thinking of buying some new furniture. It means going into debt, but Dick has a good job, and Sue works, too. Still, they have little savings, and both dislike the idea of going into debt; they have talked it over, and they agree. They remain undecided about buying the furniture. On his way home from work one evening, Dick decides to stop and talk it over with his parents. He would feel better about going ahead if his dad and mother seemed to think it was a good idea.

When he and Sue are discussing the subject again that evening, Dick says, "Mother thinks that Brocks over on Sixth Street really offers a better choice of furniture than any of the other stores, and she says we would do better on price if we would wait until August, because Brocks always has good price cuts during their August sales."

Suddenly, Sue begins to feel that it is important that they go ahead and buy their furniture now. What is his mother trying to do, anyway— tell them when and where to spend their money? Aren't they a responsible married couple earning their own living! Besides, only this morning she talked it all over with her mother over the telephone, and her mother felt that they were wise to buy their furniture now.

It depends upon how mature Sue is, whether she will make an issue of the matter. If she is fairly mature, she will not let the impulse to show Dick's mother who is running things get the better of her. If she is immature, she can use the situation to behave in a way that can turn a trifle into a real in-law problem. Research suggests that it is probably just such small matters that account for some of the in-law troubles that develop.

Many such circumstances arise in the lives of young married couples. Those who have not enough perspective on human relationships or who are immature in their attitudes will interpret as interference any interest shown by the in-laws.

Frequently, the ones who are most ready to rise and do battle with "interfering" in-laws are those who are still the most dependent upon their own families. They have not yet been weaned psychologically. Each may continue to confide in his or her own parents on all points, but resents it deeply if the spouse does.

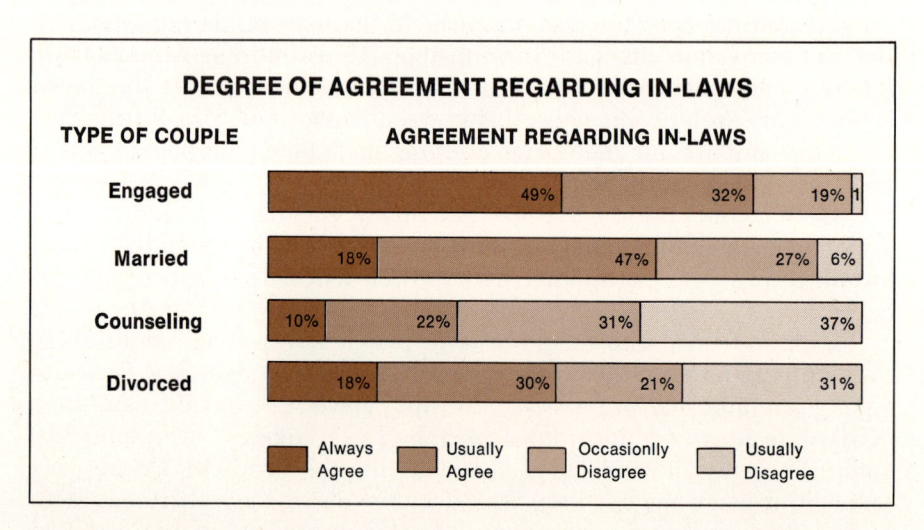

DEGREE OF AGREEMENT REGARDING IN-LAWS

TYPE OF COUPLE	AGREEMENT REGARDING IN-LAWS
Engaged	49% / 32% / 19% / 1
Married	18% / 47% / 27% / 6%
Counseling	10% / 22% / 31% / 37%
Divorced	18% / 30% / 21% / 31%

Always Agree — Usually Agree — Occasionlly Disagree — Usually Disagree

Graph 17. As reported by 122 engaged couples, 581 married couples, 155 people seeking marriage counseling, and 164 divorced people.

Thus, we see that in-law misunderstandings may arise as a natural result of normal family relationships. They arise because both the parents and the children are in a growth process. All are making the transition away from the parent-child dependence pattern that has existed for many years. Normally, they should not have to take too long to make this transition.

GROWTH TASKS FOR ALL AT THIS STAGE OF LIFE

There are certain growth tasks that must be achieved if good in-law relationships are to exist and if newly married couples are to have harmony and freedom from in-law tensions in their own relationships. There are good reasons why the special kind of growth this stage of life requires is difficult for many people.

The task of the newly married couple is threefold, and some aspects of it are contradictory. Each newly married person must (1) *build a good relationship with the mate.* Most people are aware of this task if they are at all aware that marriage makes new requirements upon them. (2) Each one must at the same time *develop a relationship with the new in-laws.* Each must make friends with them and establish an interaction that has many of the elements in relationships with one's own parents. (3) While accomplishing the first two, each must also *grow into a new kind of relationship with one's parents.* Many people are entirely unaware of this third aspect of building a good marriage, even if they consciously work to make the needed growth in the first two. There must be at least some withdrawing from the closeness to parents that may have existed in the past, in favor of giving first priority to the mate. There need not be any less affection and respect for one's parents, but it is necessary to be objective in recognizing that one now owes first loyalty to the mate and the new family unit. This automatically redefines relationships with one's own parents.

The picture is complicated by the fact that parents have equally strenuous requirements made upon them at this time. (1) They must understand and accept that their child's first allegiance is now to the new mate and that the first interest is in creating a good relationship in marriage. (2) They must accept without jealous or competitive attitudes that their child is also trying to develop happy relationships with the new in-law family. This is emotionally hard for some parents. They may not be as ready for this aspect of their child's marriage as they were to accept his or her loyalty to the mate. (3) They must work toward establishing friendly and satisfactory interaction between themselves and their new child-in-law. This means they need to be especially perceptive about the child-in-law's feelings and restrained about giving advice or asking questions. (4) They need to work to create as good relationships as possible between themselves and the other parents who have become their

It is hard for parents to "cut the apron strings" when a child marries. Most people make this adjustment, although it usually requires sincere effort on the part of both the parents and the young couple.

child's in-laws. For the two parent-in-law couples to dislike each other or to be competitive makes newly married couples' adjustments far more complicated and difficult.

One reason that these growth tasks may be especially hard for parents is that they, like their children, are in a new stage for which they may not be prepared. They must adjust to being parents-in-law and potential grandparents without having made the choice of that status themselves. To be "mother-in-law," or "grandmother," "father-in-law," or "grandfather," with all the connotations of those titles in our society, is a status *conferred* on parents by their child's decision to marry.

At the same time that parents become parents-in-law and must adjust to their new obligations, they may also be struggling with physical symptoms associated with middle-age or menopause. They may be feeling the need of special reassurance and emotional support at the very time that their children and children-in-law expect them to be more than ordinarily mature and wise.

Chapter 1 discussed the continuing growth requirements at every age in life and noted that the tasks tend to be much the same, but with different faces at different times. This is particularly true regarding in-law relationships. To think about the kinds of adjustments required equally of parents and newly married couples should help all those involved to be more understanding of each other's struggles in achieving necessary growth tasks.

THE IN-LAWS AS SCAPEGOATS

Among primitive people the "scapegoat" served a useful purpose. Sins or evils were ceremoniously placed upon an animal or person who was then driven away or punished, freeing a family or community from guilt. Something like this sometimes occurs in in-law relationships. The in-laws can be given the blame for things that it would be upsetting to admit are true in the married couple themselves.

A young wife or husband discovers traits, habits, or attitudes in the mate that are unattractive or unacceptable. But the young married person wants to approve of the mate. It is difficult and unpleasant to have to face the fact that this loved person really is, in some ways, not lovable or likable. So there are ready-made scapegoats, the in-laws, who are very likely to have those same irritating, unlikable traits.

A husband says, "Jane's mother is so prejudiced and opinionated. I can't stand the way she sounds off about things. She acts as if nobody's ideas were worth listening to except hers." Perhaps this is a tendency he has begun to notice in his wife; but he is much more comfortable if he can be angry at his mother-in-law instead. A wife says, "I don't like to associate with my husband's family. They have no interests at all except sitting around gossiping about the neighbors or watching television. I don't want our children to be like that. I just don't take the children to visit the in-laws if I can help it." Her husband was affectionate toward his family and very much like them in his ways and interests. The wife's strong antagonism toward the in-laws was really based on her feelings about her husband's interests and what she considered to be pettiness in his attitudes toward others. Thus, the true source of such difficulties can be concealed by using the in-laws as scapegoats. If the young person doesn't like the family of the fiance(e), he or she may be more likely to use them as scapegoats when they are in-laws.

Many people see things they disagree with or are critical of in the family of the one they plan to marry. But because they are in love and want very much to marry this person, they do not accept the fact that the loved one is much like his or her family. After all, we all get many of our ways, attitudes, and viewpoints from our own families. It is reasonable to recognize that when you marry, both of you will be more like your families than you are like each other. It will take time and cooperation to build your own family unit with the special ways and characteristics that you will pass on to your own children. So, during the early years of marriage, it is especially important to have attitudes that are generous and uncritical toward the mate's family. Such attitudes make for happy in-law relationships and also increase the happiness of the young married pair at an important period in their lives.

UNSUCCESSFUL ATTITUDES

Some of the comments we have from people who are having difficulty with their in-laws show clearly their lack of objectivity. One man complained bitterly, "My wife agrees with her folks, although they are ignorant, just to pacify them."

He was irritated with his wife for being agreeable to her folks, but he could not analyze his own feelings and realize that his irritation was childish. Would it help the so-called ignorance for the wife to be disagreeable to her parents? If his wife were the kind of person who behaved disagreeably to her parents, would she be the pleasant, agreeable person that he found her to be?

A wife said, "My husband's family seem to think he still belongs to them."

What does that wife want? Would she be happy if her husband's family disowned him? She has not thought that far. She is reacting in a childish manner to the fact that an affectionate relationship exists between her husband and his family. One basis for her feeling is that she is in the process of becoming established in her husband's affection. She does not yet feel entirely secure, and an element of jealousy enters into her feeling toward her husband's family. They seem so settled and secure in their relationship with her husband that she is irritated.

Sometimes, couples who marry in the teens do so against the opposition of at least one set of parents. The objections may be on the basis of the young couple's age or for other valid reasons. Once the marriage has taken place, the new parents-in-law may accept the situation and do their best to be uncritical and helpful. They want the young couple to make a go of their marriage. If the new son-in-law or daughter-in-law is immature, it may not be easy to forget the past opposition and thus hold antagonistic attitudes toward in-laws. The person who is mature enough for marriage will not hold grudges, but will work toward establishing harmonious in-law relationships.

SUCCESS WITH THE IN-LAWS

People who can be objective and flexible can have good relationships with their in-laws, just as with their own families. Some of the statements below, made by people who had happy in-law relationships, show the attitudes that are successful:

"I fit in with their way of doing things. I realize that they have developed their ways over a long period of time, so I don't try to change them."

"I ignore things that irritate me."

"I try to be sensible and not condemn them for faults when I have faults, too."

"I made up my mind to get along with them."
"I try to be agreeable and friendly to them."
"I treat them as my own family. They are wonderful people."

LIVING WITH PARENTS

Sometimes, newly married couples, especially those who marry in their teens, plan to live with their parents for a while. That arrangement is not desirable if it can be avoided. It would be better to postpone marrying until they can live alone. The early adjustments that must be made can be accomplished much more easily if there is privacy—if no outsiders, friendly or unfriendly, are at hand to observe all that is said or done.

If couples live away from their families during the first few years of marriage, they have a better chance to grow together. After they have had time to work out adjustments, they could probably live near to their respective families and get along well. People who live away from their families for a while may be able to be more objective. They can also see that their future lies in "our" family—the new family that they have formed—rather than in their relationships with their parent families.

A young student husband was very critical of his mother-in-law because he said that she kept interfering by writing letters telling the young couple how to live their lives, how to train their child, and how to make plans for the future. He felt antagonistic toward the mother-in-law and wished that she would let them live their lives as they pleased.

There is special pleasure in being a grandparent. Why does friction often arise over how to raise the grandchildren?

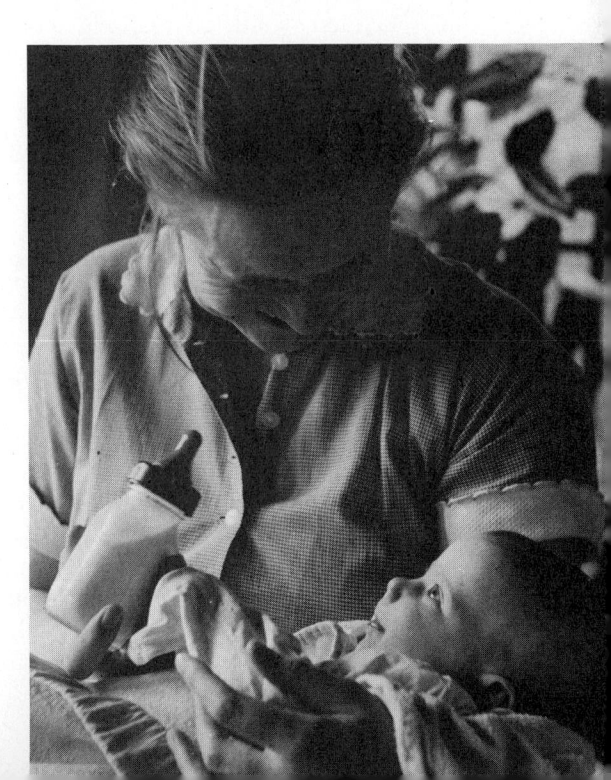

In the same conversation, this young man mentioned that every summer he and his wife and child lived at a lake with his wife's family. He was happy that they could spend the summers in the cottage. One moment, he would be discussing the horrible mother-in-law and the next talking of the comfortable summer cottage, good food, and luxuries that he was accustomed to enjoying—all provided by his in-laws. He showed immaturity and no objectivity—he wanted all the conveniences that his in-laws could provide, but did not want to be bothered with the in-laws themselves. An appraisal of the situation by an outsider would probably show that the son-in-law's resentment toward the mother-in-law was due to his own tendency to want a one-sided relationship. He wanted privileges, but was unwilling to accept the obligation to give understanding and appreciative cooperation in exchange.

SOME SUGGESTED RULES FOR GUIDANCE IN IN-LAW RELATIONSHIPS

You may have thought as you read this chapter that you have no immediate reason to be concerned about in-law relationships. Yet many of you have brothers and sisters who are married; thus, you are already an in-law. Nearly everyone becomes an in-law eventually, whether or not one marries. Before you marry, you should give some thought to ways in which good in-law relationships are built.

1. First of all, be realistic when you choose a mate. Recognize that you are marrying *into a family,* and don't marry into a background of values and attitudes you cannot accept and with which you cannot live.
2. Treat your in-laws with the same consideration and respect that you give to friends.
3. When in-laws take an interest in your life and give advice, do just as you would if any friend gave advice: if it is good, follow it; if it is not good, accept it graciously and then ignore it.
4. Remember that many times when the in-laws appear to be too concerned with your affairs, they are not trying to interfere in your life, but are sincerely interested in your welfare, and their ideas may be worth considering.
5. Look for the good points in your in-laws.
6. When you visit your in-laws, make the visits reasonably short.
7. When visiting in-laws, be as thoughtful, courteous, and helpful as you are when you are visiting other friends.
8. Accept your in-laws as they are; remember that they would probably like to make some changes in you, too.
9. Mothers-in-law have been close to their children before marriage; give them time to find new interests.

YOU AND YOUR IN-LAWS   277

10. Go into marriage with a positive attitude toward your in-laws—you believe it is a good family, and you intend to enjoy it.
11. Readjust your relationships with your own parents so that your mate will have no occasion ever to doubt your loyalty.
12. Give advice to your in-laws only if they ask for it; even then, use self-restraint.
13. Do not quote your family or hold them up as models to your spouse.
14. Remember that it takes at least two people to create an in-law problem. No one person is ever entirely to blame.
15. Make it a rule never to discuss any of your mate's faults or your marital problems with your own parents or family.

HAPPINESS IN MARRIAGE AND IN-LAW ADJUSTMENT

Those who get along well with their in-laws are more likely to achieve a high level of happiness than those who do not. Graph 18 summarizes the data from a study of over five hundred couples who were in the early years of marriage. General happiness is associated with having a good relationship with the in-laws.

Because a good relationship with in-laws means greater happiness for the married couple, as well as for both parent families, it is worthwhile to work for a good understanding before marriage as well as during the early years of marriage. Some of the evidence indicates that those

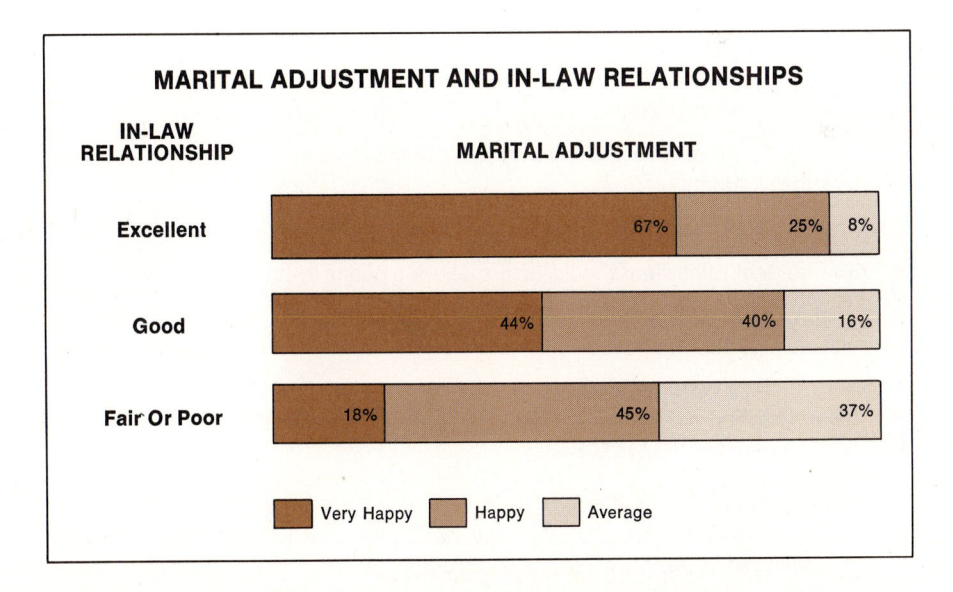

MARITAL ADJUSTMENT AND IN-LAW RELATIONSHIPS

IN-LAW RELATIONSHIP	MARITAL ADJUSTMENT		
Excellent	Very Happy 67%	Happy 25%	Average 8%
Good	44%	40%	16%
Fair Or Poor	18%	45%	37%

Graph 18. Couples who have good or excellent in-law relationships are more likely to be happy or very happy in marriage than those whose relationship is poor.

who marry young are not as successful at getting along with their in-laws as those who marry later. Therefore, teenagers who consider marrying will have to make more than the usual effort to be reasonable and understanding in their attitudes if they are to establish good relationships with in-laws.

QUESTIONS FOR REVIEW

1. "I'm marrying Jack—not his family!" How does this statement show naïveté?
2. Contrast in-law relationships in our country with those in the Orient.
3. What is meant by "the parent-child dependency pattern"?
4. What are the specific growth tasks of newly married people?
5. What are the specific growth tasks of parents when their children marry?
6. Why might the growth tasks be more difiicult for the parents than they are for the newly married couple?
7. Why might mothers be blamed more often than fathers for in-law interference?
8. How could mother-in-law jokes make for in-law misunderstanding?
9. "In-law frictions arise as a natural result of normal family relationships." Discuss.
10. Under what conditions are in-laws sometimes used as scapegoats?
11. Do you think children-in-law take as much responsibility as they can for creating happy in-law relationships?
12. Explain the differences between subjective and objective attitudes. Give some statements on in-laws to illustrate each type of attitude.
13. What factors probably make for greater in-law friction if children live with or near their parents?
14. Why do people need to live by themselves during the early years of marriage?
15. Give several rules that should help make for better in-law understanding.
16. What might explain why those who marry young may not have as good in-law relationships as those who marry later?

ACTIVITIES AND PROJECTS

1. (Special report.) Read *The Good Earth* or *The Mother,* by Pearl Buck, or *The House of Exile,* by Nora Waln. Note descriptions of parent-child and in-law relationships. Or report on some other book that pictures these relationships.
2. Analyze a case of in-law friction that you have observed. Who was most at fault, parents or children? Was a lack of objectivity evident in the difficulty?

3. Make a collection of pictures and cartoons depicting in-law relationships. Display them on your classroom bulletin board. Who is most often blamed for in-law trouble? How do the usual cartoons affect attitudes of people?

SOCIODRAMA

1. Four students act the parts of the parents and the newly married couple. Demonstrate the rather normal parent-child dependency pattern.
2. A sewing circle or bridge club meets in which wives discuss their in-law relationships. Present both subjective, destructive attitudes and objective, constructive attitudes toward the in-laws.

WORDS AND CONCEPTS

allegiance
ceremoniously
inevitable
menopause

priority
scapegoat
superficial conclusion
weaned psychologically

21 Making Decisions About Finances

After studying this chapter, you will be able to

1. Cite what studies show on the ease of reaching agreement on finances, and on the degree of financial agreement among engaged, married, counseling, and divorced people.
2. Explain the threefold nature of problems people have in connection with family finances.
3. Analyze the place of shared values in reaching agreement on finances.
4. List some advantages of keeping a realistic family budget.

When Alice and Tom were married, Alice kept her job. Before they married, they had talked over the subject of their financial plans. They agreed to have a joint bank account and to handle their finances together. They believed this would avoid the financial problems they had seen their parents have. Alice resented the fact that her father was the final authority on all money matters so that her mother had to argue to get money she needed or wanted. In Tom's family also, the father was dominant in handling the finances, but Tom saw nothing to criticize in his father's handling of the money. That seemed to him the best arrangement. He had felt that during some of the years when his father's income was hardly enough for all their needs his mother should have helped out by working at least part time as many other women were doing. Thus, when they married, he was glad that Alice wanted to keep her job.

In the first year, they were suprised and distressed to find themselves having some explosive disagreements over money. Tom was paying the rent, utilities, and other fixed expenses. Their plan was that some of Alice's earnings would provide special things they could not afford on Tom's income alone, and the rest would be saved for when they would be having children and Alice might want to stop working.

Their first serious quarrel occurred when Alice bought a new dress and coat that Tom thought she didn't need. He showed his disapproval by criticizing the dress and the way she looked in it; he went on to say he didn't think she showed good sense about spending money. Alice was shocked and angry. She told him he sounded just like her father—trying to dominate her by controlling the money—and she added that his father was just as bad and that it was no wonder his family had so many problems. Tom lost his temper, too, and said that no matter what she thought of his family, she had no business spending so much money without asking him about it. He said further that he didn't think it was much of a deal—his paying all the bills and her spending her money as she pleased.

Alice pointed out that her earnings were going into savings, and that made the quarrel worse because they had not actually accumulated any savings yet; all Alice's earnings seemed to disappear for extras and luxuries, many of which were Tom's choices.

Before the quarrel was over, they both said things they were sorry about afterward. One good result was that they both began to try to understand why they had reacted by getting so angry. They tried to figure out how they could reach a better understanding of what the other thought about the kinds of financial cooperation that were necessary in marriage.

MONEY PROBLEMS IN MARRIAGE

Alice and Tom were only coming face to face with a problem that arises in some measure in almost every marriage. Our study of over four hundred couples who have been successfully married for an average of twenty years revealed that the second most difficult problem these people had, had centered around making and spending the family income. Both the husbands and wives agreed that this had been a difficult hurdle in their effort to achieve happy marriages. However, after some years, most had reached a good understanding concerning the use of their money. They had succeeded in adjusting and compromising for harmony.

MARITAL ADJUSTMENT AND AGREEMENT ON MONEY

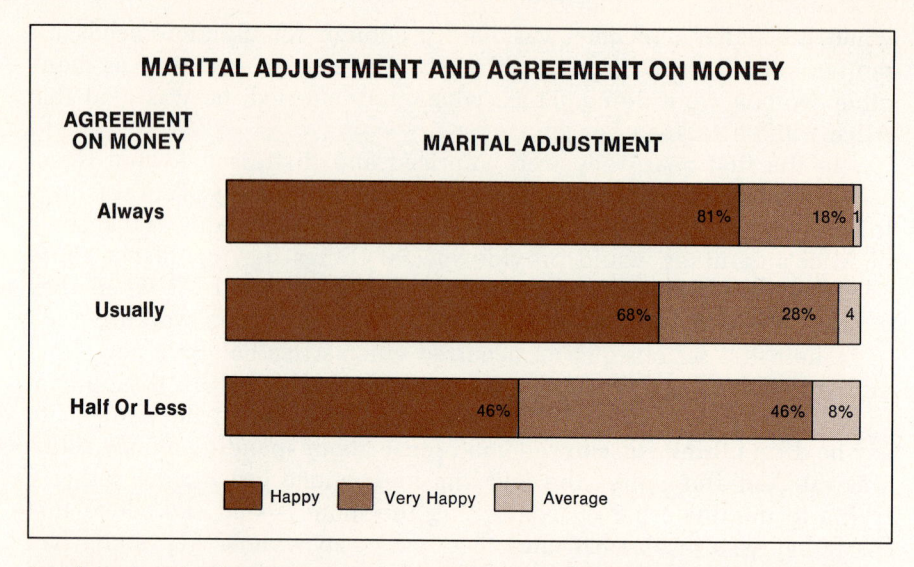

AGREEMENT ON MONEY	MARITAL ADJUSTMENT — Happy / Very Happy / Average
Always	81% / 18% / 1
Usually	68% / 28% / 4
Half Or Less	46% / 46% / 8%

Graph 19. A study of 544 young married couples revealed that those who agreed on the use of money were much more likely to be happy or very happy in marriage than those who could not agree about it.

AGREEMENT DURING ENGAGEMENT AND AGREEMENT IN MARRIAGE

In our study of married couples, couples having counseling, and divorced people, we found that all three groups listed financial cooperation as either the most serious or the second most serious problem that had arisen. These three groups and a group of engaged couples were also asked to report their degree of *agreement or disagreement* in the area of family finances. Study the pattern of their responses as pictured in Graph 20 on page 283.

The differences among the groups in their present agreement or disagreement indicate not only their real differences, but also the degree of their success or failure in setting up a good working relationship. Among the interesting contrasts is the fact that only 37 percent of the counseling group, compared to 84 percent of the engaged couples, said they always, or almost always, agree. Apparently, many couples have no idea before marriage of their attitudes or habits regarding money and its use. It is only after they are confronted with making actual choices and decisions, and cooperating to manage their income, that they discover their agreement or disagreement.

To understand that this is an area in which all married couples must work together and set mutually satisfactory policies might be helpful to engaged couples. They would then be more realistic in exploring their attitudes and habits.

MAKING DECISIONS ABOUT FINANCES

THREEFOLD NATURE OF FINANCIAL PROBLEMS

Difficulties in connection with the family income may be summarized in three main divisions. First, *many families just do not have enough money to meet all of their real needs.* In good times or bad, approximately one-third of the families in the United States do not receive sufficient income to buy the necessities of life, such as food, shelter, medical care, and an education for the children. Another third receive sufficient income to buy the necessities of life, but not enough for savings or luxuries.

A second major difficulty is due to inability of couples to agree on how to spend the money they do have. This probably causes more friction than insufficient income. Studies of marriage adjustment agree that a large income does not necessarily insure happiness. The important thing is that husband and wife agree on how to use what money they have. Two who cannot think alike on how the money should be used can be very unhappy, even though their income is high.

A third point causing difficulty for many married people is who will control the spending. When a couple gets married, they must cooperate, even though one of them takes chief responsibility for final decisions. Sometimes, couples find it hard to arrive at a satisfactory agreement on whether this responsibility should be the husband's or the wife's.

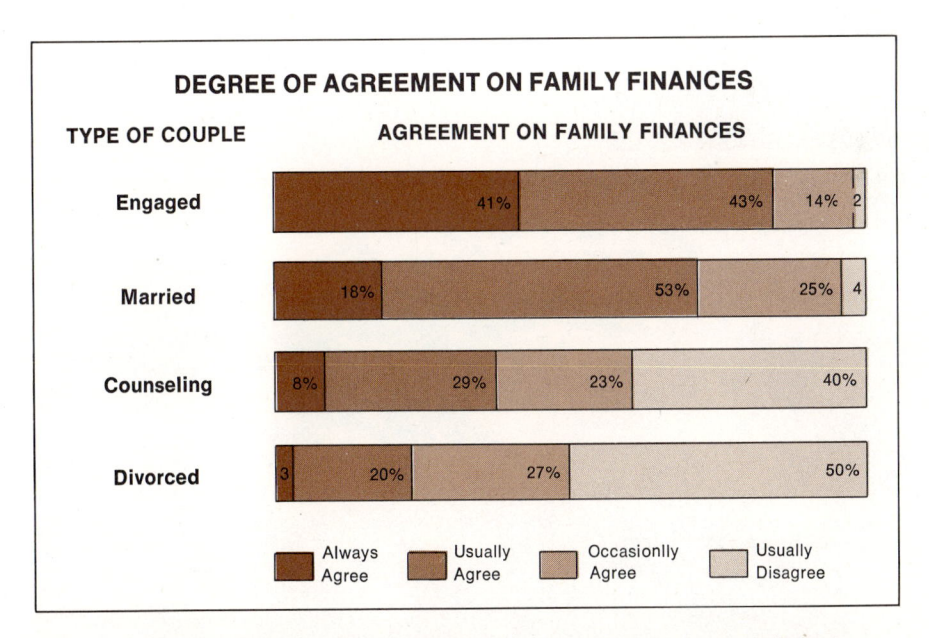

DEGREE OF AGREEMENT ON FAMILY FINANCES

TYPE OF COUPLE	Always Agree	Usually Agree	Occasionally Agree	Usually Disagree
Engaged	41%	43%	14%	2
Married	18%	53%	25%	4
Counseling	8%	29%	23%	40%
Divorced	3	20%	27%	50%

Graph 20. As reported by 122 engaged couples, 581 married couples, 155 people having marriage counseling, and 164 divorced persons.

Because it is not within our power to suggest how families may have bigger incomes, we will not give the first problem further attention. However, it is worthwhile to consider in greater detail the facts centering around the second and third major money problems. The average couple can solve these two problems.

GROWING TOGETHER ON WHAT IS VALUED

It should not come as a shock to newly married people to find that they do not agree perfectly on how to use their money. In few marriages will the two be in perfect agreement on what to buy, how much to save, and what plans to make for future buying.

The American consumer is an astute shopper who also knows how to use political pressure to protest unfair prices and practices.

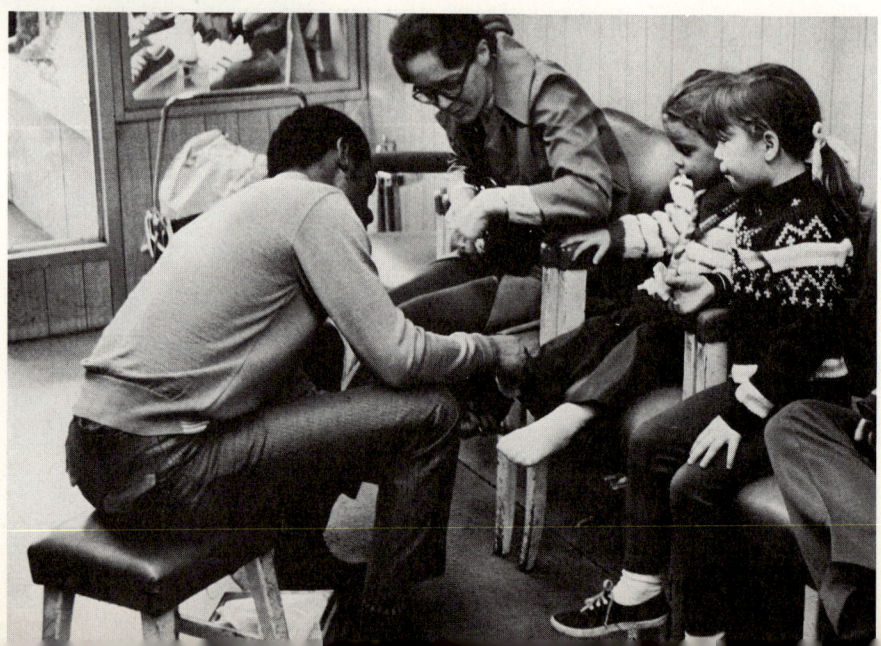

If people study each other carefully during courtship, they will observe differences in their values. Most people take into marriage the values that they gain from their respective families. The young person whose family places emphasis upon new cars, vacations, or living in the right neighborhood will tend to have similar values after marriage even though the values do not coincide with this person's earnings.

If such a person marries a mate who comes from a family who cares for entirely different things, such as saving money for their children's education, educational travel, or other cultural interests, the young people may have difficulty agreeing about how to spend their money. One may think it is ridiculous to buy a new car when it seems that the money is needed for more important things. If the couple's income is limited, their problem will be more difficult.

If two people from different social backgrounds marry, they may find even more differences. One of them may feel that it is better to economize on food in order to serve a good wine at dinner, and the other may think money spent for any form of alcohol is not only extravagant and unnecessary but immoral as well.

Similarly, if one is from a family with intellectual interests and the other is not, they may first become aware of this difference because of conflicts over money. One may feel that expenditures for books or art are almost as necessary as for food or shelter. The other may think this an extravagance, although he or she would readily spend money for movies or football games.

The thing that creates difficulty is that most of us do not question the values with which we grow up. We have no reason to examine our values critically. We accept them as right and proper, because we have always lived with them. We do not realize how much difference can exist between our own ideas concerning relative values and the ideas of our associates. Thus, after marriage, it is a rude shock to observe that things that one accepts as important and worth sacrificing for may not seem important to the mate, who would dispense with them in favor of more worthwhile things—which, incidentally, may seem entirely superficial and unnecessary to the other.

It would not be necessary for conflicts to arise if people could recognize and study their values. Couples who do this often find it is not hard to compromise. They formulate their own set of values, which may differ largely from those of either of the background families from which they have come. It is the automatic adherence to set patterns that causes the conflict. No couple can be, nor should they try to be, just like their parent families.

The following list may help you analyze your attitudes in connection with family spending. Number a separate sheet of paper from 1 to 33. Rate "A" those you think absolutely essential;"B" those that are important but not essential; "C" those that could well be eliminated for the sake of economy. Compare your rating with the way your friends rate the items. On how many do you agree? If you are dating someone seriously, discuss each item on the list and see how well you agree on their importance.

1. an apartment in a good section of town
2. owning one's own home
3. a pet (any dog or cat or other)
4. meat once a day
5. a savings account
6. continuing husband's education
7. continuing wife's education
8. college education for the children
9. going out to eat in restaurants fairly often
10. eating at restaurants on special occasions
11. an electric dishwasher
12. an air conditioner
13. two or more radios
14. television set or sets
15. subscriptions to at least one magazine or journal
16. subscriptions to at least four magazines
17. new books purchased at least three or four times a year
18. a stereo set and records
19. commercialized recreation such as movies, ball games, etc.
20. music lessons for the children
21. part of the budget for gifts and entertaining
22. part of the budget for insurance
23. part of the budget for church or charity
24. some funds for political or special interest organizations
25. new furniture
26. family vacations, such as camping trips
27. new clothes each season
28. sterling silver table settings
29. stainless steel table settings
30. concert or theater tickets
31. travel
32. a motorcycle
33. a high-priced car, good-looking as well as good for transportation

WHO SHOULD CONTROL THE MONEY?

It is impossible to make any generalizations about just who should control the money. The two will have to agree and cooperate no matter which one does the work of buying and paying bills. In few families should complete control be turned over to either the husband or the wife. Attitudes about control of the family spending will depend upon the family backgrounds of the couple.

A study of over five hundred young couples who were in the early years of marriage showed that approximately 60 percent handled their money in what they called the democratic way. But to define what financial policies are really democratic and to adhere to such policies is a problem for many couples. Solutions are complicated because family situations are so varied. In earlier times, when the husband was usually the sole earner and the wife solely a housewife and mother, responsibilities may have been easier to assign. But today, when so many wives are wage earners, roles and responsibilities are less clearly defined. Each couple must decide some basic questions for themselves. If they do not, it is likely they will encounter conflicts and frustrations.

SOME QUESTIONS TO BE FACED

In the first place, a couple should try to look objectively at their individual values. The best way to do this is to consider the standards and ways of life of their parental families. It is not necessary to be critical of one's own family nor of the mate's family. Their two families are likely to differ in many of their values and in their attitudes about using money; differences need not be categorized as good or bad. The point is for a couple to try to create their own values as a family unit. If they can do this, they can work out the answers to other more secondary questions.

One question is if they both work, how are they going to handle their two incomes? Can one think of his or her paycheck as "mine" and of the other person's as "ours"? Some people try that, and it does not make for harmony or cooperation. Moreover, can they be realistic about their actual financial situation and prospects? Many young couples get into financial difficulty after a few years of marriage because they start out on two incomes and fail to recognize that that circumstance may be temporary. As soon as they begin to have children, or if job opportunities force them to move to a location where the mate does not find a suitable job, their income may be cut in half. If they have spent money freely, especially if they have bought things on credit on the basis of their two incomes, they may find it impossible to meet their obligations.

If both continue to work after marriage, it is usually safer to make permanent financial plans based on the earnings of one, and to set their living standard on that basis. Couples who can plan carefully and make special use of the second income or save it for future emergencies will be establishing a policy helpful to their permanently good relationship in the financial area.

If two people agree on how to use their money, it will make little difference which one has more responsibility in the spending. If the wife has time for and enjoys keeping the books and paying the bills, then

One-fifth of the work force are married women, many in the early years of marriage. Today's woman who contributes to the family income learns to handle that income to best advantage.

she should do the work; if the husband is better at attending to the details, he should take over the responsibility. In general, more justification exists for the wife's taking the responsibility for handling the family finances, because studies show that the American housewife spends 80 percent of the family income. This means that the necessities such as food, clothing, and housing, for which the wife usually pays, take 80 percent of the income of the average family.

WHAT ABOUT BUDGETING?

Making the dollars go as far as they must is a puzzle in the majority of families. Many families have found that it is a help if they have a spending plan that they have carefully worked out to fit their own income and needs. This is the household budget which may or may not help, depending upon the common sense with which it is used.

We list the following points about budgeting:

1. Running a household is a business. In any business, it is necessary to plan and to keep careful records of income and expenditures. Following a budget, then, puts the family economics on a businesslike basis.
2. Budgeting helps people to decide what they value most. When they make out the budget, the married couple must take time to talk over the various needs. They must decide which are fundamental needs and which are things that can be denied.
3. A family budget serves as a record that helps the family to live within a given income. An accurate record of the family spending enables them to see just where the money is going and whether too large an amount is going for nonessentials. They can revise their spending pattern if it is desirable.
4. The budget can aid the family in achieving long-range goals. Families have immediate, operational goals—items that may be covered from paycheck to paycheck—but most families also have goals that require looking ahead. If there are children, their education requires planning. Some families save a set amount each month from the time the children are young in order to guarantee college educations. Most couples would like to own their own home. To achieve this goal, they may plan to save a certain percentage each month. Other couples want to travel. For the average family, all such future goals require a systematic financial plan.
5. In early marriage, it is a profitable, educational experience to make and try to live by a budget. It would also be a good idea if, during the engagement period, couples made a practice budget. Through this device, they would find out specifically how they agreed or disagreed about money. By trying to be realistic about details of finance ahead of time, they would improve their chances for good adjustment in this area.
6. In the early years of marriage, the budget helps couples to discuss money problems freely. Some people find it impossible to discuss money and the spending of it. If a young couple happen to have this particular problem, a budget will force them to talk about money.

This list of benefits from budgeting could be extended.

Disadvantages of family budgeting may also be listed. Most of these, however, grow out of the fundamental differences between husband and wife over the use of money and are not disadvantages of a system as such. Many people become disillusioned with their budget because it does not help them to solve all of their problems.

A budget will not increase the salary; it will not force husband and wife to value the same things and it will not settle the question of who should handle the money. It can only help people plan so that they can make better use of the money that they have and to be realistic about where their income actually goes.

THE NEED TO BE REALISTIC ABOUT EXPENSES

A complication must be noted: early in married life, while the income may still be low, it is easy to be unrealistic about a budget. Most people, when they first begin financing a household, are amazed at how much everything costs and how easily and unaccountably the money disappears.

One couple decided that they could make a substantial saving each month by giving up their apartment, which cost one hundred fifty dollars a month including utilities, and moving to a small house in a suburb. The apartment was a short walk from the husband's work, the house a forty-minute drive away. They leased the house for a year at a monthly rent of one hundred dollars.

A half year later, they were finding it nearly impossible to meet all their expenses. The utilities were not included in their new lease and now cost them fifteen dollars a month. Their telephone bill jumped because they now were charged on a unit basis when they talked with friends in their old neighborhood. Their car expenses, which had previously been low, because they had used it only for occasional pleasure trips, now were regularly at least thirty dollars a month. The husband's long drive to work also meant that they needed new tires much sooner than they had planned for in their budget. (The hidden costs of driving a car are often overlooked by people who believe that monthly payments and insurance are all that they are obliged to include in their budget.)

Next to purchasing a home, buying a car is generally a family's greatest expense. This is certainly not an item to buy on impulse. Where can you get good consumer information about new or used cars?

Further, during the first two months after this couple moved, before they were aware of the new expenses, they felt that they had made such a good gain by saving a flat fifty dollars a month on rent that they bought a new stereo. They made a down payment and contracted to pay twenty dollars monthly until it was paid for.

In the end, this couple realized that by cutting their rent fifty dollars a month, but failing to be realistic about what the move would add to their expenses, they had gotten into a very poor financial situation. They had added at least sixty-five dollars to their fixed monthly expenses in addition to unpredictable expenses such as increased telephone charges.

Because we in the United States are motor-oriented and every young person wants a car, many young families have serious difficulties over car expenses. In some marriages, during the early years, there is trouble because one feels that the other wastes money and keeps them poor by making unwise deals related to cars. To quote one wife after three years of marriage, "We'll never get ahead. Jim loves his car and spends money on it that ought to go for other things. He blocks off seeing how much it costs us to drive that car, and he won't face our financial problems. We had a good car that would have lasted a long time yet, but he had to have this one. I argued and talked, and we finally got to quarreling about it, so I just gave up. After all, I'm not going to break up my marriage over a *car*."

Actually, the factor likely to break up their marriage was not the car, but her husband's financial immaturity and the fact that they were not in agreement about how to manage money.

YOUR BUDGETING

High school students who have an income from after-school work, or from an allowance, have an excellent opportunity to learn about handling money. You can work out a plan for spending, listing the things that you know you habitually buy, as well as the needs you would like your income to cover if it were large enough. You can then evaluate the items on the list and decide which can be eliminated and which are worth sacrificing other things to have.

People who work at handling their money in this systematic way learn quickly that the budget has to be tailored to fit the person. One girl who earned money each week by baby-sitting worked out a spending-and-saving plan based on an ideal budget in a textbook; but she found it hard to follow the plan. After a time, she became disgusted with the whole idea. She told her mother that she didn't believe in budgeting and was going to drop the plan and spend as she pleased. Her mother helped her analyze her budget in relation to her special needs and habits, and together they decided what the trouble was.

She was trying to follow a plan that provided rigidly for all her spending, leaving no provision for buying on impulse. She revised the budget slightly and set aside a portion under the heading of "mad money." The money in that division was not be accounted for; thus, she would not keep any record of where it went. From then on, she was much better satisfied with her budgeting. As it turned out, some weeks she saved her "mad money" or added it to funds for some of the important things in other divisions; but knowing that it was there to be used as foolishly or as wisely as she pleased made her feel better.

CONCLUSIONS

The handling of money can be a challenge and a rewarding achievement. Or it can be a problem for the individual and a point of friction between husband and wife. Much depends upon the intelligence with which people approach the task and the understanding they have of themselves and their mates. It is of fundamental importance that those thinking of marriage discuss their values freely and make an effort to understand and appreciate the differences of similarities in their family backgrounds. It will be most helpful if they can examine the financial policies in their two parent families and decide which phases of their backgrounds they want to continue and which ones they want to discontinue.

QUESTIONS FOR REVIEW

1. What was revealed by the study of agreement on finances among engaged, married, and divorced people? How do you explain the findings of this study?
2. What are the three main types of problems that people have in handling the family income?
3. What kind of money problem seems to be the most serious in causing misunderstandings between husbands and wives?
4. Discuss some contrasts in what families value.
5. Why might a city girl have a hard time understanding the values of a farmer husband?
6. Why is it hard to understand and accept values that differ from our own?
7. Why should a couple who are both working base their financial plans upon only one of their incomes?

MAKING DECISIONS ABOUT FINANCES

8. In what type of marriage might considerable misunderstanding arise over who should control the spending?
9. Cite evidence to show that the wife should take greater responsibility than the husband for the spending.
10. What is the real purpose of a family budget?
11. List several justifications for a family budget.
12. Why do some couples become disillusioned with their budget?
13. How can the budget be misused?
14. How was it possible for the couple described in this chapter to worsen their financial situation when they moved to a suburb and reduced their rent by fifty dollars a month?
15. Can you see any value in a high school student's keeping a budget? Discuss.
16. What important principle of budgeting was brought out in the case of the girl who was having difficulty with her personal budget?

ACTIVITIES AND PROJECTS

1. Formulate a budget for yourself. Include all expenses, whether paid by you or by your parents.
2. Formulate a budget for a young couple keeping house on an income of five hundred dollars a month. Check up on average costs of housing, food, utilities, and clothing in your area, and make your budget as realistic as possible.
3. Who controls the spending of money in your family? Can you suggest another system that might work as well or better?
4. (Debate.) *Resolved:* That the husband should control the family purse.
5. Work out a budget for the cost of a car. Include all fixed expenses and all "hidden costs." Figure the total expense of the car for one year. If you present this budget to the class for discussion, will members of the class discover some cost you have not taken into consideration?

SOCIODRAMA

Two family scenes, a patriarchal family and a democratic family, in which the spending of money is the chief issue. Have both parents and children in each scene.

WORDS AND CONCEPTS

adherence
automatic
budget
disproportionate
economy
final authority

hidden costs
patriarchal family
prerogative
relative cost
superficial

Family Economics

22

After studying this chapter, you will be able to

1. Identify several sources of reliable consumer information.
2. Cite some points that the wise buyer will take into consideration when deciding where, how, and when to buy.
3. List important factors to consider when borrowing money or buying on installment plans.
4. Explain the real function of life insurance and the best kind of insurance for the average young family.
5. List several important points to consider when buying a home.

As we watch television, the commercials bombard us with "Use Little Boy Blue Soap and have beautiful hands," or "This year's model is the greatest!" On the radio, we hear from a finance company, "Let us lend you two hundred dollars just over your signature, no questions asked," or, "Try our easy payment plan and enjoy the new furniture now."

Advertising in the newspapers, magazines, on billboards, and on radio and television encourages us to buy all kinds of articles. The most effective psychological devices that have been discovered are employed to persuade us to buy, often beyond our means. The consumer has little way of knowing whether the advertised articles are of high or low quality, because extravagant claims are made for all goods.

EVERY HOME NEEDS A CONSUMER EXPERT

It takes special training to guide one through the confusion created by advertising. Because most families do not have large incomes with which to buy the necessities of life, it is important that they get the most for their money. The family shopper must know what are the best buys and be able to recognize quality.

Often it is necessary for families to borrow money in order to meet some of their needs. The consumer has to know where to borrow money at the lowest rate of interest.

Likewise, the average householder must buy protection in the form of insurance. It is important to know where adequate protection can be bought most cheaply and what protection is essential to cover particular situations and conditions.

THE WIFE AS THE CONSUMER EXPERT

In families where the wife does not have a job outside the home, she might become the expert in consumer economics. In earlier generations, the wife might not have had time to undertake the task of becoming a consumer expert. She was kept too busy with the physical work of homemaking. Today, new inventions and labor-saving devices give her relative freedom from household drudgery. She can take time to study values.

In effect, the wife who becomes a consumer expert gives the family an increase in pay. Her knowledge of quality and her wise buying of goods mean that the family has more money for other expenditures.

Husbands sometimes do not have as much time as wives to study consumer economics. If both the husband and the wife are working outside the home, both should try to become expert in this area. The responsibility in such cases should be shared or divided to fit convenience.

GETTING CONSUMER INFORMATION

With inflation, consumers increasingly demand accurate information that will protect them from unscrupulous and deceptive merchandising practices. Listed below are some agencies working to protect consumers. The addresses are given so that your class may write for materials.

1. Consumers Union, P.O. Box 3000, Mt. Vernon, New York 10550, is a private, nonprofit organization designed to help consumers get their money's worth. It buys items on the open market, tests them, and publishes the results in a monthly magazine, *Consumer Reports.* It also publishes an annual report giving a brief summary of all items tested during the preceding year and of books offering studies of life insurance, marketing practices, and medical quackery. *Consumer Reports* is the best single source of information available today.
2. Consumers' Research, Inc., Washington, New Jersey 07882, is similar to Consumers Union and publishes a summary of its findings in *Consumer Bulletin.*
3. Money Management Institute, Household Finance Corporation, Prudential Plaza, Chicago, Illinois 60601, has published twelve pamphlets: on food, clothing, housing, home furnishings and equipment, automobiles, health and recreation, budgets, savings and investments, and children's and teenagers' spending.
4. The American Institute for Economic Research, Great Barrington, Massachusetts 01230, offers information on budgeting, insurance, and other consumer matters.
5. U.S. News and World Report Series, Washington, D. C., published its first consumer book, *Planning Your Family Future,* in 1969. Write for the list of other books in the series.
6. Public Affairs Committee, Inc., 381 Park Avenue South, New York, New York 10016, publishes pamphlets covering many topics of current concern, including consumer economics.
7. Women's Division, Institute of Life Insurance, 277 Park Avenue, New York, New York 10017, has a pamphlet, "Lessons in Consumer Education for Adults," 1967. Their material on insurance is naturally biased. Read other sources as well.
8. State college or university extension services collect or develop publications to aid consumers. Many have a full-time specialist to help educate the public in consumer buying.

The federal government and some states have set up the office of consumer affairs to work for protective legislation.

SOME CONSIDERATIONS FOR BUYING

The intelligent, informed buyer knows *when to buy*. Better bargains are usually available at certain times of the year or week. Clothing may be on sale toward the end of the season. It is often possible to buy clothing at reduced prices after Christmas, because merchants may not wish to carry over their winter stock another year, or because they wish to clean up their inventory. At other times of the year, such as just after Easter, special sales on clothing allow buyers to save considerable amounts without any sacrifice of style or quality. In buying groceries, one usually finds that it pays to buy on the weekend when prices on the staples are lower.

The question also arises as to *where to buy.* The problem may be whether one should buy at department stores where charge accounts can be used or buy for cash at stores that offer "discount" prices. The one who has learned to study values and to compare prices will discover that in some cases so-called discount prices are no lower than the regular price. In other cases, substantial savings can be made by buying for cash at a "discount" store.

It is important for the family shopper to *buy according to plan* and not on impulse. The thrifty manager will check to see exactly what the clothing needs of family members are before going shopping. One will also plan meals ahead and have an accurate list of food needs before going to the supermarket. Then when shopping, one must resist buying additional items that are attractively displayed or are on sale but that are not really needed.

The young family that takes advantage of sales is practicing good family economics. Can you see the importance of this as the family increases?

JUDGING VALUES

Some consumers decide that they can never be sure whether or not an article is good by examining it, and, therefore, they make their choice on the basis of price. Some people always pay the highest price, believing that they will thereby get a good grade of merchandise. Others buy the lowest priced item, believing that they are thus getting a bargain. One thing that has been demonstrated repeatedly by such organizations as Consumers Union is that quality cannot be judged by the price of an article. Recently, one of the consumers' organizations made a test of men's shoes. After testing many qualities and brands, they found that the best shoe tested was a moderately priced brand. A highly advertised shoe that was selling for a much higher price was not so good a buy as the less expensive one. Other tests by these organizations have revealed that sometimes the most expensive article is best—and sometimes, the least expensive. Price may be one standard, but it is not the only one, and it is not always reliable.

In recent years, manufacturers of many family needs have hired experts who design attractive packages to induce the consumer to buy one brand in preference to another. Also, many items are packaged in ways that give a deceptive impression regarding quantity. Thus, the size or shape of container is not a guide any more than price is. For example, bottles are made in a variety of shapes so that an apparently large bottle may actually hold less than a more conventionally shaped one.

The federal government has become interested in the problem of deceptive packaging. However, the best protection for the consumer is still careful reading of all labels to learn exactly how many ounces are being bought, and figure the price per ounce.

The fact that an article is highly advertised is also no guarantee of superior quality. The consumer must learn to judge quality by studying information available from reliable sources.

BUYING CREDIT

At some time, most families find it necessary to borrow money in order to meet emergencies and unexpected obligations. Many American families decide to borrow money against future earnings in order to have articles for present use.

Unwise use of buying on credit leads to trouble. A study of bankruptcy was made in one California city. Bankruptcy is the last resort of failing business firms who can no longer pay their bills and stay in business. They may be forced to take this action by their creditors, or they may choose to go through court proceedings that will classify them as legally impoverished, or bankrupt. When such legal action is taken, they must declare all their assets and debts, and the court determines how the assets will be divided among the creditors.

A study of court records of bankruptcy in California found, surprisingly, that the majority of bankruptcies were by families, not businesses. Most were young families who had borrowed from finance companies or had charged more than they could pay. The last straw for many of these families was medical bills that they had not anticipated. When such unexpected expenses arose, they found themselves unable to pay the rent and utilities. Bankruptcy was the only way out for them. Yet for many of these families, bankruptcy was only a temporary solution. They were in the same difficulty a few years later. The study found that the families taking bankruptcy actually had incomes equal to the average income in their community. Their problem was that they were never realistic about how far their money would actually go. They used credit to get so deeply in debt that when emergencies arose, their situation was hopeless.

Most people need to borrow to pay for a car. On such a large purchase, credit terms from various sources should be carefully compared. How would you do this?

If a family must borrow money, it is important for them to shop for credit just as wisely as they shop for other goods. Interest rates vary from one lending agency to another, particularly because some lending agencies specialize in lending money to those who do not have good security. It is important for the family, then, to know its own financial standing. A family who has assets or securities that can be listed can usually borrow money at a lower rate of interest than if there are no securities. An ability to pay and a record of past payment on debts are important in determining the rate of interest that will be required.

When families have to borrow, they should not be misled by "easy-payment plans" or personal finance companies that advertise, "Just sign your name, no questions asked." After they have figured out their financial rating, they should investigate the possibilities and do their borrowing where interest is most reasonable. Interest rates vary from around 6 percent to actual averages of from 42 to 1200 percent at the most expensive source of lending.

A lower interest rate will cost you less. On a ten thousand dollar mortgage for ten years, here is the amount paid in interest at different rates:

at 7%	you will pay	$3,944
7½%		4,256
8%		4,568
8½%		4,870

Those who borrow from personal finance companies or small-loan companies, where the borrower just signs his name and no questions are asked, pay for this privilege in interest rates. The common charge by such companies is 30 percent interest per year. The average in the different states is from 30 to 42 percent a year. The borrower may be told that he is paying only 3 or 3½ percent on the unpaid balance, but this means that he is paying 3 or 3½ percent interest *per month,* which amounts to from 16 to 42 percent per year. This illustrates an instance where a highly advertised service is certainly not the best one for the consumer to use.

It is possible for most people to borrow from other less highly advertised sources of credit at lower rates of interest. Personal loan departments in banks charge rates much lower than the rates of finance companies. It is possible that the average individual can borrow from the bank.

Installment buying amounts to borrowing. Few people realize how much interest they are paying when they buy on the installment plan. With installment sellers, the common charge is 24 percent; but this varies from 8 to 275 percent, depending upon the business from which one buys.

For many years, the Congress of the United States has realized that because of concealed and misleading interest rates it was difficult for consumers to protect themselves against exorbitant charges. Most borrowers believed they were paying a much lower interest rate than they were actually paying. As of July 1, 1969, a federal Truth-in-Lending Act finally went into effect so that now lenders must state the *annual interest rates* on loans. This applies to credit contracts, private house first mortgages, and time-sales agreements. The popular revolving-credit charge account must state the interest charges on an annual basis. The usual interest rate has been $1^1/_2$ percent per month; now a contract at that rate must state that the real interest rate is 18 percent per year. With all interest charges stated in terms of rate per year, it is easier for consumers to shop for credit. They can compare interest charges as they compare other prices.

There are still ways in which charge account customers are required to pay too much. Some stores calculate service charges on an account *before* deducting payments each month, do not give a period of thirty days to pay with no extra service charge, and charge a minimum service fee for low credit balances. Any of these tactics results in a higher interest rate than the one stated in the contract. The Truth-in-Lending Act tries to regulate these practices, but the consumer must read the contract carefully to protect personal interests. It is best for the individual or the family not to count on government protection but to know how to figure the amount of money actually being paid when buying on credit.

THE DOLLAR COST OF CREDIT

It costs money to use credit. Take an example of a purchase and figure how many *extra* dollars your credit can cost. You want to buy a refrigerator. It costs $310 and you can make a down payment of $35. Under Dealer A's terms you would pay $17.50 a month for 18 months. Here is the way you figure the cost of credit under these conditions:

Price tag	$310
Minus your down payment	35
Leaves the balance owed on the price	$275
You will make a monthly payment of	$ 17.50
Times the number of payments	18
	140 00
	175 0
Equals THE AMOUNT YOU WILL PAY	$315.00
Now subtract the balance owed (above)	275.00
THIS IS YOUR COST OF CREDIT	$ 40.00*

* Constance Burgess, University of California, Berkeley.

Dealer B has a plan in which you would pay $16 a month for 21 months. Figure his plan in the same way. Which plan will cost you less? How much less? Do you think the additional cost is worth it?

BUYING SECURITY

One way the individual family protects itself against financial hardship is to insure against certain unpredictable losses. People insure their homes so that in case of fire or storm damage they will have some means of replacing the lost property.

It is usually more economical to buy a policy that runs for a period of from three to five years than to buy insurance for one year at a time.

Most insurance companies now sell what is called a Home Owners Policy. It applies not only to owners but also to tenants in a house or apartment. This package policy includes all the different kinds of insurance needed on a home: fire, theft, liability, and extended coverage, which not only insures for fire but also against windstorm, cyclone, hurricane, hailstorm, explosion, smoke, and damage from motor vehicles or airplanes that might crash into the house. The Home Owners Policy is cheaper than buying separate policies for such protection.

Car owners need insurance to protect themselves in case of accident. Ordinarily, a car owner should have a policy that includes personal and property damage liability. In many states, it is illegal to drive a car without liability insurance.

A seventeen-year-old boy in a state without a liability insurance requirement bought a car to drive back and forth to work at his summer job. The car was an old one, and his parents urged him to buy liability insurance before he drove the car; but he objected to spending the money, thinking that he had already spent all he could afford in paying for and repairing the car. The first day that he drove it, as he was coming home during the noon hour, he decided to offer a ride to two schoolmates who were walking along the street. He put on the brakes, then put the car in reverse and backed up with a flourish to his friends. Unfortunately, he failed to see a new convertible parked at the curb behind him. Its crumpled fender cost him far more than car insurance would have, and he still had no insurance.

Some people wish to carry accident or illness insurance on the main wage earner of the family. Need for such insurance will depend to a large extent upon one's occupation. Certain companies now have their workers fairly well covered. Some of these provide for illness as well as accident. There are also insurance plans that cover some hospital and surgical expenses. These may cover the wage earner only, or the entire family. Workers are protected by Workmen's Compensation laws if they are injured on the job and by Disability Insurance in some states.

LIFE INSURANCE

Although the Social Security Act has been extended to provide most workers with a retirement income in old age, it does not provide enough protection for the head of the family during the years of greatest responsibility. That is why many family heads carry life insurance. It has been estimated that 75 percent of American families carry some form of life insurance.

People sometimes think of life insurance as serving two purposes, protecting the dependents in case of the wage earner's death and saving money for old age. The *chief* purpose of life insurance should be *protection rather than saving.* Certain insurance policies emphasize the savings principle, but other ways are more desirable.

Several different types of insurance policies are offered by salespeople, but one type that young people, married or single, should not buy is *endowment insurance.* If you will study Graph 21 on the costs of different kinds of insurance, you will see that endowment policies give only about one-tenth the protection that the same premium would buy in a term policy.

Term insurance is what the name implies—insurance written for a certain term, or period, usually five or ten years. Like car or fire insurance, in that you renew your policy at the end of the term and do not collect on it unless you have an accident or a fire, with term insurance

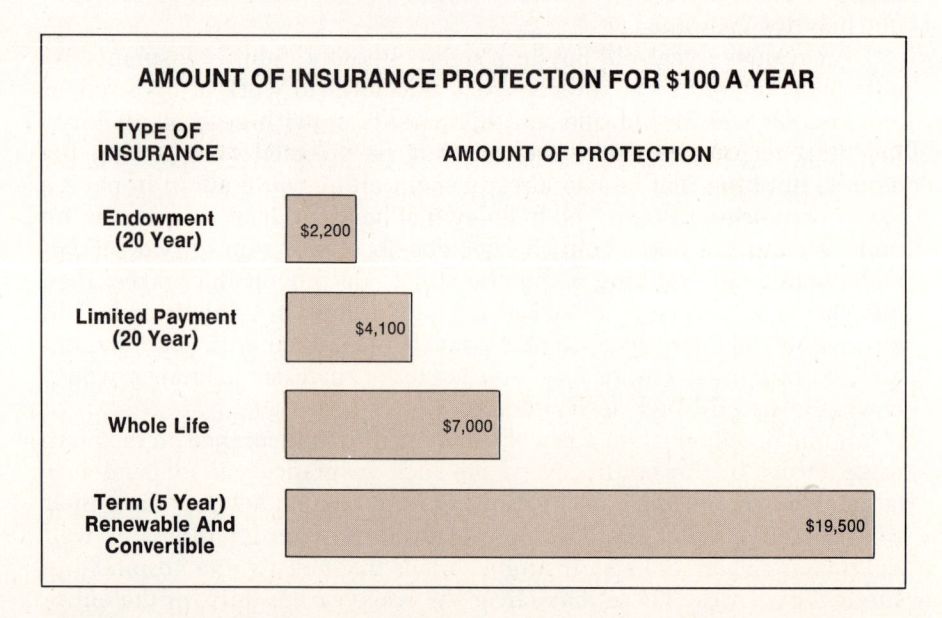

AMOUNT OF INSURANCE PROTECTION FOR $100 A YEAR

TYPE OF INSURANCE	AMOUNT OF PROTECTION
Endowment (20 Year)	$2,200
Limited Payment (20 Year)	$4,100
Whole Life	$7,000
Term (5 Year) Renewable And Convertible	$19,500

Graph 21. This graph clearly shows that insurance should be bought for immediate financial protection and not as an investment.

the amount is payable only in case of death. When you renew the policy the premium will be slightly higher, because you will be older during the next term. One should always buy insurance that is renewable without a physical examination and that is convertible to other types of policies. Today, almost all term policies are written that way. For the young family in need of the most protection while they are getting established financially, the best protection to buy is a term life insurance policy.

A type of excellent term insurance available to many people is *group insurance* provided by employers. Manufacturers, businesses, federal and state governments, and many other organizations insure their workers as a group on a term basis at very low rates. In some cases, the cost is paid by the employer; in others, the worker pays part of the cost. The worker is covered only while he remains with the organization, so usually the head of a young family needs to have additional term insurance.

Term insurance is now the most common type of insurance sold, and for good reasons. Its advantages are

1. All of the premium paid goes for protection so that the family gets the most protection for the money (see Graph 21).
2. Because the premium is based upon the present age of the insured person, one pays only what needs to be paid at that age.
3. Young families who need maximum protection can pay only a small premium but can buy adequate protection when they most need insurance.
4. The family does not have to worry about inflation or deflation of money because they are not signing up for the next thirty or forty years.

G. I. INSURANCE

When young people go into the armed forces, the government insures them under the Servicemen's Group Insurance plan (G.I. Insurance). This is good, inexpensive, financial protection for a family during military duty. When they leave the service, the policy must be converted to a regular commercial policy and the usual rates must be paid for whatever insurance is bought. Some people make the mistake of converting to endowment insurance, which gives little protection for the money. The best choice is to convert to a term policy.

The family's insurance program should be kept flexible enough to meet its needs as the wage earner goes from early marriage to old age. In general, the family head will want to carry the maximum amount of insurance when the children are small and dependent. Graph 22 shows that the dependency load of the average American wage earner is largest at the age of thirty-nine. The maximum amount of protection

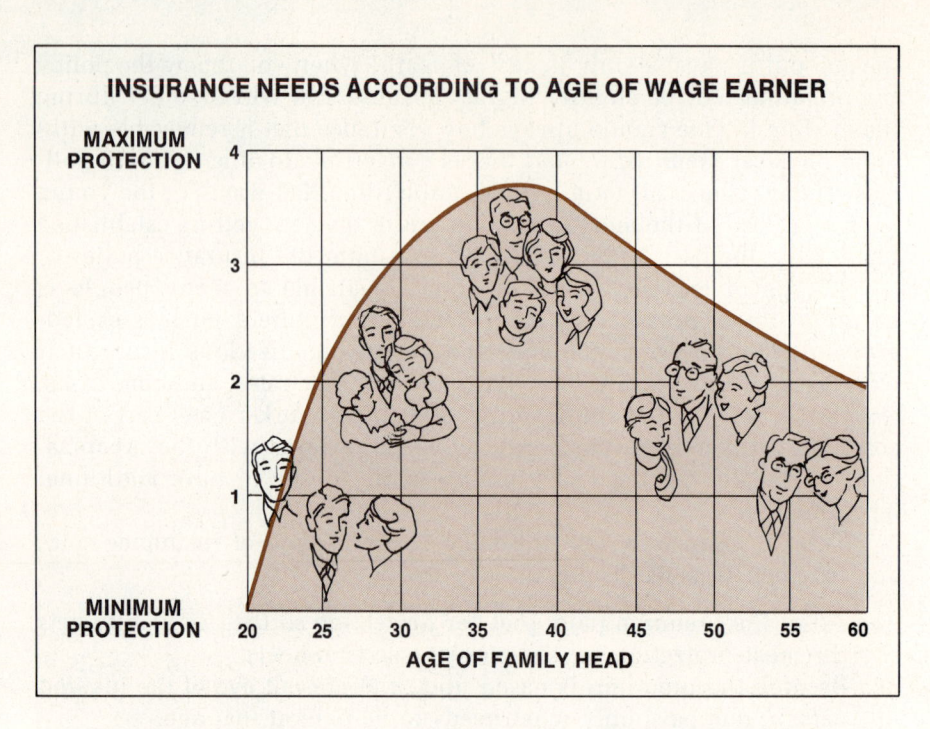

INSURANCE NEEDS ACCORDING TO AGE OF WAGE EARNER

Graph 22. Insurance purchased should provide maximum protection when the wage earner's family has the greatest need, while the children are dependent.

for the family is needed when the average head of household is between the ages of twenty-six and forty-six. As dependency load decreases after forty-six, when the children marry and leave home, the wage earner can cut down on the amount of insurance being carried or can convert some of the policies to other forms of insurance designed to build up a reserve for old age.

POINTERS IN BUYING LIFE INSURANCE

1. Young single people reading this book should not consider buying insurance at this time nor during your college years if you go to college. Most of you have no need for it. An exceptional case might be that of a young person who is in debt and whose death or injury would bring a financial hardship to the parents. If you have bought a car, and your parents have signed a note guaranteeing payment, you might take out a term policy to protect them.
2. Think separately of protection and investment. When a young family is most dependent, it should buy the type of policy (usually, renewable term) that primarily features protection and gives the largest amount for the smallest cost.

3. If income is limited, *place all insurance on the wage earner,* the loss of whom is the thing against which families need insurance.
4. Buy insurance at the lowest cost. Many insurance companies recognize that for various reasons certain people qualify for lower premiums. Women live longer than men and so they may be insured at a lower premium. People who smoke cigarettes have a higher death rate from lung cancer, emphysema, strokes, and heart and circulatory diseases. They have a shorter life expectancy, and, therefore, they must pay higher premiums for insurance in some companies. The nonsmoker is in a preferred risk group and gets a lower premium. People in certain occupations face fewer hazards and qualify for lower premiums.
5. Rather than one large policy, buy several small policies so all premiums do not come due at the same time. Pay premiums annually rather than semiannually or quarterly; this usually means a saving.
6. Don't be oversold on insurance. One of the most serious mistakes consumers make is to buy more insurance than they can carry. They become "insurance poor," and if reverses hit, they have to drop much of their insurance, and the money paid in is lost.
7. Buy only from qualified salespeople. It is also a good idea to get information about insurance from several sources.
8. Don't buy insurance on a baby unless you can afford to *after all other family insurance needs* are taken care of. New "family plan" policies, which cover the entire family, even unborn children, appeal to some people. But such policies contradict the sound principle that insurance should be upon the family head, not the entire family. Some major insurance companies refuse to sell a policy on a baby until the wage earner has adequate coverage.
9. Don't buy insurance in a hurry. Understand what you are buying. Ask an agent to put the best plan for you in outline form and leave it, along with materials from the company describing the policy. After careful study, make your decision.
10. If you buy term insurance, be sure it is renewable, renewable without an examination, and convertible to another type of policy.
11. Don't buy insurance until you need it, as you acquire dependents. It is sometimes argued that one should buy insurance early to get cheaper premiums. Actually, premium rates do not change much between ages sixteen and twenty-six. Further, to buy anything because it is cheap is not a bargain if you do not need it.

RENTING OR BUYING A HOME

People marrying today usually rent for the first few years. A good rule is that the rent should not exceed about one-fourth of the family's income. Couples are often inclined to rent apartments that are new and thus have conveniences such as a garbage disposal, dishwasher, wall-to-wall carpeting, and a balcony. Apartments in older buildings may not have these features, but they have some advantages. They may be more soundproof, have larger rooms, more closets and storage space, a yard or garden, a garage or parking space—and lower rent.

Many married couples wish to buy a home. To buy has been sound practice for many years because, with inflation, houses continually increase in value. Couples buying a home should consider the following points:

1. The purchase price should not be more than three times the family's annual income.
2. Assume that you may want to sell the house within a few years. Look for any features that would make it hard to resell. Are the rooms well-planned for an average family? Is the quality of the house equal to that of others in the neighborhood?
3. If buying a newly built house, check for such factors as the possibility of flooding in heavy rainfall or sliding during a wet season, cracks in any walls, window leaks, adequacy of the heating system. Is the house in an area that will increase or decrease in value?
4. If buying an older house, check the wiring, plumbing, heating system, and understructure to see that it meets today's code requirements. It may pay to call in an expert to appraise the structure.
5. In many areas, the buyer should have an expert inspect the property for termites and other wood-destroying organisms. The buyer pays the cost of inspections, and the seller must pay for repairing any damage discovered.
6. Consider what immediate repairs or changes in the structure would have to be made, and count the cost of additional furniture and equipment needed, rugs, curtains or window shades, and redecorating. These expenses are a part of the initial cost just as the down payment is.
7. Shop for the most favorable financing available. The real estate agent can help with this. Consider the advantages of paying down as little as possible and paying off the loan over as long a period of time as possible with the lowest interest rate that can be had.
8. Offer a reasonable price, not necessarily the asked price, for a house. Most houses up for resale have an asking price and a price at which the owner expects to sell. The latter depends upon individual circumstances.

By considering all factors carefully and buying their first home with reasonable caution rather than impulsively, young couples may make a considerable saving on this long-term investment.

FAMILY ECONOMICS

Chapter 21 discussed the necessity for husband-wife agreement on using the family income and on the division of the responsibility for handling their money. This chapter offers specific information for the family as consumers. In all matters discussed here, the young single person will do well to be prepared with information that will help to avoid unnecessary financial problems later. It is especially necessary to evaluate one's attitudes and prejudices concerning money and its use. Attitudes will affect the future security and the success of marriage.

QUESTIONS FOR REVIEW

1. Why is it more necessary today than formerly for the family buyer to have a knowledge of consumer economics?
2. Who should be the consumer expert in the family? Discuss.
3. Give several sources of information for consumers.
4. Cite some points that the wise buyer will consider in deciding *when* and *where* to buy.
5. "I always buy the article that costs the most; then I know I am getting the best." Discuss.
6. Do you think manufacturers should be prohibited from packaging products in ways that make it difficult to judge the amount of the contents?
7. "Nationally advertised brands are the safest buys." Discuss.
8. Is it the families with the lowest incomes who file for bankruptcy? How do bankrupt families differ from solvent families in the same community?
9. How do you account for the large difference in interest rates charged by different lending agencies?
10. What are the provisions of the Truth-in-Lending Act? In what ways may charge account customers still pay extra charges in some stores?
11. Why is it especially important for those who drive cars to carry personal and property liability insurance?
12. What is the real function of life insurance?
13. What is the best kind of insurance for the average young family to buy? Should insurance be carried on all family members?
14. Give several points to remember when buying life insurance.
15. If you were to buy life insurance now, would you qualify as a "preferred risk" and thus be eligible for a lower premium?
16. What are some advantages in renting a newly built apartment? An older one?
17. Give several key points for buying a house.

ACTIVITIES AND PROJECTS

1. Pay attention for one evening to advertising on radio. Keep a list of the claims that are open to reasonable doubt.

2. At a grocery, buy several cans of a certain vegetable: the lowest-priced, the highest-priced, and a medium-priced brand. Open the cans and have your family decide by taste and appearance which is the best buy. Is there a difference in the amount of solid matter as against liquid? Remove the labels and number the cans before testing, so no one will be influenced by price or brand.

3. Go to a grocery and select three jars of some item. They should have identical contents but be packaged in different shapes so that their size is deceiving. Do the same with three boxes. Report to class on your observations.

4. John and Mary have been married seven years; they have four children and several debts. Should they have life insurance? If so, what type of policy would you recommend? Should the insurance be on John, Mary, the children, or some on each?

5. Henry is a senior in high school. He still lives at home and has no debts or dependents. Should he carry life insurance? If so, what kind?

6. Send to: The New Jersey Office of Consumer Protection, 1100 Raymond Blvd., Newark, New Jersey, for the illustrated checklist, "To Buy or Not to Buy—How Do You Decide Which Used Car to Buy?" Post it on the class bulletin board and, after all have seen it, have a panel discussion on buying a used car.

7. If your state or locality has an office of affairs, consumer or equivalent, write to learn what laws have been enacted to protect consumers.

8. Investigate the various types of credit. Find out from a bank or department store how credit can be established.

9. Discuss with a real estate agent the points given on buying a house. Obtain additional information, including some on legal fees, property tax rates, school tax, garbage collection tax, necessary household equipment. What are some of the hidden costs?

WORDS AND CONCEPTS

praise
bankruptcy
consumer economics
convertible
deceptive
Home Owners Policy
inflation
interest rate
investment

liability insurance
medical quackery
premium
revolving-credit charge account
solvent
term insurance
Truth-in-Lending Act
unscrupulous
wage earner

Avoiding Divorce

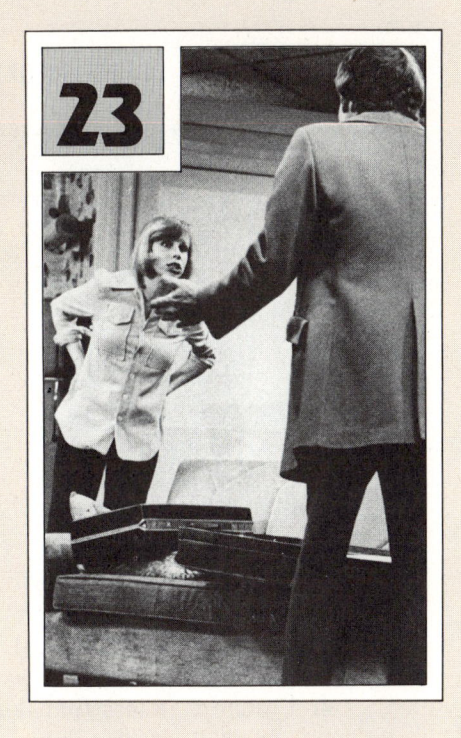

23

After studying this chapter, you will be able to

1. List factors that have an effect on whether or not people will dissolve or endure an unhappy marriage.
2. Describe the necessary procedure one goes through to get a divorce in most states.
3. Give the two basic concepts of no-fault divorce, and distinguish these from adversary proceedings.
4. Discuss the function of Conciliation Courts.
5. List some specific personality traits related to marital unhappiness.
6. Outline the questions those considering divorce should ask themselves.

It is much more challenging to consider the subject of divorce honestly and thoroughly in a discussion with people in their teens than with a group of older people who are already married. The reason for this is that the time to take a realistic look at divorce is before you marry. Those who clearly understand the nature of divorce will try to choose mates more wisely. They will know that, once married, the task is to work through any problem that may arise, for divorce is no easy way out. They may go into marriage with a stronger determination to build for success.

RATIO OF MARRIAGES TO DIVORCES

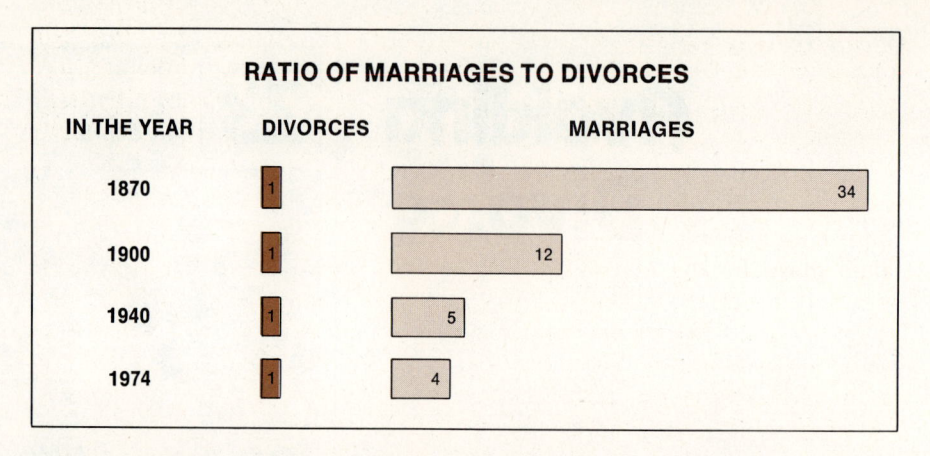

IN THE YEAR	DIVORCES	MARRIAGES
1870	1	34
1900	1	12
1940	1	5
1974	1	4

Graph 23. The ratio of divorces to marriages in four different years. The divorce rate had steadily increased.

A few generations ago, it was not necessary for those thinking of marriage to give thought to the subject of divorce, because divorce was a rare occurrence. In 1870, there was only 1 divorce for every 34 marriages. In 1900 the ratio was 1 in 12 marriages; in 1940 it was 1 in 5; and today it is less than 1 in 4.

In 1870, divorces were so rare it meant a scandal; the divorced person was usually in disgrace. The increasing frequency of divorce with the passing of time and some change in social attitudes have resulted in less stigma for those who divorce.

The great increase in divorce does not mean that marriage unhappiness has increased so extensively. It means that now when people are not happily married they are inclined to seek a way out through divorce. It means something more, however, and this second fact is the one that is of concern to us here. The present frequency and legal ease of divorce may mean that many couples, who *could* find happiness together if they would remain married, now turn to divorce. Some of these couples might be fortunate if no divorce were possible.

MARRIAGE FAILURE COMES EARLY

The failure of a couple to adjust usually comes early in marriage. Although most couples are or think they are in love with each other when they marry, many become discouraged in the early months or years of marriage.

More people divorce in the third year after the wedding than in any other single year; and half of all divorces are secured during the first six years of marriage. But marriages fail long before divorces occur. The psychological break comes when one or both partners conclude that the situation is hopeless. At this point, they may separate, but it usually takes longer for them to become ready to undergo the stress of the complications involved in divorcing.

A California study analyzed the length of time from the wedding to the separation of couples who finally filed for divorce or annulment. It found the first year of marriage to be the most common one in which these couples had separated. Almost half of all these separations had taken place by the end of the fourth year of the marriage. (Graph 24 shows this pattern.) Clearly, disillusionment is not delayed for many couples who should never have married each other in the beginning. While separation and divorce also occur between couples married for many years, these are, statistically, the exceptions. Many of the longer married couples also had the psychological break much earlier, but for various reasons, they could not bring themselves to seek divorces until years later.

WHY UNHAPPY MARRIAGES CONTINUE

There are many reasons why some people in unhappy marriages wait years before they divorce, and in some cases never divorce. In fact, it is not necessarily the unhappiest couples who do divorce. Because of certain circumstances people may continue in a marriage that is very

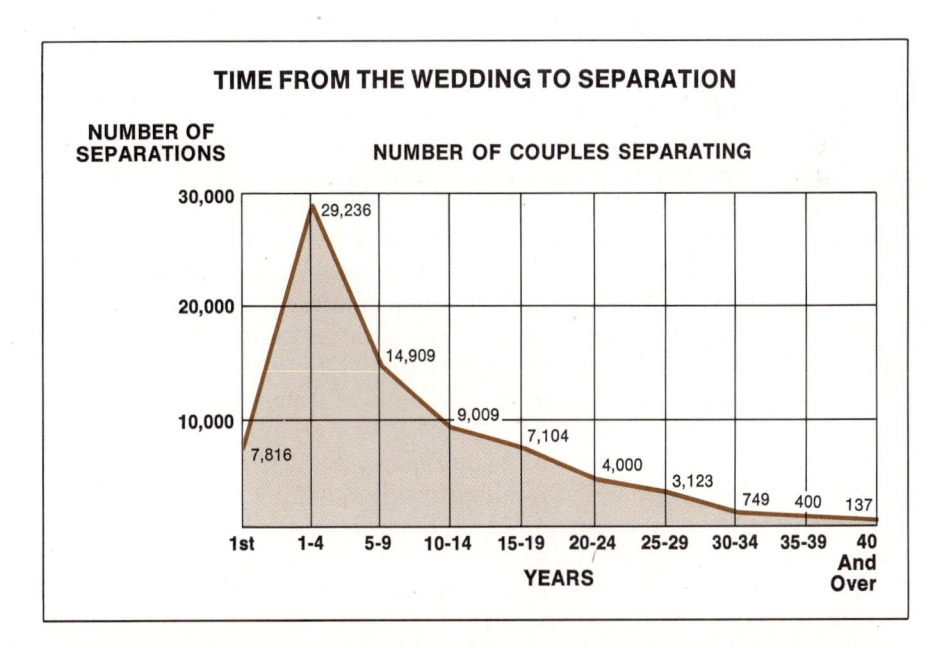

TIME FROM THE WEDDING TO SEPARATION

Years	Number of Couples Separating
1st	7,816
1-4	29,236
5-9	14,909
10-14	9,009
15-19	7,104
20-24	4,000
25-29	3,123
30-34	749
35-39	400
40 And Over	137

Graph 24. Length of time from wedding to separation of 69,292 first marriages among couples filing for divorce, separate maintenance, or annulment in California in 1966.

unhappy. In studying many unhappy marriages, we found that people who were very religious were more likely to remain married than were people who were indifferent to religion. Women who had little education or who had no vocational training were more likely to remain married than were women who had more education and who had a job or profession.

We found that people who were from families with a history of divorce were quicker to end an unhappy marriage through separation and divorce than were people whose families did not have a history of divorce. Divorce becomes an accepted way out of an unhappy marriage to those who have seen it in their own families, while it takes time for the person from a family that has no divorces to accept the idea of divorce. The latter will struggle longer to save their marriage, refuse to accept divorce as a solution, and possibly remain in the unhappy marriage. A religious couple may be very unhappily married and yet never seriously consider divorce. A nonreligious couple from a family surrounded by divorced relatives may divorce, although their marriage might not be as unhappy as that of the religious couple.

THE DECISION TO DIVORCE

The decision to divorce is emotionally disturbing, if not traumatic, to most people. During the courtship period leading up to engagement and marriage, a couple tends to emphasize and build upon their similar interests, their needs for each other, and their ways of looking at life. If couples notice differences before marriage, they often refuse to face them realistically. They think the differences will go away after they are married. Day-to-day living, however, forces people to come to grips with their differences. The less well people know each other before marriage, the more likely they are to have differences. The previous research (see page 174) on length of acquaintance and engagements shows a higher degree of happiness for those who were well acquainted before marriage.

The period of courtship leading up to marriage is one of greater and greater emotional involvement. This process continues after marriage for those who continue to find congeniality in their relationship. For those who begin to discover many points of differences, the process becomes one of *alienation.* It is a process of growing out of love, the reverse of what was experienced before marriage. It is a process of love turning to dislike, happiness to unhappiness; of feeling needed and then unwanted; of desires being met and then denied; of encouragement changing to discouragement and hope to despair. The alienation leading up to separation and divorce may come quickly, or it may continue over a period of years.

If there were many danger signals in a relationship before marriage, a couple might not be so disillusioned after marriage. One or both soon may come to realize that they should never have married, that there were too many conflicts. Couples struggling through the period of alienation behave in ways that they themselves do not always understand. Society tends to give more guidance on how to fall in love than it does on how to fall out of love. Everyone "loves a lover" according to the poets, but who loves or understands the one falling out of love?

Couples whose relationship is falling apart often move between being in love and being out of love. The couple did have much in their relationship that was good, or they would not have married in the first place. As they go through alienation, they often weigh the good and the bad in trying to decide what to do. It is typical that they have serious quarrels and then make up, or that they separate and then come back together. Verbal attacks are made upon each other that are sometimes forgiven, but not necessarily forgotten. Each may have a brief love affair with someone else.

As the relationship deteriorates, there are more thoughts of divorce. Because of the disapproval of divorce, it is difficult for people to admit to their friends and family that they have made a failure of their marriage. If the parents opposed the marriage, the person may be in greater turmoil because it is hard to admit that the parents were right. People who have a strong religious orientation may suffer because their beliefs are not compatible with divorce. Some weigh the merits of the bad marriage they are in against the possibility of living a single life should they not be able to remarry.

The decision to divorce does not come easily for most people. Today, even though the stigma against divorce has been largely removed, people still take marriage seriously, and the process of dissolving a close relationship like marriage is difficult. People often develop emotional and physical symptoms that are not easily understood by themselves or others. People going through the turmoil of a failing marriage may be difficult to live or work with. They may have more health problems, may become sexually promiscuous, or may drink excessively. If there are children, they may become the victims of the unreasonable behavior of their parents, while the parents' decision to divorce becomes more difficult because they want to do the right thing for their children. They are faced with the decision to stay married for the sake of their children or, possibly, to get a divorce for the sake of their children. Their decision is difficult.

DIVORCE LAWS

When a marriage reaches the breaking point, by custom it tends to be the woman who seeks and is granted the divorce. Under our present laws, three out of four divorces are awarded to the wife. Many authorities who have studied divorce in our society believe that the divorce laws need rewriting. To end a marriage that has failed, the wife—or husband—should not be forced to make charges and accusations against the mate. Such charges are seldom the true reasons for the failure of the marriage.

The way the law works on this point is shown by the words of a young woman going through the process of divorce after seven years of marriage. After a very short acquaintance and whirlwind courtship, she had married a man who was extremely immature and inadequate as a husband and as a father to their two young sons. She struggled through much emotional turmoil, but at last decided to divorce.

After conferences with her lawyer about the upcoming court proceedings, she said, "I'm afraid I won't be able to go through with what he says I'll have to do in court. He says I will have to charge Phil with some offense, such as adultery, mental or physical cruelty, fraud, drunkenness, desertion, or neglect. He told me that these may not be the causes of the trouble in our marriage, but they are the charges the court accepts as reasons for divorce. He said that today when people divorce, one usually charges the other with mental or physical cruelty. I told him that Phil had not committed any of these offenses and that it would be better to agree to a divorce. He then informed me that agreeing to a divorce constitutes an illegal act called *collusion*. To agree to divorce is illegal because a divorce is based upon *adversary* proceedings that assume guilt and innocence. I must prove in court that Phil was guilty of doing harm to me or the children. I'm used to telling the truth. It's hard for me to lie. Phil has not been cruel to me. He has done the best he could. But being married to him means that I have to be responsible for three little boys—not two. You can't treat a husband as if he were a son! I get all twisted up trying to pretend that one of the little boys is a man and the head of the family. I can't raise my sons this way—it's absolutely impossible. I asked my lawyer why I couldn't just say in court that Phil did the best he could, but our marriage was impossible. But the lawyer says there would be no divorce then. I have to charge Phil with something, and cruelty is the usual choice. Not only that, but I have to have a witness in court to swear that this is the truth about Phil."

Laws are no longer appropriate that require that for a couple to divorce, charges must be filed and one or the other person must be shown to be the offender. There are many reasons why marriages fail. Realistic divorce laws must recognize this and they must be designed to help find solutions to the problems involved for a couple, their children, and society.

Increasing concern about divorce laws arises because today the majority of divorcing couples have children, and the effect of parental conflict and marital break-up is likely to be terribly damaging to children. It is suggested that unhappy couples have competent counseling help. The needs of all the family members—the children and the husband and wife—can thus be considered before the decision is made whether to end a marriage or to make further efforts to keep it intact.

NO-FAULT DIVORCE

Many years ago, authorities working with families who had problems recognized the need for change to a better way of dissolving unhappy marriages than through adversary proceedings. In 1969, California completely changed the concept of divorce from adversary to one of *no fault.* The court is no longer interested in guilt or innocence but whether or not there are *irreconcilable differences* that make it impossible for the couple to live together. If the court decides there are irreconcilable differences, the marriage is dissolved. No fault on the part of either party is the concept applied to marriage failure when considered in terms of irreconcilable differences rather than from guilt or innocence. Since California passed this pioneering divorce reform law in 1969, nine other states* have passed similar laws, and more states will doubtless pass revised laws reflecting the new concept.

Most states adopting the new code for ending marriages use the term *dissolution of marriage* rather than *divorce.* Some states still use the word *divorce* as synonymous with *dissolution of marriage.* In California, if after counseling the court finds there are irreconcilable differences, and there are no chances for reconciliation, the marriage is dissolved, and the decree becomes final in six months. In Iowa, dissolution is granted if "there has been a breakdown of the marriage relationships to the extent that the legal objects of matrimony have been destroyed, and there remains no reasonable likelihood that the marriage can be preserved." The new Texas Family Code adds *insupportability* as a reason for divorce. Insupportability is defined as "discord or a conflict of personalities that destroys the legitimate ends of the marriage relationship and prevents reasonable expectations of reconciliation."

All of the new divorce codes reflect two new concepts about failing marriages. The no-fault concept recognizes that there are neither innocent nor guilty parties in a failing marriage. In most cases, the two people should never have married in the first place, and each was equally responsible for having decided to marry. The second concept in the new reform recognizes that it is the psychological break in a relationship that is responsible for the real ending of a marriage not the legal termination through divorce. If the marriage has reached the point where there are irreconcilable differences or if discord or conflict of personalities has destroyed the legitimate purpose of the marriage, then psychologically there is no reason for the marriage to continue.

---

* The states are Arizona, Colorado, Florida, Iowa, Kentucky, Nebraska, Oregon, Texas, and Washington.

One argument against the reform in divorce laws is that it will result in more divorces than have occurred under adversary proceedings. Some argue that laws should be passed to make divorce more difficult rather than easier. The no-fault divorce laws have not been enacted long enough in most states to answer these questions, but the evidence accumulating in California sheds some light. When the new law went into effect in California, divorces increased by 46 percent during the next year. However, in the same year, the waiting period for divorce was reduced from one year to six months. This change alone would result in an increase in divorce. Before the waiting period was reduced, many California couples went to Nevada for a quick divorce. After the new law went into effect, they divorced in California. There has been no percentage increase in divorce over that of the first year after enactment. As the laws become enacted in other states, more information will be gathered that will help answer the question of whether or not no-fault divorce laws lead to more divorces. We should stress that divorce is not always bad; it does make it possible for people to get out of destructive marriage. Our goal, however, is to improve the courtship process and to extend premarital education so that fewer people get into marriages that are likely to fail.

CONCILIATION COURTS

People who have serious difficulties in their marriage tend to struggle for some time before they will admit to others that they are having problems. They do not seek outside help early and when they do, it is often from unqualified people. They may talk to friends and family, when actually they should be talking with trained marriage counselors. Several states following the new divorce procedure have set up Courts of Conciliation. These function as an aid to people trying to decide about divorce. When people go to the court to petition for a separation, the court may first require that the couple go to a marriage counselor associated with the court. This is more likely to be required if the couple have minor children. The marriage counselors work with the couple in helping them to decide whether or not their marriage should be dissolved. The counselors also advise the judge before he makes his final disposition of the case. In states having Conciliation Courts, couples can go for marriage counseling before starting action for a divorce. Marriage counselors associated with courts do not have enough time to work with couples for more than a few sessions. If a couple needs extended counseling, they must go to a private counselor. The number of couples having serious marital problems indicates a strong need for more qualified counselors. People need expert help in trying to decide whether their marriage should be dissolved or has some chance of happiness.

WHAT IS DIVORCE?

Divorce has been appropriately called "the unhappy opposite of a wedding." The wedding is the legal, official beginning of a marriage, and weddings are traditionally happy occasions. In contrast, divorce is the legal seal that officially ends a marriage, and divorces are almost always traumatic in some way for everyone concerned.

Because there are many divorces, some people hold rather casual attitudes about divorce. They may assume that divorce is a fairly easy way out for those whose marriage does not give them what they had hoped for. But outside observers cannot know the bitterness that almost inevitably is a part of divorce. People who have married, intending to love and cherish each other until death, and who have tried for months or years to make a permanent union of their lives, cannot easily break their relationship and publicly acknowledge failure. Even the worst of marriages usually have some bonds that can be broken only through a painful process of disillusionment and struggle.

It is true that in many cases divorce is the only logical course of action. It represents an attempt to meet problems by changing circumstances and trying to reorganize one's life. But because one can never "go back and start over," a marriage that has ended will be a permanent factor in the divorced person's future experiences.

CAUSES OF DIVORCE

The official causes of divorce as listed in court records all over the country fall under a few main headings as shown in Graph 25.

These are not necessarily the real causes of divorce. They are merely, under present laws, the reasons given by people who seek divorce. If a couple have in fact been cruel to each other, *why* have they been so? Why are they unfaithful? Why do they desert each other? The reasons go back far into the personalities of the two who marry.

Chapter 3 discussed the various ways people meet their problems. It pointed out that the habitual ways people have for reacting to life situations will have much to do with what kind of partners they will make in marriage. Before you marry is the time to examine your behavior patterns and to begin working to change ways or habits that are handicaps. Throughout this book we have emphasized the importance of also looking at the personality of the one you plan to marry, because the roots of unhappiness might already be present in some people before they ever marry. They will create problems for themselves and for others wherever they go. Divorce will not solve their problems; therefore, one good way to avoid divorce is to avoid marriage to a person who has

LEGAL REASONS FOR SECURING DIVORCES

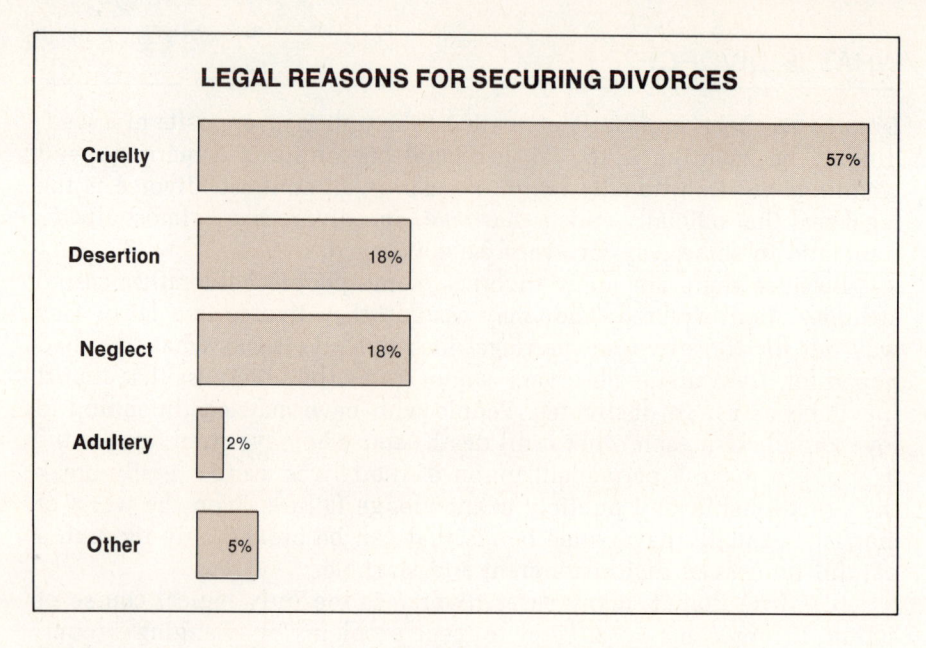

- Cruelty: 57%
- Desertion: 18%
- Neglect: 18%
- Adultery: 2%
- Other: 5%

Graph 25. Legal reasons used for securing divorces, as reported in 21 states.

personality problems. Census data on marriage and divorce show that people who have failed in one marriage are more likely to fail in a second, and those who have failed in two marriages are more likely to fail in a third. Graph 26 summarizes a study of the divorce rate according to how many times people have been married, and it charts the increases in failure with the increasing number of previous marriages. This emphasizes the necessity to look clearly at your own marriageability, if you would avoid divorce.

However, those who can recognize in themselves the roots of unhappiness may overcome their handicaps. It is true that the experiences of early childhood help or hinder personality growth; we may develop traits that make it hard to be good wives or husbands, but we can overcome these disadvantages.

Two sociologists who have studied growth and life experiences said, "We do not believe that the early personality is so irrevocable as the crack of doom. There certainly is no reason for a fatalistic view concerning man's ability to break the mold of his childhood learning. Admittedly, this learning often sets the pattern for many later responses toward people—but old men learn to change their habits of living; selfish men learn to sacrifice. Even cowards, under a powerful surge of hope, or in new situations, or by gaining insight, learn to stand and to hold their ground. The adult outgrows his fears. . . ."*

---

* W. Allison Davis and Robert J. Havighurst, *Father of the Man*. Boston: Houghton Mifflin Company. 1947.

Thus, those who have weaknesses or faults that will make it hard for them to adjust well in marriage can, nevertheless, have happy marriages if they are determined to succeed. The important point is that they must know that the fault is within themselves, not in marriage, and perhaps not in the person they have married. That is why divorce is not necessarily a solution to marriage problems.

SPECIFIC PERSONALITY TRAITS AND DIVORCE

In an attempt to get at the personality traits that make for unhappiness in marriage, L. M. Terman asked 792 couples to rank the most common grievances each mate had against the other. The complaints were ranked according to their seriousness in causing difficulty in the marriage. The twenty-eight most common ones are listed in Table 11. If you study the list given by husbands and wives, you will notice that most of the grievances are based upon personality traits in the individual, traits that were present before marriage.

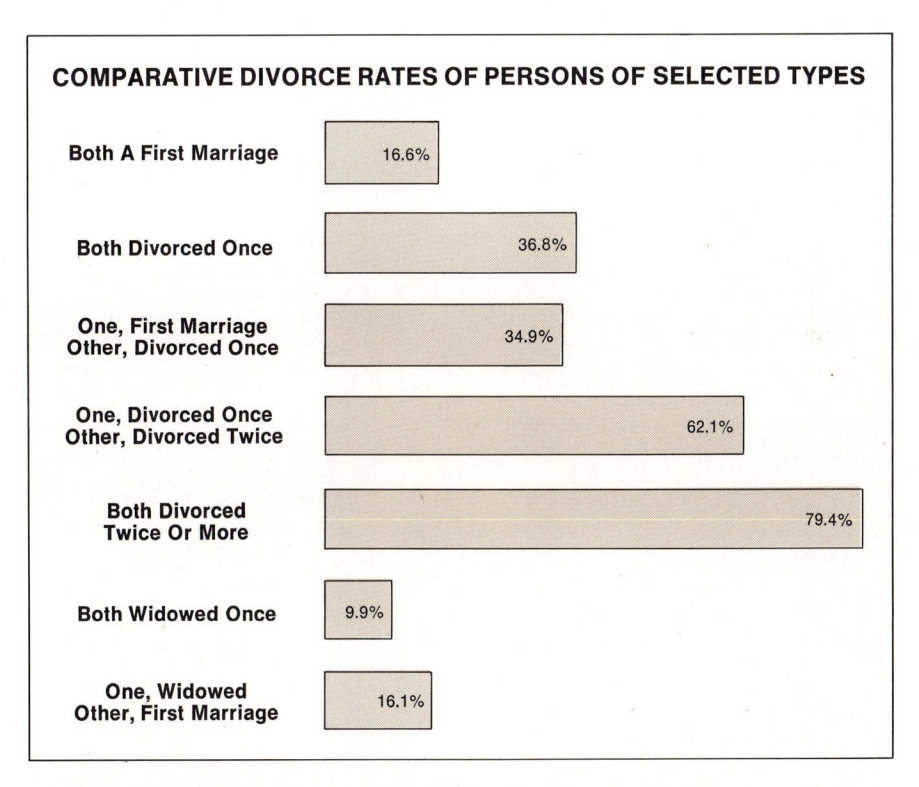

COMPARATIVE DIVORCE RATES OF PERSONS OF SELECTED TYPES

Both A First Marriage	16.6%
Both Divorced Once	36.8%
One, First Marriage Other, Divorced Once	34.9%
One, Divorced Once Other, Divorced Twice	62.1%
Both Divorced Twice Or More	79.4%
Both Widowed Once	9.9%
One, Widowed Other, First Marriage	16.1%

Graph 26. Although this study was done a number of years ago, subsequent ones yield essentially the same profile.

To illustrate, the husbands ranked first in order that their wives were nagging, not affectionate, selfish and inconsiderate, and complaining. Selfish dispositions and complaining attitudes toward life are not traits that suddenly develop after marriage. They were present before, but these husbands did not see them, did not want to see them, or did not consider them serious. In marriage, they loom large as causes of trouble.

Our study of a large number of couples who were successfully married for some years revealed that these couples explained their success in marriage on the basis of certain personality traits. They mentioned most often affection, understanding, ability to give and take, cooperation, and willingness to talk things over.

Table 11 MARITAL GRIEVANCES ACCORDING TO SERIOUSNESS*

ORDER LISTED BY HUSBANDS	ORDER LISTED BY WIVES
1. W. nags me.	1. H. selfish and inconsiderate.
2. W. not affectionate.	2. H. unsuccessful in business.
3. W. selfish and inconsiderate.	3. H. untruthful.
4. W. complains too much.	4. H. complains too much.
5. W. interferes with hobbies.	5. H. does not show his affection.
6. W. slovenly in appearance.	6. H. does not talk things over.
7. W. is quick-tempered.	7. H. harsh with children.
8. W. interferes with my discipline.	8. H. touchy.
9. W. conceited.	9. H. has no interest in children.
10. W. is insincere.	10. H. not interested in home.
11. W.'s feelings too easily hurt.	11. H. not affectionate.
12. W. criticizes me.	12. H. rude.
13. W. narrow-minded.	13. H. lacks ambition.
14. W. neglects the children.	14. H. nervous or impatient.
15. W. a poor housekeeper.	15. H. criticizes me.
16. W. argumentative.	16. H.'s poor management of income.
17. W. has annoying habits.	17. H. narrow-minded.
18. W. untruthful.	18. H. not faithful to me.
19. W. interferes in my business.	19. H. lazy.
20. W. spoils the children.	20. H. bored with my small talk.
21. W.'s poor management of income.	21. In-laws.
22. In-laws.	22. H. easily influenced by others.
23. W. has insufficient income.	23. H. tight with money.
24. W. nervous or emotional.	24. H. argumentative.
25. W. easily influenced by others.	25. H.'s insufficient income.
26. W. jealous.	26. H. has no backbone.
27. W. lazy.	27. H. dislikes to go out with me.
28. W. gossips indiscreetly.	28. H. pays attention to other women.

* Rank order as given by 792 couples. Lewis M. Terman, *Psychological Factors in Marital Happiness.* New York: McGraw-Hill Book Company. 1938.

Because of the comparative ease of obtaining divorce today, some marriages that might have succeeded end in the courts.

LACK OF PREPARATION FOR MARRIAGE AS A CAUSE OF DIVORCE

An important cause of divorce that does not show up in the court statistics is that many people are not prepared for the realities of married living. Couples go through the courtship period thinking that everything will be perfect after they marry. They may have no special personality problems, but cannot be realistic when it comes to building good husband-wife relationships. When they meet unanticipated problems in their marriage they become discouraged and do not know how to handle the situation. People who were well balanced before marriage may become quite disorganized when their marriage is not going well.

Better preparation for marriage and family living would help these people adjust to marriage. They do not have the handicaps of those who, in addition to a lack of preparation, also have basic difficulties in their personalities that make it hard for them to get along with others.

ALTERNATES TO DIVORCE

Suppose two people are unhappily married; they differ on a number of points, and they have almost no friendly companionship. They feel that they will never be able to agree, and both are becoming so emotionally disturbed that they are looking hopefully toward divorce. Would they not be happier apart?

Before they divorce, there are some questions they should consider as dispassionately as possible.

1. What is ahead in my life after the divorce? Life at present looks drab to an unhappy person, but will a future of being alone be less drab?

2. If I remarried, have I learned enough so that I could make the second marriage a success?
3. What possibilities for real happiness would there be in the future that are not present now?
4. What are the good things that will be lost to me if I divorce?
5. Are the bad things so bad that it is worth giving up the good things to escape them, or do the values in this marriage really outweigh the ills? Would it be worthwhile to put up with some of the problems in order to keep the other values?
6. Am I looking at marriage in a mature, adult manner—not as a highly emotional experience, but as a working relationship, which requires self-sacrifice, loyalty, and cooperation in order that mutual needs may be met?
7. Is infatuation with an outsider the reason for wanting a divorce?
8. Is a qualified marriage counselor available? Marriage counselors know the universal problems of marriage adjustment. They may be able to help one decide whether the marriage should never have taken place or whether some way may be found to work through present difficulties to a better relationship.

If no marriage counselor is available, there may be others who could help. Usually, it is better to seek counsel from a qualified person who is not personally involved in any situation related to the marriage. Relatives and friends, who are greatly interested, can hardly help being prejudiced and are generally unable to be objective. Their counsel, no matter how well meant, may not be as sound as that of a disinterested but qualified outsider. Some ministers have taken special training in counseling and some doctors have also taken training in this area, although counseling is not ordinarily a part of medical training.

QUESTIONS FOR REVIEW

1. Why should divorce be considered in a study of personality adjustment and marriage?
2. What is the ratio of marriages to divorces at present? How does this compare with the ratio in 1870?
3. Is the increase in divorce an accurate measure of the increase in marriage unhappiness? Explain.
4. When in marriage is failure most likely to occur?
5. Is it always the unhappiest marriages that end in divorce? What factors influence people to dissolve or endure an unhappy marriage?
6. Contrast behavior during courtship with that of alienation.
7. What are some of the thoughts that people have as they look at a deteriorating marriage?

8. What are the most common years for marriages to fail psychologically?
9. Why is the woman more likely to ask for the divorce?
10. What is the procedure for getting a divorce in most states?
11. How do adversary proceedings differ from no-fault divorces?
12. What are the two basic concepts in no-fault divorce?
13. Do you think no-fault divorce will result in more divorces? Explain.
14. What is the purpose of the Conciliation Courts?
15. In what respects is divorce the unhappy opposite of a wedding?
16. What do court records show as the causes of divorce?
17. What are some of the real causes of divorce?
18. Why is divorce often no solution to a problem?
19. Cite some personality traits that cause serious trouble in marriage. What personality traits make for good adjustment?
20. What are some questions that couples who are considering divorce might ask before going ahead with a divorce?

ACTIVITIES AND PROJECTS

1. Consult or write to your state department of vital statistics, and report upon the ratio of marriages to divorces in your state; in your city.
2. Make a poster to display in class that brings out the chief factors making for an increase in divorces.
3. What are the grounds for divorce in your state? Consult your state laws on marriage and divorce. How could your laws be improved?
4. To prevent divorce, would it be better to make it more difficult to get a divorce or more difficult to marry? Discuss.

WORDS AND CONCEPTS

adversary
alienation
collusion
conciliation
dissolution of marriage
divorce proceedings
insupportability

intolerable
irreconcilable differences
irrevocable
mandatory
no fault
stigma
traumatic

24 Adjusting to Divorce

After studying this chapter, you will be able to

1. Point out new problems one is likely to have after divorce.
2. List the advantages of ending an unhappy marriage.
3. Discuss special problems that should be faced when a person who has never been married considers marrying a divorced person.
4. Explain the statement, "Some marriages should end for the sake of the children."
5. Describe reactions of children to divorce in terms of their age at the time of the divorce.
6. Discuss reactions of children in terms of how happy or unhappy they saw their parents' marriage prior to divorce.

Divorce does not always remove problems, but exchanges a new set of problems for the old. One can afford to think carefully a long time before deciding if the new set will be any easier to take. The problems that a divorced person faces may seem far away and unimportant to the one who is emotional about his marital trouble. He tends to think only of escape from the present. In reality, a divorce requires major adjustments just as great as marriage requires—adjustments often harder to make because there are two together to adjust in marriage, while in divorce one struggles alone and without the rewards that come in marriage.

What are some of the problems after divorce?

1. The person will still have to live with himself or herself. If he or she is discontented, inwardly insecure, or distrustful and suspicious, these traits will cause trouble whether the person is married or single.
2. The divorced person faces readjustments of personal life. Even two who do not get along very well together are still more dependent upon each other emotionally than they may realize. It is often an emotional shock to try to adjust again to living as a single person, alone, after having been married.
3. Divorce requires changes in one's social life. It becomes necessary to make new friends and to find new interests. A man may have less difficulty here, because "extra" men are usually scarce in social groups and thus are in demand; but the woman often feels that she is a "fifth wheel" for whom there is no place in social groups. "Extra" women may not be as much in demand.
4. Divorce creates or increases financial problems for both men and women. The woman must plan for her own support and provide for her future economic security. Alimony is seldom sufficient to allow freedom from financial worries. The man's obligation to share his income with the former wife and children sometimes means that he cannot remarry and undertake the support of two families. If he does remarry and have a second family, the second family usually must accept a lower standard of living and make sacrifices.
5. Both will almost unavoidably suffer emotionally from the divorce. As one woman expressed it, "If he had died, people would grieve with me. He is gone; but people only look at me and expect me to go on as if nothing had happened. I can't even admit that I grieve.

DIVORCE MAY OFFER NEW HOPE

Throughout this book, we have emphasized that making a wise choice of a mate through a long, mature courtship is essential to a happy marriage. We recognize that many people do marry who should not, that they had failed to learn what they should have learned during courtship. For some of these marriages, the most constructive outcome is divorce. Society gains more, in general, from happy rather than from unhappy marriages. What are the advantages in ending an unhappy marriage?

1. The individual may regain a degree of emotional health not experienced in years. Many people are emotionally destroyed by the conflict and the indecision that they experience when going through the psychological failure of a relationship. They may be unhappy, depressed, and difficult to live with because they cannot adjust to a bad relationship.

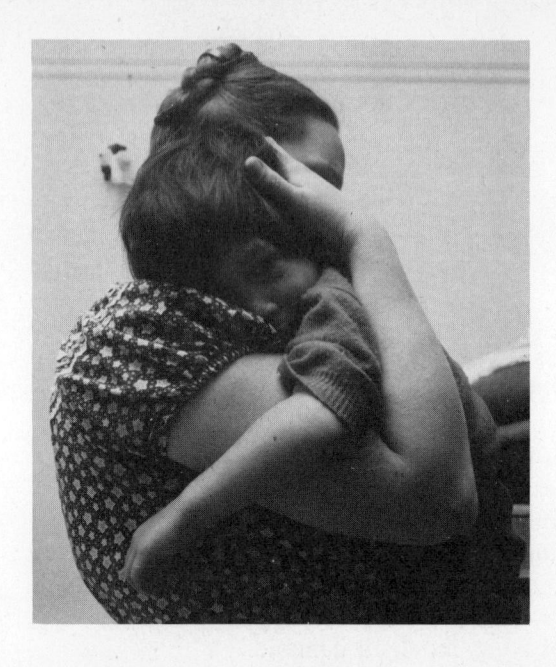

Divorce always offers new problems in exchange for those it attempts to remedy, especially when children are involved.

2. The person may experience a general improvement in physical health. It may be easier to work and to sleep. With the cessation of worry and indecision, there may be fewer physical signs of ill health, such as headaches or stomachaches, and there may be a noticeable increase in energy.
3. It is often true that divorce itself is not difficult; it is the indecision leading up to divorce that is disturbing. With the act of divorce, the person may feel relieved that it is finally over. Often, in looking back, people cannot understand why they waited so long to make the decision to divorce when they can now see that the marriage had been destructive for some years.
4. Divorce gives people a chance to remedy a mistake. Couples who marry very young, who marry because of pregnancy, or who were too immature may end a bad marriage. It is not too late for them to continue their education, make plans for a different future, and become mature before making a second marriage.
5. Often, relationships with family and friends become strained in a bad marriage. Once the marriage is broken, the person may be happy and rebuild relationships with friends and family.
6. If there are children, their emotional security may improve after the divorce, especially if the predivorce years were characterized with much open hostility and conflict.
7. The individual may remarry and substitute a happy marriage for an unhappy one. The marriage rates for divorced men and women are higher for all age groups than they are for the single person. Almost all women who divorce under twenty-five and most men who divorce eventually remarry. Although divorced people who remarry have a higher divorce rate than people married only once, at least half do find happiness in a second marriage.

MARRYING AFTER DIVORCE

The prevailing divorce rate in the United States means that in more and more marriages at least one of the pair has previously been married and divorced. Statistical analyses of census records show that about one-fourth of all marriages involve a previously divorced person. The records also show that there is a tendency for divorced people to marry divorced people and that these marriages have a much higher rate of failure than marriages that are a first for both. Whatever the reasons for the first marital failure, the breakup inevitably leaves scars that will be a factor in a second marriage.

Sometimes, a young person contemplating marriage to a divorced person accepts without question explanations of the previous failure, such as the first wife or husband was unfaithful, or "didn't understand me," or "couldn't get along with my family," or "was selfish," or "was financially irresponsible," or any one of many other reasons that put the blame for the marital failure upon the previous mate.

Marriage failure is almost never the fault of one person alone. Just as it takes two cooperating to make a good marriage, so a bad marriage results because both people fail in mate choice, in ability to grow up to life's responsibilities, or in realistic adjustment to marriage. The divorced person who blames the ex-mate rather than accepting a personal responsibility will tend to repeat the same pattern in a second marriage. In fact, such a person is likely to have unrealistic expectations that put undue strain on the second mate.

For the person who considers marrying a divorced person, there are some special facts or circumstances that should be faced. These factors will affect the marriage and in some cases are sufficient reason to decide against the marriage.

1. Parents and family tend to be less approving of marriage to a divorced person than to someone never married before. Parental disapproval is a factor that should be considered in any contemplated marriage. Parents' doubts will affect the marriage; moreover, their views may be based on reliable conclusions about the chances for success.
2. A previously married man may have financial responsibilities toward the former wife or children. If the husband in a second marriage must pay alimony or child support, the financial obligations may put strain on the new marriage. Few men can support two families adequately.

    Sometimes, even with the best of planning, the second wife must work outside the home as might not have been necessary if her husband did not have to divide his earnings. The financial problems in second marriages often become a source of tension.

3. If the formerly married one has visitation rights with the child or children, further emotional complications arise. The second wife wonders if her husband sees the former wife when he visits the children, and may resent the exchange of telephone calls or letters that must sometimes take place with the former wife over matters related to the children.
4. Other emotional tensions may arise regarding the formerly married one's former in-laws. The first marriage is a fact to be lived with. It represents months or years of the person's life which were committed to a marriage that failed. The two families were involved, as families always are when a marriage between their members unites them. Their interest in and involvement with the ex-wife or husband usually does not suddenly end with a divorce.
5. When adjustments must be made and problems arise, it is not possible for the two people to view the situation as they could if this were a first marriage for them both. The formerly married one's view is influenced by past experience. This may or may not help in being objective about present problems. One may think there is evidence of another failure in situations that would be viewed more optimistically if a painful disappointment had not already been experienced.
6. The statistical evidence suggests caution about marriages after divorce. Records show that among people who have divorced once, the median duration of marriage before the first divorce was 6.5 years; if both had been divorced once before, the duration before divorce was 3.5 years; and if both had been divorced twice, the duration of the marriage before the next divorce was only 1.7 years.

There are several possible explanations for the increase in divorce rates of successive marriages after divorce. The person who resorts to divorce as a solution cannot see other possible solutions and may be quick to divorce again, instead of attempting to solve problems more constructively. In addition, personality traits that contributed to the first failure are a continuing handicap in succeeding marriages. And still another factor, perhaps the crucial one, is that while all marriages require growth and adjustment, marriages after a divorce definitely do have more ready-made special problems and complications. To make a success of these marriages, people need to be more adequate, more adjustable, and more wise in mate choice than the average. The evidence seems to show that a large percentage cannot meet that requirement.

Possibly, all people who divorce should be required to register for classes in marriage education, or be required to go for marriage counseling before they are permitted to remarry. In these classes, the divorced should learn that rather than remarrying too soon, as they tend to do, they should take longer to get acquainted before entering the second marriage. They would learn to recognize danger signals in relationships, learn more about their personality needs, and learn about other characteristics that would help them be successful in a second marriage.

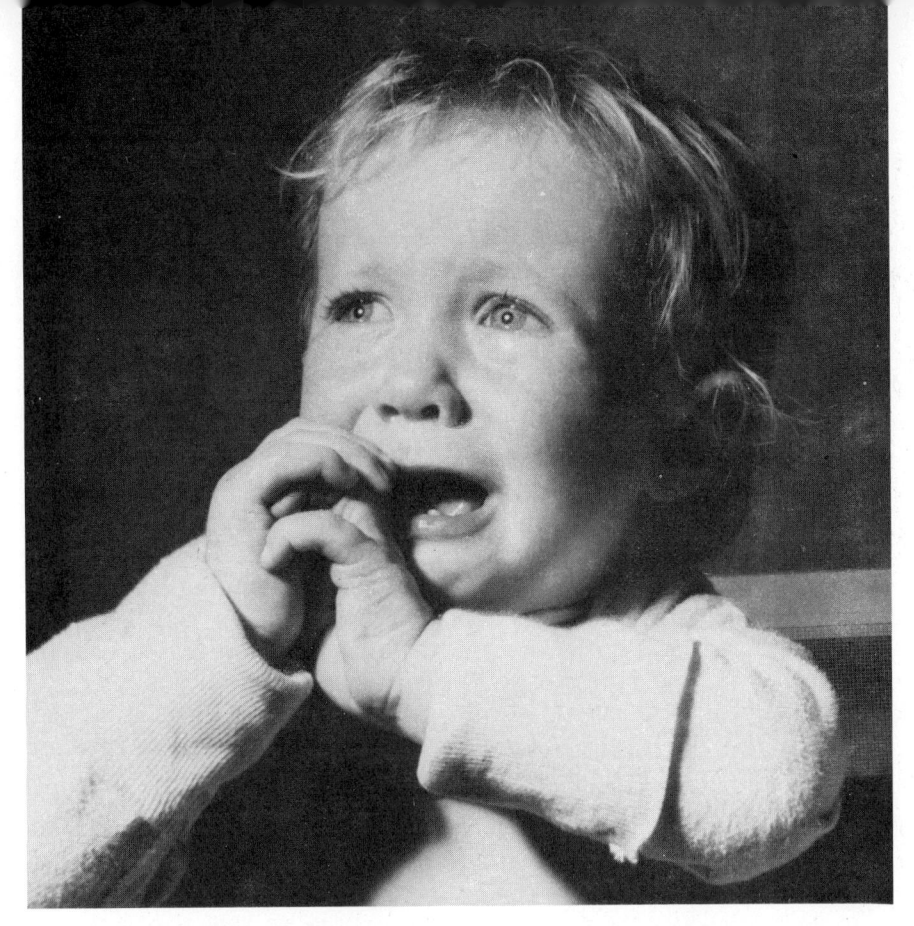

Each year, children in approximately 400,000 homes are affected by divorce.

CHILDREN AND DIVORCE

Before discussing children from divorced homes and the effects of divorce upon them, we should make it clear that it is the unhappy home that is destructive to children. Whether the unhappy marriage is ended by divorce or continues is not the main consideration as far as the children are concerned. There is some evidence to suggest that the children who continue in an unhappy home are more disturbed than are the children who are freed from the unhappy home through divorce. As more research is done on successful and unsuccessful parenthood, it will become clearer that some unhappy marriages should end in divorce "for the sake of the children."

The breakup of the parent's marriage is almost always painful to the children. There is a tendency for those looking at divorce to think that all children from divorced homes are affected in the same ways. The children are stereotyped as being from broken homes. We studied three hundred children, all of whom were from divorced homes, and learned that divorce affects children in many different ways. There certainly is no justification for stereotyping.

Divorce and Age of Children

Marriage failure tends to come in the early years of marriage when the children are young. If the divorce does come when the children are young, the parent who gets custody may remarry and rear the children in a happy home. If this person does not remarry, but is a wise and adequate parent, the children may still be better off than in an unhappy home. In either case, the very young child may not be disturbed adversely by the divorce.

In our study of the three hundred children from divorced families, we found that one-third were too young to remember the family before the divorce. We found that children who had been eight or older suffered most from the family unhappiness and divorce. Those who had been older reported feeling less security, more unhappiness, and more awareness of predivorce conflict than did the children who had been younger. At the time of the divorce, they had felt more upset, had felt a greater threat to their feelings of security, and had felt a greater loss in prestige in facing their friends. They had felt that they had more often been "used" by their parents during and after the divorce. Among those who had been very young, less trauma was felt from most of these circumstances.

How Children Viewed Home Before Divorce

One of the findings in our study was that the effect of divorce upon the children is dependent upon how the children viewed the parents' marriage before they learned of the impending divorce. It is often assumed that divorce is preceded by open conflict between the mother and father and that the children always know that there is trouble. This, however, is not always the case. Some mature parents may find that they have wide differences that make it impossible for them to live with each other, and mutually agree to divorce. They may face their failure rationally and without emotional outbursts, quarreling, or chronic conflict. Further, they may know that it would be damaging to their children if they did show open conflict.

Our research found that approximately one-third of the children did see their homes as closely united and happy before they learned of the divorce. It was children from these homes that experienced the most trauma in terms of loss of security, being upset, and in not being able to accept the fact that their parents would divorce. The children who had seen their homes filled with conflict and hostility reacted entirely differently. Over half reacted by feeling it "was best for all concerned" when they learned of the impending divorce. This does not mean that these children were not upset when they learned of the planned divorce; they were in many ways, but it was not the blow to them that it was

ADJUSTING TO DIVORCE

to the children who thought their homes were happy. In Table 12 we summarized the responses of the children from the happiest and unhappiest homes as viewed by the children before the divorce and how they reacted when they learned of the divorce.

Table 12 CHILDREN'S REACTIONS WHEN LEARNING THEIR PARENTS WOULD SEPARATE OR DIVORCE

Reaction	1/3 Happiest	1/3 Unhappiest	Total*
	Percentage		
Thought it was best for all concerned	19.7	54.1	34.4
Couldn't believe that it had happened to us	42.6	16.4	33.3
Fought against it and tried to prevent it	13.1	11.5	14.2
I was happy	1.6	14.8	6.0
I was unhappy and upset	52.5	57.4	51.9
I was worried and anxious about my future	14.8	27.9	20.2
Hated father	4.9	19.7	8.7
Hated mother	1.6	8.2	3.3
Did not understand	18.0	8.2	12.0
Indifferent	6.6	3.3	4.9
Miscellaneous reactions	19.7	11.5	15.3

* Total represents two-thirds shown, plus one-third of sample not shown. As reported by 183 children of divorced parents.

The dissolution of their parents' marriage is hard for older children to accept, as is the upheaval in their own lives. Children need both parents, but in a happy, peaceful home.

Although the immediate reaction to divorce by those who thought their homes were happy seemed to be most traumatic, it does not necessarily mean that the long-range effects would be as serious as for children from chronically unhappy homes. The child who has known years of security, love, and unity in a family is more likely to recover from tragedy. This child is likely to be able to weather a serious blow such as the parents' divorce and still reach normalcy in feelings and thoughts.

Parents "Using" Children During Divorce

Our research also found that some divorcing parents are unwise because in various ways they "use" the children before, during, and after the divorce. This puts an unnecessary strain on the children. Again, it is the children who saw their parents as unhappily married who were more likely to feel they were "used" by one or both parents during the parental conflict. In Table 13, we have summarized ways in which chil-

Table 13 WAYS IN WHICH CHILDREN WERE USED BY DIVORCED PARENTS

Way in Which Parent "Used" Child	$1/3$ Happiest	$1/3$ Unhappiest	Total*
		Percentage	
One tried to get information from me about the other	21.3	41.0	21.0
Asked to testify against one parent in court	4.9	21.3	7.8
Asked to back up one parent or other in family quarrels	1.6	31.1	9.8
Not permitted to talk to one parent	—	3.3	1.0
Not permitted to see one parent	3.3	8.2	4.1
One told untrue things about the other	18.0	42.6	17.6
One gave messages to me to give to the other	9.8	11.5	7.1
I was used as a go-between in quarrels	—	13.1	3.7
One or both played on my sympathy	14.8	52.5	25.8
Neither ever used me	60.7	24.6	44.4
Miscellaneous responses and too young to remember	4.9	9.8	20.0

* Total represents two-thirds shown, plus one-third not shown, plus 112 respondents who were too young to remember family before divorce but old enough to remember postdivorce years. As reported by 295 children of divorced parents.

dren reported they were used by their parents. It is hard to understand how parents can draw their children into the family conflicts and use them as "go-betweens" in getting information. However, it must be remembered that the parents are living under an emotional strain and also that they may actually be more immature in their behavior than their children are in their development. The child who has gained a degree of objectivity about personal relationships may be able to stay uninvolved in the parental conflicts. Children sometimes react by trying to do something that will save the parents' marriage. It might be better to strive for detachment and try to learn things from the situation that will help them learn how to avoid making a marriage that would have similar problems.

CONCLUSION

As we have said, divorce is a sad thing from any viewpoint. It is better for you to be aware of the truth about divorce before you marry. Just as we study both nutrition and disease in an effort to build health intelligently, so it is necessary to look at marriage failure as well as marriage happiness in order to know how to build successful marriages.

The majority of marriages are happy. Even some couples who divorce find that they were happier while married, and regret their divorce. In other cases, divorce is the wisest choice. The sound attitude is to choose a mate wisely and then go into marriage ready to accept the responsibility for creating happiness.

QUESTIONS FOR REVIEW

1. What are some of the new problems often faced by those who divorce?
2. What are some of the possible advantages for those who divorce?
3. What are some of the special problems that might arise when a person who has never been married before marries a divorced person?
4. Can you explain the fact that statistical records show that people who have failed in one marriage are more likely to fail in a second marriage than never-before married people?
5. Why might people who have been divorced need education for marriage more than people entering a first marriage?
6. What is meant by saying that some marriages should end for the sake of the children?
7. How does the age of children at the time of the parents' divorce affect children?

8. Do all children in marriages that end in divorce see the marriages as unhappy before they learn of the impending divorce?

9. Contrast the reactions to divorce of children who thought their parents were happily married with children who thought their parents were unhappily married.

10. What are some of the specific ways in which divorcing parents "use" their children?

ACTIVITIES AND PROJECTS

1. (Report.) Visit a divorce court for a few hours, and report to the class. Note particularly the causes given for seeking the divorce; the effect of the divorce upon the children, if they are present; who is given custody of the children; and what the financial settlement is.

2. Ask a minister, rabbi, or priest to give the class his views on divorce.

SUGGESTED READINGS FOR THE UNIT

American Institute for Economic Research. Great Barrington, Massachusetts 01230. The Institute publishes a series of helpful books for consumers priced at $1.00. Some of the titles are: *How to Avoid Financial Tangles, Life Insurance From the Buyer's Point of View, How to Invest Wisely, The Rubber Budget Account Book.*

Beyer, Glenn H., *Housing and Society.* 1965. New York: The Macmillan Company.

Bowman, Henry A., *Marriage for Moderns.* 1974. New York: McGraw-Hill Book Co.

Chambers, H. G., and V. Moulton, *Clothing Selection.* 1969. Philadelphia: J. B. Lippincott Company.

Craig, Hazel T., and O. D. Rush, *Homes with Character.* 1966. Boston: D. C. Heath and Company.

Consumers Bulletin, Published by Consumers' Research, Inc., Washington, New Jersey.

Consumers Reports. Published monthly by Consumers Union, P. O. Box 3000, Mt. Vernon, New York.

Duval, Evelyn Millis, *In-Laws: Pro and Con.* 1954. New York: Association Press.

Faulkner, Ray N., and S. Faulkner, *Inside Today's Home.* 1968. New York: Holt, Rinehart and Winston.

Fitzsimmons, Cleo, and N. White, *Management for You.* 1969. Philadelphia: J. B. Lippincott Company.

Hamilton, David B., *The Consumer in Our Economy.* 1962. Boston: Houghton Mifflin Co.

Klemer, Richard, and Margaret Klemer, *The Early Years of Marriage.* Pamphlet No. 424. New York: Public Affairs Committee.

Krantzler, Mel, *Creative Divorce*. 1974. New York: M. Evans and Company, Inc.

Landis, Judson T., and Mary G. Landis, *Building a Successful Marriage,* Fifth Edition. 1973. Englewood Cliffs, N. J.: Prentice-Hall, Inc.

Logan, William B., and Helen M. Moon, *Facts about Merchandise*. 1967. Englewood Cliffs, N. J.: Prentice-Hall, Inc.

Milt, Harry, *Young Adults and Their Parents.* Pamphlet No. 355. New York: Public Affairs Committee.

Nickell, Paulina, and J. M. Dorsey, *Management in Family Living.* 1967. New York: John Wiley and Sons.

Rhodes, Kathleen, and Merna A. Samples, *Your Life in the Family.* 1964. Philadelphia: J. B. Lippincott Company. Unit 4, Chaps. 16–19.

Rutt, Anna H., *Home Furnishings.* 1961. New York: John Wiley and Sons.

Troelstrup, Arch, *Consumer Problems and Personal Finance.* 1970. New York: McGraw-Hill Book Company.

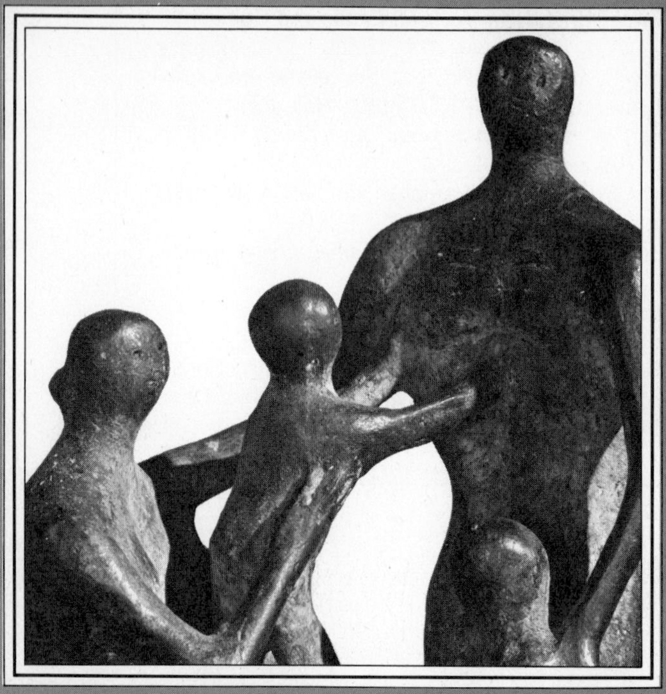

part five

WHEN YOU BECOME A PARENT

Oh, God of the Sunrise,
as I have given myself to my babe,
wilt Thou watch over and protect him
through the night.
If he awaken when the sun greets the earth,
he will grow to be a man
and will take upon himself
the responsibilities of a man in the world.

Allunde, Swahili Lullaby-Prayer

25 Approaching Parenthood

After studying this chapter, you will be able to

1. Appraise some of the positive and negative aspects of experiences related to becoming a parent.
2. Discuss steps one should take in preparing to be a successful parent.
3. Explain the "natural childbirth" approach to pregnancy and delivery.
4. Describe the stages of the birth process.
5. Analyze the adjustments necessary between husband and wife during pregnancy and after the birth of the child.

It is difficult to perceive ahead of time exactly what life's most significant experiences will be. The conception we have of parenthood before we experience it is likely to be inaccurate in either of two directions. One may hold idealized, romantic views and so undertake the task without being prepared for the work and responsibility that are a part of being a parent. In contrast, some people, seeing parenthood from the outside, wonder why anyone wants to have children. They see young parents giving up their freedom to carry heavy responsibilities and older parents worrying about their children or having a hard time meeting expenses.

Both contrasting views include some elements of truth. Parenthood is not the carefree, romantic experience it sometimes appears to be in magazine pictures or advertisements. On the other hand, few of us can appreciate ahead of time the unique rewards and the enrichment of life that come to people who are successful parents.

POSITIVE REWARDS OF PARENTHOOD

To be able to contribute positively to the physical and emotional growth of a baby and to watch the child's normal development toward becoming an adequate person brings great satisfaction to parents. To be a successful parent means one needs to be able to meet constant challenges to one's intelligence, flexibility, and ingenuity. These challenges probably require more growth from an individual than is required during any other part of life. Whenever we meet and cope with them in satisfactory ways, the sense of achievement is as great as the task. Gradually, as children grow into adults, parents' responsibility decreases, and eventually, people who have been able to accomplish their parental task find in their children congenial friends and associates who share a common background.

The positive, happy side of parenthood is a *result of adequacy as parents.* It is not an automatic consequence of giving birth. People who would experience the joys and rewards of being parents must be prepared also to understand and accept the responsibilities and unselfish sacrifices involved.

BEING REALISTIC ABOUT PARENTHOOD

A young mother who had happily anticipated her first baby's arrival found herself a month later physically exhausted and overwhelmed by the continuous responsibility of caring for a tiny infant. She said, "My marriage is happy. I had seen some unhappy marriages, and I did a lot of thinking before I married. I think I was prepared. But I had not thought through the subject of being a parent, and I guess I wasn't ready for it. The hardest adjustment is that I never in my life before had to be responsible for anyone but myself, and suddenly, here I am with this helpless baby depending on me night and day, twenty-four hours of every day. I get scared when I think about having this responsibility for years and years—until the baby is grown up and I'm an old lady!"

This girl was taking her responsibility very seriously and trying to be as good a mother as she was capable of being. She had not yet had a chance to experience the rewards of seeing her baby grow into a healthy, happy child and adult. Her feeling of disillusionment with parenthood is an aspect of becoming a parent that is experienced by many

The 2 A.M. feeding finds many a couple exhausted. This "ordeal" ends when baby can take enough food to last out the night, but the demands of being a good parent go on for many years.

people, both mothers and fathers. In our culture, most of us are not prepared to be realistic about parenthood.

Better preparation for parenthood would help many couples to make an easier transition from the honeymoon stage of marriage into their new status as parents. And, with more knowledge about what parenthood means, couples who have not been able to make their own adjustment and create a good relationship might be inclined to postpone having children until they are more ready for the task. People who have achieved their own growth tasks and have been able to create a good marriage have reason to be confident that they can cope with the growth tasks that are involved in being successful parents.

PARENTHOOD AS CRISIS

For all couples, even in the best of marriages, to become parents brings many new adjustments. Until they are parents, a husband and wife have been absorbed in working out their two-way interaction. Now, another personality is involved. Even before birth, the new baby is a factor in the relationships of the couple. E. E. LeMasters, writing about "Parenthood as Crisis" makes the point that we must consider the family as a small social system and that to add a member to this small social group forces a reorganization just as much as does the removal of a member by death or divorce. After interviewing many new parents about their feelings and their experiences, he concluded, "It is the arrival of the first child, rather than marriage, that forces the young couple to take the last painful step into the adult world."

LeMasters and others who have studied families have concluded that a large percentage of couples do make the required adjustments to parenthood. They establish a new interaction pattern when they have a child; they accept their obligations, and they and their children become successful families. But the situation in a family, as in a marriage, is never static; more adjustments must be made as children grow older. There is constant need for the parents to be flexible and to keep maturing. If they do keep growing, their own marriages will be happier, and their children can become emotionally healthy people.

PARENTHOOD AS A PROFESSION

It was once assumed that little formal training was necessary for those who would enter any profession. A man might read up on laws and begin practicing as a lawyer; one who had a knack for mixing herbs could begin practicing as a doctor without benefit of any other training or degrees; the person who felt "called" could just leave his plow or his workbench and begin to preach. Standards have changed so that now people must go through specified courses of academic training, and they must also pass examinations and be licensed by the state in which they would practice their profession. Requirements are spelled out in detail so that one can know when one is ready to begin the chosen work.

Parenthood is more demanding and more permanent than other jobs and professions, and yet most people still take on the job without special preparation. There are no restrictions on who can become parents and no defined course of study by which people can prepare themselves.

HOW CAN ONE PREPARE?

Rather than to go blindly into the parental role, the first step is probably *awareness of the need to prepare.* Then, for many people, *courses in school provide good opportunities to study and learn.* The course in which you are studying this book has probably opened up new areas of thought and information that can help you as a parent. There is opportunity in such courses to consider many vital questions related to parenthood. You will never get all the answers in any course or in any book, but part of preparation is reading, thinking about, and discussing such questions as the following: What are the needs and rights of children at each age? What are the responsibilities of parents? Is it enough to provide food, clothing, and shelter? Are these things as important as, or more or less important than, the obligation to provide for the emotional needs of children? How *can* people meet the different needs that children and infants have? What rights do parents have? If some of these rights seem to conflict with a baby's or a child's rights, whose rights have priority? Why?

Another important step in preparing to be a successful parent is *thoughtful assessment of one's own background.* The person who thinks back over his or her own development and the impact of parents and their child-rearing methods, need not be negative or critical of one's own parents. The need is to be objective about how the ways of parents affect children. We can try to be objective in assessing our background and in determining where we might do better with our children. We can set up policies for ourselves that may increase the probability of our doing better. Almost all of us have at least as many and probably more advantages than our parents had. We should be able to learn from their experience in addition to other learning opportunities available today.

Courses such as this one in the methods of natural childbirth help to prepare prospective parents for the birth of their child.

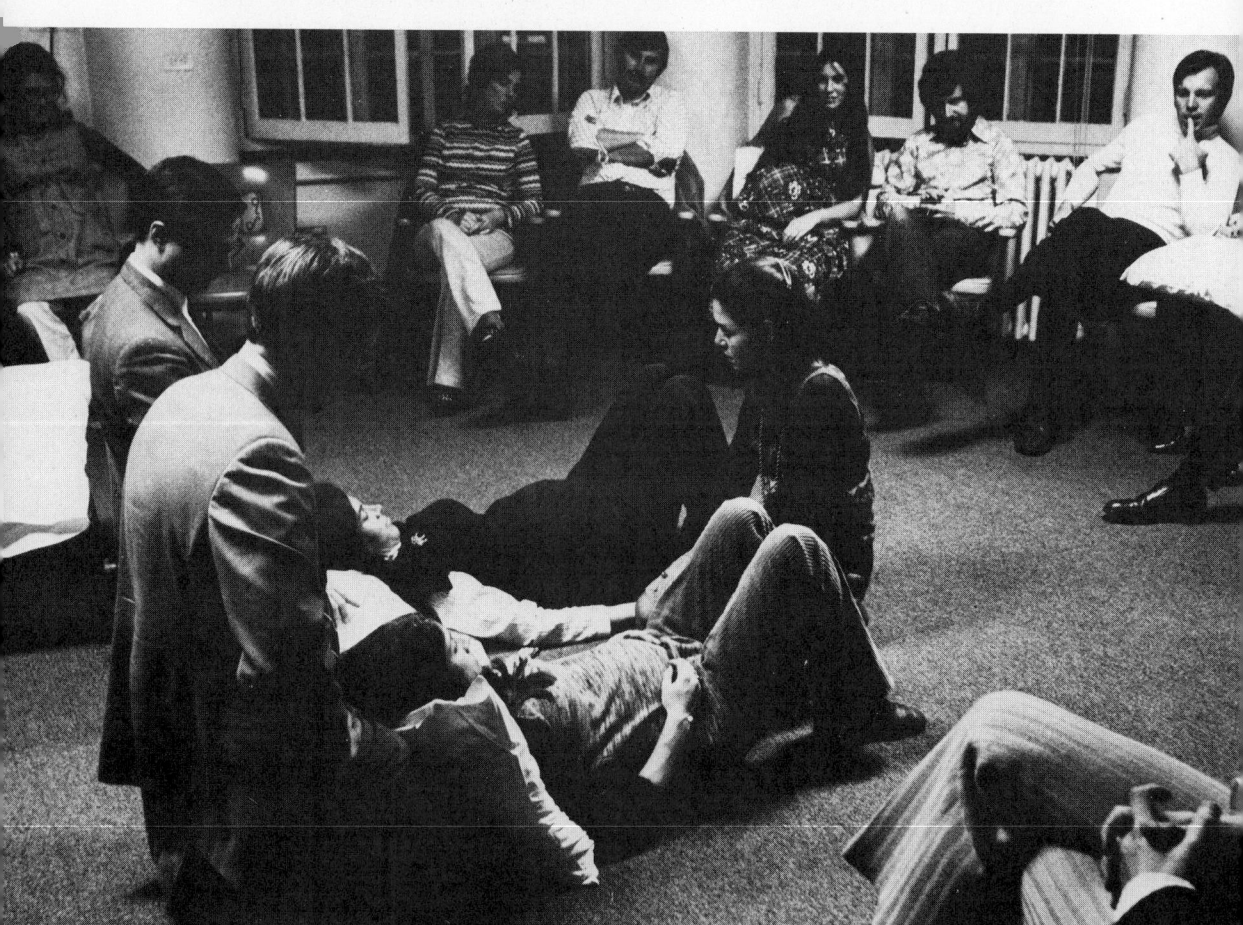

Perhaps the most essential step in preparing for parenthood is to grow up first: to achieve the important tasks of the earlier stages of life before becoming a parent. Chapter 7 included Christensen's research that shows the greater success of marriages in which couples do not become parents too early. The child is fortunate who is born to parents who achieved their growing up tasks before they married, who have already learned to cooperate, and who are prepared to welcome and work together to rear the child.

Sometimes, the coming of a baby brings out the immaturity of one or both parents. A father may be jealous because the mother seems too preoccupied with the baby. If he is self-centered, he may not sense the extent of his wife's and his own new responsibilities. He would probably not recognize his feelings as jealousy of a baby; he could not admit to having such feelings. He may just feel resentful and unhappy, and behave unreasonably toward his wife and even toward the baby. If the mother is immature, that will show up now also. Mature self-discipline is necessary if a new mother is to cope with the added work and loss of freedom that motherhood brings.

After a baby comes, neither parent is free to think first of his or her own selfish wishes. To put one's own needs in second or third place requires maturity, regardless of age. It is important to assess one's own progress toward maturity before undertaking parenthood.

Basic in preparing for parenthood is to choose wisely the person who is to share one's parenthood. If you marry, you probably will have children; most people do. The one you marry is going to spend more years as your co-parent, the father or mother of your children, than as just your mate.

Two who marry must recognize that it takes two people, a man and a woman, to meet the needs of a child. Being parents is not solely the mother's or the father's task.

Fathers and children are sometimes cheated because of a tendency for mothers to take most of the responsibility for child rearing. Fortunately, there is an increasing tendency for fathers to take more part in caring for the children and to enjoy their privilege of parenthood. In the days when men worked ten or more hours a day, six or seven days a week, and women did not hold outside jobs, it was logical that fathers had little to do with child care. Because of today's shorter work week and the fact that women hold outside jobs, more parents now share these responsibilities. This necessity for both to be involved in the nurture of the child needs to be understood as part of the preparation of both marriage partners for parenthood. The emotional growth of a child is likely to be healthier when the father willingly accepts some of the nurturing tasks formerly thought of as "mothering."

The man and woman who work together, pooling their knowledge, discussing points that puzzle them in an effort to understand their children, will find new happiness and enrichment in their own relationship, and they will be able to contribute far more to the development of their children than either of them alone could possibly do.

Community programs also provide learning opportunities for students and for people who are already parents. Even people who have prepared as well as they can will find help if their children attend cooperative nursery schools in public school systems. Parents whose children go to the nursery schools take part in group discussions. Of benefit is the fact that at least one member of each couple must regularly assist in the school. Thus, the parents have the advantage of seeing their child with other children and of seeing other parents in active association with children. They can learn by the good examples and by the mistakes of other parents.

Many communities recognize that because stable families and healthy children are essential to the survival of our society, parent education must be provided. Therefore, a variety of classes or learning groups are available for parents.

APPROACHING THE FIRST CHILD'S BIRTH

In past generations, childbirth was a taboo subject. Women tended to approach childbirth with unfounded fears because they had heard tales about the pains and dangers, but had little accurate knowledge of the process. Now medical research has advanced, and many taboos have disappeared. Accurate information about childbirth is available to the public.

Many doctors feel that part of the pain of childbirth is due to physical tensions resulting from fear and ignorance and not to factors actually or necessarily a part of the process itself. These doctors have observed that mothers who have accurate knowledge of the birth process are able to be more relaxed and less tense, and the normal action of giving birth can proceed less complicated by fear-induced reactions.

The term *natural childbirth* is generally used to distinguish this new approach to childbirth from traditional childbirth. In traditional childbirth, it was the doctor who "delivered" the baby. Anesthetics were routinely used at certain points whether or not the mother especially needed or desired them. The mother was usually not conscious at the moment of her baby's birth. Only later, when she wakened, did she learn if she had had a boy or a girl. In some areas, doctors still adhere to traditional ways, but increasing numbers of doctors and mothers now prefer natural childbirth.

In natural childbirth, the emphasis is upon the mother's role in giving birth, not the doctor's role in delivering the baby. Anesthetics are given only if the mother needs and wants them. She is prepared ahead of time with accurate knowledge of the process of giving birth. She is ready to cooperate fully and is usually aware of the moment of her

Children who grow up in happy families are more likely to choose mates wisely and in turn have happy homes.

child's birth. Studies of thousands of mothers who have gone through a series of sessions in preparation for childbirth show that the average length of labor is much shorter, and there are fewer complications for mothers who are thus prepared. The "prepared" mothers understand the muscular contractions that push the baby from the mother's body; thus, they do not consider these rhythmic contractions simply as "pains." The physical effort involved, which is sometimes intense and exhausting, is still endurable when the reasons for it are understood. Some young mothers report that they felt discouraged during the birth when progress seemed slow and the contractions continuous, but they still look back upon the experience not as an ordeal, but as an achievement.

The current emphasis upon helping mothers and fathers toward a good understanding of just what is going to take place and upon the mother's role in giving birth is in contrast to the former practice of placing major emphasis upon anesthetics and the doctor's role in the birth of a child.

PREPARING PROSPECTIVE PARENTS FOR THE BIRTH

The exact plan for preparing prospective parents varies with different doctors and depends upon whether the plan is for natural childbirth or whether the approach is traditional. Some instruction emphasizes the birth; others include child care. The minimum level of preparation includes only the mothers. In such plans, the mothers meet in groups early in pregnancy and hear a lecture by an obstetrician explaining the facts concerning pregnancy and birth. Later, about six weeks before the babies are due, the mothers hear another lecture and have an opportunity to ask questions on points on which they may be in doubt. At that time, they also visit the hospital to see a delivery room.

A few years ago that plan was a progressive step in parental preparation. Some doctors objected that even that took too much of the busy obstetrician's time; others answered that the obstetrician's time was well invested because of the benefits to the mothers. But when the medical profession became actively interested in natural childbirth, many of them realized quickly that they were leaving out an important half of those concerned in the birth—the fathers.

In some areas, community agencies work with the medical profession to offer a series of classes for expectant fathers and mothers together. These classes include material on the reproductive systems of men and women; the beginnings of life; prenatal development; explanation of the birth process; the mental, physical, and emotional aspects of pregnancy for both the father and the mother; importance of correct diet for the mother and the child; demonstrations of all phases of infant care and feeding.

Couples attend the classes together. The basic purpose of the pre-birth instruction is to free both parents-to-be from fears and anxieties resulting from old-wives'-tales. Through the classes, the mother learns how and when to relax during the birth and the father learns to give emotional support and reassurance conducive to relaxation when she most needs it. She will have exercises that will strengthen muscles to be used in giving birth. She will practice the kind of breathing that will be needed at the crucial time.

Whether parents who go through the classes together will have natural childbirth or whether their baby will be born with the traditional reliance on the doctor to deliver the baby will of course depend upon their doctor and his or her attitudes and upon the facilities and policies of the hospital. They will know early in the pregnancy what their alternatives are, and can plan accordingly.

PRESENCE OF THE FATHER AT THE BIRTH

In some hospitals, the father can remain with the mother to give her emotional support and to encourage her throughout the birth. Many doctors who have a special interest in the emotional as well as the physical well-being of new parents and their babies feel it is much better for fathers to be present. One said that he is convinced that the expectant father who is with his wife at the supreme moment is certainly able to give her better emotional support than any resident doctor possibly can. Another said that his experience with over four thousand fathers in the delivery room has convinced him that a helpful husband has a calming effect on a woman as effective as any strong medication. Usually, the father can be present during labor even if not during delivery.

Some hospitals still do not allow fathers in the delivery room, and some women feel their husbands should be "spared the ordeal." However, an interesting study compared the experiences of two groups of women, those who chose natural childbirth with their husbands present, and another group who chose the traditional method of delivery with more anesthesia and husbands not present. This study found that women whose husbands stayed with them saw their husbands as strong, competent, helpful, and capable, in brief, as generally supportive. The women whose husbands did not remain with them were more likely to see their husbands as dependent and in need of protection.*

STAGES OF THE BIRTH PROCESS

During the pre-birth classes, films and lectures are used to acquaint expectant fathers and mothers with the facts about the three distinct stages in childbirth. The first stage begins when, after approximately nine months of pregnancy, hormones in the mother's body trigger the mechanisms that start the delivery of the baby.

When a baby is ready to be born, the mother feels labor pains or cramping sensations that alert her that the time has come for the birth. The muscles of the uterus have started a series of contractions that usually last from two to twenty hours. The first stage of labor is the longest. For many women it is the most trying because of its duration. During this state, the cervix, which is the opening to the uterus, or womb, is gradually opening or dilating, so that the baby can emerge. At first, the contractions may come every ten or fifteen minutes, but as the cervix dilates, the contractions come at shorter intervals. During this stage of labor, the mother consults with her doctor as to when she should check into the hospital. There is nothing she can do to hasten the birth even though she may be in this stage of labor for many hours. The best thing she can do is to relax and allow her muscles to do their work. Any attempts to bear down to force the baby out of the uterus during the first stage of labor only tire the mother and use energy she will need at the second stage of birth. At this time, involuntary muscles do all the work. A mother can no more hasten this part of the birth process than the involuntary muscles of the stomach can be hastened by conscious effort in the digestion of food.

After the cervix has opened, the second stage of labor begins. At this point, the mother will be taken into the delivery room. During this stage, the baby will be expelled from the mother's body through the birth canal.

---

*See the articles by Tanzer, Newton, and Meerlow, listed under suggested readings at the end of this unit, for detailed reports on the subject of fathers and natural childbirth.

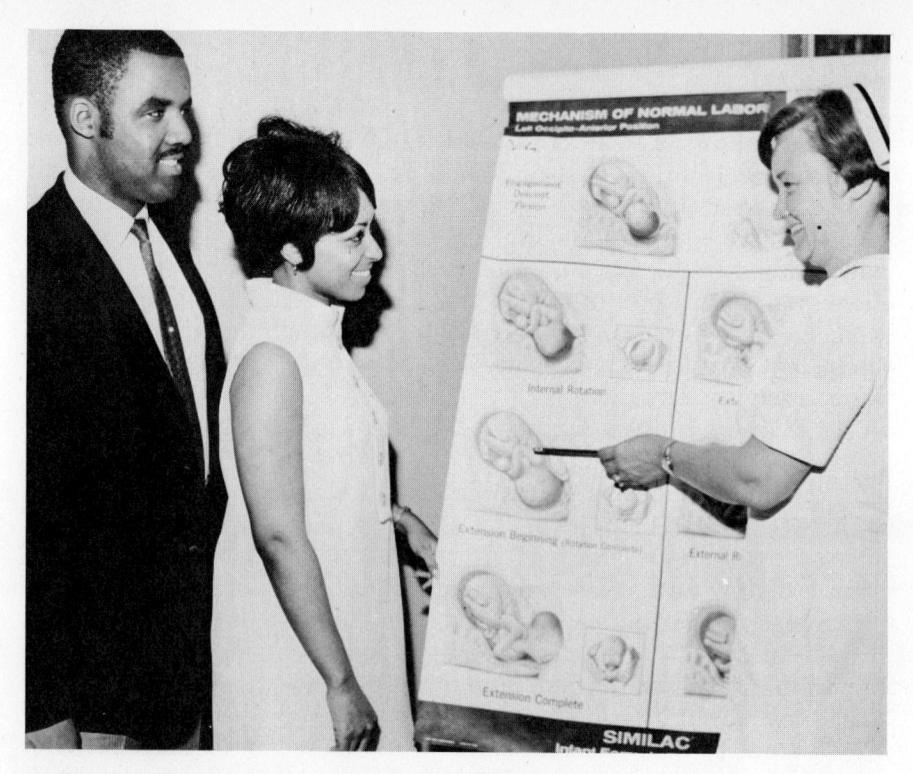

Good medical care during pregnancy and accurate information about labor bring assurance to both prospective parents.

Even though parents have chosen natural birth, doctors always stand ready to give medication during the second stage of delivery if mothers wish it. But although it is available, many mothers prefer not to have medication that would dull their awareness of the moment of their child's birth. This second stage is usually short, from a few minutes to an hour or so. In classes for natural childbirth, the mother will have been taught how she can aid the birth process at this time through bearing down to help the muscles move the baby through the birth canal. She will also have learned how to breathe as an aid in delivery.

The third stage of labor comes shortly after the baby has been born, when the placenta, or "afterbirth," is expelled. There is no pain, and most mothers are hardly aware of this as a separate stage.

New mothers and fathers who have made use of the opportunities to prepare themselves for the coming of the baby can approach the experience of birth with a measure of confidence. In most cases, the classes will also have helped them to become more nearly ready to take care of a tiny new infant. Both parents will have learned something of how to bathe, feed, and diaper a baby, not only by watching demonstrations but by having a chance to practice these tasks themselves. Fathers who feel capable of caring for the children and meeting their needs will always feel that they have shared in a positive contribution to their children's development.

Even if such preparation did nothing for the child's welfare, it would be a valuable experience for the parents. It gives them the experience of working together and building habits of cooperation in the first tasks of parenthood.

UNDERSTANDING EACH OTHER DURING PREGNANCY

Education for parenthood should also help couples to understand each other during pregnancy. During the first pregnancy, some husbands and wives have their first real difficulties. Some wives become irritable and wish to be treated as if they were ill or helpless. This may be due to a lack of knowledge about pregnancy and birth. Pregnancy is not an illness, and in most cases, the mother is in the very best of health. Nevertheless, physical changes are taking place and hormonal changes do affect emotions and behavior. The hormonal changes cause some pregnant women to become depressed, to worry about whether or not the baby will be normal, and to worry about whether or not they will live through childbirth. Often they find themselves crying easily and without known cause. If these exaggerated emotional states are experienced, they should be recognized as being caused by hormonal changes associated with pregnancy. Husbands should help the wife by giving reassurance and understanding and try to realize she is having a difficult time emotionally.

Hormonal changes also occur after the birth of the baby, and some women have emotional turmoil they do not understand. One of the most common types is called *postpartum depression.* Women who have this depression find it hard to understand, especially if they have looked forward to the birth of the baby. Medication has been developed that may help while her hormones are readjusting after the birth. Many women, however, have no such reactions.

We studied 212 couples who had gone through their first pregnancy and found that more than half the wives noticed no change in their health, one-third said their health was better, and only one in ten said her health was poorer. More than half the wives in our study reported having nausea (morning sickness) during the first three months of pregnancy, but only 15 percent during the last three months of pregnancy.

Sexual adjustment is often affected by pregnancy. In our study of the 212 couples, one-half of the wives and three-fourths of the husbands reported they saw no change in their sexual desire during the first three months of pregnancy, but both husbands and wives reported a rapid decrease in sexual desire during the last six months of the pregnancy. In one-fourth of the marriages, the wives reported a marked or complete lack of sexual desire during early pregnancy. When this happens, it may create a serious problem in sexual adjustment; the wife may feel guilty because she does not feel like participating in intercourse, and the husband, because of his sexual frustration, may lose perspective on the overall adjustment in their marriage. In general, however, our study found that young husbands tended to identify with their wives during the first pregnancy and to adapt their sexual urges to conform to the desires of their wives. The study found that within about six weeks after the birth of the baby, sexual desire returned to the prepregnancy level, and normal sexual relations were reestablished.

During pregnancy, most women need more time for rest and for outdoor exercise than they may have been accustomed to; and they must pay particular attention to eating a well-balanced diet both for their own sake and so that their child may develop to its full potential. More and more is being learned about how important prenatal environment is to an individual's total pattern of growth and development.

Both the husband and the wife need to show consideration and understanding for each other during pregnancy—possibly even more than at other times. The prospective child is a new development in their lives, and, like all stages of progress, it will require adjustments of both. If they do make the adjustments, they will gain fresh insights, and their marriage will be enriched. They may discover qualities in each other's character and personality that they had not yet known or appreciated.

When a wife discovers she is pregnant, a new relationship develops between a couple as they look forward to their new status as parents together. How can they now reinforce their feelings for each other?

APPROACHING PARENTHOOD

QUESTIONS FOR REVIEW

1. Discuss some inaccurate conceptions of parenthood.

2. In what ways is parenthood one of the most significant experiences possible in life?

3. Contrast romantic and realistic concepts of parenthood.

4. Do you think the reaction of the young mother quoted in the text was typical of many young mothers after the first baby is born?

5. How do the requirements for entering the profession of parenthood differ from the requirements for entering other professions? Is such a difference logical?

6. Through what ways can one prepare to be a better parent?

7. Do you think people of high school age are mature enough to look objectively at how their parents reared them and to evaluate what was good or bad in the methods and policies?

8. Why is it so important to be emotionally mature before becoming a parent?

9. Do you think people approaching marriage consider how the prospective marriage partner will function as a co-parent in the future? Discuss.

10. Why is it necessary for fathers to have a share in caring for the children?

11. Why do doctors think that classes in preparation for childbirth shorten labor and lessen the pain?

12. Why should fathers attend classes in preparation for childbirth?

13. What are the arguments for and against the father being present in the delivery room?

14. Just what takes place in the mother's body during the first stage of labor? What can the mother do to hasten this part of the birth process?

15. What happens during the second stage of labor? What can the mother do to aid the delivery process at this stage?

16. Why are new adjustments between the husband and wife required during pregnancy? After the birth of the child?

ACTIVITIES AND PROJECTS

1. Report on educational opportunities for parents in your community.

2. Report on cooperative nursery schools or kindergartens in your community. What are the obligations of parents whose children attend?

3. As a class, visit a nursery school. Pay special attention to types of the children's behavior that you have noticed in yourself or in other adults.

4. Write an essay on "The Ideal Parent," or on "My Assessment of Myself as a Future Parent."

5. Does your community have a class for expectant parents? If so, ask the director to talk to your class about the work being done.

6. Read one of the magazine articles listed in the suggested readings at the end of this unit that would apply to this chapter. Report to the class. If the magazines *Psychology Today* and *Child and Family* are not available in your library, consult the *Reader's Guide* for current articles on natural childbirth, and report to the class.

WORDS AND CONCEPTS

alleviate
anesthetics
dilate
emotional climate
natural childbirth
nurture

obstetrician
postpartum depression
rhythmic contractions
social system
static situation
taboos

New Parents and Emotional Growth of Children

26

After studying this chapter, you will be able to

1. Discuss the basic needs of babies with special emphasis on their need for love.
2. Explain the implications of the thought that parents should respect their child as an individual.
3. Give the chief aim of all child training.
4. Analyze why keeping a sense of perspective is important in child training.
5. Describe two basic means of helping children develop good habits.

Babies have essential needs that must be met if they are to grow normally. They need food, sleep, and love. No one of the three can be said to be any more essential than the other two. Most parents are immediately conscious of their child's need for food because the infant will cry, fuss, and disturb the household when hungry. The infant's need for sleep will be satisfied also, because most babies will sleep if given a reasonable chance. If parents provide a comfortable place for the baby to sleep, protection from the cold and heat, and nourishment, usually the baby will sleep soundly, becoming accustomed to noise or other disturbing factors.

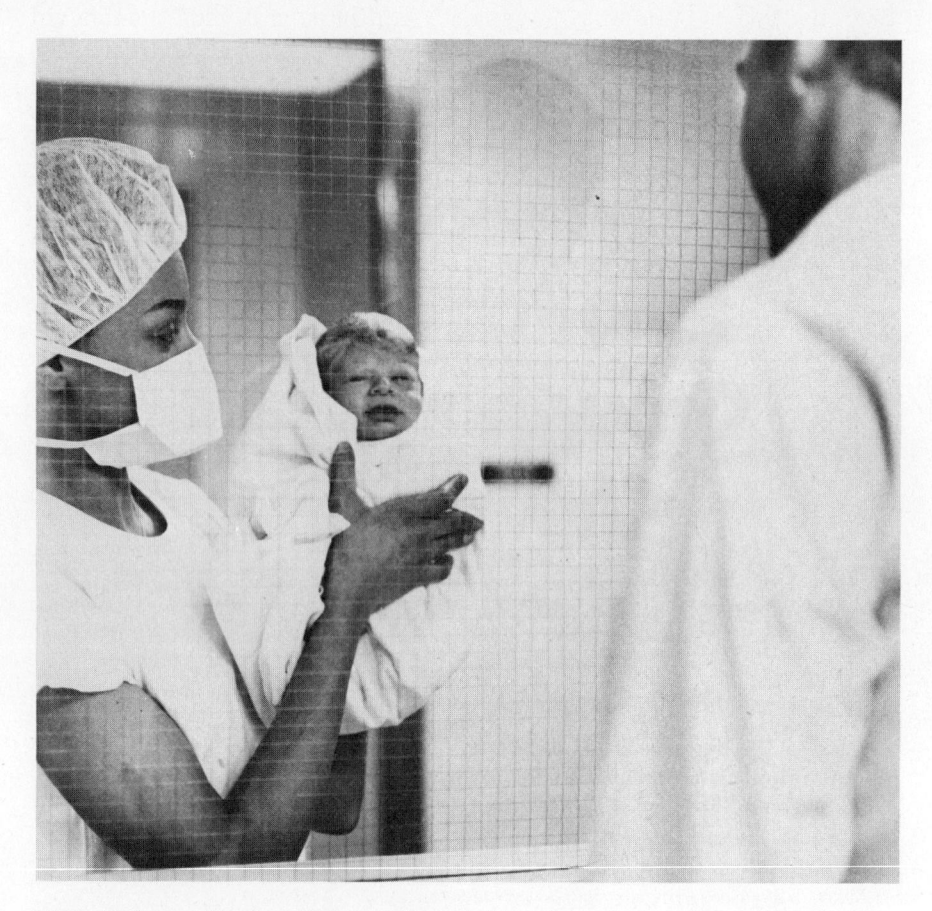

Many fathers still view their newborn babies through the glass windows of antiseptic nursery wards. Even so, there is no sight more wondrous.

THE CHILD NEEDS LOVE

The child's need for love clearly is less understood by some parents. Sometimes, parents are so busy providing for the tangible needs of the child that they are unaware of an immense need for love; but it has been demonstrated that warmth of affection is just as important to good physical growth as are a warm bed and enough food. In one foster home, a specific test was made. Someone was assigned the responsibility for giving to each baby in a selected group what nurses call T.L.C. (tender, loving care). Every day, someone rocked and cuddled these babies and gave them special loving care. It was found that the babies who were shown love and were cuddled as a regular part of their care developed much more satisfactorily than those who were faithfully cared for, but not cuddled or given love. The "loved" babies had better appetites, gained weight more rapidly, and excelled the other babies in general physical well-being and in personality growth.

A young mother complained, "I had to spend so much time holding the baby and rocking him today, that I didn't get anything done at all." She meant that she didn't get any housecleaning or sewing done. But surely, rocking and cuddling a restless, temporarily unhappy baby was more important and longer lasting in consequence than sewing or housecleaning.

That is true of many of the tasks of parenthood. One may not be able to see a specific accomplishment at the end of a day; but patient and loving care of a baby or young child builds a healthy personality in the child. No other work a parent can do is worth so much. A mother and a father need to hold their baby close in their arms often. The newborn is adjusting to the shock of coming into a cold, impersonal world after being cradled within the mother's body.

A healthy baby who is given warmth of love from the beginning of life feels secure and gradually begins to distinguish between the parent and the rest of the world. Attitudes and responses to the larger world and to other people arise from a feeling of security or insecurity in relation to the parents. Thus, socialization begins gradually, and it does not end with infancy. A young child's need to be held and cuddled continues for months or years. The two-year-old who suddenly becomes naughty when a parent is especially busy or preoccupied with a new baby is probably reacting to the withdrawal of needed and desired loving attention.

Parents sometimes fear they may spoil children by rocking them at bedtime when they are "too big" to be rocked. But "spoiled" children are more probably ones whose emotional needs are not being met.

CHANGES IN ATTITUDES ABOUT INFANT CARE

A generation or two ago, hospitals gave a new mother instruction about how to bathe the baby and other points of physical care. She was impressed with the importance of keeping everything that came near the baby perfectly clean and antiseptic. She was given a mask to cover her face during the short period of time that she had the baby with her in the hospital room. Cleanliness and good physical care are important, but they were emphasized so much that no recognition was given to the important matter of the affectional relationship that needs to develop between the parents and the newbaby.

Many hospitals now use a "rooming-in" system, where the baby is kept in the room with the mother, rather than being kept in the nursery. The mother is urged to breast feed and give warmth and affection from the beginning, so that the baby will not experience the shock that otherwise comes with emerging at birth into a cold world. Because the baby is in the mother's room, the father can see the baby at every visit. He does not have to content himself with looking at his child through a glass window. Thus, both parents can begin to get acquainted with their child during the first days of the baby's life.

Because maternity wards in older hospitals have been constructed on a plan that does not permit the baby to stay in the room with the mothers, rooming-in is not always possible. But many hospitals are making or have made the necessary changes so that babies can be with their mothers much of the time. The medical profession now generally recognizes that new babies should be with their mothers, and as rapidly as they can do so, hospitals will put the knowledge into practice.

EACH CHILD GROWS IN HIS OR HER OWN WAY

All parents are interested in the growth of their children. Sometimes, parents are overanxious on this point. They may worry or wonder because their baby is seven months old and has no teeth while the baby across the street is only four months old and has three teeth. They fear that their child is not normal at eleven months because he or she sits and plays happily in the playpen or crib while some other baby at that age is walking and climbing.

The time at which a child's teeth appear and the age at which walking starts are simply a part of an individual pattern of development. Such patterns are likely to be characteristic of a family; that is, the children may be early or late in teething or walking, just as they may tend to be mostly blue eyed or brown eyed or to have other particular family characteristics.

The truth is that it does not matter at all whether a child gets his teeth at four months or at eight months or later, if the child is healthy and happy and growing at his own pace. Parents who worry or fret because their baby does not get his teeth as soon as some other baby may be the same parents who, when their child is sixteen, will be making the teenager unhappy by their discouraging comparisons with other teenagers.

It is almost impossible for parents to speed up a child's development, but by their anxiety, they can retard it. A child usually will develop in a unique way and at a personal speed unless treated in ways that will be a handicap. To push and prod a child or to try to mold a certain or different sort of person is destructive. Parents' pressure upon a child or their anxiety about the rate of the development they desire is perceived by the child as no confidence in him or her. The child is likely to begin to feel the parents' disappointment or anxiety. As a result, even a young child's self-concept may be damaged and hinder development. In order to nurture a healthy personality growth, it is most important that parents enjoy and respect their child as an individual.

BASIC AIMS OF CHILD REARING

Sometimes, discussions that deal with personality development of children are discouraging because they point out the pitfalls along the way. The subject need not be discouraging, but rather challenging. The early chapters of this book considered the traits that we have or need to develop, and some of the undesirable traits or habits that we need to work to eliminate in ourselves. As you look back upon your childhood, you can see mistakes your parents may have made. You may be able, when you become a parent, to avoid some of these. You can look ahead intelligently and consider what are the important and desirable traits that you wish to see in your own children. Some things definitely help or hinder the healthy personality growth of children. By this time, you are probably aware of some habits or attitudes in your own personality that you would like to change so that you might avoid passing them on to your children.

The chief aim of all child training is to help the child to be an independent, responsible person who can function effectively within the environment. It might be better to say that the aim of child training is not to hinder the child's growth. Sometimes, parents are so intense in their desire to do right by their children that they overdo their training. They do too much hovering, too much supervising, and especially, too much criticizing. They attempt to fit the child into a pattern that exists in the parent's mind, but has not been cut to fit the child. In such cases, the effect may be to hinder the development of a well-rounded personality in the child.

SENSE OF PROPORTION

A sense of proportion is important in child training. Some specific personality traits are desirable and worth working for; other traits, that might seem desirable to a parent, are not of permanently fundamental significance. For example, an intense parent who considers cleanliness of major importance may deal with children within the household too rigidly in an attempt to train them to be neat and clean in all their habits. Another who believes in the value of table manners may make every meal an unhappy occasion by constantly criticizing and supervising the children's eating.

Cleanliness and good table manners are all right, just as are many other habits for which parents may struggle and strain, but parents need to have a sense of proportion about these things. It is important for the children to eat their meals happily and to feel that they are a welcome addition to the social circle at the family table. What if they do sometimes spill their milk or eat with their fingers while learning?

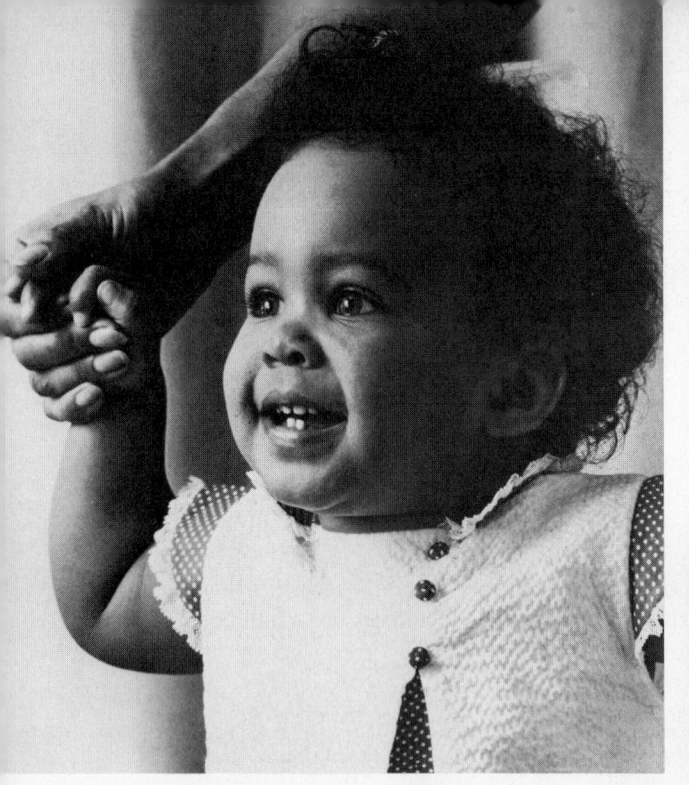

(Left) Given warm affection, each child will develop into a happy, productive person in his or her own way. (Right) Isn't it more important for a child to enjoy food and family companionship than it is for the child to use the right fork at the table?

FORMING GOOD HABITS

It is true that children should develop good habits so that the details of daily living will become routine. Such good habits can be developed primarily by two means:

1. *By example.* Sometimes, parents tell a child over and over what to do and how to do it, when they could accomplish more by setting a good example. Cleanliness, eating habits, courtesies such as saying "please" and "thank you," all come naturally after a while to children who associate with adults for whom these things are a habit. Some parents are in too big a hurry. They urge and coerce and defeat their own aims. They might more readily accomplish their purpose if they would *be* the kind of people they want their children to be.
2. *By getting cooperation* so that an effort is made by the child to form the desirable habit. Habits cannot be put on a child like a garment. They can only be built from within. A small child will work to form satisfactory habits if others are doing so, or if pleasure and approval are the rewards. One parent said to another, "How do you make

Encourage children to "do their own thing" with little overt supervision.

Johnny do what he should do?" The other answered, "I don't. I doubt if you ever can *make* anyone do anything. It seems to me you can only lead and guide and encourage and hope. Johnny is usually reasonable. He seems to be strong-willed in making himself do what he decides is the right thing to do."

A child will work for improvement in habits when there is some point in doing so. If the child realizes that putting away toys after playing with them makes them easy to find next time, the habit of putting them away will be encouraged. A parent may inspire "won't power" instead of "will power" by scolding and showing impatience about play things being put away or by going ahead and doing it instead of letting the child do such things, however long it may take.

Impatience is a handicap in dealing with children. Some adults want action, quick and prompt. They fail to realize that to a young child time means almost nothing. So, parents may become impatient and scold or punish when a child fails to do things in an adult way. Through their impatience, they provoke resistance in the child, who decides not to cooperate and without thinking it out in so many words may show the attitude, "Let them make me do it if they can." Thus, progress toward developing good habits is slowed or blocked.

BEDTIME HABITS

In some families, much conflict centers around sleeping and eating habits of young children. Putting children to bed should not be used as a punishment. Going to bed should be handled in such a way that the children look upon bed as a pleasant, comfortable place that is entirely their own. Children may hate their beds and resist being put to bed if someone has been cross and impatient when putting them to bed, or if being put to bed is used as punishment.

In one family, the children had a puppy whose rights they had been taught to respect. When the puppy became tired of playing or if the children were too rough with him, he would run to his basket in the corner and curl up as if for a nap. The two children, three and five years old, would sit patiently beside his bed with the explanation, "We won't bother him while he rests in his bed." Sometimes they would say, "Snips is tired and went to his bed for a nap. We'll have a rest, too." And they would settle down in their own beds for brief naps. Naps and bedtime were not a problem in that family.

EATING HABITS

Poor eating habits in healthy children are almost always a reflection of the attitudes of the adults who are around the children. If parents make too much fuss or constantly offer too much food, little children learn quickly that they can create a sensation or get special attention by pushing away their food and refusing to eat. They are aware at once that the adults are anxious and tense about their eating, and it becomes more pleasant and interesting to refuse to eat than to eat. Some parents hover anxiously over their small children, watching for each bite to go into the child's mouth as if it were a matter of life or death. Such a performance always puzzles or amuses other people who cannot imagine why eating should be such an emotional matter. But such situations really are not funny. To build in children unhealthy attitudes about eating is to give them an unnecessary handicap in life. Some fat people who struggle against obesity are products of overanxious parents who conditioned them early to look upon eating as a way to win parents' approval or as an escape from unpleasantness.

Healthy children should be given *small* servings of nourishing food and second or third helpings if they want them. But whether they eat much or little should not occasion comment. There is no virtue in overeating and nothing sensational about a light appetite. The attitude to work for is that we eat for nourishment, and we are fortunate if we have enough nourishing food for our needs. Eating is one of our natural processes, and not a subject for comment or a device for attracting attention. If children look upon it otherwise, it is because of the example or policies of those about them. Research studies have shown great variation in the amounts of food necessary for health and growth in different individuals. What is enough for one may be far too much, or not enough, for another. Thus, a child must be allowed to choose how much to eat and should never be urged or coerced.

Older children copy the adults in the family. Some families have the habit of commenting freely at the table on what foods they like or dislike, as if such food preferences were a fascinating concern to all present. A good rule in any family is that a compliment to the one who cooked the meal is always acceptable, but any other comment on the food is out of place. The world is full of interesting topics suitable for conversation at the family table.

FAMILY TABLE TALK

Many families do not realize how important table conversation is. The kind of talk that goes on can greatly influence the attitudes and feelings of children. The parents of a three-year-old worried because the child had a poor appetite, dawdled over food, sometimes refused to eat at all, or after eating sometimes vomited. The parents habitually used mealtime as the place to discuss their worries and troubles or to argue about their differences. It never occurred to them that this kind of mealtime conversation might be the basis for the child's eating troubles. They thought all such talk was not understood by the child. But even babies respond to the spirit of the conversation, whether or not they can understand the words. Table conversation, pleasant or unpleasant, affects all of us at any age. It is worthwhile to try to make mealtimes happy occasions in family life.

One couple was forced to take stock of their dinner-table conversations and try to correct some of their habits when their three-year-old son began imitating them at dinner. He sat twisted in his chair, leaning close to his plate looking exactly like his father. He kept up a running conversation in a low voice, repeating the words and tones of the parents as they talked.

He was not aware they were noticing what he was doing. He was only amusing himself, occupying himself with the little private game, because he was not included in the conversation and was ignored at the table unless he misbehaved.

For the first time, the parents realized what some of their table habits were. They had habitually discussed problems or unpleasant subjects while they ate. "Please" was a word absent from their conversation, and the only comments they addressed to their children were admonitions such as, "Be careful," or "Clean your plate," or "Keep your feet off your chair."

When they saw their mealtime as reflected by their three-year-old, they decided to change and to establish different customs.

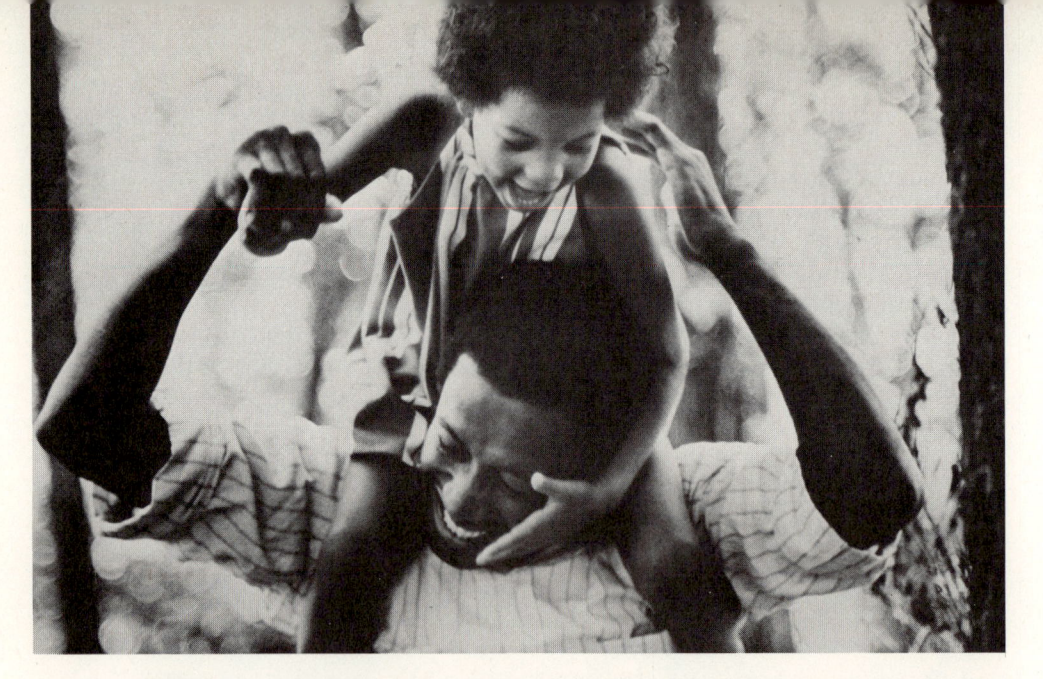

Ideally, parents and children grow mutually. This little girl will always remember a happy childhood. Is it safe to say that she has a good foundation for helping her own children to become positive individuals?

In many families, the only time most family members are in each other's company for any length of time is often during the one or two meals that they may have together. As you read this, you may think of the mealtime customs you have at home. If there is bickering, argument, discussion of troubles and worries, or just no talk at all, can you personally do anything to improve this situation? It is not necessary to think unfavorably of your parents if conversation at meals is not constructive, for all family members can tak responsibility for what goes on. But it is important that you think about such matters now, before you establish your own home. In the family that you establish, you can work to build elements that contribute to a happy home and the healthy emotional growth of children.

OVERALL GOALS

In this chapter, we have been considering aspects of the emotional growth of children. This may help new parents to decide about their overall purposes and to understand that during the infancy and early childhood of their children, they establish habits of family interaction that are significant in their children's personality development. No two families are alike. Each parent functions according to his or her special capacities and abilities. But parents can begin to create a home situation conducive to the best development of their children if they have thought through the many aspects of child rearing and if they are consistent in working toward their overall goals. Always it is necessary to be flexible.

Wise parents learn that they do make mistakes. No one of us can be all-wise in the way we deal with children. But successful parents do not give in to defeat or discouragement but keep trying. They become able to acknowledge mistakes and to change habits or policies that prove to be unwise. They continue to learn from their children as their children learn from them.

QUESTIONS FOR REVIEW

1. What are the basic needs of babies? Which one is sometimes overlooked?
2. What was found about the importance of giving loving care to children in the foster home?
3. Will rocking "spoil" a child? Discuss.
4. What is the purpose of "rooming-in"? Do the hospitals in your city operate on this plan?
5. Why are parents concerned if their baby does not walk, talk, or get teeth as soon as some other baby does? Is the concern justified?
6. Explain what is meant by the statement that parents must respect their child as an individual.
7. What is the most basic aim of successful parenthood?
8. "A sense of proportion is important in child training." Discuss. Give instances to clarify your points.
9. Discuss two ways of developing good habits in children. Which do you think is more effective? Can you give an illustration?
10. Give some rules for helping children form good sleeping habits.
11. Give some rules for helping children form healthy and acceptable eating habits.
12. How might table talk affect the development of children?

ACTIVITIES AND PROJECTS

1. Anonymous class study. Each class member writes examples of two kinds of table conversation that would have opposite effects on the children in the family.
2. Observe the behavior of your smaller brothers or sisters or of the children of friends or neighbors. Report on actions you observe that are normal in children but childish in adults.

SOCIODRAMA

1. Show a series of family scenes demonstrating some right and wrong ways to train children.

2. Show two families with contrasting mealtime habits: one family whose table talk would have positive effects on the attitudes and personalities of children and one whose interaction would have negative effects.

WORDS AND CONCEPTS

coerce
consistent
obesity

self-concept
sense of proportion
tangible

Discipline and Guidance in Child Development

After studying this chapter, you will be able to

1. List priorities parents should have in order to establish consistent patterns in child rearing.
2. Analyze how lack of discipline or guidance is related to habitually naughty behavior on the part of a child.
3. Discuss the importance of being able to distinguish between feelings and actions and between discipline and punishment.

In some families, the little children are reasonable and cooperative. The parents seem to have positive ways of handling the daily affairs of living so that there are very few situations that provoke outbursts of temper, screaming, or resistance to reasonable rules or suggestions. In other families, the opposite situation exists. The small child is habitually resistant and uncooperative, kicks and screams frequently, and interrupts constantly when others talk. Mealtimes and bedtimes are battles. Such disagreeable behavior has various causes. It may be that the parents themselves are aggressive and in conflict in many matters. The children are merely expressing their version of the family norm.

Or it may be that parents take such behavior for granted as normal childhood and make little effort to set a happier standard. The parents may hold confused ideas about how much freedom to allow. They don't want to inhibit, so they go to the other extreme and do not help the child use self-control. Psychologists have concluded that among these too-permissive parents are some who have inner doubts about their own feelings toward their children. They may not be sure enough of their love for the child to be able to be consistent in disciplining. If they ever restrict the child, it may be only when they are responding to their own angry feelings and not when limits of behavior actually need to be set if the child is to make growth toward maturity. The parents should strive to have a quality of love that would enable them to help the child learn self-control, and the child would then be happier and more secure. In other cases, the child's unpleasant behavior may mean that the parents are too arbitrary, demand too much, and create too many frustrations. The child may react with resistance and aggressive behavior.

CONSISTENCY IN CHILD REARING

As early as they can in the life of their child, parents must establish a pattern of consistency in dealing with each individual child. To ignore certain kinds of behavior one day as if it were of no consequence and to react with anger to the same behavior on another day confuses the child and contributes to feelings of insecurity. Parents must first try to think together about their priorities in child training. What are their basic aims? Their primary goals should be (a) *to help the child grow steadily and happily toward maturity,* (b) *to help the child develop inner strengths that will enable the child to make a good adjustment outside the family unit, and* (c) *to enjoy the child rather than to have friction during the childhood years.* If they can so define their purposes, they have a guideline helpful in being consistent. They can see that some types of behavior are annoying, but not significant, and can be treated lightly. Others may indicate a trend in the child's development that suggests that this child needs help. To these, the parent must be alert. Naturally, a parent feels distraught sometimes when a child behaves in embarrassing or frustrating ways; but if the response to the child's behavior is emotional only, a parent cannot be consistent. The child will observe that some actions are acceptable on days when the parents are in a peaceful frame of mind but unacceptable on other days. The child will then have no basic guidelines for his or her own behavior.

LACK OF GUIDANCE MEANS TROUBLE FOR A CHILD

Whatever the cause of parental inadequacy, the habitually "naughty" child has his or her own motivations. Nearly always, the personal needs

(Left) To be secure, children must feel accepted and approved in what they learn to do. High school students who work with children come to understand themselves as well as to help the little ones. (Right) Children develop confidence if they are allowed to do things for themselves.

of the child are not being met. The child becomes unhappy and, in time, is handicapped by the unacceptable behavior. A necessary factor in building security and self-confidence in children is for them to see and feel that they are accepted and approved rather than rejected and disliked. Little children, even more than the rest of us, are keenly aware of, and responsive to, the feelings of other people. If nearly everyone around finds the child to be provoking, the child is conscious of their feelings, and will not be happy or comfortable. In such situations, most children have no idea what to do about the uncomfortable feelings, and they do the thing that only adds to their unhappiness: they exaggerate and increase the very behavior that has caused the trouble. Naturally, a small child cannot figure out rationally, "These people disapprove of certain acts of mine, so I will start being good." Rather, these vague feelings of discomfort lead the child to fight back at the world with more unpleasant behavior. The child probably does not know why he or she misbehaves. Help, not punishment, is needed.

Children need the help of parents who show love and who try to use wisdom and understanding in dealing with them. They must help their children behave in ways that will add to good feelings about themselves and that will not bring disapproval from other people.

The feelings children have in response to constant disapproval are harder on self-development than it would be to learn to control their actions. Parents are human in their feelings. No one likes to be called names or to be kicked, even if the offender is a four-year-old and one's own child. For parents to allow such behavior and simply control themselves does not help the child. No one else in the world is going to tolerate that kind of behavior from the child later; so if the parents help the child to learn to behave in acceptable ways, they are helping him toward more frequent experiences of feeling accepted and liked by other people. These "good feelings" will in turn help the child to develop more inner security and more confidence in his ability to meet life adequately. The approach must be positive. Punishing can never be as productive as leading, praising, and guiding with love.

Parents and others who deal with children need to understand clearly, themselves, the *distinction between feelings and actions*. It is natural to become angry or provoked, to want one's own way, and to feel like fighting to get it. It is possible to help even young children begin to learn that in this complicated world we must become able to accept our feelings but must control our actions.

When little Billy struck angrily at his mother and said, "I hate you!" she said, "Billy, sometimes I feel pretty angry at you, too, but in this family we don't strike each other. You just go outside and kick your football around until you feel better." She led him firmly outside and shut the door.

On another occasion, Billy was feeling cross and irritable after a long rainy afternoon in the house. He expressed his feelings by quarreling with the other children who had come to play. He kicked over one child's block house, and tore up another child's crayon picture. His mother put him in a separate room, saying, "Billy, the other children have a right to play without your messing things up for them. They don't like this rainy day any better than you do. You'll just have to find a better way of letting off steam." Billy took the suggestion literally, and in a few minutes, he came beaming out to suggest that they all have a game of leap frog. The living room was soon in wild disorder, but Billy's mother kept out of it. She could see that Billy was really trying to find a "better way of letting off steam."

Such examples suggest that there is a middle way that helps a child develop well. A child need not be allowed to run wild and misbehave in such ways that one is often in trouble. Nor is it necessary to suppress and try to make the child feel that he or she must be an angel-child who never has any mean or unpleasant impulses.

The point is that we live in a civilized and complicated world. The sooner we learn as individuals to respect the rights of others and to behave with as much decency and consideration for others as we can, the smoother life will be for everyone. Parents who love their children try to help them learn these things early. Whether we call it discipline or loving guidance does not greatly matter.

SELF-CONFIDENCE

Of greatest importance to the child's whole life adjustment is the development of self-confidence. How does it happen that some people feel inadequate in almost all of life's situations? They try to compensate for their feelings of inadequacy by being aggressive or belligerent. Or they are hesitant and withdrawn because of their fear of failure, never venturing into any activity that might challenge them.

Parents can help their children build self-confidence. This is not done by encouraging the child to think that he or she is always right. Rather it is based upon acceptance of and respect for the child as a person. If parents have accepting and supportive attitudes toward each other and toward the child, he or she will be better able to build on his or her own special strengths. The child can develop attitudes that, with the passing of time, will allow working with confidence at overcoming weaknesses or handicaps that may have been acquired.

An eight-year-old child tried to help by washing the dishes. When the mother saw the results, she ignored the fingermarked glasses and damp plates and praised her child for the shining forks and knives and for being helpful. She said, "I am so lucky having a child like you in the kitchen with me." The mother's sense of proportion helped her to realize that fingermarked glasses were of no consequence compared to the pleasures of having a child who was helpful and a good companion. Such incidents contribute to the feelings about self that one has as he or she grows through childhood.

If a child can read only one line in the book well, it pays to praise the fine reading of that line; it will help the child to feel confident that, by working at it, one can some day be a good reader.

The child develops confidence if allowed to do things without help. The three-year-old who insists on dressing without help may emerge with the shirt on backward and shoes on the wrong feet, but with face beaming and showing pride in the achievement. The child feels wonderful about having done it all alone. Progress is being made. But what if the older members of the family all burst out laughing when they see the child and someone says, "Here, you've got it all wrong; let me put these things on you right." The child's confidence is damaged and pride is spoiled. Less interest may be shown in doing things without help after that. A parent who says, "Here, let me do it for you," very often should pay attention to whether or not the child is being deprived of the satisfaction of achievement.

Other damaging words are "You're too little." If the child really is too little for what is being attempted, there are better ways for the parent to give assistance. But many times, parents underestimate a child's ability. The child who has self-confidence and is not under parental pressure is likely to be ready for higher levels of accomplishment than parents may realize.

How does the responsibility and discipline of a job help a youngster grow? Will the child make mistakes in business transactions? Do adults?

VALUE OF PRAISE

The value of earned praise cannot be overestimated. Not only is it effective in building self-confidence but it also gets constructive results in all the learning situations in childhood. Praise encourages the desire to improve, to continue in the ways or activities that have earned the praise. Criticism has the opposite effect. Criticism is not merely a waste; it is definitely destructive. It defeats its purpose, for it actually destroys the incentive to grow and learn.

Twelve-year-old Peter had a paper route. He did well at building it up, kept adding new susbscriptions, and was faithful in delivering the papers and careful in his collections. But he had never had any money of his own to spend before, and he had not learned to save. His weekly earnings were usually spent so soon that he even had difficulty saving enough to pay his regular bill for papers when the circulation manager came to collect each week.

His parents criticized him severely for his carelessness in handling his money. They compared him disparagingly to another boy who had a paper route and was systematically saving his money. Peter's father told him, "A fool and his money are soon parted." It never occurred to the parents to praise him for his faithfulness and punctuality in delivering his papers, or for his pleasant way of dealing with people, or his success in adding new customers.

Finally, he gave up his route in discouragement. Years later, this boy told a counselor, "I have never been able to do one single thing well in my whole life. I'm just a fool and a failure." His parents had failed to praise him and had concentrated on criticizing not only once but habitually. They built in him a consciousness of his weaknesses and no awareness of his abilities or good points. The counselor was able to help him begin to evaluate himself more accurately and to begin to develop some self-confidence, but the boy was handicapped by his parents' failure to appreciate the importance of praise and to comprehend the damage that criticism can do.

CONSTRUCTIVE VERSUS DESTRUCTIVE TRAINING

To point out sins and failures is almost always to be destructive. It is better to concentrate one's attention upon the good points even if a child does only one right thing in a whole day of activities. However, if the parents can find only one good thing in a child's whole day's activities, something is seriously wrong with the viewpoint of the parent. We find what we are looking for, and we tend to create what we seek.

A news columnist wrote: "I don't know about you, man. But I was brought up to feel unworthy. Maybe worthless. At home I would do this,

Most children need pets. Through caring for pets, a child may learn to think of the needs of others. The devotion of a pet also serves to add to the child's feeling of security.

that, or the other thing and my mother would say, as usual, 'Ah, you'll end up in Sing-Sing.' And away from home I would go to church and sing with the congregation, 'Oh, Lord, I am not worthy. . . .' And I wasn't kidding. I wasn't worth a nickel and I knew it. How I ever would fit into the great grown-up world where people wrote books, and built houses, and repaired plumbing, and sailed boats, and planted trees, I could never figure out. I had daily assurance that I was a misfit—which certainly did not fit me for *not* being one. . . . We are all, to be sure, imperfect. Overemphasis on that point can hardly do any good to the growing young animal. . . . Life is to be lived. The essential ingredient for this great adventure is confidence that it can be lived, and well. The job of instilling that confidence in a child is the parent's most important function."*

The point is that parents need to be positive rather than destructively negative. They need to find the capacities and potentialities that are there and that can be encouraged and built up. To say or imply to a child that one is "bad" or "stupid" or "selfish" does only harm. It creates in the child or makes permanent these traits that might need changing.

All this implies that the parent needs self-discipline. When feeling tired, overworked, or full of tensions, the parent may feel like saying to a child, "You're bad." It requires self-discipline to think intelligently about what would be most effective in accomplishing good results in the child, and to act according to the wise decision rather than to give way to impatience or a tendency to criticize.

A mother once said to her child, "You are a dirty, bad boy," when he came in from playing in the mud. He answered, "And I think you are a dirty, bad mother." She was shocked and said, "Say you are sorry you said that." Her son answered, "You tell me you are sorry first. You called me names first."

The mother said afterward, "I realized we were both acting like four-year-olds, but he *is* a four-year-old, and I am twenty-six."

Being parents is not so complicated for people who have the habit of working at keeping their relationships in good order with all those about them—their own parents, their friends, and the mate in marriage.

AGREEMENT BETWEEN PARENTS

Our study of four different groups of couples on how well they agreed on child training brought out the fact that a large percentage of engaged couples think they will agree on child training, and far fewer of married couples find when they have children that they do agree (see Graph 27).

---

*Charles McCabe, *San Francisco Chronicle*, 1968.

DISCIPLINE AND EMOTIONAL GROWTH OF CHILDREN

DEGREE OF AGREEMENT ON CHILD TRAINING

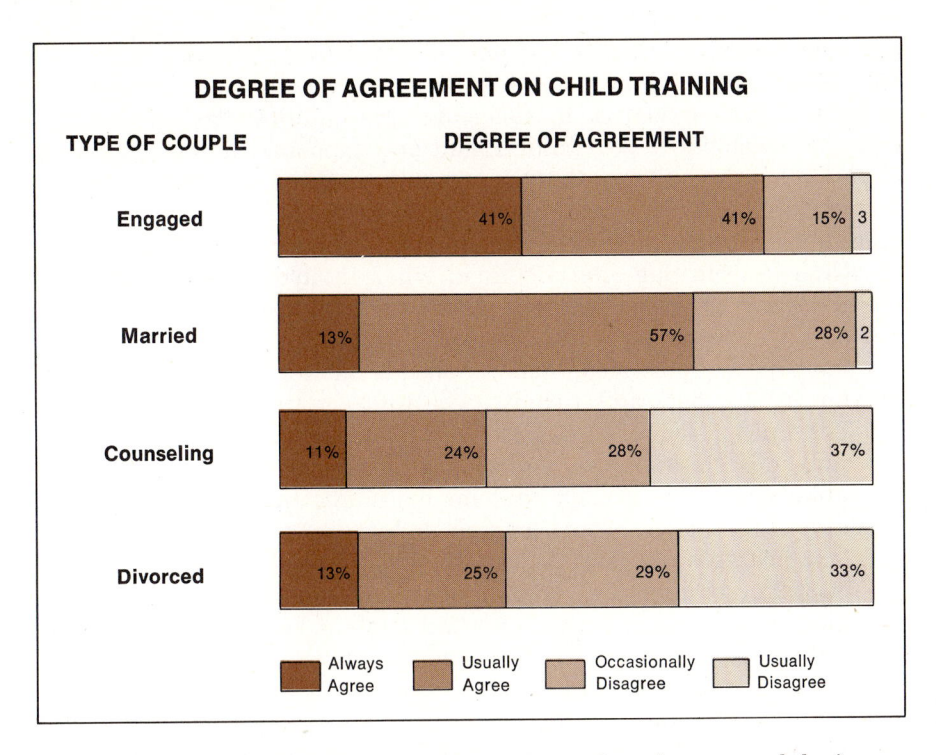

TYPE OF COUPLE	DEGREE OF AGREEMENT
Engaged	41% / 41% / 15% / 3
Married	13% / 57% / 28% / 2
Counseling	11% / 24% / 28% / 37%
Divorced	13% / 25% / 29% / 33%

Legend: Always Agree / Usually Agree / Occasionally Disagree / Usually Disagree

Graph 27. As reported by 122 engaged couples, 581 married couples, 155 people having marriage counseling, and 164 divorced persons.

The study showed that married couples did not discover how much they differed until after they had the children. They just assumed that because they loved each other, they would love the child and would agree on child rearing, even though they may have different attitudes about other matters. When they discovered their differences, new adjustments were required.

Parents who want their children to grow into happy and useful adults will stand together whether or not they agree entirely. They will talk over their ideas about what is right for the children; they will then present a united front.

It is natural that two people who marry and later have children may not agree about bringing up children any more than they agree always on the use of money, or on other points. Each one will reflect the attitudes and methods that prevailed in the parental family. If you will stop to consider some of the families you know, you will see that in almost every home the ways of dealing with children differ.

In one family, the father's word is law; when he speaks, no one argues. In another family, the father may attempt to make decisions or rules, but finds himself overruled by his wife. If he refuses the children permission to do anything, they only have to go to their mother, and she will give the permission. The children know that their parents do not agree on many things, and they learn to pit one parent against the other to get their wishes. In some of these families, the parents will argue, one defending the children and one opposing. If you have been in such a home, you know that the atmosphere of the home is not happy. The children may have more freedom of action than some other children, but life is not so pleasant for them.

Nine-year-old Sue often declined when invited to a certain home. When her mother asked why she was not willing to go to Jane's house, she said, "Jane's house is too dark and dirty."

Sue's mother protested. "Jane's house is much nicer than ours. Why do you say it is dark and dirty?"

The child answered, "Well, it seems dark and dirty to me, because her mother is cross and her father is gruff. When Jane wants to play, her father says, 'Yes, yes, go on,' and her mother says, 'No I need you to help me. You have played enough today,' and then her folks argue, and Jane just goes out to play, but she doesn't have much fun."

In still other homes, the parents seem to agree. Their children know that the parents will talk over important matters, and that the decisions will not be changed by one or the other independently.

These couples do not agree by accident. When they first became parents, no doubt they found, as others do, that each had his or her own ideas about bringing up children. But they have made the effort to get together in their views.

Our research with parents of young children, as well as among those whose children are grown, showed that disagreement over the training and disciplining of the children had been a major problem with many couples. Both parents may feel inclined to defend their ideas about child training, although neither may have a reliable basis for these theories. But some couples realize early that it is better for their own and the children's happiness if they can agree. They establish the practice of talking over their points of difference and trying to understand each other's viewpoint. Then, after they compromise, they support each other so that the children have the security of two parents who are for rather than against each other, with both trying to do what is best for the children.

Those who have studied large numbers of children have concluded that children are happier and better adjusted to life if their parents present a united front in child training—even if the methods the parents use are not the best, and even if the parents are too strict in their discipline.

Thus, early in marriage, couples need to form the habit of talking things over without having to quarrel. It is easier to form that habit while children are little and the problems are such matters as the best place for the baby's bed or how much to pay a baby sitter. Later, when the problem is how many nights a week a child can have the car, or how late a child should be allowed to stay out on weekday nights, parents will find it hard to get together if they have not established a pattern of solidarity. For now, the children can get into the argument, too, and the children already know whether or not they can "divide and conquer" their parents.

PERSPECTIVE ON DISCIPLINE AND GUIDANCE

In this chapter, we have attempted to give a philosophy of child discipline and guidance. We have presented the ideal, recognizing that parents cannot always measure up to this ideal. It is natural to make mistakes. The most successful parents will recognize that they have made some mistakes with their children and may feel guilty. But it is amazing how tough children are, and the fact is that they may not be seriously affected by an occasional mistake. Further, children soon learn to recognize when their parents have had a bad day, and have been issuing commands or giving unjustified punishments. In a way, children are quite forgiving of their parents when the parents are unwise. But the parent may feel guilty just the same. In trying to give parents perspective on child rearing, one authority told them to remember that an occasional mistake will not ruin the child; it is the making of mistakes day after day that destroys the child.

QUESTIONS FOR REVIEW

1. What may be indicated by aggressive misbehavior by a young child?
2. What questions might parents ask as guides in establishing consistent patterns in child rearing?
3. What does "naughty" behavior in a child often indicate?
4. Explain: "The naughty child needs help, not punishment."
5. "Punishing can never be as productive as leading, praising, and guiding with love." Discuss.
6. What is meant by the statement that people need to make a distinction between *feelings* and *actions*?
7. Distinguish between *discipline* and *punishment*. Find the exact meaning of *discipline* in the dictionary.
8. Why is it important to build self-confidence in a child? Give some examples of parental actions that can either help or hinder the child in building self-confidence.

9. What is easier to give, praise or criticism? What are the effects of each upon a child?
10. Illustrate what is meant by "constructive" and "destructive" methods. Earlier in the text, we discussed the "looking-glass self." How does the term apply to the discussion here?
11. Why is it difficult for some parents to agree about how to train and discipline their children?
12. How do both parents and children benefit when parents agree on training and discipline?
13. In summary of this chapter, what should be the chief aims of parents in child rearing?

ACTIVITIES AND PROJECTS

Have you ever observed a family in which the parents seldom agreed on how to train the children? If so, what effect did it have upon the children? Report your observations to the class.

SOCIODRAMA

1. Two family scenes. In the first, the parents constantly disagree in front of their children. In the second, the parents present a united front. Show the resulting behavior of the children.
2. As if this were a television show, two boys act out the parts of a father and a five-year-old son. Show ways that the father interacts with his son that are positive or that are destructive. How do many actual television shows portray such relationships? Discuss.
3. Two children act the parts of a parent doing household tasks, with a young child helping. Show positive or destructive ways of interaction.

WORDS AND CONCEPTS

arbitrary
belligerent
compensate
discipline vs. guidance

parental inadequacy
potentialities
priorities in child training
supportive

The Second Baby 28

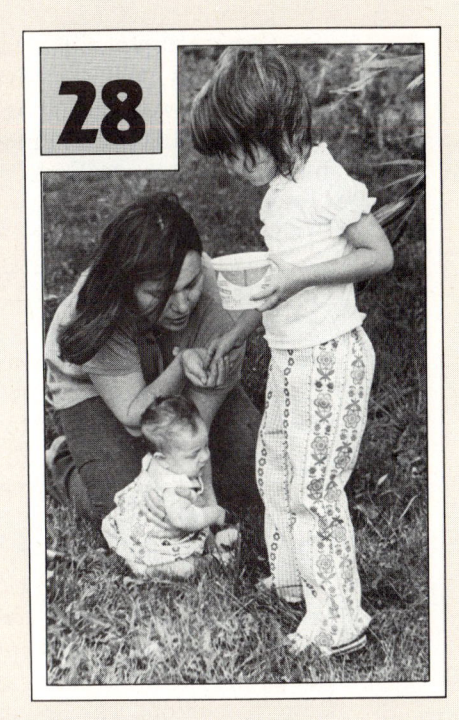

After studying this chapter, you will be able to

1. Give some common reactions of children to the birth of a baby sister or brother.
2. Discuss ways in which parents can help the older child adjust happily to the new baby.
3. List specific types of questions that children of different ages ask about sex and reproduction.
4. Give specific points on when and how to answer questions children ask about sex and reproduction.
5. Explain the dilemmas parents face in discussing sexual deviation with children.

Just as the coming of the first baby presents new challenges for married couples, so the coming of the second baby again changes many things in the family. Most young parents have the benefit of frequent consultations with a physician about the growth and development of their child. They also have books or pamphlets to consult when they are puzzled about things. Thus, almost all parents have been warned that they must prepare the first child for the coming of the second. Some who have told the toddler that there is to be a small sister or brother believe the matter is thereby taken care of, and are shocked and disillusioned if the older one shows dislike or animosity toward the baby. Some parents think that it is not natural for a child to show antagonism toward a tiny, helpless baby. They punish the child if he or she is unkind or tries to hurt the baby.

Other parents will say proudly, "We told Nancy ahead of time about the new baby, and we have had no problem with her at all. She goes on with her own activities just as she did before. She doesn't pay any attention to the baby, but she would never do anything mean to him like some other small children do to new babies."

OLDER CHILDREN REACT IN VARIOUS WAYS

Children have different ways of showing or not showing their feelings about a new brother or sister. It is safe to say that in every case there is some definite reaction to the coming of the new one, whether or not it is apparent. The first child does not always react with negative feelings directed specifically at the new baby. If the older child is happy and secure in the parents' love, the response to the new baby may be positive, especially at first. The child may find it exciting and pleasant to share "our" new baby. However, many children who have looked forward to the promised sister or brother are disappointed when they discover that the new one is not good company, but only a tiny baby who sleeps much of the time, and in addition, requires so much attention from the parents. The first child has been living in a world that revolves around him or her, and has been the center of attention. After the coming of the baby, the child's world does change. No matter how wise and loving the parents are, they cannot get around the fact that they now must share their time and attention with two children. So even the child whose initial response to the baby was positive may later have second thoughts about the new one.

Some children react negatively from the beginning. They may try to eliminate the baby by force. The new baby has to be protected from them. Other children may ignore the baby, trying to pretend that nothing serious has happened—that there really is no new baby around. Still others will try to win back their place as the center of attention by being extra good. They show great pride and loving concern for the baby in the hope of winning favor with the parents who seem so devoted to the infant. If parents are understanding, they can give such a child the love and reassurance needed so that gradually this outward show of caring becomes established as a part of the older child's real feelings for the new family member. The new baby then is another happy experience shared with the parents. But if the parents are too preoccupied with the new baby and the older child's needs are not met, this child may shortly conclude that being good is not accomplishing anything, and may then revert to babyish ways such as thumbsucking or bedwetting. Some children will become unusually naughty in order to get their parent's attention. Even punishment and disapproval are better than being ignored in favor of the baby.

Children have different ways of showing their feelings about baby brothers and sisters. Does this picture give a clue as to how this little boy feels?

UNDERSTANDING THE CHILD'S FEELINGS

For parents to understand the reason for a child's actions is helpful to both parents and child. They must recognize that the arrival of the new baby forces a rearrangement of relationships. Daily routines change. No one in the family behaves exactly the same as before, and this can be upsetting at any age.

Parents, without ever knowing they are doing so, tend to change in their behavior toward the first child. One reason for this is that all at once the first one seems to be such a big child in contrast to the baby. Unconsciously, they begin to expect more of the firstborn than they have been. While the older child feels the same as ever, except for needing more reassurance than usual, the parents begin to make more demands and to expect suddenly more than is fair for this child's age. So the child's troubled feelings increase. Sometimes, the mother who is involved with the new baby sees only that the older child is being difficult. Her show of irritation when reassurance is what is especially needed can create real problems where none existed.

WHAT CAN BE DONE ABOUT IT?

A preventive measure is to try to be as accurate and as realistic as possible when preparing the first child for the coming of the second. When parents talk about the new little brother or sister who is to be born, the first child naturally is thinking of an immediate playmate. Reality can bring disappointment or disillusion. While parents and child are happily looking forward to the new baby's coming, parents should help the child to understand that at first the baby will be tiny and helpless and will need a lot of care, that for a while the baby will just sleep or cry, and that only later will the baby grow up to be a playmate. At least, one part of the child's disillusionment could thus be avoided.

Whatever the older child's reaction to the new baby, the child can be helped to outgrow any negative feelings and to adjust happily. Above all, the parents must continue to show their love for the older child, and show it no matter what the older child does. At the same time, a small child cannot be permitted to hurt the baby; parents have to be alert to the needs of both children. While they avoid situations in which the older child might harm the baby, they must realize that the more difficult the older one is, the more that child needs love. A few moments taken at the right time to drop everything else and sit down to rock and cuddle the older child, can accomplish more than a whole day of protecting the baby from harm and scolding or reprimanding the child for misbehavior. To withhold love is always destructive.

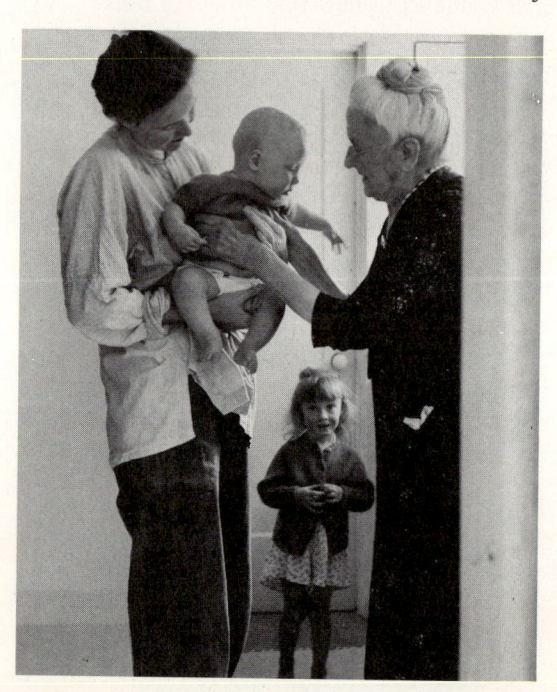

Does this picture give any clue as to how the little girl feels about her baby brother?

At any age, if sudden outbursts of naughtiness occur, special understanding is needed. "Badness" always means a child is having feelings with which help is needed. Parents should help the older child cope with bad feelings and to control actions. The parents should realize that they are expecting too much in the way of grown-up behavior from a child who is still the same as before the baby came.

Fathers are especially important at such times. The father must spend time with the older child in new and pleasant activities. These new activities should not be in connection with the baby. It is no fun for the older child to help entertain visitors who want only to admire the baby. The child would rather go with the father on an excursion or do some other things that are in a big child's world that excludes babies.

No matter how busy the mother is, she can arrange things so that she has some time for the older child. She should spend this time happily with him or her, letting it be felt that she enjoys this child's company and that he or she has a special place in her affection. Her attitude during the time that she is with the older child is much more important than the actual amount of time she is able to spend.

It is not only when the baby is "new" that parents need to be alert to the needs and feelings of the older one. Many children anticipate joyfully with their parents the coming of the new brother or sister and are positive in their feelings all through the early months when the infant is "our baby." Then as the baby outgrows infancy and becomes a toddler, the older child may become disenchanted with the whole business. The little one suddenly begins to represent interference and competition. For the first time, both of the children, but especially the older, must come to terms with feelings of jealousy and aggressiveness that may occur between siblings.

It is important to a child's whole life adjustment that he or she be helped to have a healthy emotional attitude toward brothers and sisters, especially the one next younger.

SEX AND REPRODUCTION

Answering Questions

The coming of a new baby when the first one is two, three, or four years old usually presents an excellent opportunity for the parents to begin building in their child wholesome attitudes concerning sex and reproduction.

Little children are very busy learning about their world. They can think of a multitude of questions to ask about everything they see about them. Many of their questions are just for the purpose of getting their parents to pay attention to them. One little boy, after having asked a

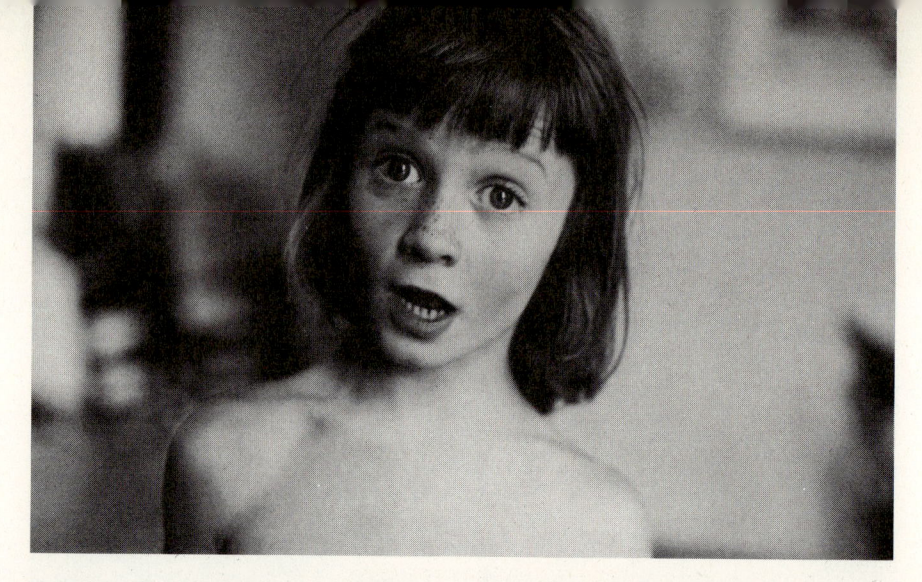

Parents who answer their children's questions, whenever they arise and whatever the subject, build confidence and healthful attitudes in their children.

long series of questions that his father had answered as well as he could, was heard to murmur to himself, "Let me see, now what can I ask him?" The child was clearly using questions as a way to get his father's undivided attention.

However, many, perhaps most, questions are evidence of the child's expanding interest and desire to know how everything works. Even if no new baby is coming, most children will begin asking questions about reproduction by the time they are three or four. Many people make a mistake at this time because they try to evade these questions. They had not expected them so soon.

Parents may try conscientiously to answer all the questions the child asks, but they react differently when the child begins to ask questions that deal with reproduction. The child sees at once that this subject has emotional implications; it seems to be somehow different from other subjects about which the parents are more cooperative when the child asks questions. At that point is to be found the beginning of the unhealthy attitude some people have about sex.

Children have a right to the most honest, straightforward answers that parents are able to give. Whether questions are about what the sun is made of or how far it is to the moon or where babies come from, there should be no difference.

If parents make sure ahead of time that they have the facts of sex and reproduction straight scientifically, they can more nearly answer a child's questions without embarrassment. The child usually wants to know the answer to just what is asked. Only that need be answered. It is not necessary to sit down and have a facts-of-life conference when the child asks a simple question such as "Where did you get me, Mother?" The child of three, four, or five, would be bored with a long explanation. As a child grows older, more specific questions will be added and more detailed answers will be required.

THE SECOND BABY

Specific Questions Children Ask

We asked 581 mothers to list the specific questions their children had asked about sex and reproduction and also to give the age of the child when the question was asked. The information is summarized in Table 14. Parents who have some idea of the type of questions that are quite universally asked by children of different ages can prepare themselves ahead of time by being informed and willing to answer when questions come.

Parents who refuse to answer questions or who show embarrassment when questioned force the child to go elsewhere for information. Research has revealed that a great many young people do get their only information about sex and reproduction from associates and from undesirable sources rather than from their parents.

Table 14 QUESTIONS ASKED BY CHILDREN REGARDING SEX AND REPRODUCTION*

QUESTIONS ASKED	Age of Child	Percentage of Children Who Asked
Origin and growth Where did I come from? Where did my brother (sister) come from? Where did you get me? Where do babies grow?	2–5	43
Body structure and function Why is brother (sister) different from me? What is that? (referring to genitalia) What are those? (referring to breasts) Why do boys and girls look different?	2–5	25
Birth of babies How do babies get out? How are they born? How do they know when to come out? Are babies born through the navel?	6–9	25
Fertilization and mating How do babies get in? How does the egg get fertilized? Where does the sperm come from? How are babies made? How is the seed planted? Do you have to be married to have a baby?	6–13	5

* As reported by 581 mothers in Landis study in 1967.

Pointers in Giving Reproduction Information

Some points about giving reproduction information follow:

1. Questions should be answered when they are asked, regardless of whether or not the child seems too young.
2. Exactly what is asked should be answered. If other questions follow, they too, should be answered, but there is no point in going into an extensive discussion if the child asks only a question or two and is satisfied with the answers.
3. Whichever parent is asked should answer. It is not sensible to give the father responsibility for certain questions and the mother responsibility for others.
4. Most important of all is the attitude with which the questions are answered. Parents need to try to answer questions about reproduction willingly and as accurately as they try to answer the child's other questions.
5. In discussing sex and reproduction with children, the accurate scientific or medical terms should be used for bodily functions and for parts of the body rather than using baby talk or street language that will be unacceptable later. If children learn the precise words from the beginning, communication will be much easier and more natural later, when both parents and children would be uncomfortable trying to discuss anything related to sex without the appropriate terms. To use accurate terminology with young children will eliminate one of the blocks to discussing sex behavior or facts of reproduction with older children.
6. If questions about sex are answered wisely when children are young, communication will be established that will enable parents to help their sons and daughters understand the emotional aspects of sex later. As people grow up, they become aware that sex functioning is more than reproduction. Sometimes, people who have as children known the facts about reproduction still do not develop wholesome attitudes toward sex.

Sex impulses and their pleasurable expression are an important factor in marriage, aside from reproduction. Many parents find it hard to interpret that fact to their children, and so they ignore it. Their sons and daughters, then, may not be prepared to understand their own emotional drives as they go through adolescence. Because sex functioning is a valuable part of personality makeup, it is important that people know not only the facts of reproduction but also that they learn to understand and cope with their sex drives. When the time comes for marrying, people have an advantage who have some understanding of sexuality and who have achieved a balance between their sexual-emotional drives and the other pressures and obligations upon them.

Informing the Child About Sexual Deviation

Studies show that few parents inform their children about sexual deviation, and yet many children have experiences with adult sexual deviates. Our study of 1800 university students found that one-third of both men and women had one or more experiences with adult sexual deviates when they were children. The most common experience girls reported were with exhibitionists and people who made sexual advances to them, and boys reported approaches by homosexuals as being most often made. Most parents are fearful that children may have experiences with adult deviates, and yet parents find it difficult to explain to the young child what may happen and how to handle the situation. Parents face dilemmas. They want the child to have an accepting attitude toward others and yet want to warn the child that not all people can be trusted. Parents want children to have normal attitudes toward sex and yet want to guard the child against unpleasant and possibly traumatic sexual experiences.

As in all areas of sex and reproduction education, parents should use a rational and unemotional approach. Children are taught that there are honest and dishonest people, people who can be trusted and people who cannot be trusted; and they should also be told that there are people who have unhealthy and warped attitudes toward sex. Children should be told how to cope with these people if they are encountered. The child should be encouraged to tell the parents of any incidents. Sometimes, when children do tell their parents about an encounter with a deviate, the parents do harm to the child by the shock and horror they register. Children are sometimes warned against "strangers" and what they might do, but improper sexual advances are often made by neighbors, relatives, or people known to them. This fact makes it doubly hard for parents to prepare their children against deviation. The best atmosphere for answering all questions about sexual behavior—normal or abnormal—is one in which parents and children can discuss the subject openly and without embarrassment. If this atmosphere can be created early in the lives of the children, then the most difficult problems can be discussed freely between parents and children.

Positive Effects of Childhood Information on Sex and Reproduction

Parents sometimes fear that if they freely answer their children's questions about sex and reproduction, the children might be more likely to experiment. Research studies show that the opposite seems to be the case. The more information children get from their parents, in contrast to getting information from other sources, the more likely children are to have desirable attitudes toward sex and the more likely they are to uphold the standards of society.

ATTITUDE OF YOUNG PEOPLE TOWARD SEX

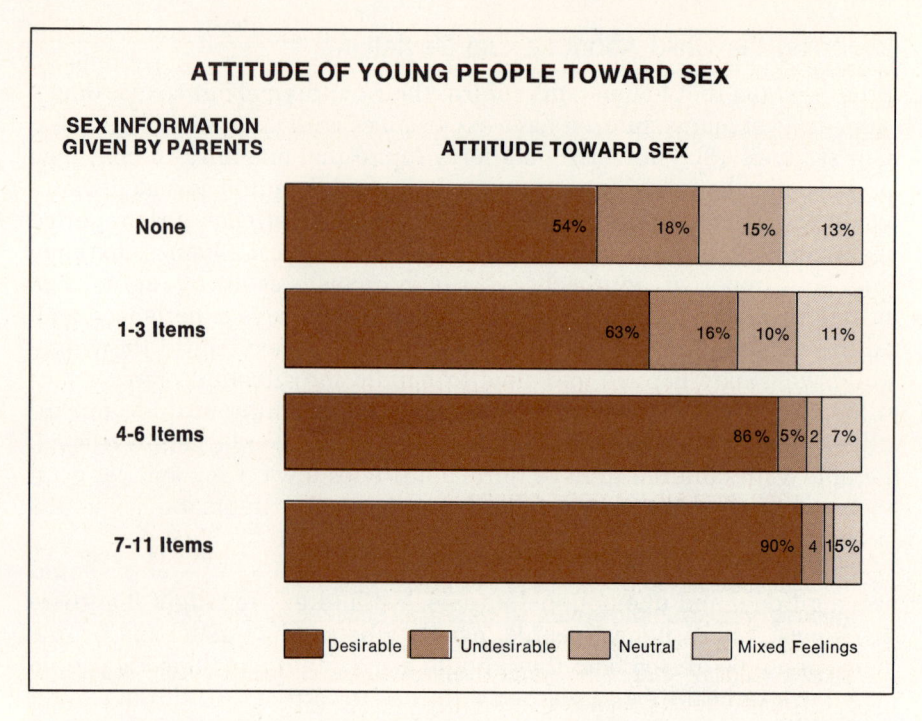

SEX INFORMATION GIVEN BY PARENTS — **ATTITUDE TOWARD SEX**

Sex Information	Desirable	Undesirable	Neutral	Mixed Feelings
None	54%	18%	15%	13%
1-3 Items	63%	16%	10%	11%
4-6 Items	86%	5%	2	7%
7-11 Items	90%	4	1	5%

Graph 28. Attitudes were rated according to responses of 3000 students to a check list of items, such as: "Sex is dirty and vulgar." "Sex is for mutual husband and wife enjoyment."

Graph 28 summarizes one study of three thousand students in which we asked the students to list the items of information on sex and reproduction they had received from their parents; and we then related their responses to the attitudes they expressed toward sex in husband-wife relationships. About 90 percent of those who had received complete information from their parents held positive attitudes in contrast to 54 percent who had had no information from their parents.

PARENTS' UNCERTAINTIES AS CHILDREN GROW UP

As children approach adolescence, parents who have not been able to answer their children's questions and have not established a good understanding with their children begin to worry. It is hard for some of you to understand why your mothers sit up until you return from a date; why you can't stay out until two or three o'clock in the morning; why some parents think there is too much freedom in expressing affection between boys and girls. It is true that while their children are approaching adulthood, parents tend to worry about their children's behavior. Young people ask, "What's wrong with Mom; what's wrong with Dad? Don't they trust me?"

In most cases, it is not lack of trust. It is just that many parents wonder whether or not they have done well enough through the years in helping their children to have an understanding of the emotional aspects of growing up and to develop wholesome attitudes. They regret that they do not have good communication with their children on this subject, but they do not find it easy to bring up the subject now. Any mention of behavior is likely to cause the child to feel that he or she is not trusted. It is too late now to discuss such topics if they have not been freely discussed long ago.

Yet parents understand and appreciate the strong drives with which young people must cope. They feel inadequate at a time when they would especially like to help. Thus, they may appear to be critical and overly anxious about where the children are and what they are doing. They may be tense, and the children think they are hard to get along with.

PARENT-CHILD UNDERSTANDING

If parents and children are to have a good understanding and be able to help each other when the children are approaching adulthood, good understanding must have begun when the children were young. That is why it is worthwhile for parents to try to be honest and objective in answering questions young children ask about all subjects, including sex and reproduction.

In fact, simple honesty between parents and children is a basic necessity if good relationships and healthy personalities are to develop. Successful parents have to be able to say, "I don't know," if they honestly don't know the answers. And then they must show a sincere desire to learn the things they don't know. They have to be able to say, "I was wrong," without feeling that it is so terrible to be wrong or to admit it. The only "terrible" thing would be to refuse to admit weaknesses or mistakes and to try to fool oneself and others into thinking one is perfect or all-wise. This basic honesty does not shake the child's confidence in the parent, as some people might fear. Rather, it helps the child to develop confidence in his or her own ability to face facts and do something about them. The child learns that weaknesses or errors do not have to be fatal, but can be steps in growth if a lesson is learned.

QUESTIONS FOR REVIEW

1. Why may the older child experience some feelings of hostility toward a younger child?
2. Can parents prevent the antagonism by telling the older child that he or she is to have a baby brother or sister? Discuss.

3. Give some of the common ways in which older children react when a baby is born. Which reaction is most likely and which one least likely to be recognized by parents?
4. What specific things can parents do so that the older child will not develop strong, permanent feelings of hostility toward the new baby?
5. When should children be told about sex and reproduction?
6. What are the specific questions children ask about sex and reproduction at different ages?
7. Why do some parents find it difficult to answer children's questions about reproduction?
8. What important phase of sex development do parents usually fail to discuss with their preadolescent or adolescent children?
9. What are the dilemmas faced in discussing sexual deviation with children?
10. What are some of the most common experiences children have with deviates?
11. What are some of the reasons why it is difficult for parents to tell their children about sexual deviation?
12. Why would you expect children who receive most of their sex and reproduction information from their parents to have more positive attitudes toward sex?

ACTIVITIES AND PROJECTS

1. Describe the reaction of a first child to the arrival of a second child in a family you know well.
2. (Report.) "The most common questions children ask about sex and reproduction, and how to answer them."

WORDS AND CONCEPTS

animosity
exhibitionist
homosexual
hostility

sexual deviation
siblings
solicitude

Adoption 29

After studying this chapter, you will be able to

1. Describe the changes made over the last twenty-five years regarding the qualifications required for adoptive parents.
2. List some unsound reasons for adopting.
3. Distinguish between positive and negative ways of telling a child she or he is adopted.
4. Discuss the progress made and the reforms needed in laws concerning children born to unmarried parents.

People approaching marriage are sometimes more concerned about planning to control the number of children they will have than about any possible inability to have children. Yet it has been estimated that from 6 to 15 percent of marriages are sterile from biological causes. A great many people approach middle age deeply disappointed because they have been unable to have children or because they have had only one. It used to be assumed that if no children were born the fault was with the wife. Research shows that in sterile marriages (marriages in which pregnancy has never occurred) both members are usually relatively infertile. More, but by no means all, of the factors are found in the woman, but in most cases, the responsibility for the childlessness cannot be placed wholly upon either partner.

In less enlightened days, few couples would admit that they could not have children. Now people are more likely to seek medical aid, for they know that many minor causes of sterility can be corrected. In recent years, progress has been made in finding the causes of infertility. The medical research that developed the oral contraceptive had as its first purpose to discover how hormones could be used to correct infertility. The research continues, and many couples who formerly would have remained childless now can become parents. Fertility specialists report successful treatment of from 25 to 60 percent of treated cases.

ADOPTING CHILDREN

If they cannot have children or have only one child, some couples consider adoption. There are laws to protect adoptive children, because the state recognizes that some who would adopt children are not qualified for parenthood. Laws set certain standards that prospective adoptive parents must meet before they can adopt a child.

In the 1940s and 1950s there were far more people who wished to adopt than there were babies available. Sometimes, qualified couples had to wait for years before a child was placed with them. The difficulty was due in part to the rigid requirements set by agencies responsible for protecting the interests of children. In recent years, however, policies have changed. Requirements about homeownership, income, education, religion, and age are less rigid, and rightly so, for these are not necessarily the most important qualifications of good parents. Besides, people who would adopt are changing toward more willingness to adopt children who are past the infancy stage and children who have handicaps requiring special care.

These changes would seem to lead to a balance between the number of adoptable children and couples ready to adopt. During the early

It is important to be honest about adoption. But the subject should not be overemphasized to make a child feel different from others.

1960s, a better balance actually occurred. Couples did not have such a long wait after applying for a child to adopt; and fewer children remained unchosen, except among minority groups. However, changes in the birthrate again began to affect the number of adoptable children. By the late 1960s, couples in some areas were again being disappointed because of difficulties or long waits. By the 1970s, there were far more couples seeking to adopt babies than there were babies available. Even when there are children who need homes and couples who want children, there are always some children who remain homeless because of physical or emotional factors or for other reasons. Adoption agencies now encourage couples to consider adopting older children, children of mixed races, and children who are handicapped. The enlightened view is that every child needs parents who will love and care for him or her regardless of physical, religious, or racial facts. Some couples, because of humanitarian motives, deliberately seek to adopt children with background handicaps rather than trying to find a child who resembles themselves.

UNSOUND OR SOUND MOTIVES FOR ADOPTING

Couples need to examine their motives as honestly as they can before adopting a child. If they want a child because they believe that having one will help hold a shaky marriage together, they are expecting the impossible. Any child, whether adopted or born to a couple, is an added responsibility that will complicate life. If two people cannot make a success of their marriage, they should not consider involving a child in their problems, either by birth or by adoption.

If the married pair are immature in their ways of meeting problems —if they tend to make alibis and blame others when things go wrong— they should not adopt. Such people would be likely to blame the adoption, or the child's heredity, instead of accepting their full responsibility for providing the emotional climate necessary for the child's growth to maturity.

If they want to adopt to provide companionship for a child they already have, they are likely to give more attention to the first child's needs than to the adopted child's. They should not adopt unless they can love each child individually.

If they wish to adopt to have a child to carry on the family's business or continue the family's achievement socially or professionally, they are likely to try to fit the adopted child into a mold that may not be right for him. In such a case, they are inviting disaster.

The only sound basis for adopting a child is if the couple hope to enrich life for themselves and for the child, are capable of giving a full measure of love, and are willing to accept the problems and responsibilities of parenthood along with the enrichment.

HONESTY ABOUT ADOPTION

Adopted children should know that they are adopted. Children become interested in their origin at very young ages, and the parents must be ready to answer as honestly as possible when asked such questions as, "Where did you get me?"

It is absolutely necessary that there be honesty between all parents and children, but especially if the child is adopted. Only if there is honesty can a child make good emotional growth and become able to cope with troublesome feelings while growing up. Parents who avoid the truth because it is hard to answer questions will block communication and create needless doubts and fears. But some parents who want to be honest and want the child to feel secure and happy about his or her origin make too much of a story of the adoption. They tell of hunting for and "choosing" the child with much more emphasis than they would ever give the subject if the child had been born to them. Without intending it, they succeed in overimpressing the adopted child that he or she is different from other children.

Certainly, this part of the adoptive parents' task is hard. They must see that the child knows that he or she is adopted, so that the child will never have to learn it unhappily later. At the same time, they must help the child to have good feelings about self and origin. The truth is that there are two faces to adoption—just as there are to every other important experience in life. In the background of every adopted child are some regrettable and sad events, or the child would not have been available for adoption. On the other hand, he or she *is* a chosen child; the parents went out of their way to find and adopt him or her. The child did not just "happen" to them.

People who have the capacity to love and accept a child and to create happy family relationships, should be able to handle the difficult task of helping the adopted child to know and understand about her or his adoption. They can best do this if they love the child freely and wholeheartedly. A child who never doubts the parents' love and honesty can better accept whatever facts are learned.

FEELINGS ABOUT ADOPTION

Sometimes, when adopted children reach the teens, they go through a period when they attach any feelings of unhappiness and insecurity they may have to the fact that they are adopted rather than having grown up with their "own" parents. Some of them worry and wonder about their natural parents and go to considerable efforts to learn all they can about their background. For the adopted child who is troubled with questions and doubts about her or his background, it is helpful to recognize that no one, adopted or not, has every circumstance of life just the way it might be wanted. Everyone probably has some fact in experience or background that one should try to come to terms with, if she or he is to make the best of life. People growing up with the parents who gave them birth often have just as many dissatisfactions. They can look around and see other families who are more desirable or more fortunate; they might easily wish at times that they had been born to different parents.

This may also be a difficult time for the adoptive parents. It is hard for them to cope with the feeling of being rejected by their teenage child. All those involved—the adoptive parents and the adopted child—need special understanding, love, and patience during the adopted child's teens.

CHILDREN BORN TO UNMARRIED MOTHERS

Many children to be adopted are among the approximately 300,000 babies born each year to unmarried mothers. Some of these children are kept and reared by their mothers or their mothers' parental families. Others are cared for in foster homes under the supervision of welfare agencies until they are either adopted or become old enough to be self-supporting.

Is it fair that any child should be branded illegitimate because of a mistake the child's parents made?

In the past, the child of an unwed mother did not have equal rights with children born to married parents. The child's birth certificate, a public record, recorded the birth as "illegitimate." The child was not guaranteed the same rights of support, and limitations were placed upon the right to inherit from the father. It is now recognized that all children should have certain rights regardless of their origin, and efforts are being made in nearly all states to revise old laws to guarantee them equal rights.

Changing outmoded laws is always a slow process, and many of the states still have done little about laws that discriminate against children born to unmarried parents. However, the trend is in the direction of correcting the inequities. A number of states now issue what is called a "wallet card" birth certificate that gives only the information needed for identification: name, sex, date and place of birth.

Some states have passed laws that remove all limitations based on illegitimacy. Under old laws, a child of married parents inherited from the father automatically, but a child born out of wedlock did not inherit unless the father voluntarily acknowledged and legally provided for the child. New laws give the child of unmarried parents the same inheritance rights that other children have.

Progress is being made toward providing the same maternity care for unmarried as for married mothers so that they will come safely through the birth experience, and their babies will have a good chance for a healthy start in life.

MORE REFORMS NEEDED

Little progress has been made in some reforms that are needed. These have to do with establishing the paternity of a child and enforcing paternal as well as maternal support and responsibility. At present, in most states, the mother must bring legal action in order to establish the paternity of her child. Many unwed mothers are not in a financial or an emotional position to take such action, and an injustice results for the child. In some European countries, the state assumes the responsibility for determining who is the father of a child of an unmarried mother; the mother need not take action. The state also requires the father to meet his financial obligations. At present, in the United States, most of the states have laws requiring the father to support the child, but the laws are ineffective because the mother must bring action to collect the child support if the father does not pay. If she cannot take legal action, she may seek help from welfare agencies that may try to collect from the father. Under that system, a father may avoid his obligations by moving away from the area and becoming hard to find.

Society has a stake in every child, whether or not the parents are married, and acceptance of that fact means that the state must act to protect children rather than leaving it to the mother alone.

Why should any child be made to stand outside the circle of life's activities—especially if it is because of the circumstances of his or her birth?

In an ideal society, all couples might be expected to become mature, marry, and create a healthy home atmosphere before they have children. As individuals in a less than perfect world, we can at least approach the ideal by preparing as well as we can for marriage and parenthood. We can try to achieve the maturity necessary in order to meet the challenges of successful child rearing.

QUESTIONS FOR REVIEW

1. What percentage of couples find it physically impossible to have children?
2. If a marriage is sterile, who is at fault?
3. Why are there fewer children available for adoption now than there are people wanting to adopt?
4. What changes have been made in the qualifications of people before they can adopt? In the types of children that are now considered adoptable?
5. Discuss negative or unsound reasons for wanting to adopt.
6. How should parents who have adopted a child tell the child about her or his adoption?
7. What are some special problems that may arise for both the adopted child and the adoptive parents as the child reaches the teens?
8. What important reform should be made in laws concerning children born out of wedlock?

ACTIVITIES AND PROJECTS

1. What are the laws and regulations concerning adoption in your state? Investigate and report to the class.

2. What has your state done to protect the child born to unmarried parents? In your state, are births recorded as legitimate or illegitimate? Is a "wallet card" birth certificate sent to all citizens? Investigate and report to the class.

3. Ask a social worker who handles adoptions to talk to the class about changes in attitudes toward "matching" adoptive parents and children, and about the balance or imbalance between numbers of adoptive parents and adoptable children in your state.

WORDS AND CONCEPTS

adoptable children
adoptive parents
humanitarian motives
inequities
infertility
oral contraceptive
paternity
sterility
"wallet card" birth certificate

The Successful Family

30

After studying this chapter, you will be able to

1. List factors students consider basic in contributing to their childhood happiness.
2. Discuss the most common factors causing unhappiness in childhood.
3. Examine ways in which the death of a loved one can be handled constructively with children to help them avoid permanent emotional damage.
4. Describe the qualities that are important in a good mother whether or not she has an outside job.
5. Analyze the ways in which the needs of old people are the same as those of young people.
6. Describe the basic elements of a successful family.

This book began with a discussion of the needs we have throughout life, no matter what our age. Although these needs do not change, the circumstances of life do change; our choices of solutions become limited and our directions somewhat more circumscribed as we grow through the succeeding stages. At each stage, we tend to be absorbed in the problems that are prominent in our lives at that moment. It is helpful if all members in families can have a perspective that enables them to appreciate the problems and needs of family members who are in other stages and circumstances of life.

The successful family fulfills the basic needs of all members at each age. When our needs are not met, we have different ways of reacting, according to our stage of life. The three-year-old may throw a dish to the floor to force the family to recognize that he or she is present at the dinner table; grandfather, who is far past the dish-throwing stage, may insist upon expressing his political views at great length. The child may show a desire for security by worrying about whether his or her parents might die and go away; grandmother's concern for her security may show in her worry about her health—her fear that she may not be able to take care of herself in old age. This chapter will review some aspects of the different parts of the life cycle through which each of us goes. With an understanding of the range of needs and capacities of the different individuals within any one family, we can hope to have a useful perspective as we live our way through the successive parts of life.

HAPPINESS OF CHILDREN

We have stressed the necessity for giving love and affection to children from the time they are born. Children learn to fit into the social world—to cooperate and to consider the needs of others—more reajily if they are in families where warmth and affection underlie all training and discipline. Such children are more likely to be happy people with confidence in their ability to cope with life's problems.

Two large groups of university students have given us some information about the things that they remember bringing happiness to their childhood. Table 15 gives the fifteen factors that they mentioned most frequently.

Most of the items that the students mentioned had to do with situations within the family that brought love, recognition, and security to them. *For their parents to have had a happy marriage was of first importance.* Parents sometimes deprive themselves of many things in order to give their children "advantages," but the greatest advantage you will ever be able to give is to build a good marriage and provide your children with a happy home.

Homes in which the parents are in unhappy conflict may injure the child even more than homes that are broken by divorce. Studies of delinquent children show that homes that are broken by death or by divorce may be less damaging to children than homes in which the parents live in conflict.

The students mentioned their parents' expression of love for them as second most important. Many parents who devotedly love their children fail to show their affection in ways that the child can understand. To provide food, clothing, and shelter and to give them gifts does not

Table 15 STUDENTS' RANKING OF HOME CIRCUMSTANCES THAT BROUGHT GREATEST HAPPINESS AT AGE 5 TO 12

1. Happiness of parents.
2. Parents' expression of love for me.
3. Sense of family's interest in me.
4. Sense of parents' trust.
5. Mother a good cook.
6. Companionship with parents.
7. Family unity and fellowship.
8. Meals always on time and house always clean.
9. Family able to provide adequate financial means.
10. Pride in accomplishments of family.
11. Pleasure in doing things together as a family.
12. Parents' approval of friends.
13. A religion in the home.
14. Family cooperation.
15. Feeling that I had a responsible part in our family.

necessarily come through to the child as love. These are simply part of the world the child lives in. Experience does not allow the child to realize it could be any other way. The child must be told he or she is loved, and touched with loving hands. Children do not take love for granted as much as adults do, and in all stages of life it matters to people to be told in words as well as by actions that they are loved. A complaint by many married people is, "Now that we are married, he (she) expects me to take love for granted—doesn't show enough affection."

Several of the other items that the students said had brought them happiness indicate that it is necessary for the child to feel that he or she counts in the family. *Family unity and family approval* mean much to children.

Most of the factors mentioned as bringing happiness to children are things within the power of all parents to provide. They do not depend upon income.

FACTORS MAKING FOR UNHAPPINESS DURING CHILDHOOD

Table 16 lists the most common factors causing unhappiness in children, and Table 17 shows the most common worries or anxieties of children.

Many children worry unnecessarily over their physical appearance. Often, a child who feels that he or she is homely or has a conspicuous feature that ruins his looks is just as handsome as other children who feel no handicap. The reason for this feeling is not to be found in his or her actual appearance but in the fact that members of the family have been thoughtless. They have joked or remarked about the features without realizing the effect upon the child. The child begins to feel homely whether or not it is true.

If you will carefully examine these lists, you will see that most of the factors listed are situations that could be alleviated or prevented if families understood their effect upon the children. It is worthwhile for you to think objectively of those things now. You will be better able to avoid them in the lives of your children.

Almost the only unhappy situations not within the power of parents to avoid are serious illness and death.

The functioning family does as much as possible toward maintaining the health of the family through reasonable routines of diet and sleep and by making use of available medical care. Nevertheless, death of a loved one will unavoidably occur in the experience of some children. A grandparent, an aunt or uncle, even a parent may die. Death is a most difficult part of life for parents to handle with children. At such a time, they themselves will be extremely upset emotionally, and the emotional depression of a parent is likely to be terrifying to a child, even if the child personally might not be so acutely aware of the death.

Table 16 STUDENTS' RANKING OF HOME CIRCUMSTANCES THAT BROUGHT GREATEST UNHAPPINESS AT AGE 5 TO 12

1. Death and illness in the family.
2. Parents' quarreling.
3. Conflict with parents' views.
4. Quarreling of brothers or sisters.
5. Inability of parents to see my point of view.
6. Loneliness.
7. Misunderstanding in the family.
8. Parents' unhappiness.
9. Quarreling with parents.
10. Feeling of being misunderstood.
11. Being compared with other children.
12. Parents nagging me.
13. Lack of companionship with parents.
14. Fear that parents would separate.
15. Father hard to get along with.
16. Lack of association with those of my own age.
17. Lack of adequate finances.

Table 17 STUDENTS RANKING OF CIRCUMSTANCES THAT CAUSED ANXIETY DURING CHILDHOOD

Physical Features	Worries Reflecting a Need for Security
1. Afraid I would be homely. 2. Crooked teeth. 3. Awkwardness. 4. Too fat or too slim. 5. Wearing glasses. 6. Complexion. 7. Unattractive hair. 8. Not growing any taller.	1. That our house would burn. 2. That my father would die. 3. That my mother would die. 4. That brother or sister would die. 5. That I would die. 6. That I was adopted. 7. That my parents would separate. 8. Being kidnapped. 9. That the world would come to an end.

Conditioned Fears	Losing Face Before Others
1. Darkness. 2. Lightning and thunder. 3. Animals, snakes, bugs. 4. Being left alone. 5. Fires. 6. Deep water. 7. Being locked in closets. 8. Old, empty houses. 9. Fear of not getting to heaven. 10. Fear of going to hell. 11. Fear of being punished by God. 12. Ghosts.	1. Scolding before other children. 2. Had to perform before others. 3. Parents made me apologize for things. 4. Parents bragged about me. 5. Did not dress as other children did or had to wear hand-me-downs. 6. Teasing. 7. Being left out of things. 8. Couldn't do things others did. 9. Mother always let everyone know I was the baby.

HELPING CHILDREN WHEN A LOVED ONE DIES

Even sorrow and death can be somewhat eased for children if parents are prepared. At least a child's experience with death can be handled so that its overall effect on the child can be toward constructive growth rather than being altogether traumatic.

Parents should be honest about their grief. Children can perceive emotions. If the parent expresses no sorrow when his or her own parents or some close relative dies, but tries to hold in and cover personal feelings, the child can become frightened and insecure. The child may imagine that the feelings are directed toward himself or herself or that some unknown disaster is looming that is too horrible to understand. If the child sees the parents experiencing grief, and the parents share it with the attitude that "This is hard for us, but we will bear it to-

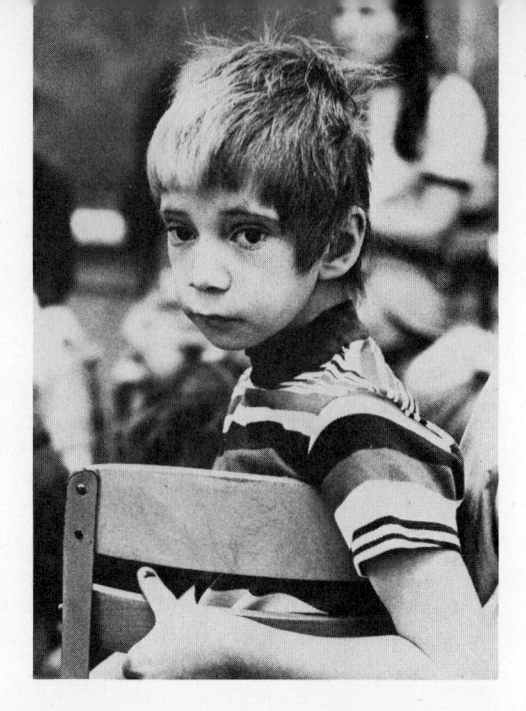

Helping a child come to grips with the idea or fact of death gives the child security in his or her expanding adjustment to the world.

gether," the child can endure personal grief and not lose feelings of security and trust in the parents.

Many parents try to hide death from children and avoid any discussion of it, even when there is a death in the family. They do so mainly because they don't know what to tell the child. Such questions as "Where is he gone?" "Where is he now?" "Will he come back?" "Why did he go?" and others are painful because the questions go to the root of the parent's own bewilderment about death. Parents who are religious have somewhat less of a problem than others. If they honestly believe that death represents the entrance of a loved one into eternal life, they can answer a child's questions with some confidence. But if a parent is not a believer in heaven or an afterlife, it is better not to use those ideas as an answer to children's questions. Children sense insincerity or lack of conviction if the parent does not really believe the explanations. Many parents do not have any specific religious faith; and their personal philosophy may not include overall concepts about the larger meaning of life and death, the continuity of the human race, and the universe we live in. They have nothing to say to a child at the time of a death, so they try to hide their feelings. Because of this, the child may suffer from feelings of guilt lest the sorrow which is felt may be in some way the child's fault.

Earlier, in the discussion of answering questions about sex, it was emphasized that it is important to be able to say "I don't know" if that is the only honest answer. The same applies to questions about death. There are many things that we do not know. Whether or not the parent is a believer in immortality, and whatever philosophical view one has about life and death, there remain many aspects for which one has no certain answers. To some of a troubled child's questions, a parent can only say honestly, "I don't know."

The parent does know some things that can help a child to accept death. The parent knows that a loved one's life is ended, that every life ends, and that we grieve when someone dies because we wish life did not end. We want those we love to be with us, and we feel great sadness when they die. A child can accept, more easily than an adult, that this is the way things are. The child is occupied with encountering many new things in the world and so may not find death shocking or amazing. The child's suffering is partly a reflection of the feelings of the family, and also, a result of any new adjustments that must be made if death causes changes in daily life.

When parents acknowledge death truthfully, most children think at once, "If every life ends and everyone dies sometime, are *you* going to die and leave me?" A parent can answer truthfully, "I hope to live with you for many, many years yet, until you are grown up and have your own home and have some little children of your own, and maybe years and years longer even than that. Most people do live that long." Such an answer can help to relieve a child's fears.

We see, then, that if parents have thought ahead about the matter of death, as they think of many other contingencies, they can help the child to develop attitudes and feelings of security that will enable her or him to go through the universal experience of loss through death without receiving permanent emotional damage.

FACING YOUR VOCATIONAL FUTURE

You should now be ready to look ahead and think seriously about your vocational future. Many people your age are wondering whether to go to college after high school or to get started at once in some job. Some of your friends may know that they would like to go to college, but they do not have the means, and their parents cannot afford to send them. A study of opinions of several thousand high school students showed that the majority of them want to get more training either in college or in a business or trade school. The occupational aspirations of the same high school seniors and their chances of finding employment in these jobs do not always coincide. The studies showed that many more young people expect to go into certain fields than can possibly enter these occupations; that is true especially of those who hope to enter a profession.

Many girls do not know if they should prepare for a vocation outside the home or think entirely of marriage and a family. Most girls plan to marry. Ninety-five percent of women have married at least once by the age of forty. If they do not marry, they must be prepared to support themselves. If they marry, should they plan to work after marriage? Most girls cannot know for sure years ahead of time whether or not they will

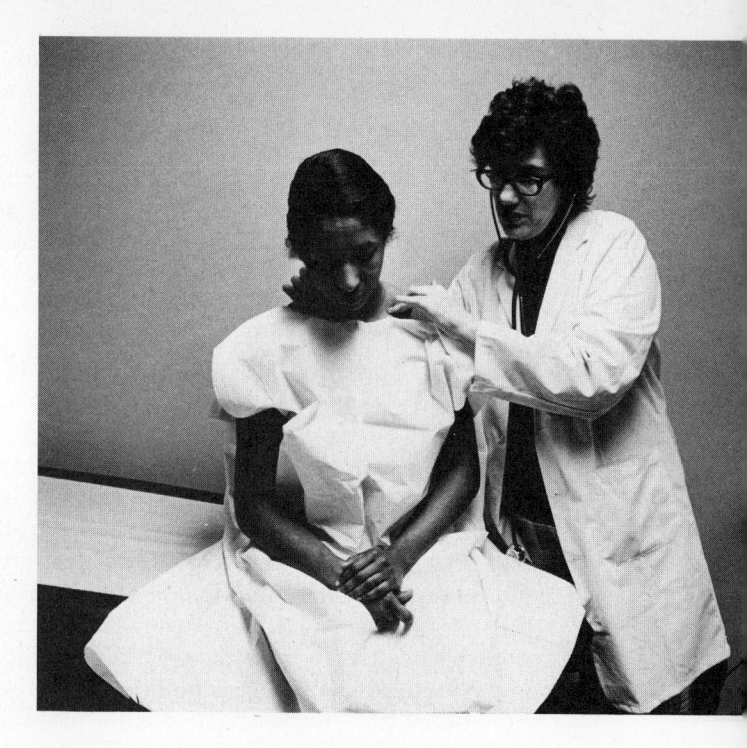

What shall my vocational aims be? Shall I become a doctor? a laboratory worker? an office employee? What education do I require to attain my goal?

work outside the home after they are married and have children. In practice, more and more women do work outside the home. The cost of living is such that many families feel they need two incomes. Even if the family could do very well on the earnings of the husband, many women still feel the need to have some special work of their own, outside their work at home. It is becoming accepted that girls should have the education and training to be self-supporting and perhaps to support dependents, just as much as boys should.

WORKING MOTHERS

Many girls have conflicting feelings about a future vocation because they fear that a woman cannot hold an outside job and also be a good wife and mother. But to be a good mother involves far more than simply working or not working, staying home with the children full time or being away from them part of the time. *The quality of a mother's relationship with her children, her love for them, her understanding of their important needs, and her maturity as a person are the things that will determine how well she does as a mother.*

Some women can happily be full-time mothers and homemakers and do well at rearing emotionally healthy children. Other women can hold outside jobs or have a professional life outside the home and be equally as successful as wives and mothers. Research studies of working mothers and their children have found that the attitude of the mother toward her work, whether it is at home or outside the home, has much effect on her performance. The woman with unhappy, negative attitudes is not likely to be a good mother. She might do better by her children if she spent only part of her time with them and spent part of her time in productive work away from home. Her children would probably make better growth with a competent sitter, or in a nursery school, than with an unhappy, irritable mother who is not contented with her task.

Another research finding is that some mothers with full-time jobs actually spend more *meaningful* time with their children than some full-time mothers do. It was found that these successful working mothers were aware of the need for companionship with their children; and when they were with their children, they used the time in ways constructive to their children's growth. Some other mothers had the children with them full time, but much of the time was spent in ways not productive for the children. That is, the child might be taken along while the mother shopped or did other duties that had no interest and that were physically tiring for the child. Or the mothers were heavily involved in social life or other outside activities that took as much or more time from their children as would be spent on a job.

Thus, it is apparent that to work or not to work is not the crucial question. The crucial point is that every young person, boy or girl, should be prepared to earn a living, to support dependents if necessary, and to function adequately as a parent when that time comes, regardless of what kind of work is chosen.

PARENTS IN THE HAPPY FAMILY—MIDDLE AND LATER YEARS

We have emphasized the importance of a wise choice of a mate if people are to be happily married, good parents. We have considered the fact that it takes time for two people to learn to live well together; that people are happier if they respect each other; and that the growth of love depends upon understanding and companionship and the habit of settling differences through friendly discussion rather than quarreling.

Couples who have this kind of relationship will be likely to have the same kind of understanding and appreciation for the needs of their children. In the family that approaches the ideal, there is a good husband-wife relationship and good parent-child relationships.

Children sometimes fail to recognize the rights of their parents. Parents should not have to do all the sacrificing in the family. With increasing maturity, people become able to take their part of the load. All family members need to share in making the sacrifices that are required from time to time in almost every family.

We asked two large groups of old people when they felt they had been happiest in life. The majority of both the men and women said that for them the happiest time had been during the early and middle years of marriage, before their children had left home. This may seem surprising to you. Those same parents may not appear to be having as much fun as you have. But these people who have tried all of life's stages reported that their real happiness and contentment in life were more closely associated with marriage and family living than with any other of their life experiences.

Many a working mother who recognizes that she must use her available time to establish a loving, secure relationship with her child gives more of herself to her family than some non-working mothers.

HOW SONS AND DAUGHTERS CAN HELP PARENTS

When the last child has left home, parents face readjusting to a type of living that is somewhat like their early married life. Just as they had to learn to live with each other early in marriage, now they must adjust to living again as two instead of as a family of four or five. This new stage may be more difficult for the mother than for the father.

Some couples find this adjustment difficult. They may have become so accustomed to interacting with the larger family circle that the two, as a pair who fell in love and married, have lost some of their closeness. The father's work and the mother's responsibility toward the family may have crowded out much of their private companionship. So in this stage, they must recreate a new level of interaction. If they do, this stage of life can be happy for them. It will also be easier for them to let the children live their lives without interference.

Children, now as always before, need to understand the problems of the parents and to be adult in their attitudes. Children need also to consider whether or not they have developed a mature independence from their parents. This independence involves not only freedom to live one's own life, but an obligation to let the parents live theirs. Sometimes, young grandmothers who would like to be free to go about with their husbands are imposed upon by their children, who think of their own convenience first.

One such grandmother said, "I can hardly make plans of my own because my daughter brings her baby over for me to take care of whenever she wants to go somewhere. I hate to refuse to help, but often I have to give up my own plans at the last minute because Sally wants me to keep her baby for her." Sally's view was, "Mother's always glad to keep the baby. She has nothing else important to do."

REMARRIAGE OF PARENTS AND GRANDPARENTS

One way for parents or grandparents who have been alone to continue to have lives independent of their children is through remarriage. It is still true that society frowns upon the remarriage of older people. Children may have a hard time understanding why a parent would want to remarry. If an inheritance is involved, children may oppose remarriage for that reason. The desire to be married is strong in adults of all ages, and if people are in good health, this continues to be true into old age. The reasons for marrying may be altered with age, but the need for companionship, affection, independence from children, and emotional support continues throughout life.

As people enter middle and old age it becomes much easier for men than women to remarry because of an unequal sex ratio. Women live longer than men, and for this reason, by age fifty, there are many more widowed women than men. When men are widowed, they tend to remarry soon partly because the sex ratio makes it possible. They may also feel more of a need for someone to take care of them than does a widow. There is not a great amount of research about the widowed, but available research shows that most of the widowed who remarry had been happily married the first time and that they usually make a happy second marriage. Their success may be explained in that they have had the experience of one happy marriage; they know how to choose a compatible partner a second time and they know how to make the necessary adjustments in marriage.

Widowed people often marry someone they have known for many years. They may have known each other as neighbors, friends, or may have been related by marriage. It is not unusual for a man to marry a sister-in-law or for a woman to marry a brother-in-law.

GRANDPARENTS—OLD AGE

The time comes when the needs of old people must be faced. Some families are responsible for the financial care of the aged; others must provide a place for them, or see that they have mental or physical care. In some families, caring for the aged members creates a family crisis.

Some of you are in families where three or even four generations are living in the same home. In some of your homes, the needs of all are being met, and the situation is happy. In others, the presence of the grandparents or of another older relative has necessitated adjustments with unhappy results.

Because average life expectancy has increased greatly during the last fifty years, a large percentage of people live to be grandparents and great-grandparents. More research is needed on the problems of the aged. Present research tells us some important things, however, on how to make old people happy.

Chiefly, younger family members must remember that the needs of old people are the same as their own. Grandparents want security, independence, recognition, and affection. They want to be treated with respect and consideration, just as you do.

Old people would rather live alone independently if possible. They want to live their own lives just as much as they did in their teens or in their thirties. It is not ever easy to be dependent on others and dominated by them.

If grandparents must live with their children, it is better to provide a place in the home that is their own private and particular headquarters. In some homes, it is possible to divide the house so that the grandparents have their own rooms and cooking facilities. In this way, the two families can be near each other, but they can live independently.

After a grandfather has retired, the warm bond between him and his grandchildren, or great-grandchildren, has the time to ripen into happy days for both generations.

This prevents friction arising over such things as how to train the children, differences in cooking and eating habits, and different interests.

Grandparents are happier if they are healthy, have regular work or have hobbies that take up their time. Like the rest of us, they want to know that they are useful and count for something in the lives of those around them. Sometimes, people make the mistake of doing too much for the old people in their homes. As one old person said, "Too many children are willing to buy a rocking chair for their aged parents and then let them rock themselves to death in it."

Just as the small child is hurt and the child's personality damaged by ridicule, so the old person suffers from lack of respect or an attitude that implies that grandmother or grandfather is out of date and has silly ideas.

The truth is that old people usually have ideas that are worth hearing. They have lived through many experiences that the rest of us have yet to work our way through. They have made some practical observations on life that would be a help to us. True, the newest slang or the latest fads in dress may seem peculiar to an old person; but if grandparents can tolerate our absorption in things that seem to them to be unimportant, we also can well afford to be generous regarding their interests.

THE HAPPY FAMILY

It all adds up to this: in a happy family, all members will show respect and affection for each other. They will try to understand each other's viewpoints and will make an effort to help meet each other's needs. Whether one is eight, eighteen, thirty-eight, or eighty will make no difference. The family member who is "difficult" is showing a need for love and understanding.

Today, there is public concern about high crime rates, alcoholism, drug use, and mental and emotional breakdowns. A variety of solutions are proposed to solve these problems. We must recognize that many of these maladjustments go back to the family, the basic unit in our society. Young people who marry wisely and establish happy homes will not only be insuring their own personal happiness but they will be making a positive contribution toward solving the problems that plague our world.

QUESTIONS FOR REVIEW

1. What is a successful home?
2. What are some chief divisions in the family life cycle?
3. What factors seem to be most important for the happiness of children?
4. Discuss some preventable factors that bring unhappiness to children.
5. Study the list of things that cause anxiety during childhood. Check the ones that troubled you. What others would you add to the list?
6. Discuss reasons why parents find it so difficult to help children when death occurs in a family.
7. What are some rules for helping the child to grow and to avoid permanent emotional damage when confronting the death of a loved one?
8. Discuss the statement that girls as well as boys need to prepare for a vocation that will enable them to earn a living and support dependents.
9. List characteristics that are important in a good mother, whether or not she has an outside job.
10. How might parents and children reach better understanding?
11. What is the happiest period in life, according to a large group of old people?
12. What is one way of insuring that one will be happily married and will be a good parent?
13. Cite some of the problems that parents face when their children leave home.

THE SUCCESSFUL FAMILY

14. In what ways are the desires of old people the same as those of young people?
15. Cite several factors that are important to the happiness of old people.
16. How is building a good marriage a positive contribution not only to the individual and his or her children but to society in general?

ACTIVITIES AND PROJECTS

1. Investigate facilities in your community for the care of old pegple and what help they can get through Social Security, Medicare, and other programs. Are these adequate?
2. List anonymously the thing that creates the greatest happiness in your home, the thing that creates the greatest unhappiness, and the things that cause anxiety in your life. Have a class committee summarize the results. How do they compare with the results summarized in the tables in this chapter?

WORDS AND CONCEPTS

"advantages"
affection
afterlife
alleviate
circumscribe

contingencies
differentiate
immortality
life expectancy
mature independence

SUGGESTED READINGS FOR THE UNIT

Aldrich, C. Anderson, and Mary M. Aldrich, *Babies Are Human Beings.* 1962. New York: The Macmillan Company, Collier Books.
Baker, Katherine Read, and Xenia F. Fane, *Understanding and Guiding Young Children.* 1975. Englewood Cliffs, N. J.: Prentice-Hall, Inc.
Bean, Constance A., *Methods of Childbirth.* 1972. New York: Doubleday & Company.
Caplan, Frank, *The First 12 Months of Life.* 1973. New York: Grosset and Dunlap.
Carson, Ruth, *So You Want to Adopt a Child.* Pamphlet No. 173A. New York: Public Affairs Committee.
Child Study Association of America, *Sex Education and the New Morality.* New York: Columbia University Press.
———, *What to Tell Your Children About Sex.* New York: Child Study Association of America.

Eckert, Ralph, *Sex Attitudes in the Home.* New York: Association Press.

Flanagan, Geraldine Lux, *The First Nine Months of Life.* 1962. New York: Simon and Schuster, Inc.

Genne, William H., *Husbands and Pregnancy.* Handbook for Expectant Fathers. 1965. New York: Association Press.

Glaser, Barney G., and Anselm L. Strauss, *Awareness of Dying.* 1965. Chicago: Aldine Publishing Company.

Goodrich, Frederick W., *Infant Care: The United States Government Guide.* 1968. Englewood Cliffs, N. J.: Prentice-Hall, Inc.

———, *Preparing for Childbirth: A Manual for Expectant Parents.* 1966. Englewood Cliffs, N. J.: Prentice-Hall, Inc.

Hurlock, Elizabeth B., *Child Growth and Development.* 1968. New York: McGraw-Hill Book Company.

Hymes, James L., *How to Tell Your Child About Sex.* Pamphlet No. 149. New York: Public Affairs Committee.

Landis, Judson T., and Mary G. Landis, *Building a Successful Marriage,* Fifth Edition. 1973. Englewood Cliffs, N. J.: Prentice-Hall, Inc.

LeShan, Eda A., *You and Your Adopted Child.* Pamphlet No. 274. New York: Public Affairs Committee.

McKain, Walter C., "A New Look at Older Marriages," *The Family Coordinator.* Vol. 21, No. 1, Jan. 1972. Pp. 61–69.

Meerlow, Joost, "Mental First Aid in Pregnancy and Childbirth," *Child and Family.* Vol. 5, No. 4, Fall, 1966.

Morris, Sarah, *Grief and How to Live with It.* 1972. New York: Grosset and Dunlap.

Newton, Miles, "New Methods for Easing Childbirth," *Child and Family.* Vol. 5, No. 4, Fall, 1966.

Osborne, Ernest, *When You Lose a Loved One.* Pamphlet No. 269. New York: Public Affairs Committee.

Peterson, Eleanor M., *Successful Living.* 1968. Boston: Allyn and Bacon, Inc. Chs. 22–32.

Read-Dick, Grantly, *Childbirth Without Fear.* 1959. New York: Harper and Row.

Rowe, Jane, *Parents, Children and Adoption.* 1966. New York: Humanities Press, Inc.

Scheinfeld, Amram, *Your Heredity and Environment.* 1965. Philadelphia: J. B. Lippincott Company.

Shuey, Rebekah M., E. L. Woods, and E. M. Young, *Learning About Children.* 1969. Philadelphia: J. B. Lippincott Co.

Spock, Benjamin, *Baby and Child Care.* 1968. New York: Pocket Books, Inc.

———, *Dr. Spock Talks with Mothers: Growth and Guidance.* 1961. Boston: Houghton Mifflin Co.

Tanzer, Deborah, "Natural Childbirth: Pain or Peak Experience?" *Psychology Today.* Vol. 2, No. 5, Oct. 1968. Pp. 16–21.

Your Child from One to Six. Washington, D. C.: Department of Health, Education, and Welfare, Children's Bureau.

INDEX

INDEX

A

Ability, intellectual, 6, 14, 24
Abortion, legalization of, 102
Adaptability, 146
   importance in marriage, 244–5
Adjustment in marriage, 235–45
   adaptability, importance, 244–5
   areas requiring, 237
   after baby arrives, 342–3
   compromise, 240
   after divorce, 329–30
   engagement, adjustment during, and, 173–4, 176–7
   in-law relations, *see* In-law relations
   length of courtship and, 174–5
   money problems, 281–4
   during pregnancy, 351–2
   quarreling and, *see* Quarrels
   sexual, 258–66
   time required for, 237–9, 258–9, 261–2
   types of, 240–2
Adolescence and family conflict, 124–5
Adopting children, 391–7
   honesty about, 394
   motives for, 393

Age at marriage, 96–7
   divorce rate and (graph), 167
   financial problems and, 163–6
   happiness and, 164
   parental interference and, 163–4
   pregnancy and, 97
   responsibility and, 95
Age for marriage, 160–3
   legal, 221, 223
   love and, 169
   maturity and, 161–3
Age stereotyping, 2–3
Agreement:
   in areas of living (graph), 177
   as marriage adjustment, 240
   on use of money, 282
   between parents, on child training, 374–7
   prenuptial, 205
   on religion, 201–2
   on sexual relations (graph), 259
Alcohol:
   dating and use of, 113
   making decisions and, 113
   as a depressant, 109–10
   driving and, 112, 113
   greater acceptance of use among teenagers, 109
   increasing use of among teen-

agers, 109
malnutrition and, 110
muscular coordination and, 112
narcotic effect, 110
overweight and, 110
    research concerning, 109–12
Alcoholism, 110, 112
    symptoms of, 112
American Cancer Society, 117
American Institute for Economic Research, 297
Annulment, legal grounds for, 225
Approach to marriage, 86–7
Automobile:
    costs, 290–1
    driving and drinking, 112, 113
    insurance, 303

B

Bankruptcy, 299–300
Behavior:
    during engagement, 194
        patterns, 11–14, 17–23, 30–44, *see also* Problem solving
Biological inheritance, 11–14
Borrowing, interest rates, 301–3
Budgeting, 288–92

Buying, *see* Consumer economics

C

Catholic-Protestant marriages, 203–5
Child training, 355–65, 367–77, 379–89
    agreement between parents, 374–7
    aims of, 359
    bedtime habits, 362
    consistency in, 368
    constructive vs. destructive, 373–4
    discipline in, 368–70
    eating habits, 362
    family conversation and, 363–4
    guidance, importance of, 368–70
    habits, forming good, 360–1
    individual development, 358
    needs of child, 355–7
    personality growth, 359
    praise, importance of, 372–3
    self-confidence, developing, 371
    sense of proportion in, 359
    sex questions in, 383–8
Childbirth:

Childbirth (cont.)
  approaching, 346–7
  fathers and, 348–9
  hormonal changes in mother before and after, 351
  natural, 346–51
  preparing for, 347–8
  sexual adjustment of parents after, 351–2
  stages of, 349–50
Children:
  adjustment of older, to baby, 379–83
  adopted, 391–7
  divorce and, 331–5
  happiness of, factors making for, 399–401
  of mixed marriages, 204–5
  needs of, 355–7
  training, see Child training
  unhappiness of, factors making for, 401–5
  of unmarried mothers, 395–6
Chromosomes, 13
Cigarettes, see Smoking
Common-law marriages, 219–20
Communication:
  about death, 403–5
  during engagement, 192–4
  between parents and children, 134
  parents' worries and, 131–4
  responsibility for, in families, 134
  about sex, 132
Compliments, 53–5
Compromise, adjustment in marriage, 240
Conciliation Courts, 318
Conference, family, 254–6
Consumer economics, 295–309
  buying, considerations for, 297–8
  buying a home, 307–8
  consumer information, getting, 296–7
  credit, buying, 299–303
  insurance, 304–7
  interest rates, 301–3
  renting a home, 307–8
  security, family, 303–7
  values, judging, 299
Consumers' Research, 297
Consumers Union, 297
Coordination, narcotic effect of alcohol on, 112
Credit, buying, 299–303
Customs, marriage, 219, 227–9

D

Danger signals:
  dating and, 82–87
  during engagement, 179–85
  failure to recognize, 181–5
  quarreling and, 83–84
Dating:
  age for, 126
  alcohol and, 113
  asking for dates, 64–5, 67
  blind dates, 68
  danger signals in, 82–87
  evaluating dating experiences, 62–71, 74–89
  expenses, 67–8
  discovering families through, 78–80
  family car and, 128
  family patterns and, 78–9
  family understanding and, 124–34
  functions of, 74–89
  hours to be in, 129
  implications for growth in, 89
  as learning, 74–5, 89
  love and, 80–2, 209–17
  mate selection, see Mate selection
  parents and, 86, 126–30
  problems, student's statements of (table), 64
  qualities of a good date, 69–71

refusing a date, 65–6
rules that help in, 64–8
as self-discovery, 75–6
sex and, *see* Sex, premarital
steadily, 87–9
uncertainties in, 63–64
understanding love through, 80–2
Daydreaming, as problem solving, 37–8
Death, children and, 403–5
Defeat, admitting, in problem solving, 31–2
Dependability, desirable habit, 52
Differences:
  individual, 24, 26–28
  between mates:
    in background, 155–7
    over child-rearing, 374–7
    economic, 155
    in education, 155
    in nationality, 155–7
    physical, 155
    in race, 156, 224–5
    in religion, 157, 203–6
    research concerning, 376
  in motivation for premarital sex, 98
  in rates of development in children, 358
  social, between boys and girls, 27
Direct attack, as problem solving, 31–2
Discipline, in child training, 368–70
Divorce:
  advantages of, 327–8
  adversary, 316
  age at marriage and, 166–7
  alternatives to, 323–4
  causes, 319–23
  children and, 331–5
  collusion, 316
  comes early in marriage, 312–3
  Conciliation Courts and, 318
  decision not to, 313–4
  decision to, 314–5
  dissolution of marriage, 317
  family background and, 141–5
  grievances of husbands and wives (table), 322
  insupportability, 317
  irreconcilable differences, 317
  laws, 315–8
  legal reasons for, 319–21
  marriage preparation, lack of, and, 323
  mate choice and, 143
  new problems after, 326–7
  no-fault, 317–8
  personality traits and, 321–2
  rate and marriage-preparation courses, 143
  rate and religion, 198, 199, 203–4, 205
  remarriage after, 329–30
  teen-age marriages and, 166–7
Drugs:
  addicting and nonaddicting, 121–22
  dependence upon, 118, 121
  laws and, 121
  problems associated with using, 120–1
  side effects of, 118–9

E

Economics, consumer, *see* Consumer economics
Educational differences, in marriage, 155
Emotional maturity:
  moods and, 20–3
  traits indicating, 161–3
Emotions:
  nutrition and, 21–2
  physical bases of, 21–2
Engagement, 173–85, 187–95
  adjustment during, 174–9

Engagement (cont.)
  agreement during, 176–7
  breaking, 188
  broken, emotional adjustment to, 187, 188–90
    reasons for, 187, 188
  danger signals during, 179–85
  length of, for adjustment in marriage, 174–5
  preparation for marriage during, 192–4
  problems to discuss during, 191–2
  purpose of, 178–9
  readiness for, 178
  sexual behavior during, 194
  separation, effect on, 170
Environment, and personality, 13–14
Evaluating dating experiences, 62–71, 74–89
Expenses, dating, 67–8

F

Family:
  background and mate choice, 141–5
  conflict, 124–34
    over dating, 126
    over hair and dress, 130–1
    over hours kept, 129
    and maturing, 126
  functions, 11
  happiness of parents:
    health and, 144
    mental health and, 144
    parent-child conflict, lack of, 141, 144
      religion and, 198–201, 202, 204–6, (graph), 206
  income, see Money problems in marriage
  inheritance from, 11–14
  table talk, 363
  understanding during dating years, 124–34
  values, 10
Fear, coping with, 40–1
Focus on You,
  behavior habits, 43–4, 56–7
  dating behavior, 71–2
  evaluation of dating, 90
  family understanding, 134–5
  maturity for marriage, 170–1
Functions of dating, 74–89

G

Generation gap, 125
Genes, 13
Grandparents:
  growth tasks of, 25
  needs of, 409–11
  remarriage of, 409–10
  role of, 410–11
Growing up, challenges and problems, 3–14, 25–6
Growth tasks, 3–14, 25–6
  family conflicts and, 126
  of grandparents, 25
  in-law relationships and, 271–2
  of new parents, 341
  of parents, 8
  of teenagers, 5–8
  of teenagers' parents, 8

H

Habits:
  arguing, 51
  boasting and bragging, 51
  borrowing from others, 52
  cheerfulness, 53
  compliments, giving honest, 53–5
  contradicting others, 51
  cutting remarks, making, 52
  dependability, 52
  flattery, 54

gossiping, 48–9
grudges, holding, 47–8
jealousy, 49–50
laughing at others, 51
punctuality, 52
rights of others, considering, 55–6
sarcasm, 52
sportsmanship, 55
word of honor, keeping, 52
Happiness in marriage, 235
   adjustment during engagement and, 173–4, 176–7
   age at marriage and, 163–7
   age differences and, 154, 155
   agreement on religion and, 201–2
   agreement on use of money and, 282
   approach to marriage and, 86–7
   confidence before marriage and (graph), 85
   educational differences and, 155
   family background and, 141–5
   high school marriages and, 168
   in-law relations and, 277–8
   maturity and, 161–3
   mixed marriages and, 155–7
   parental approval and, 86, 152–4
   personality and, 145–8
   sexual adjustment and, *see* Sexual adjustment in marriage
   teen-age marriages, problems, 163–7
   time to adjust and, 243–4
Health:
   family background, 144
   mental, family background, 144
   problem solving and, 41–2
High school, marriage while in, 163–7
   attitudes of schools on, 168
Homogamy, in mate selection, 154
Honeymoon, 229
Hours to be in, dating, 129

I

Immaturity, trait characteristics, 162–3
Income, family, *see* Money problems in marriage
Independence:
   developing, in children, 359
   from parents, 126
Infant care, *see* Child training
Inheritance:
   biological, 11–14
   family, 11–14
In-law relations, 267–78
   friction in, causes, 268–71
   growth tasks, 271–2
   guidance in, rules for, 276–7
   happiness in marriage and, 267–8
   immaturity and, 270
   living with parents and, 275–6
   success with, 274–5
In-laws as scapegoats, 273
Institution, family as, 11
Insurance:
   auto liability, 303
   health, 303
   home owners, 303
   life, *see* Life insurance
Internationality marriages, 155–7
Interracial marriages, 156, 224–5

J

Jealousy, 49–50
Jewish-Gentile marriages, 205–6
Judgment, narcotic effect of alcohol on, 110

L

Laws, marriage:
  age for marriage, 221, 223
  annulment and, 225
  for common-law marriage, 219–20
  interracial, 224–5
  license requirements, 225–7
  mental qualifications, 220
  physical qualifications, 220
  relatives, prohibition, 223–4
  by states (table), 221
  void and voidable marriage and, 225
  waiting period, 221 (table), 226–7
Life, stages of, 2, 3–5, 8, 9
Life insurance, 304–7
  buying, pointers in, 306–7
  endowment, 304
  G.I., 305–6
  group, 305
  need for, as protection, 304
  policies, types, 304–5
  purpose, 304
  term, 304–5, 307
Love:
  age and, 213, 214
  assessing, 214–7
  components of, 210
  need for receiving, 18, 210, 356–7
  personality needs, satisfaction of, 211–2
  physical attraction and, 210–1
  relationship with others, looking at, 213
  romantic concept, 235
  types of, 214
  understanding need for, 80–2
  unselfish nature of, 212–3

M

Marriage:
  adjustment in, *see* Adjustment in marriage
  age for, 160–3, 221, 223
  approach to, 86–7
  ceremonies, 227
  common-law, 219–20
  customs, 219, 227–9
  educational differences and happiness in, 155
  engagement as preparation for, 192–4
  failure comes early in, 312–3
  family background affects, 141–5
  happiness in, *see* Happiness in marriage
  honeymoon, 229
  internationality, 155–7
  interracial, 156, 224–5
  Jewish-Gentile, 205–6
  laws, *see* Laws, marriage
  legal qualifications for, 220
  marriageability, 146–8
  mate selection, *see* Mate selection
  maturity for, 161–3
  mental qualifications for, 220
  minimum-age laws, 223
  mixed, and problems, 204–5
  money in, *see* Money problems in marriage
  officiant, 227
  parental approval, 86, 152–4
  physical qualifications for, 220
  planning the wedding, 227–8
  premarital examination, 227
  relatives, prohibition, 223–4
  religion and, 197–206
  to avoid separation, 170
  versus singleness, 9
  social implications of, 9–11
  success, maturity and, 163–8
  teen-age, by state, 222 (graph), 223
  teen-age, problems, 143–6, 163–8

INDEX

Marriageability, 146–8
  traits associated with, 147
Mate selection:
  age differences and, 154, 155
  agreement on religion, 201–2
  economic status, differences and, 155
  educational differences and, 155
  family background and, happiness of parents, 141–5
  health, 144
  mental health, 144
  parent-child conflict, lack of, 141, 144
  friends, mutual, 151
  homogamy in, 154
  internationality marriages, 155–7
  interracial marriages, 156, 224–5
  likes or opposites, 154
  marriageability, 146–8
  mixed marriages and, 155–7
  parental approval, 86, 152–4
  personality needs, meeting, 148–9
  recreational interests, 149–50
  social interests, 151–2
Maturing:
  and family conflict, 126
  rates of, 7–8
Maturity:
  emotional, 20–3
  marriage success and, 161–6
  traits, indicating, 161–3
Menstrual cycles, moods and, 22
Mental health:
  family background and, 141–5
  marriage success and, 144–5
Mixed marriages:
  Catholic-Protestant, 203–5
  divorce in religious, 203–5
  interracial, 156, 224–5
  Jewish-Gentile, 205–6
  mate selection and, 155–7

prenuptial agreement, 205
Money problems in marriage:
  agreement on, during engagement, and, 282–4
  agreement on, happiness and, 282
  area for adjustment, 281–4
  borrowing, interest rates, 301–3
  budgeting, 288–92
  control of spending, 286–8
  time to adjust on values, 284–6
Monogamy, 219
Moods, emotional maturity and, 20–3
Moral codes, 94–5
  definitions, 94–5
  during engagement, behavior, 194
Mother-in-law, see In-law relations

N

Narcotic effect of alcohol, 110
Narcotics, see Drugs
National Safety Council, 112
Natural childbirth, 346–51
Needs, fundamental:
  at all ages, 18–20
  of babies, 355–7
  meeting, in the successful family, 399–400
No-fault divorce, 317–8

O

Old people, see Grandparents
Orgasm, 262–3
Ovum, 13

P

Parental approval:
  of dress and hair, 130–1
  of mate choice, 86, 152–4

Parenthood, 340–52, 355–65, 367–77, 379–89, 391–7
  adjustments:
    after baby arrives, 342–3
    during pregnancy, 351–2
  agreement between parents, 374–7
  child training, see Child training
  childbirth, see Childbirth
  as crisis, 342–3
  overall goals of, 364–5
  preparing for, 343–6
  realistic approach to, 341–2
Parents, see also Parenthood:
  approval of mate choice, 86, 152–4
  conflicts with:
    age for dating, 126
    causes, basic, 125, 131–2
    clothes and hair, 130–1
    children's demands, unreasonable, 132–4
    family car, use, 128
    hours to be in, 129
    lack of, in family history, 141, 144
  happiness of, in family history, 141–5
  in-law relations, see In-law relations
  living with, 275–6
  prospective, preparing, 343–6
  remarriage of, 329–30, 409–10
  rights of, recognizing, 408–9
  understanding of teen-agers, 124–34
Personal appearance, 51
Personality:
  compatibility of, in marriage, 148–9
  development, 17–27
  divorce and, 321–2
  emotional maturity, 161–3
  environmental and, 13–14
  growth of, 42–3, 358
  habits, see Habits
  matching of, in marriage, 148–9
  meeting problems and, 30–1
  needs, fundamental, 18–20
  traits, 51
    adaptability, 146
    divorce and specific, 321–2
    flexibility, 146
Physical attraction, 210–1
Physical makeup, inherited traits, 11–14
Physical qualifications for marriage, 220
Popularity:
  personal standards and, 104–5
  personality and, 46–57
Possessions, popularity and, 132–4
Postpartum depression, 351
Praise, importance, child training, 372–3
Pregnancy:
  adjustments during, 351–2
  health and, 351–2
  hormonal changes, during and after, 351
Premarital examination, 227
Premarital sex, 92–105
  abortion and, 102
  guilt feelings and, 100
  motivations for, 98
  personal standards, 104–5
  pregnancy and, 101–4
  responsibility and, 93–5, 100–1, 102–4
  society's interest in, 102–4
  youthful marriage and, 96–7
Prenuptial agreement, mixed religious marriages, 205
Problem solving, 30–43
  compensation, 32–3
  daydreaming, 37–8
  direct attack, 31–2

INDEX

fear, coping with, 39–1
frustration, feelings of, 30–1
giving up, 33–5
health and, 41–2
personality integration and, 42–3
rationalization, 36–7
regression, 35–6
retreat, 35–6
steps in, 42
Puppy love, 214

Q

Quarrels, 83–4, 247–56, 281
as a danger signal, 83–4
during engagement, 180–1
family conference as substitute for, 254–6
function in early marriage, 248–50
habitual pattern of behavior, 251
marriage adjustment and, 247–56
money problems and, 281
physical factors and, 253–4
tension relief, 251–2

R

Racial differences, in marriage, 156, 224–5
Rationalization, problem solving, 36–7
Recreational interests, 149–50
Regression, problem solving, 35–6
Relatives, marriage of, prohibition, 223–4
Religion:
agreement on, 201–2
divorce rates and, 198, 199, 203–4, 205
family background and, 200
family living and, 198–200
marriage and, 197–206
prenuptial agreement, 205
Remarriage:
after divorce, 329–30
of grandparents, 409–10
of parents, 409–10
Reproduction, 346–52

S

Security, family, *see* Consumer economics, insurance
Self-confidence, developing, child training, 371
Sex:
answering children's questions concerning, 383–8
premarital, 92–105
questions children ask about, 385
Sexual adjustment in marriage, 258–66
biological basis of sex drive, 260
childbirth and, 351–2
differences in sexual arousal, 264
frequency of sex, 264
frustration, causes of, 265
happiness and, 259–60
orgasm, 262–3
physical changes and, 263
physical sexual development and, 262
pregnancy and, 351–2
problems in, 262–5
social conditioning about sex, 260–1
strength of sexual drive, 263–4
study of, 258–9, 261–2
testosterone, 263
time for, 258–9, 261–2
Smoking, 114–7

Spending, *see* Consumer economics; Money problems in marriage
Sperm, 13
Standards, *see* Behavior
Sterility, 391–2

T

Testosterone, 263

U

Unmarried mothers:
  aid to dependent children and, 103
  maternity care for, 395–6

V

Vocational choices, 405–6

W

Waiting period, before marriage:
  for marriage license, 226–7
  by states (table), 221
Wedding:
  ceremony, 227
  planning, 227–8
Working mothers, 406–7

Y

Yale University alcohol studies, 110